Horrid Spectacle

Medieval & Renaissance Literary Studies

HORRID SPECTACLE

Violation in the Theater of Early Modern England

Deborah G. Burks

Duquesne University Press Pittsburgh, Pa.

Published in the United States of America by

DUQUESNE UNIVERSITY PRESS
600 Forbes Avenue
Pittsburgh, Pennsylvania 15282

Library of Congress Cataloging-in-Publication Data

Burks, Deborah G., 1963–
      Horrid spectacle : violation in the theater of early modern England /
Deborah G. Burks.
            p. cm. — (Medieval & Renaissance literary studies)
Includes bibliographical references.
      ISBN 0-8207-0341-9 (acid-free paper)
      1. English drama—Early modern and Elizabethan, 1500–1600—
History and criticism. 2. Sex crimes in literature. 3. Christianity and
literature—Great Britain—History—16ᵗʰ century. 4. Christianity and
literature—Great Britain—History—17ᵗʰ century. 5. Politics and
literature—Great Britain—History—16ᵗʰ century. 6. Politics and
literature—Great Britain—History—17ᵗʰ century. 7. English
drama—17ᵗʰ century—History and criticism. 8. Rape victims in
literature. 9. Women in literature. 10. Rape in literature. I. Title.
II. Medieval and Renaissance literary studies.
      PR658.S4B87 2004
      822'.3093556—dc22
                                                                        2003019475

∞ Printed on acid-free paper.

Reason observing which way I was bent,
Did stay my hand, and ask't me what I meant;
Will you, said shee, thus waste your time in vaine,
On that which in the World small praise shall gaine?
For shame leave off, sayd shee, the Printer spare,
Hee'le loose by your ill Poetry, I feare
Besides the World hath already such a weight
Of uselesse Bookes, as it is over fraught.
Then pitty take, doe the World a good turne,
And all you write cast in the fire, and burne.
Angry I was, and Reason strook away,
When I did heare, what shee to me did say.
Then all in haste, I to the Presse it sent,
Fearing Perswasion might my Book prevent.

— Margaret Cavendish, "The Poetess's hasty Resolution"

Contents

III. Renegotiating the Rhetoric of Abusive Sexuality

Acknowledgments

I have incurred many debts in the course of this project. First, to those who taught me, challenged me, inspired me: Lewis J. Owen, William B. Worthen, Frank Whigham, Elin Diamond, Emily Bartels, Ann B. Coiro, Thomas Van Laan. Next, to colleagues who have responded to portions of this book as it developed: Colleen Hobbs, Anne Herzog, Anne Rea, Emily Detmer, Nancy S. Weitz, John N. King, Christopher Highley, David Frantz, Phoebe Spinrad, John Norman, James Phelan, John Hellmann and David Adams. I owe a great deal to my colleagues in the English Department and in the administration at The Ohio State University's Lima Campus, who have supported this work in large and small ways: William J. Sullivan, Violet I. Meek, Phillip Heath, William Ackerman, Duane W. Roller, Beth Sutton-Ramspeck and Nan Arbuckle, in particular, have my sincere gratitude. Special thanks also to James Bracken and staffmembers of the OSU libraries, particularly those whose work in the Rare Books collection and OSU's Foxe Digital Project have facilitated my study of Foxe's *Acts and Monuments*. Grants of time and funding from my institution have made it possible to complete this project. My students deserve thanks, as well, especially the members of my Shakespeare and early modern women writers seminars; their responses have sparked much rethinking and have gently shaped many moments in this text. This book would not have been written without the support of Louisa Fuller and Lucia, Darnall, Marilyn and Sarah Burks. For their examples, love and generosity, I am deeply grateful. Finally, I want to thank John Wurster for his support, his good humor, his sense of perspective and his patience. This book is dedicated to him, with love.

Introduction

In her study of the politics of the Restoration stage, Susan J. Owen asserts that in the political language of the Exclusion Crisis, we see elements of political discourses still in use in England and the United States at the turn of the twenty-first century:

> This period represents our own history in the making. . . . [In England, the language of Toryism lingers in] the idea of the unity of the upper and middle classes in an aristocracy of taste, as against the lower classes and radicals who attack "true culture," for instance, or the use of ideas of sexual deviation as an image of political disorder. In the United States the Whig language of republican virtue and radical Protestantism is equally in use in political discourse.[1]

Only the first of elements Owens mentions (the "aristocratic" alliance of the upper and middle classes) may legitimately be said to have arisen in the political crucible of the Restoration.[2] The others (the ideologies of republican virtue and radical Protestantism and the association of sexual deviation with political disorder) predate Tory/Whig factionalism by more than a century.

The conflicting ideologies of aristocracy and citizenship, of royalism and republicanism did not spring into being *ex nihilo* in the middle and late seventeenth century. Along with the imagery of sexual disorder, which was indeed a central motif, these ideas are the remains of earlier periods, earlier politics. It is the project of this book to reenvision Restoration drama's historical and political place by redefining the usual historical and literary period

1

within which we imagine it to belong. Where some recent studies have tended to propose the Restoration as a discreet, isolated moment of time, and others have figured it as the first segment of a long eighteenth century, this study considers Restoration drama (and the political discourses in which it participated) to have been situated at the end of a long seventeenth century, a century of political developments and discourses that supplied the Restoration with ideological and metaphorical constructs ready for use.

Richard Helgerson has pointed out that "in early modern England the language of politics was most often the language of religion."[3] We might also observe that the language of religion was often overtly political. This was true not only because political writers adopted religious language to promote their secular aims, but also because religious writers entered the political arena to achieve religious ends. Furthermore, this was true not only of the official language of the state and the state church, which mingled the two discourses in order to reinforce their hegemony, but it was also true of opposition speech. Because the institution of religion and the institutions of the state were intertwined, religious dissent was figured as a political act both by those who voiced it and by those in authority against whom dissent was directed. Likewise, political dissent was often construed as a matter of sacred obligation by those who committed it, and as a transgression of sacred obligations by the state in its response.

The English church's position was that social and political docility were duties owed by the people to the king and to their God. It was a position articulated frequently from the nation's pulpits by ministers obliged to read certain authorized homilies. When, in 1623, the church re-issued *Certaine Sermons or Homilies appointed to be read in Churches . . . by Authority from the Kings most Excellent Majestie*, the book's purchasers read words they had heard from their local pulpits since childhood:

> praised be GOD, that we know the great excellent benefit of GOD showed towards us in this behalf, GOD hath sent us his high gift, our most dear Sovereign Lord King James, with a godly, wise and

honorable Counsel, with other superiors and inferiors, in a beautiful order, and godly. Wherefore, let us subjects do our bounden duties, giving hearty thanks to GOD, and praying for the preservation of this godly order. Let us all obey even from the bottom of our hearts, all their godly proceedings, laws, statutes, proclamations, and injunctions, with all other godly orders.[4]

First published in 1547 by authority of Edward VI and reauthorized in turn by Elizabeth I, James I and Charles I, this "Exhortation concerning good Order, and obedience to Rulers and Magistrates" taught generations of English subjects their places in God's creation.

It is clear, however, that this lesson met with some resistance. Though the writer of this homily attests to the orderliness of creation, his tone is both admonitory and defensive. As though the beauties of good order might prove insufficient in and of themselves to entice England's Christians to obedience, the homilist threatens his listeners with a horrifying vision of the alternative:

[W]here there is no right order, there reigneth all abuse, carnal liberty, enormity, sin, and Babylonical confusion. Take away Kings, Princes, Rulers, Magistrates, Judges, and such estates of God's order, no man shall ride or go by the highway unrobbed, no man shall sleep in his own house or bed unkilled, no man shall keep his wife, children, and possession in quietness, all things shall be common, and there must needs follow all mischief, and utter destruction both of souls, bodies, goods, and commonwealths.[5]

In the absence of a king and system of orderly justice, men are vulnerable to violations of all kinds: their persons and their possessions (including wives and children) will surely be ravaged by violence. If order fails, abuse will prevail: souls, bodies and goods will all be ravished.

Beautiful order or all abuse: at the homily's opening the choice seems perfectly clear, but it quickly becomes apparent that the issue of order was a fraught and complex matter for the English church. The homilist finds it necessary to argue that God ordains princes, then pauses to address a possible objection to the administration of justice in a principality, saying that

the places of Scripture, which *seem* to remove from among all
Christian men, judgment, punishment, or killing, *ought to be
understood* that no man (of his own private authority) may be judge
over other, may punish, or may kill. But we must refer all judgment
to God, to Kings, and Rulers, Judges under them, which be Gods
officers to execute justice and *by plain words of Scripture*, have
their authority and use of the sword granted by God.[6]

The homilist anticipates that some of his hearers will invoke
certain familiar passages of Scripture (for instance, "Justice is mine,
saith the Lord" or "Thou shalt not kill") to argue that the Bible
forbids human authorities to commit violence, even in the name
of justice, an argument that effectively denies the legitimacy of
kings, rulers and judges. Apparently the words of Scripture were
not sufficiently plain to convince all English subjects to accept
the authority and the violence of those who held power over them.
This homily, which was commissioned by the church hierarchy
and authorized by the Crown, seems to anticipate substantial and
sophisticated resistance to its message. Ironically, it also institu-
tionalizes those arguments for resistance by reiterating them each
time the homily is preached or reissued from the press.

Clearly this homily was written for a nation of churchgoers
familiar with a range of arguments against monarchy. Particularly,
the homilist concerns himself with the issue of whether it is
necessary for Christians to obey an evil prince or magistrate. To
this the homilist responds with the biblical example of David, who
refused to injure King Saul despite the many wrongs Saul had
committed against David. The homilist asserts that although there
may indeed be evil princes, "we may not in any wise withstand
violently, or rebel against rulers, or make any insurrection, sedition,
or tumults, either by force of arms (or otherwise) against the
anointed of the Lord, or any of his officers: But we must in such
case patiently suffer all wrongs, and injuries, referring the judgment
of our cause only to God."[7]

Preached first to the subjects of Edward VI, this sermon teaches
the sort of passive resistance John Foxe ascribes to so many of the

Protestants who chose martyrdom during the reign of Mary I, and herein lies the crux of the problem that troubles this homily — and which troubled seventeenth century English society. The homilist does not doubt that evil princes exist and he does not dispute that subjects may suffer terrible wrongs at the hands of such authorities. These are large concessions, and they are merely the beginning. Who was to decide which kings were to be obeyed? Granting that "we must rather obey God than man," and conceding that "we may not obey Kings, Magistrates or any other, (though they be our own fathers) if they would command us to do anything contrary to God," the homilist walks a difficult tightrope. In post-Reformation England where the Bible was available in English to all who could read, disagreements over God's word arose regularly. The homilist enjoins obedience to temporal authority, yet acknowledges the grounds on which many seventeenth century English subjects would question that authority. Even as he threatens terrible punishment for any who resist, withstand or rebel in deed or even in thought, the homilist grants that wicked authorities sometimes oppress good subjects. He insists on physical compliance and submission to king, church and law, while crediting conscientious objection. Specifically, he releases English believers from any fear that Scripture enjoins them to submit to "the pretensed or colored power of the Bishop of Rome, for surely the Scripture of God alloweth no such usurped power, full of enormities, abusions, and blasphemies," but this is a template for resistance that could be (and was) applied to the English church and state by those who believed those institutions were perpetrators of "enormities, abusions, and blasphemies."[8]

At the heart of this homily are two twinned axioms. The first holds that God ordains hierarchical order, placing power in the hands of a few over the lives of the many. The second concedes that the exercise of human power sometimes turns to abuse or is experienced as abuse by the powerless. Just as the homily "Of the state of Matrimony" concedes that for women marriage is often a lifelong sentence of suffering, this homily on obedience accepts that the lot of subjects is to submit to wrongs and injuries.[9] God's good gift of kings, princes, magistrates, judges and an orderly society could be more burden than boon. Despite its assertions to the contrary, the homily tacitly accepts that, from the point of view of the subject, authority and order may be experienced as violation. The idyll of natural order in the homily's opening lines comes to seem rather like its horrible alternative.

The rhetoric of these homilies (both the "Exhortation concerning good Order" and "Of the State of Matrimony") was effectively turned against the state church and the Crown at the end of the civil wars, when it was evoked to authorize the reform of the church and the execution of the king. A representative and effective articulation of this argument appears in Elizabeth Poole's prophetic testimony, which in 1648 she delivered to Cromwell and the army's General Council, then published as *A Vision Wherein is Manifested the Disease and Cure of the Kingdome*. Poole acknowledges that the king is the country's "Father and husband, which you were and are to obey in the Lord." She asserts that he is "the head of her [the country's] body," and concedes that "you were given [to the king as] a helper in the body of the people."[10] She also accepts the orthodox instruction that wives are subject to their husbands even if those husbands are violent: "You never heard that a wife might put away her husband, as he is the head of her body, but for the Lords sake suffereth his terror to her flesh." However, it is Poole's thesis that her king has indeed proved an abusive husband to his people, and although the wife may not divorce ("put away") such a husband, nonetheless she may appeal to God and God's vice-regents to intercede.[11]

At this point, however, Poole is careful to evade the orthodox identification of the monarch himself as God's earthly vice-regent and the state church's ecclesiastical courts as the judiciary to which a wife might appeal her husband's mistreatment. The analogies she has chosen inevitably raise these associations, but for the express purpose of overturning and reassigning them:

> if he will usurpe over her, she appealeth to the Father-hood for her offence, which is the spirit of justice, and is in you [the General Council of the army]; For I know no power in *England* to whom it is committed, save your selves (and the present Parliament) which are to act in the Church of Christ, as she by the gift of faith upon her, shall be your guide for the cure of her body, that you might therefore commit an unsound member to Satan (though the head) as it is flesh; that the spirit might be saved in the day of the Lord.[12]

The General Council of Cromwell's army (or perhaps the present Parliament — she mentions both, but doesn't choose between them because the two bodies were struggling for authority with regard to the disposition of the king's person) will fill a role parallel to that once played by the state church's ecclesiastical courts in cases of spousal abuse in order to excommunicate the offending husband and will fill the role of God's vice-regent once played by the king and his courts in cases of treasonable abuse to the state, in this case to try and punish the offending king.

Poole makes evocative use of the traditional patriarchal metaphors for English kingship in order to illustrate the king's rule as a type of sexual violation. The king perverted his relationship as father/husband to his nation "when he forgot his Subordination to divine Faith hood and headship, thinking he had begotten you a generation to his own pleasure, and taking you a wife for his own lusts," she writes, charging the king with (metaphorical) incest with his children and fornication with his wife, using them for his sexual pleasure rather than as his helpmeets and fellow Christian souls. Furthermore, she depicts the king's violation of his nation/spouse as a murderous rape in which he threatens to pierce her "bowels with a knife or sword to take [her] life."[13]

Poole exhibits her mastery of polemical discourse in her careful manipulation of gendered images and pronouns. At one moment, the "you" she addresses is the masculine General Council, in the next it conflates with the feminine nation, identified throughout the text according to the convention that makes countries and ships female entities under the command of male kings and captains. The "you," which is at one point God's vice-regent on earth, is at another the woman, Abigail, who, in the Old Testament, defies her wicked husband to support David when he is persecuted by King Saul: "Put your swords into [God's] hands for your defence," she instructs her listeners, "and feare not to act the part of *Abigal*, seeing *Nabal* hath refused it (by Appropriating his goods to himselfe) in relieving *David* and his men in their distresse [1 Sam. 25]; it was to her praise, it shall be to yours, feare it not."[14] The gendering of this passage is complex: the members of the General Council are like the faithful woman Abigail, who defies an evil husband. Like her they will be rewarded for defying an evil, unworthy spouse, who, like Charles I, is guilty of "appropriating his goods to himself" and denying his resources to the worthy ones who both deserve and dearly need his succor. It is worth noting two more things about this analogy: first, although Poole identifies the council with Abigail, she leaves room for them to see themselves and/or their leader, Cromwell, as David, though the latter is initially a figure for the loyal people of England. Thus Poole executes a clever escape from the possibly diminishing effect of the Abigail identification in her anecdote. Second, for those familiar with 1 Samuel, Abigail and David's story has a sequel: after God takes vengeance on the ungrateful Nabal, Abigail becomes David's bride. In Poole's use of the analogy, then, the anecdote anticipates the replacement of one evil husband/sovereign with an infinitely better one. As David is to Nabal, so will the Cromwellian government be to Stuart monarchy.

Poole's demonstration of her rhetorical ability progresses from the skillful manipulation of biblical material to the incendiary deployment of violation imagery when she transforms the "you" addressed by the text into the king's battered bride locked in a desperate struggle for self-defense: "you may hold the hands of your husband, that he pierce not your bowels with a knife or sword to take your life." In context, addressed to Poole's primary audience of army officers, the image not only feminizes them as vulnerable women in the hands of a violent husband, but, insofar as they do not relinquish their sense of themselves as men, the image also threatens these officers with anal rape at the hands of a king who recently had tried his best to sheath his weapon in their bowels on the field of battle.

It is perhaps unsurprising that while Poole's prophecy helped Cromwell mobilize support for his policies, neither Cromwell nor the General Council felt moved to heed her instruction that they must not kill the king, their rapacious spouse.[15] In this one regard, Poole refuses to break free of orthodox understandings of monarchy and subjecthood: she reviles the king as having broken faith with his God and country, but she will not endorse regicide. On this subject, she varies not a degree from the instruction of the homilies of matrimony and obedience:

> You have all that you have and are, and also in Subordination you owe him all that you have and are, and although he would not be your Father and husband, Subordinate [to God], but absolute, yet know that you are for the Lords sake to honour his person. For he is the Father and husband of your bodyes, as unto men, and therefore your right cannot be without him, as unto men. . . . For know this, the Conquest was not without divine displeasure whereby Kings came to reigne, though through lust they tyranized: which God excuseth not, but judgeth; and his judgements are fallen heavy, as you see, upon *Charles* your Lord: Forget not your pity towards him, for you were given him a helper in the body of the people . . . although the bond be broken on his part.

She urges her countrymen, that "as the Lord revenged his owne cause on [Nabal], he shall doe on yours; *For vengeance is mine, I will repay it, saith the Lord* [Rom. 12:19]."[16] It is ironic testimony to the power of the state church's doctrine that Elizabeth Poole, prophet and member of the radical sectarian Particular Baptist conventicle, proved a more faithful student of orthodox religious teaching than the politicians she sought to advise.

As the "Exhortation concerning good Order, and obedience to Rulers and Magistrates" hints, a key source of this rhetoric of violation, which the homilist employs to threaten would-be rebels and which Poole directs against her monarch, is to be found in Reformation polemical protests against Roman Catholicism. Violation imagery was a characteristic of Protestant print from its very earliest days; it came to be shared by religious and political writers alike and was employed to articulate dissent as well as to maintain the status quo. Writing from exile during the last days of Henry VIII's reign, John Bale used the relatively young technology of print publication to reach out to what he hoped would be a socially broad audience of readers. Bale's boisterously belligerent prose style and his vigorous pose as the little fellow taking on powerful giants combined with his penchant for alliterative phrasing to make his tracts memorable. He styled himself a latter-day David taking on the Goliaths of Henry's church, whom he described as "belly-gods," "mitered moody idols," "terrible termagants of antichrist's holy household," "horned whore-mongers" and "lecherous locusts leaping out of the smoke of the pit bottomless" — among other things.[17] Bale's strategy was to cast all laypeople as fellow victims of the avaricious violence of the greater clergy; his readers, then, were to see themselves as members of a community of the oppressed that crossed class lines to unite all of England's true believers. To the gentlemen and aristocrats among his hoped-for readers, Bale suggested that their willingness to countenance the social and political pretensions of the bishops had made them no better than bawds to these ecclesiastics, "convey[ing them] in the dark a piece for [their] pleasure." To the rest of the reading classes, he suggested that their priests were to be reviled because "those shorn sorcerers of that Sodomitical kingdom" were seducing men's wives as well as copulating with "boys, bitches, and apes."[18]

One of Bale's early colleagues was Anne Askew, one of those examined and executed for maintaining reformed opinions near the end of Henry VIII's reign. Like Bale, who shepherded her writing into print after her death, Askew realized the affective potential of violation imagery when shaping her account of her treatment at the hands of male authorities, particularly Edmund Bonner, bishop of London, and the Lord Chancellor Thomas Wriothesley.[19] When she recounts Bonner's attempts to interrogate her, she casts him as a rather comically impotent would-be seducer who sets a time for Askew and several witnesses to appear before him, then summons the young woman two hours early in order to pressure her privately. In her telling of the episode, Bonner feigns a chivalrous concern for her, indicating that he "was very sorry for [her] trouble" and urges her "boldly to utter the secrets of [her] heart, bidding [her] not to fear in any point. For what so ever [she] did say in his house no man should hurt [her] for it." Askew sees through the bishop's faux chivalry, refusing either to be seduced or intimidated into incriminating herself with an unguarded admission. She ascribes a similar blend of fair promises and physical intimidation to the secular officials who, "withal their power and flattering words, went about to persuade me from God. But I did not esteem their glosing pretences." Even when racked, Askew steadfastly refuses to name any "ladies or Gentlewomen" who share her religious beliefs, and her fortitude under this extremity of torture elicits a ferocious response from her interrogators: "Because I lay still and did not cry, my Lord Chancellor and Master Rich took pains to rack me with their own hands, till I was nigh dead."[20] As I will demonstrate in greater detail in chapters 2 and 3, Askew's representation of this episode suggests that the physical frailty of her female body, combined with her willful refusal to obey the demands of her torturers, arouses a peculiar sort of rage in these men, who break the decorums of class and office and take over control of the rack from the hirelings who have failed to break Askew's will. All of the lord chancellor's masculine wiles are impotent against Askew: neither his "many flattering words" nor his furious violence succeeds with this woman. Askew uses the gender politics of her situation to portray the unscrupulous bloodthirstiness of her persecutors. The genius of her work is that it manages to convey the vulnerability of all Protestants, male as well as female, to these tyrants of church and state, who would not mitigate their violence even when dealing with a mere woman.

Askew's and Bale's innovative and influential use of the press to disseminate opposition opinions made them pioneers in popularizing political speech. The violation rhetoric in which they chose to couch their critique of Roman Catholicism and Tudor government echoes across a century and a half of England's renegotiations of its social and religious settlement with church and Crown.[21] Together, Bale and Askew provided generations of writers (religious and secular alike) with a peculiarly effective mode of political language. Ironically, this rhetoric was employed not only to articulate radical dissent, but also to maintain the property-based social hierarchy, as it was when the male landed classes adopted it to resist what they perceived as dual threats to their estates from the Crown above and from the women and servants of their households below (see chapter 4). This book demonstrates the durability and adaptability of violation as a figure for disruptions of the normative relations among superior and subordinate members of the society, revealing how this rhetorical and visual trope linked discrete political discourses sometimes in fortuitous but often awkward ways.

Because this study focuses specifically on a rhetoric of victimization (albeit an unusual rhetoric of victimhood with emphasis on the mental and moral strength of the sufferer), I must stress that it is not my argument that early modern women specifically, or early modern subjects more generally, were merely victims or that they saw themselves as mere victims. Indeed, my study attempts to show that the rhetoric of violation was a strategic tool, a savvy representational strategy meant to mobilize powerful, real political action.

Rape and violation imagery provided a way for writers to figure their experience of political and social vulnerability. In a century when the literate, propertied men of the Parliament and the literate, politically active leaders of religious reform (both men and women) were formulating a sense of individual rights to property and to faith in the face of perceived threats from the state and the state church, it is notable that so many of these writers (many of them men) use a language of bodily seizure and violation to articulate their sense that their rights have been infringed upon. In other words, the ubiquitous use of rape in the rhetoric of the page and in the action of the stage intimates not only that English writers posited the individual's bodily integrity and mental distinctness as foundational to English law and social relations, but that they perceived the violation of their rights to property and to religious faith as an outrage analogous to the violation of a woman's body in rape or to the violence suffered by the male body in castration. Indeed, in the property-based hierarchy of English society, male sexual intactness was fundamental to the preservation of a line of blood heirs and was, therefore, a powerful emblem for the most fundamental vulnerability of a family estate to assault from without. Similarly, female sexual intactness, figured both as bodily wholeness (the hymen's intactness or rupture was taken as a physical marker of a woman's sexual status) and as the absence of taint from sexual congress, was essential to the preservation of blood purity in the family line. However, while it is easy to see how fears of women's sexual vulnerability were related to property concerns, it is surprising to find so many male writers figuring rape not as an oblique threat to men through their women, but as a direct analogy for how it felt to be a male subject vulnerable to the depredations of the powerful.

The importance of virginity or sexual intactness in Elizabethan culture, where the queen mobilized virginity as a figure for her own unassailable primacy and as a metaphor for the inviolable separateness of her island nation, has been the subject of studies by Philippa Berry, Helen Hackett and Carole Levin.[22] In this context, virginity was obviously fraught with contradictory tensions for male subjects: it was emblematic of the integrity of the family and its possessions, but it was also the primary emblem of the Crown's power to which they were subject. Elizabeth tempered her rhetoric of virginity with an insistence that she was married to the state and to her subjects for their collective happiness, but of course her chastity was a mixed blessing as it brought political uncertainty for the future along with a comforting measure of present security against the foreign domination a royal marriage might have entailed. In contrast to "the barren virgo/virago iconography of Elizabeth's reign," James I's revision of the sexual emblems of monarchy was equally a matter for ambivalence.[23] Elizabeth's role as virgin/wife juxtaposed her claims to absolute power as prince against her acknowledgment of a relationship with her subjects. For male subjects, Elizabeth's metaphor placed them in the role of husband, which, despite the question of what it meant for husbands to be subject to such a wife, allowed them an imaginative position of privilege. James's desire to be seen as the father of his new nation — or as its bridegroom, the role he adopted for his 1603 entry into London, left his male and female subjects in the metaphorical position of wives or children. In this context, Parliament's affinity for the language of rape seems quite logical as an articulation of the property-owning subject's struggle against James's claims of prerogative ownership over English persons and property. As Elizabeth Poole's tract written on the eve of Charles I's execution shows, the figure of a monarch as abusive husband came to signify the dire conflict between Stuart kings and their subjects.

Clearly, when Elizabethan and Jacobean plays staged representations of sexualized violence they were engaging a set of images already imbrued with political significance. Specifically, these images had been freighted with partisan meaning by Reformation polemicists who, following Bale's lead, used this rhetoric of violation to articulate the vulnerability of Protestant Christians in Henry VIII's and, later, Mary I's England.[24] This imagery remained an important element of Protestant self-representation after the accession of Elizabeth I, when it came to be used not only as a critique of Roman Catholicism, but of the Elizabethan state and ecclesiastical hierarchy as well. John Foxe's *Acts and Monuments of these latter and perillous dayes* was the most substantial and widely read work to articulate this Protestant rhetoric of violation, and although Foxe deliberately casts his work as an instrument of support for Elizabeth and her church, the text and its memorable illustrations provided plenty of material for use by more radical reformers. A notable instance of this can be seen in the mid-seventeenth century writings of John Bastwick, Henry Burton and William Prynne, who were fined, sentenced to life imprisonment and suffered the loss of their ears as seditious libelers for applying the imagery of violation, dismemberment and bestiality to Charles I and the ecclesiastical hierarchy of the state church (see chapter 6).

In the hands of playwrights, too, this imagery served various purposes. A number of playwrights starting with Bale and Foxe employed the stage to further the Reformation project. This group of Protestant partisans later included Thomas Middleton and Thomas Dekker, who used violation imagery much as they found it in the works of polemicists like Bale, Askew or Thomas Scott, an influential opposition writer of their own generation, and in the pages of Foxe's *Acts and Monuments*.[25] In other hands, this same imagery was turned to other purposes. As I argue in chapter 2, in *Measure for Measure*, Shakespeare deploys elements of this Protestant critique of abusive authority, borrowing identifiable catch phrases from polemic, but uses it to assert that citizens of all sorts are vulnerable to the power of those in authority, regardless of religious affiliation. While this imagery was often used in print and onstage to mount politically radical attacks on the institutions of church and Crown, it was also used for more moderate political purposes to urge reform of church and state by writers committed to maintaining a loyal posture with respect to the king. I argue that this is the case with James Shirley, whose 1641 play, *The Cardinal*, urges a change of royal policy in order to mollify the radical opposition. A similar case could be made for the work of

Margaret Cavendish and Aphra Behn, who critique the personal and political behavior of Charles II and royalist men, though both of these women positioned themselves as royalists.

This imagery was never the exclusive possession of Protestant writers, who had borrowed it and reworked it for their purposes.[26] At the latter end of the seventeenth century, when Aphra Behn recycled a still recognizable version of this material in *Oroonoko*, she transformed it in order to mount an early critique of the corruption of British colonial officials in the New World, white men who broke faith with her central character, the "royal slave," Oroonoko. In her characterization of the villainy of these European men, Behn emphasizes: (1) their willingness to break their word (not only verbal promises, but written contracts), (2) their ruthless violence, and (3) their sexual predation toward female slaves, all of which she presents as evidence of the paradoxical barbarity of these supposedly civilized authority figures. Their barbarity is denoted by their zest to violate the bodies and wills of those in their power. Thus, Behn treats sympathetically Oroonoko and Imoinda's decision that Imoinda should die rather than face ravishment by their captors. When she describes Oroonoko's death, Behn makes it clear that his executioners mean to dishonor the slave by inflicting torturous pain and by violating his bodily dignity. Oroonoko denies them this victory, maintaining that any sort of death is preferable to life in such a place and that pain is immaterial so long as the punishment leads to honorable death.

> Turning to the Men that bound him, [Oroonoko] said, *My Friends, am I to Dye, or to be Whip'd?* And they cry'd, *Whip'd! No; you shall not escape so well*: And then he replied, smiling, *A blessing on thee;* and assur'd them, they need not tye him, for he would stand fixt, like a Rock; and indure Death so as shou'd encourage them to Dye. *But if you Whip me,* said he, *be sure you tye me fast.*
>
> He had learn'd to take Tobacco; and when he was assur'd he should Dye, he desir'd they would give him a Pipe in his Mouth, ready Lighted, which they did; and the Executioner came, and first cut off his Members, and threw them into the Fire; after that, with an ill-favoured Knife, they cut his Ears, and his Nose, and burn'd

> them; he still Smoak'd on, as if nothing had touch'd him; then they
> hack'd off one of his Arms, and still he bore up, and held his Pipe;
> but at the cutting off the other Arm, his Head sunk, and his Pipe
> drop'd; and he gave up the Ghost without a Groan, or a Reproach.[27]

Ironically, the colonists do not see that for Oroonoko, whipping
would be a worse punishment than death because it humiliates
the captive, forcing him to submit to bodily violation while refusing
him the ennobling reward of death. Instead, the colonial authorities
subject him to a version of the standard English execution for
traitors: dismemberment and quartering. Key to this sentence is
the severing of the man's sexual members while he remains alive
to suffer the pain and to see this symbol of his manhood destroyed.
Oroonoko maintains a stoic dignity throughout, refusing to reward
the executioner or the crowd with any sign that their brutality
disturbs him. Thus, Behn designs this scene of punishment for her
readers not as a testament to Oroonoko's criminality, but to his
nobility and to his tormentors' depravity.

Behn's use of the rhetorical strategies of martyrology demonstrates the portability of that idiom for use in new contexts and
for use in the service of various (and competing) causes. English
Protestants borrowed the forms and conventions of martyrological
literature from a longstanding Roman Catholic tradition. John Foxe
drew directly from the Roman Eusebius, chronicler of the persecutions and harassments suffered by early Christians. Foxe's
work in its turn supplied images to English imaginations and
strategies to English writers, who appropriated them for new and
not necessarily compatible purposes. Indeed, to say that Behn, who
may well have leaned toward Roman Catholicism herself, echoes
Foxe is merely to observe the paradoxical, politically heterodox
influence of that work.[28] Oroonoko's unperturbed acceptance of
torture and death echoes the calm command with which Foxe's
martyrs faced their deaths.[29] It is reminiscent, for instance, of the
Acts and Monuments account of Thomas Cranmer's fortitude in
holding his right hand in the flames so that it would burn before
the rest of his body, or the report of several women who went

willingly to their deaths without needing to be bound to the stake. Certainly, *Acts and Monuments* remained influential, receiving new editions in 1641 and 1684. However, for Behn and her readers, this rhetoric of abuse also resonated from the pages of texts produced in several fresher contexts, where it had been used to great effect, for instance, to villainize Irish Catholics who rebelled against English colonial rule, or to malign royalists throughout the civil wars and during the Interregnum (see chapters 6–8). Thus, when Behn wishes to crystallize her readers' sense of the injustice done to Oroonoko, she gives him a martyr's death at the hands of a collection of "inhumane . . . Justices" and a "rude and wild . . . Rabble," all led by "one Banister, a wild Irish Man," who had been set on by the work's chief villain, the "faithless" deputy governor of Surinam, William Byam, himself a royalist exile from England.[30]

Characteristically, Behn reveals her ambivalence about her own royalist allegiance, echoing the critiques of the parliamentary and "godly" (Puritan) opposition, while nevertheless holding to an ideal of royal character.[31] In this novella, she suggests that an African slave may be more royal, more noble, more honorable than any of the white men in the colony of Surinam.[32] This critique of British men recurs in Behn's plays, where it is not African slaves, but women who suffer the predations and faithlessness of simultaneously appealing and unscrupulous Tory rakes.

This book seeks both to convey the local specificity of individual authors' use of the imagery of violation and to explore the complex ways in which later writers negotiated their own use of this material, which came to them already laden with cultural significance. The first section of the book considers the relation of Protestant print to two plays that are not themselves devoted to polemical ends. Thus, the first chapter looks closely at the Protestant use of violation imagery, particularly as it was mobilized by Foxe. I follow this with a chapter on *Measure for Measure* (1604), which sees Shakespeare borrowing from Protestant polemic with truly provocative results, mixing and muddling the roles of abuser and victim so that a nun and her brother, a known fornicator, are victims of the tyrannous and rapacious abuse of a man identified as a "precisian." To complicate matters, the siblings are also victims of the blameworthy meddling and mismanagement of the duke, who spends most of the play disguised as a friar. This play does not dodge the religious politics of Shakespeare's day, but it does refuse to offer a simple endorsement of either the reformed or the Counter-Reformation position, offering an independent view instead. Although much has been written about the duke and his deputy, my reading of the play is new in its attention to Shakespeare's deliberate manipulation of key elements of Balean and Foxean polemic to fuel his critique of power's capacity to corrupt regardless of political or religious affiliation. It is a vision of the danger all subjects face as potential victims of shifting policies in a state where power pools in the hands of a few. In the third chapter, I discuss George Chapman's similarly shrewd appropriation of Protestant materials in *Bussy D'Ambois* (ca. 1604–7). In that play, we find Chapman mimicking the conventions of polemic, particularly its representation of women's suffering, in order to manipulate his audience's empathy for purposes that seem only obliquely politicized. Although Chapman's plot resonates with topical concerns about King James's policies, the play seems to have mobilized the discourses of martyrdom principally for the playwright's commercial gain: Chapman recognized a winning formula and capitalized on it. One effect of these plays was to dissociate the rhetoric of violation from Protestant politics, while disseminating its affective critique of power to new audiences.

The second section of the book begins and ends with discussions of politically resonant plays: Thomas Middleton and William Rowley's *The Changeling* (1622) and James Shirley's *The Cardinal* (1641). As with the Shakespeare and Chapman plays, these two are acutely attuned to the issues of their day without being simplistic political allegories. I argue that *The Changeling*'s concentration on rape and on the complicity of women with their rapists was enmeshed in Jacobean England's discussion of subjects' rights, a political debate that appropriated violation rhetoric for new uses. The play is not merely a tale of aristocratic corruption, but taps into a much broader concern about property rights. It was not only the Crown that seemed to threaten men's ownership of their property, however. Each Parliament of James's reign considered legislation that sought to protect men from the treachery (and simple vulnerability) of their women. In this sense Middleton and Rowley's play, which contains no king and is not about the abuse of power by the great, can nonetheless be seen to contribute to English anxiety about material rights.

Paired with this analysis of *The Changeling* is a chapter on Arbella Stuart Seymour, whose uniquely unhappy experience as a potential heir to the English throne, as a woman and as a property owner whose rights had been infringed by the Crown (her estate was jointly swallowed by Queen Elizabeth and King James) makes her just the sort of anomaly that allows us to read the anxieties of other, less extraordinary subjects more clearly. Her collected letters, which make pointed and effective use of the tropes of violation, shed important light on the tangle of gender and status ideologies at the heart of *The Changeling* and the culture that produced it. While Stuart Seymour's letters were not public documents, they were nevertheless political. The author writes as an individual subject convinced that she suffered the very depredations complained of by Jacobean MPs. Stuart Seymour appeals to the Crown for the return of the title and property which were her patrimony, skillfully mobilizing the language of subjects' rights and the imagery of Protestant martyrdom to articulate her profound sense of violation.

The Cardinal, another rape play, brings the study to a new stage in its consideration of abusive authority. This chapter takes up the political crisis of 1640–41, giving particular attention to the propaganda generated by an increasingly well-organized "godly" party opposed to the Crown and the ecclesiastical hierarchy. This literature takes Jacobean subjects' rights discourse a step further, reaching back to Tudor Protestant polemic not only for its rhetoric of violation, but also for its perception that the survival of Protestantism hinges on the actions of its readers. While James Shirley's play is contemptuous of the "short haired men" of the godly party, it is also highly critical of the Crown's inability to reform the English church. Although it does not share their antimonarchical sensibilities, the play does share with the godly propagandists a key conceit when it represents the abuses of the ecclesiastical hierarchy as rape and emasculation, as a violation of the wills, bodies and rights of English subjects. Shirley redeploys this rhetoric of abuse in the hope of altering the trajectory of its critique. Thus we see James Shirley, chief dramatist for the King's Men in their later years, joining with certain conservative members of Parliament in appropriating the godly party's rhetoric for considerably less radical ends. Unlike his more militantly Protestant fellow writers, Shirley's investment in the issue is less spiritual than pragmatic: he urges the Crown to reform its own abuses before reform is imposed on it from without. This play is more open about its political agenda than any of the others discussed in this book, but this is a matter of degree and opportunity: the play appeared in a period one propagandist labeled the time "when men think what they list and speake and write what they think." I argue that 1641 was a year when men like Shirley wrote what they thought in the hope of moving the king away from policies that had pushed the nation to the brink of war.

This study is also concerned with the gender implications of the political valences of violation as represented on England's stages and as invoked in political tracts and speeches. After all, the political discussions of subjects' property rights and the statutes that addressed the crime of ravishment were put forward by and for men, though both concerned and were concerned with women. *The Changeling* (1622) and *The Cardinal* (1641) both demonstrate that early modern men understood violation as an imposition targeted at men, as a threat to masculinity and masculine interests. In *The Changeling*, we encounter a father, a murdered fiancé, the fiancé's brother, and a husband, all presented as victims of a ravishment, a crime they define in such a way as to place blame not only on the ravisher, DeFlores, but also (equally) on the ravished woman, Beatrice-Joanna. While the later play, *The Cardinal*, seems to credit the suffering of the female victim, the cardinal's attempt to rape the duchess is one violation among many in the play, all of them crimes against property-owning subjects, all of them perpetrated by a power-hungry prelate and countenanced by a weak king. Violation, the rape included, is still a crime against property as presented here, and it is still overwhelmingly represented as a threat to masculinity rather than to women or their femininity. To this end, the play principally figures the duchess as an aristocratic subject whose property the cardinal covets; her gender figures in the same way it did in *The Changeling* — her female body is the vulnerable point of access to the aristocratic estate under attack by the cardinal.

Although early modern men constructed rape and property law as matters of masculinity and although these male playwrights used rape as a means to articulate the vulnerability of male subjects, these plays and laws (and the political discourses that also appropriated the rhetoric of ravishment) had real consequences for the lives of early modern women. Those women's lives are not available to us through the female characters in Jacobean or Caroline drama, even when those characters are sympathetically drawn, so it seems appropriate to include in this section some attention to three actual women: Lady Elizabeth Hatton, her daughter, Frances Coke Villiers, and Arbella Stuart Seymour. All three were privileged, all three found themselves exploited for their property, all three found that the law was, in practice, a flexible institution manipulable by powerful men who found it convenient to deny these women even those rights the statutes apparently accorded them. Their experiences, the reports and actions of the men who judged them, and the collected letters of Arbella Stuart provide us with an alternate view of ravishment and of early modern subjects' rights.

The final section of the book traces how this durable imagery of violation, which was so effectively deployed against Stuart monarchy and against the royalist forces during the civil wars and the Interregnum, was recuperated by writers like Margaret Cavendish, John Dryden and Aphra Behn to support the Restoration. Though it was not without difficulty, this project was crucial to the reestablishment of the Stuart monarchy and to the recuperation of aristocratic ideology. I argue that these royalist writers struggled to renegotiate the meanings of violation, attempting to wrench this imagery and plot material free of its long-established association with political and religious opposition. This problem is central to much of Cavendish's work, which offers an early and uniquely awkward version of royalist mythology. Cavendish was ambivalent about marriage and about the sexual double standard that was indisputably at the heart of her culture, an ambivalence that shows through both her fiction and her plays. This ambivalence bubbles up through the fissures in her fiction in her representations of masculinity. While we do not have any reason to suppose that she wished to undermine the royalist cause, her characterizations of aristocratic men create an uncomfortable paradox. As one whose family suffered devastating losses of persons and property to parliamentary violence, as a former gentlewoman-in-waiting in Henrietta Maria's service, and as the wife of a royalist commander, Cavendish has reason to uphold all symbols of the royalist cause, but as a woman, she implicitly distrusts the central symbol of that cause: the aristocratic man. Thus, she and the antimonarchists share a rhetoric of violation in which the villains are royal and royalist men. In her play, *The Convent of Pleasure* (1668), and the novella, "Assaulted and Pursued Chastity" (1656), Cavendish manages to recuperate the lustful, deceitful, overbearing princes who play her "romantic" leads, but only halfheartedly.

Dryden's heroic drama (I focus on *The Conquest of Granada*, 1672) is less divided in its efforts to recuperate the notion of monarchy from the opprobrium cast upon it by Interregnum writers who had successfully portrayed kings, especially Stuart kings, as vicious, tyrannical and sexually corrupt. Charles II's sexual ostentation complicated matters for his dramatic apologist, but Dryden does his best first to make aristocracy and monarchy appear dashing (putting a positive spin on the court's sexuality), then to mythologize aristocrats and monarchs as people of great deeds and grand passions, the best of whom could exercise control over their fierce emotions.

Cavendish was not the only woman for whom this myth was less than comfortable. The final chapter considers Aphra Behn's *The City Heiress* (1682). There, as in most of Behn's plays, we find Tory rakes portrayed simultaneously as objects of desire and as treacherous betrayers of women. These characters are fictional counterparts to the gentlemen and aristocrats who were exiled for the royal cause and who lost their estates in the process. Thus, the plays justify the unscrupulous behavior of these characters as a survival instinct: they are socially elevated men forced to use their wits — and their sex appeal — to survive their current economic crisis. Behn does romanticize and excuse these men, but she is ambivalent about them. She demonstrates that Tory ideology — and Restoration sexual license — benefited men far more than women and, in fact, benefited men at women's expense. Thus, violation remains a key image in the rhetoric of dissent, though in Behn's case, it is a means only of articulating a minority position from within Toryism.

What this study attempts to chronicle is the way violation imagery passed from genre to genre, from writer to writer, from one cause to another, because the history of this recycling is a key piece of the history of seventeenth century political discourse. By tracing the various iterations of this rhetoric of violation, we begin to recapture a sense of the seventeenth century as a continuous series of moments and movements, a sense of continuity that has been lost to students of literature because of the way we tend to break the period into isolated pieces.

Literary periodization is not alone to blame in the fracturing of the seventeenth century and is not the only barrier to be

surmounted in a project that proposes to trace the trail of borrowings, reactions, reconstructions and reformations of such a durable
form of cultural currency as this imagery of violation. The ascendancy of "revisionism" among historians of the seventeenth century
has made it easier to work with a fractured vision of the period.
Not wishing to commit the cardinal error of implying a teleological
view of the years leading into, through and out of England's civil
wars, historians and literary critics alike have felt it safer to simply
divide the period and pass lightly by the ways in which poets or
playwrights or politicians or propagandists of later moments
echoed, rejected or reappropriated their predecessors. The powerful
(and correct) insight of revisionist historians is that history should
be seen not from the vantage of the present, from which angle the
current of events will appear to flow inevitably to the present point,
but that historians should attend to the contingencies and multiple
possibilities inherent in each historical moment, remembering always that what occurred was not inevitable.[33] Thus, it is a sensitive
matter to talk about the influence of earlier events or earlier writers
on later ones. Nonetheless, while one would not presume to say
that because John Foxe and John Daye published (and continued
to reissue) their influential martyrology, the civil wars were
inevitable, we may certainly see how deeply that work influenced
playwrights, politicians and propaganda hacks throughout the
seventeenth century, among them the political activists, who in
the early 1640s recycled Foxe's rhetoric of abuse to fan flames of
discontent within the nation. And it is certainly in keeping with
the notion that events are contingent and that cultural institutions
are shaped by multivalent forces to trace the various and often
incommensurate uses to which this potent imagery was put.

As deployed by Bale, Askew and Foxe, by Shakespeare, Chapman, Middleton, Stuart Seymour and Shirley, by Prynne, Burton,
Bastwick and others, the influence of this imagery extended well
beyond the bounds of party or religious affiliation. One reason the
propaganda of the 1640s was not merely the marginal noise of a
radical fringe was that this discourse of violation had already been

appropriated and disseminated for wider political and artistic purposes. By the 1640s, this rhetoric was familiar, but rather than losing its power with age, in this new iteration it met with a broad audience of readers predisposed to imagine themselves as the propagandists would have them: as victims of an abusive church and state, as vulnerable bodies subject to violation by the powerful. Because this imagery had such a powerful and persuasive life in the literary and political works of the civil wars and the Interregnum, these same images haunted Restoration writers, troubling their efforts to revivify monarchy and nobility and royalist literature.

This study reads theatrical texts in relation to other contemporaneous genres of writing, most of them nonliterary. My premise that the theater was a site of political and religious discourse insists that these disparate texts may usefully be read together, and yet it is worth considering whether the tools of literary analysis are appropriate for use on texts that fall into other categories. Frances Dolan argues that these tools are not only appropriate, but necessary when considering early modern documents such as court records, and her logic applies equally well to the case of the heresy proceedings compiled in Foxe's *Acts and Monuments* or to the published speeches of members of Parliament. "I now view court records," Dolan writes, "as themselves representations, shaped by occasion and convention, rather than as standards against which to check the accuracy of, say, plays. Published accounts of trials can stand as one example of how indistinguishable are 'documents' and 'representations.'"[34] In fact, the representational strategies of such texts sometimes make historians quite queasy about the validity of such evidence. Kevin Sharpe, a historian of the Jacobean period who has increasingly incorporated literary evidence into his analyses of the period, merits attention when he exhibits his disapproval of parliamentary speeches as useful evidence for historians. He has two particular concerns: first, that such publications must not be taken as representative, as they represent only the opinions of the most vocal MPs (the ones who took the floor to make speeches for or against a bill); second, that they are distorted by rhetorical conventions contemporaries knew to dismiss:

> [W]e should remember with Francis Bacon that "many in this house who speak not are as wise as others that do speak." Excessive concentration on the evidence of speeches may lead us to forget many silent back-benchers. . . . We may also ascribe too much importance to the rhetorical embellishments with which arguments were decorated. Undoubtedly rhetorical form is evidence that the historian cannot afford to ignore, but it is not evidence that he should use uncritically, especially since contemporaries often dismiss it as part of the ritual of parliamentary debate. James I frequently told his parliaments to "avoid rhetorick." . . . Sir Thomas Wentworth shared his sovereign's impatience with some members, urging his colleagues in 1614, "let us then leave the orators and become doers." Robert Bowyer dismissed "a long discourse of Sir William Morrice" as "to little effect" and was content to summarize a half-hour speech by Sir William Seaton in a half-page, passing over "some preamble."[35]

As mine is a study of the "rhetorical embellishments" with which early modern texts were "decorated," Sharpe's critique cannot pass unremarked. To be fair, literary scholars as well as historians ought to heed both of Sharpe's warnings (1) that the conditions of early modern publication (and the vagaries of time which have claimed some texts while allowing others to survive) ought to be considered lest we misrepresent the prevalence of certain opinions; (2) that rhetorical embellishments must be considered in relation to the contexts and conventions that shaped their use. Sharpe's critique, however, seems to be weighted toward dismissing political language as "embellishment" and *mere* "decoration." Where historians are comfortable discussing political strategies and alliances, they are less at ease with the language of the documents in which those alliances were forged and those strategies executed.

This is one area in which literary critics have something to offer historians. By considering the rhetoric of political speech as an important act in its own right and as a discourse related to other public and private modes of speech, we gain a fuller understanding of the period. The evidence of partisan speeches, of propaganda pamphlets, of popular literature, of Protestant polemic, while obviously requiring interpretation, is nonetheless crucial evidence of the attitudes, prejudices and opinions that shaped events. Dolan offers a particular example of how indispensable such evidence is when she discusses the challenges of recovering any accurate sense of what occurred during the Gunpowder Plot. "In regard to Catholics in seventeenth century England, the [popular] representations of events such as the Gunpowder Plot are not less reliable forms of evidence — colorful elaborations on or illustrations of less slippery 'facts' — but, for the most part, the only available evidence."[36] Indeed, while such materials may not provide certain evidence of *what* happened among Guy Fawkes and his fellow conspirators, they do supply crucial evidence of English Protestant *perceptions* of English Catholics. Furthermore, they attest to the ways in which the press was used to influence attitudes, religious affiliation, national identity and public policy. I draw on the same varieties of text on which Dolan relies, and for the same ends. Mine is a study of the political voices of the period, among them those of MPs, propaganda hacks, radical Protestants and play-wrights, each writing in a distinct genre shaped by conventions, embellished by rhetoric, but each an important voice within a turbulent period.

Frank Whigham has described the active role of the stage in the "daily social intercourse" of early modern England, noting that dramatists

> do not simply write about social activity, they write social activity. . . . Playwriting is of course a symbolic and abstracted activity, the playwrights themselves analysts of a kind. But the discourse they employ is one not of abstraction but of embodiment, perhaps reembodiment, not only physical (for I speak now of the written records, our mediate access to early modern performances) but linguistic. The words and actions of their created characters tend very much toward the locus of practical consciousness: sometimes groping (in soliloquy, author and character often in tandem) toward theoretical discursivity; much more often, exactly dramatizing the felt or disturbed or presumed — but known — provisional realities

of capacity and limit in their social world, by acting with them, on them, instrumentally and effectively. And in turn the auditor's multiple and conflicted relations to such acting are not only determined by, but capacitate, social action outside the playhouse.[37]

This description makes the broadest case for the role of the theater within daily social life; my work makes a more particular argument about the political function of the stage within the daily intercourse of the English nation. Plays initiated, continued, echoed and replied to the debates — about domination and subjection, rule and rights, prerogative and property holding, sovereignty and citizenship — that were central to the events of the period.

With regard to the role of the stage within the political arena of Tudor and Stuart England, T. H. Howard-Hill asserts that "many recent writers on English political drama . . . [hold] an anachronistic belief in the importance of popular opinion. . . . At this time in modern scholarship it is difficult to find anyone who does not believe that James's court [trembled] before the might of the English theater: *Vox theatri, vox dei.*"[38] Howard-Hill raises an important issue when he accuses critics of claiming too much political effectiveness for English drama without being able to document real evidence of these effects. It is a legitimate qualm, and his documentation of chronological and factual errors in recent literary historical studies is sobering. In any case, his critique calls for a more careful articulation of the claims being made here for the social and political position of the stage within seventeenth century English culture. I maintain that the theater *participated in* political culture. Its voice was not unitary: from play to play, playwright to playwright, company to company there was a good deal of political variety. The theater was certainly not always a platform for opposition, but it was a platform for the voices of politically engaged writers and performers, and it was an auditorium for politically sensitive audiences. As for the theater, so for the press, which was at various moments more and less free to articulate a range of political opinion.

This study belongs to the current iteration of new historicism in its attention to the participation of the written word and the enacted text in the dynamic systems of early modern English culture. Early new historicist studies were justly criticized for attending too narrowly to the cultural elite (the aristocracy, the court, the Crown) and for recapitulating the processes of power they ostensibly sought to expose through their preference for canonical texts, which they viewed principally in relation to these sources of power and capital. The current study joins more recent work that considers the theater as a "popular" art with a diverse constituency and with social and political affinities not exclusively bound to the elite.

While this study by no means ignores or neglects canonical texts or the voices of the social elite, it examines those voices, those texts, for their interplay with the active, astutely political voices of others in early modern England — the voices of women, the voices of City dwellers, the voices of clergy and layfolk. Literate England — or more broadly still, political England — was a socially diverse nation to which and within which London's theaters contributed politically inflected art and entertainment. Even in the final section of the book, which treats writers generally held to have been royalist in their politics, violation remains a politically charged plot element. In Dryden's work, we see the cultural elite's reappropriation of imagery long used against it; in Behn's work, we see a more ambivalent use of rape and coercion. Although both writers worked to earn their living and had economic reasons to curry favor with the court, Dryden was far more successful. Behn's relation to the Crown, first as a foreign spy, then as a writer, was less generously rewarded. As a woman, too, she stood in awkward relation to the intellectual and political elite, never fully receiving the welcome she sought.

In Behn's work as in Cavendish's, we find an old rhetorical convention resurrected and given new resonance as it is exploited to make fresh points about gender politics. Importantly, this book addresses women writers in company with their male peers; it has seemed crucial in this study of the literatures of violation to view women's writing and women's experience as having been enmeshed with the experience and writing of men. Like Wendy Wall, whose book on authorship and the print trade, *The Imprint of Gender*, centers on a series of gendered tropes through which early modern writers and publishers defined "reading, writing, and publishing by generating various representations of women," I felt it imperative that my study do more than merely examine the way male writers used women's experience metaphorically to describe their own situations. As with Wall's study of publication, my study of the political discourses of violation is a study of a particular mode of cultural expression in which the central imagery treats women's experience as a *trope*. Thus, "in order to prevent the category of 'woman' from becoming visible in this work solely as a metaphor for the insecurities of a patriarchal order," I have attended to the ways in which female as well as male authors mobilized these tropes.[39] In the same way that this book considers private and political writing alongside literary texts with the intention that the disparate motives, modes of address and methods of transmission of each type of writing will serve as foils one for another, this study also addresses the work of women (Askew, Stuart, Cavendish and Behn) alongside the work of men (Foxe, Shakespeare, Chapman, Middleton and Rowley, Shirley and Dryden) without segregating or prioritizing either gender group.[40] These juxtapositions clarify our consideration of each text, each genre, each political moment.

I

Acts and Monuments
of Violation

ONE

Spectacles of Violation
ENACTING THE WITNESS OF WORD AND WOODCUT

You see now your doinges so wicked can not be hid, your crueltye is come to light, your murthers be euident, your prety practises, your subtyle sleightes, your secrete conspiracies, your fylthy liues are sene, and stincke before the face both of God and man.
— John Foxe, "To the Persecutors of Gods truth, commonlye called Papistes, an other preface of the Author"

John Foxe's Rhetoric of Violation

England's religious settlement under Elizabeth may have been determined in the relatively closed circles of church, court and Parliament, but it would be difficult to overestimate the extent to which these decisions were shaped, spurred and goaded by the polemical literature that made its way into the public realm of print. Protestant polemicists seized on imagery of violation to plead their case against Roman Catholicism, the great "Whore of Babylon." Although this rhetoric was not a new creation of Elizabethan writers, it flourished in the years following the brief but exceedingly traumatic period of the Marian Counter Reformation.[1]

Protestant polemic quickly found its most substantial expression in John Foxe's martyrology, *The Actes and Monuments of these latter and perillous dayes, touching matters of the Church, wherein ar comprehended and described the great persecutions & horrible troubles, that haue bene wrought and practised by the Romishe Prelates, speciallye in this Realme of England and Scotlande from the yeare of our Lorde a thousande, unto the tyme nowe present.* Foxe's work offers a uniquely powerful account of the violence that the Reformation and Counter Reformation inflicted on the populace of Europe, especially England. First published in 1563, the scope of the work was unparalleled and grew more vast with each subsequent edition.[2] In each of his four English editions, Foxe had two aims: first, to construct a comprehensive Christian history of the world which would prove that the Roman Catholic Church was the Antichrist and that the vulnerable, beset Protestants of Europe were God's elect; and second, to document the monstrous evil of the Roman Catholic Church through an overwhelmingly comprehensive catalog of the horrors it had perpetrated against Protestant martyrs.[3] This second section is the more powerful and more important of the two, as is attested by the fact that the work was popularly called "The Book of Martyrs," not *The Actes and Monuments of these latter and perillous dayes.*

Among the prefatory materials in the first English edition of the work (1563), Foxe includes an open letter to "the Persecutors of Gods truth, commonlye called Papistes," which begins with an appeal to "see" the violence committed against Protestants by Roman Catholic persecutors:

> Beholde your own handy woorke, consider the nomber almost out of nomber of so many, silly & symple lambes of Christ, whose bloud you haue sought and suckt, whose lyues you haue vexed, whose bodies you haue slayne, racked, and tormented, some also you haue cast on dunghils, to be deuoured of Foules and Dogges, wythout mercy, without measure, without al sense of humanity. See I saye and behold here present before your eyes, the heapes of slayne bodies, of so many men and wemen, both old, yonge, chyldren, infantes, new borne, maryed, unmaryed, wyues, wydowes, maydes, blynde

men, lame men, whole men, of al sortes, of al ages, of al degrees, Lordes, Knightes, Gentlemen, Lawyers, Merchauntes, Archbishops, Bishops, Priestes, Ministers, Deacons, Lay men, Artificers, yea whole householdes, and whole kyndredes together, Father, Mother and Daughter, Grandmother, Mother, Aunt, and Chylde. &c. whose woundes yet bleedynge before the face of God, cry vengeaunce.[4]

With its attention to bodily distress and its very particular enumeration of victims ("men and wemen, both old, yonge, chyldren, infantes, new borne, maryed, unmaryed, wyues, wydowes, maydes," and so on), this preface could almost be mistaken for a description of early modern tragedy. Consciously theatrical and deliberately spectacular, this letter previews the strategy Foxe will use throughout the work as he molds his material to resemble a tyrant play in which his Roman Catholic antagonists star as villains who "sought and suckt" the blood of their victims, the poor, simple Protestant "lambes of Christ."

When he enjoins the Papists to "beholde your own handy woorke . . . see I saye and behold here present before your eyes, the heapes of slayne bodies . . . whose woundes yet bleedynge before the face of God, cry vengeaunce," Foxe speaks of the pages of his text as though they are a stage upon which the final scene of a tragic drama has just been played and where the corpses lie dead for his readers to "consider." Though he has only words at his disposal to create the image, Foxe attempts to render a vivid picture of the dead, "the nomber almost out of nomber of so many, silly & symple lambes of Christ, whose bloud you haue sought and suckt, . . . whose bodies you haue slayne, racked, and tormented, some also you haue cast on dunghils, to be deuoured of Foules and Dogges, wythout mercy, without measure, without al sense of humanity." The bodies Foxe depicts are not simply dead; they have been abused in ways that demand the reader's attention and command her imagination. Foxe carefully constructs this abuse as violation: the imposition of violence on helpless innocents.

Foxe's anatomy of violation depends on the notion of *will*: the persecutors seek to impose their wills on their victims. Foxe describes these abusers as willful, a concept that carries two senses as it describes both deliberate, intentional acts as well as acts committed at whim. In the passage above, the appeal to consider the "nomber almost out of nomber" works not only to establish the magnitude of the crimes, but also to suggest that the violence was impersonal, unmotivated except by a zeal to do harm. It is worth noting that in this passage and in many (though not all) of the accounts in the *Acts and Monuments*, Foxe is careful to avoid any suggestion that the victims defended themselves against their tormentors. By attributing all of the action and intention to the villains while presenting the victims as already dead, *this* passage cultivates the notion that the dead in no way provoked the violence that befell them: the Papists "sought" out their victims, pursuing, vexing, torturing, then murdering those who in their "silly and symple" innocence appear to have done nothing to initiate the conflict — they are merely passive recipients of violence, bodies to which horrible things have been done. The will to engage, the will to harm, is thus entirely seated in the victimizers.

This is not to say that Foxe's martyrs lack will. Not at all. Unlike the helpless dead of this preface, most of the victims who people the *Acts and Monuments* achieve the status of martyrs by asserting their wills against the violence meted out by their persecutors. As the violators seek to impose either conversion or punishment, the victims assert their wills by remaining steadfast in their beliefs, even to the point of death. In other words, Foxe constructs martyrdom as a battle of wills won by the victim. Although the persecutors succeed in violating bodies, they cannot ravish the souls of the faithful.[5]

According to Foxe, when the Roman Catholic authorities found Protestants to be spiritually inviolable, they turned in their frustration and fury to break bodies instead. This is another habitual element of his rhetoric of violation. To return to the prefatory letter to the Papists, Foxe turns them from mere executioners into monsters by asserting that their violence went beyond the mere meting out of the prescribed punishment for heresy (burning at the stake, which itself Foxe holds to be inhuman), but extended to blood sucking, "racking" and "tormenting." Finally, he accuses them of desecrating the bodies of their victims (presumably ones that were not burned to ashes) by "cast[ing them] on dunghils, to be deuoured of Foules and Dogges."

Hand in hand with this portrait of Roman Catholics as lacking "al sense of humanity" is another of Foxe's standard devices of vilification: beginning in the prefatory letter to the Papists and extending throughout his martyrological manifesto, he depicts them as practitioners of "manifest whoredome," whose sexual monstrosity is an inextricable element of their evil dispositions. Sexual perversity (the "styncking Camerine of [their] unmaidenly lyues") is not incidental in Foxe's critique of Papist behavior, and it is not incidental in his text. Foxe shares with early modern dramatists the insight that officialdom's wall of secrecy might also confer impunity for sexual abuses. These writers recognize that revelations of secret sex crimes carry more potency than other types of official misconduct. The reason is not only that sex is inherently captivating, but that sexual abuse crystallizes the charge that these villains took pleasure in persecuting their victims. Thus, in print propaganda and onstage, sexual abuse became emblematic of all kinds of tyranny.

Together Foxe and Bale established a polemical style that shaped English political and religious critique for more than a century. The most influential Protestant writer of the previous generation, Bale had fled to Europe in the latter years of Henry VIII's reign to avoid being tried as a heretic.[6] Once established overseas, Bale became a leading propagandist, whose works were printed in Europe, then smuggled into England. Bale's characteristic mode was to attack the hypocrisy and violence of England's ecclesiastical authorities, who, he believed, secretly intended to reunite the English with the Roman church. In his *Epistle exhortatorye of an Englyshe Christiane unto his derelye beloued contreye of Englande against the pompouse popyshe Byshoppes therof as yet the true membres of theyr fylthye father the great Antichrist of Rome*

(1544), Bale depicts the bishops as a self-serving group whose ambitions were for worldly power and riches rather than for the spiritual good of the English people. Thus, Bale portrays clerics as simultaneously indulging their own flesh while oppressing the people:

> The good workes that we beholde in youre daylye conuersacyon for all youre bolde bragges of good workes are by the fylthye frutes of the fleshe as Saynct Paule doth call them. For we se nothynge in you but hawtynesse, vayneglorye, couetousnesse, pryde, hatred, malice, mannis-slaughter, banketynges, glotonye, dronkenesse, slowthe, sedicyon, ydolatrye, wytchecrafte, fornicacyon, lechere, lewdenesse, besydes youre fylthye feates in the darke whan women are not redye at hande.[7]

Both Bale and Foxe address their antagonists directly, accusing them openly of the deeds they might wish to hide. The implication of this passage is that the clerics he accuses are free to indulge themselves because they hold all worldly power and know that they will not be held to account. Thus, the imagery of fleshly corruption becomes a testament to the powerlessness of any human agent to prevent these vicious churchmen from using their power to serve their whims.

Elsewhere in the *Epistle exhortatorye*, Bale elaborates on the charge that shedding innocent blood is among the pleasures in which Roman Catholic clerics love to indulge. One of his favorite rhetorical devices is to cast England's clerics as fell beasts who devour God's hapless flock:

> not onlye the bloudy bearwolfe of Rome, but also the most part of ye other Bysshoppes & stoute sturdy canons of cathedrall churches, with other petie prowlers and prestigiouse Prestes of Baal his malignaunt members in all realmes of Christendome, speciallye here in Englande, doth yet rore abrode lyke hongrie lyons, frete inwardlye lyke angrie beares, and byte as they dare lyke cruel woules, cloysteringe togyther in corners lyke a swarme of adders in a donge hyll or most wylye subtile serpentes to upholde and preserue theyr fylthy father of Rome, the head of theyr bawdye brode yf it maye be. (2v)

Though Bale's penchant for alliteration may be distracting, it should not be thought that he chooses words merely for the sake of their initial consonants. His juxtaposition of "petie prowlers" and "prestigiouse Prestes" highlights his chief complaints about England's clerics: that they were both petty and personal in their targeting of victims; that they were subtle in their pursuit and in their prowling after evidence to use against those they would convict of heresy; and that they were absurdly concerned with prestige, while already possessed of too much worldly power. Insofar as they are like bears, wolves and lions, these clerics are dangerous predators, but their predation may also appear in a more devious form, as the serpent images suggest. Bale warns that these men are to be feared not only for their open violence, but also for their covert attacks that strike victims unawares. The snake metaphors also caution that these men are skillful false persuaders like the "subtle" serpent of Genesis, chapter 3.[8]

When Bale comes directly to his charge that the bishops of the English church are murdering innocent people for failing to espouse the doctrine of the Roman Catholic Church (despite the ostensible separation of the English church under Henry VIII), his imagery of abuse makes use of the rhetoric of violation to communicate that the body can be forced to submit, but a faithful will and spirit never capitulate even to the most horrendous force:

> Ye call euermore upon the earthly gouernours, as ded Symon Magus youre predecessour upon the Emperour Nero, to slee the Gospels preachers; else will not theyr kyngedome endure (ye saye). Christ willed non to be brought to his fayth by compulsyon. Nether used the Apostles to enforce anye manne ther unto. It is not oure maner (sayth Saynct James the more unto Hermogenes) to cause anye manne to take oure beleue unlesse he be willynge. And you lyke tyrauntes more cruell than the Turke constrayne menne to professe youre false fayth by diuerse kyndes of deathe. (16)

For Bale, the sexual grossness of Henry's crypto-Catholic clergy cannot be separated from their quest to assert their wills over those who would resist their theological coercion. The "ranke rable of

Romystes" are both "cruell captaynes and shorne sorcerers of that sodomytycall kyngedome"; they are both worldly magnates and the pope's minions (23v).

Foxe does not exclusively or even principally frame the abuses committed by Roman Catholic authorities as sexual, in which regard he departs from the example of his mentor, who couched his critique largely in these terms. However, Foxe's use of this tactic is an important component of his overall presentation. These two influential writers set the tone for much of the polemic that followed. Foxe's intention at all points is to demonstrate that the pope and the ecclesiastical hierarchy used whatever means they could to force Protestant heretics to recant their firmly held opinions. Foxe views this effort to impose Roman orthodoxy on God's "symple lambes" as violation. At every turn, Foxe wishes his readers to see the heresy proceedings as a battle of wills between faithful Protestants and the hypocritical authorities of the church, who in their zeal to violate the heretic's will did not hesitate to violate his body.[9]

The Witness of Word and Woodcut

In *Acts and Monuments,* Foxe demonstrates a clear sense of the dramatic potential of his material. A playwright himself, Foxe brought to the writing of narrative history the stylistic and presentational techniques of stage practice, which he adapted to his work's printed medium. In her recent study, *Staging Reform, Reforming the Stage: Protestantism and Popular Theater in Early Modern England*, Huston Diehl contends that Foxe shapes and selects his materials as a dramatist would.[10] Diehl notices this especially in his decision to print the transcripts of ecclesiastical and civil trials and interrogations in dialogue form rather than paraphrasing or narrativizing his sources: "Printed as dialogue — like the scripts of plays — these examinations lay out the arguments of both the martyrs and their persecutors in a way that highlights the dramatic conflict between them. By thus adopting the techniques of a playwright, Foxe renders the theological con-troversies of the Reformation immediate, accessible, and rele-vant to his audiences."[11] However, as anyone who has seen the work would immediately acknowledge, the sections of dialogue, the vivid descriptions, the declamatory asides—the text—are the lesser elements in *Acts and Monuments'* theatrical display. Through the woodcuts, the printer John Daye contributed spectacle to the work, heightening the visual and agonistic aspects of the text so that the printed word complements and is completed by these remarkable illustrations. The Book of Martyrs is in reality a collaboration between these two men, and its dramatic qualities are the result of the combined witness of word and woodcut.

Again and again in *Acts and Monuments*, Foxe's text and its woodcut illustrations work together to depict the Marian per-secutions as the fruit of an unholy alliance between church and state authorities. The result is a picture of individual tyranny and collective abuse of power on the part of England's highest officials. In his editorial preface to the documentary evidence he assembles concerning "the martyrdome and burnyng of x. faythfull and blessed Martyrs, v. men, and v. women burnt at Colchester. V. in the forenoon, and v. in the afternoone for the testimony and wytnes of Christ Jesus and his glorious Gospell," Foxe writes:

> Among the manyfolde matters mentioned in the hystoryes of this booke, I marvaile more at the great ouersight of some, then at the malicious myndes, and monstrous doinges of others. It hath bene alwaies sene since Sathan broke lose, that prelates haue persecuted the poore people of Christ: but in my minde *this is moste to be lamented, that noble men, men of honour, and worship woulde bee made suche ministers to serue the affections of these tyraunts*, as they were in the sorowful dayes of the late quene Mary. For if thou diligenly marke (good Reader) herein the labours of every state and degree in al tymes and yeares, who then sitteth so styl in worldly security, as doth the bloody byshops, unles it be to practise pestilent policy, to bring such worthy men to serue their slauishe slaughter, to the poysoning of Christen soules, as here in this history thou mayest se, to the great griefe of a good hart. (Italics added)[12]

Here and throughout the work, Foxe bemoans the cooperation of secular authorities with the ecclesiastical hierarchy. Like Bale, who writes of the seductive voice of the fair-seeming church, which like "the mermaydes songe [is] swete, yet . . . full of payson (as are your honyed rhetoryckes) & leadeth them unto deathe whych geueth them thereof yᵉ hearynge," Foxe insinuates that honorable noblemen have been seduced into serving the "affections of these tyraunts" (24). Bale noted the affinities between the proud prelates of his day and the upper classes, "great lordes and ladyes, lerned menne and stowte lawers, gentylmenne, great doctours, & soche as hath fat benefices, with a bende of bolde braggers or blasphe-mouse swearers abought ye to wayte upon youre tables, to holde up you tayles in the strete, to kepe youre houndes and horses, and to conueye you in the darke a pece for youre pleasur" (22).

Not only is this a critique of the worldliness of religious men who, in the Protestant view, should be the least worldly of all men, it is also an attack on the power bloc of combined secular and sacred authority. Both writers see that secular authority has somehow been brought to serve the church and both attempt to dismantle the alliance by presenting it as a subversion of societal order. In the passage quoted above, Foxe seeks to make great lords and other powerful lay people see that their power would increase if they did not submit themselves "slavishly" to ecclesiastical authority.[13] While it is not an appeal to the purest instincts of its audience, it is a wholly Protestant argument: the reformers held that each soul could approach God directly without the intervention of a priest; thus, the upper classes (all people, in fact) had no need to court the favor of churchmen who could neither harm nor enhance their chances of entering heaven. The sexual insinuations in Bale's version of the argument are icing on the cake, contributing to make the clergy less appealing: not only are they depicted as sexually corrupt (seeking "in the darke a pece for [their] pleasur"), but also sexually corrupting, making bawds and prostitutes of the (aristocratic) laity to "serue [their] affections."

Foxe's account of the heresy proceedings against William Sawtrey, a fifteenth century Wyclifite priest, is characteristic in its treatment of the complicity of church and state. According to this account, Sawtrey was a priest who fell afoul of the bishops of his day for offering to preach to Parliament a sermon "inflamed with the zeale of true Religion . . . for the commoditie and profit of the whole Realme" (1563 ed., 141). Unfortunately for Sawtrey, his case came to trial in the first year after Henry IV's usurpation of the throne. The result, according to Foxe's second edition, was that "As king Henry the i.i.i.i. . . . was the first of all English kinges that began the unmercifull burning of Christes saintes, for standing against the Pope: so was this W[illiam] Sautre the true and faythfull Martyr of Christ, the first of all them in Wicliffes time, which I finde to be burned in the raygne of the foresaid king, which was in yᵉ yere of our lord 1400" (1570 ed., 1:619). Sawtrey's case is not singular among Foxe's martyrs, except for its chronological significance: it is the first account of an English Christian put to death for his resistance to papal supremacy, and it is the first place in the text where Daye inserted an illustration of a martyr burning at the stake.[14] Although a few illustrations precede this one, the Sawtrey woodcut is the first to depict a living, gesticulating, speaking body being consumed by flames[15] (fig. 1.1).

We do not know whether Foxe and Daye collaborated in the decision to include this illustration, but it perfectly underscores Foxe's treatment of the episode. The body is chained to the stake and engulfed in flames, which even lick up from his head and his fingertips. The upstretched arms simultaneously communicate suffering and religious fervor; the victim imitates Christ on the cross as he spreads wide his arms. Although he calls for mercy, this figure appears calm. Rather than cast his eyes to heaven with his appeal, he looks directly forward — at the reader. His words, then, are ambiguous. Is he asking for mercy for himself, or does he ask on behalf of other Christians, or does he beg mercy for his persecutors? The steadfast martyr's gaze is as unsettling as the artist's depiction of the riotous flames; the effect is horrifying.

Fig. 1.1. The burning of William Sawtre. From Foxe, *Acts and Monuments* (1570), 1:618. Courtesy of the Rare Books and Manuscripts Library of the Ohio State University Libraries.

The horror of this execution is absolutely Foxe's point; thus, he includes the king's "terrible decree" (1563 ed., 142), which in its English translation calls for Sawtrey to "be put into the fyer, and there in the same fyer really to be burned, to the great horrour of this offence and the manifest example of other Christians" (1563 ed., 143). Clearly, Foxe's text deconstructs the king's decree, rendering the incident so that the execution itself appears to be a "horrible offence" and reversing the "manifest example" taught by the episode. Where Henry IV intended the execution to teach his Christian subjects to avoid heresy, Foxe transforms the event into a witness of Sawtrey's victimization by the Crown, an event that teaches Christians to persevere in faith even in the face of persecution. Foxe intends that his readers understand not only the horrible suffering of burning martyrs, but also the horror of a state that would put its subjects to such an awful death in its attempt to constrain (Foxe would say corrupt) the Christian conscience.

Finally, in the passage accompanied by the marginal gloss: "Admonition to Princes," Foxe concludes his account with this bit of editorializing:

> Thus it may appeare howe kynges & princes haue bene blynded & abused by ye false prelates of the churche, in so much that they haue bene their slaues and butchers, to slay Christes poore innocent members. See therfore what daunger it is for Princes, not to haue knoweledge and understanding them selues, but to be led by other mens eyes, and specially trusting to suche guydes, who through hypocrisie both deceiue them, and through crueltie devoure the people. (1563 ed., 143)

Foxe insists on the tyrannical connivance of the king with the church hierarchy, a connivance that in Henry IV's case resulted from Henry's reliance on support from the church in order to maintain his grasp on the throne. Foxe warns, however, that any monarch might play this role if inadequately prepared to withstand the deceptive wiles of false prelates. In the 1570 edition, Daye repositioned the illustration so that the woodcut appears directly beneath the "Admonition" as though to punctuate its point (fig 1.1).

The woodcuts never miss an opportunity to cast Roman Catholic clerics of all types in the villain's role. For instance, in the illustration accompanying the account of William Tyndale's execution (fig 1.2), an appropriately sinister-looking monk stands on each side of the scaffold, observing and perhaps directing the proceedings (1563 ed., 519). (See especially the tonsured figure on the right side, who is depicted leaning forward and gesticulating animatedly. His fellow on the opposite side reveals only a ghoulish face.)

Like Foxe's text, the illustration also indicts secular authorities for their role: here, secular gentlemen occupy the foreground, some of them armed as officers of the state (of Flanders, in this case), and a secular official is strangling Tyndale as he ties him to the stake. The illustrator indulges in a bit of irony, too, as he shows that the state is not quick enough in stopping Tyndale's breath to prevent him from expressing his challenge to the church and state: "Lord open the king of Englands eies." Tyndale's speech is significant: although he is clearly speaking of the need for *religious* reform, he aims his words at the king of England, Henry VIII.

More commonly, as in figure 1.3 illustrating the hanging of three martyrs, the woodcuts depict clergymen directing the proceedings. This particular illustration puts the cleric at front and center, giving the reader a clear view of his robe, stole and four-cornered hat. The square cap, which was a particular target of Elizabethan antivestmentary attacks, appears among the crowd in figure 1.2 (look just over the shoulder of the hooded monk on the left side). It becomes ubiquitous in Foxe's text, appearing as the counterpart to the distinguishing signifiers of monks: the cowl and tonsure. In fact, the woodcuts forge this connection quite deliberately: English and Roman Catholic clerics merge to become two flavors of the same evil. Wherever the viewer looks, a square cap, a cowl or a tonsured head is sure to appear. Always, these are the marks of a sinister figure. Often, their wearers are depicted in the midst of some abusive deed, as in the illustration of Edmund Bonner, Marian bishop of London, burning the hand of Thomas Tomkyns during his imprisonment as he awaited execution (fig. 1.4).

Fig. 1.2. The execution of William Tyndale. From Foxe, *Acts and Monuments* (1563), 519. Courtesy of the Rare Books and Manuscripts Library of the Ohio State University Libraries.

Fig. 1.3. The hanging of three iconoclasts. From Foxe, *Acts and Monuments* (1563), 496. Courtesy of the Rare Books and Manuscripts Library of the Ohio State University Libraries.

Fig. 1.4. "The sharp burning of Thomas Tomkyns' hand, by cruel Boner himself, who not long after burnt also his body." From Foxe, *Acts and Monuments* (1570), 1101. Courtesy of the Rare Books and Manuscripts Library of the Ohio State University Libraries.

Although it depicts an unusually large number of clergymen in attendance on this torture, the illustration is typical in its representation of the victim's fortitude during his ordeal. Tomkyns's figure appears small compared to the clerics, who would tower above him if they stood up. By contrast with his well-balanced and composed facial features, the collected clerics are grotesque: all have squinting or leering eyes, bulbous or beaklike noses. Bonner is particularly unappealing in this caricature, which exaggerates his bloated jowls. The only clergyman who is not giving his full attention to Tomkyns's torture is the one in the middle rear, who scowls at the jailer — apparently because the scene has moved the jailer to tears. While this jailer is more sympathetic than the clerics, he is impotent to stop the proceedings, and he does not appear to have the gumption to try. There can be no doubt where the viewer's sympathies ought to lie.

There is a tension in *Acts and Monuments* between an impulse to portray the martyrs as strong, unshakeable souls and an impulse to emphasize their vulnerability in order to convey more forcefully the overwhelming power and evil of their persecutors. The wood-cuts reveal a similarly divided approach: in some the illustrator aims to show the fortitude and fearlessness of the martyrs, while others emphasize (even sensationalize) the suffering and distress of the victims. While the stories and illustrations do not equate these categories with gender, gender is a significant element in both types of account.

Where the text wishes to emphasize the fortitude of Protestant martyrs, it can heighten that effect when the martyr is a woman. Hugh Latimer and Nicholas Ridley went to the stake like brave men, an impression etched in the minds of generations of readers by Foxe's report of Latimer's last, courageous words: "Be of good comfort, master Ridley, and play the man. We shall this day light such a candle, by God's grace, in England, as I trust shall never be put out" (1570 ed., 2:60). Rose Allin, however, appears in *Acts and Monuments* as a young woman whose fortitude in the face of official intimidation and physical suffering exceeded all expecta-tions (fig. 1.5). Like Thomas Tomkyns and Bishops Latimer and Ridley, Allin transforms the persecutors' flame into a light that exposes their hypocrisy. But she is a woman, which, for the early modern writer and audience, makes her strength and patience a far greater tribute to the power of faith at work in the believer's soul.[16]

Like Allin, Anne Askew was a young woman who refused to be intimidated or swayed by the men who interrogated, tortured and condemned her. In both cases, the woman's youth combines with her gender to render her bravery the more remarkable. One of the most famous of Foxe's martyrs, Askew went to the stake as an extraordinary woman, a woman who so transcended her society's expectations of feminine behavior (weakness, fearfulness) that she was reported to have inspired the men who died with her. Foxe concludes his account of the execution with this observation:

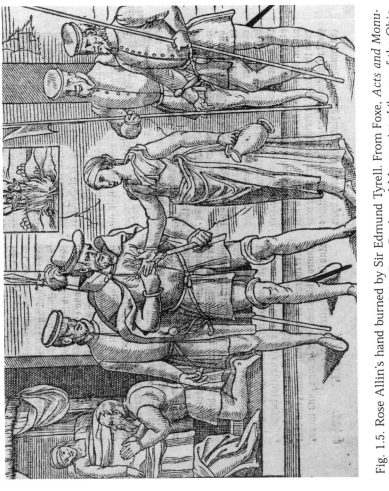

Fig. 1.5. Rose Allin's hand burned by Sir Edmund Tyrell. From Foxe, *Acts and Monuments* (1563), 1544. Courtesy of the Rare Books and Manuscripts Library of the Ohio State University Libraries.

It happened well for [these men], that they died together with Anne Askewe. For albeit that of them selves they were strong and stout menne, yet through the example and praier of her, thei being the more boldned, receyved occasion of more greater comforte, in that so painfull and doolefull kynde of death, not only beholdyng her invincible constancie, but also oftentimes stirred up through her perswasions, they did set apart all kynde of feare.[17]

Throughout her narrative, Anne Askew emphasizes her gender for two strategic reasons: first, to make her persecutors seem more monstrous for their unchivalrous treatment of a woman, and second, to make her triumph the greater when all of their authority and all of their masculine self-possession fails to break Askew's spirit.

Gender could also be used to quite different effect. When Foxe wished to horrify his readers or wished to heighten the emotional effect of an account, womanly fear and distress was a trump card to be played. Figure 1.6 illustrates Foxe's account of the execution of three women unjustly convicted of heresy during the Marian persecutions. (Foxe concedes that the three did not even hold heretical opinions, but he uses their case to illustrate the blood lust of the authorities who would proceed in such a case.) Here the text and the woodcut work together to capitalize on the vulnerability of these "sely" women (1563 ed., 1544). In the text, they are the victims of the "crueltye of the Deane [of the Isle of Gurnsey] and his accomplices," and of the king's officers, the "honourable counsel" of the Crown, and of the king and queen themselves, to whom the women appealed their case. All of these authority figures are described as "bloody, furious, and fyrye Papists," whose "malicious hatred" led them to conspire to deprive these women of their property and their lives (1563 ed., 1544–46).

The monstrosity of the "Papists" and the suffering of the women crystallize in the episode's most amazing feature: the persecutors put to death not only these three women, but also burned a newborn child. The woodcut conflates two moments during this sensational event, showing the birth of the child from its mother's

Fig. 1.6. Three women of Guernsey and an infant burned at the stake. From Foxe, *Acts and Monuments* (1563), 1544. Courtesy of the Rare Books and Manuscripts Library of the Ohio State University Libraries.

ruptured womb and also depicting the attending bishop in the act of throwing the infant back into the fire to die with its mother. The bishop is shown pulling back his distinctive long sleeve to improve his range of movement as he casts the child into the fire. Beyond signifying the bishop's perverse use of his authority, this gesture and the pulled back sleeve amount to a parody of birthing scenes, in which the cleric-midwife raises his garment not to receive the infant from its mother, but to cast the child away.[18]

Foxe's accompanying text provides the reader with this account of the atrocity:

> At the tyme that the sayd good poore women were burning in the fyrye flames aboute them, the wombe of the sayde Paratine [Massye], shee beyng great with childe, brake with the heate of the sayde fyre, and thereby issued foorthe of her bodye a goodlye man chylde, which was taken up, and handled by the cruell tormentours, and after they threw most spightfullye the same chylde into the fyre agayne, wher it was burned with the sely Mother, Graundmother, and Aunt, very pitifully to behold. (1563 ed., 1544).

The baby, of course, is a propaganda coup: here is a truly innocent death and an extraordinary villainy committed by the authorities. The author and illustrator work deliberately to use the gender of the women, especially the pregnancy of the one and her motherly distress at the fate of her child, to heighten the contrast between the martyrs and their powerful persecutors.

The nakedness of the women is also significant. The woodcut is quite careful not to unduly eroticize its treatment of the scene. For instance, while the bare shoulders and the revealed nape of the neck of the woman on the left-hand side and the draping of her hair over her shoulder might be read as a sexual treatment of the female body according to early modern pictorial conventions, it would be difficult to argue that the exposed breasts of the central figure are in any way eroticized (they almost seem anatomically misplaced). If the illustrator has used some of the conventions of beauty in his portrayal of the first woman, he seems intent on coding the figure of the second woman in terms of her distress rather than in terms of her beauty or her desirability.

However, despite the illustrator's care not to arouse his viewers, he suggests that the male figures within his illustration may find the scene arousing. Consider the expressions and line of sight of the two secular officers at the right of the drawing: they appear intrigued with the proceedings, though perhaps no more so than the corresponding figures in the Tyndale illustration (fig. 1.2). Or consider the prominent codpieces on two of the men at the left of the illustration. Again, this is not the only illustration depicting men in codpieces, but it seems that in the context of this scene, this element of masculine dress receives heightened attention. As one looks from the cleric to the baby, it is difficult not to look at the one man's codpiece: the baby's hand points the eye in that direction.

Among the woodcuts, the most obviously sexualized treatment of abuse occurs in the illustration of Bishop Bonner flogging a Protestant martyr, "The ryght Picture and true counterfeyt of Boner, and his crueltye, in scourgynge of Goddes Saynctes in his Orchard" (fig. 1.7). This illustration appears in the middle of a section of *Acts and Monuments* entitled, "An other Chapiter or treatyse concerning such as were scourged and whypped by the papistes, in the true cause of Christes Gospel," which begins on page 1682 near the end of the 1563 edition. The chapter reaches back to the "tyme of Anne Ascue," the end of Henry VIII's reign, then runs chronologically through the stories of several people who were scourged during their examinations for heresy. In the first two accounts, Bishop Bonner receives mention, but plays no more than a walk-on role, stopping to peek into a prison cell to taunt a printer's apprentice jailed for publishing a book called *Antichrist*. As the section progresses, however, Bonner plays an increasingly central role, becoming the principal antagonist. Where the first two accounts culminate in whippings carried out by secular authorities, the latter cases detail Bishop Bonner's penchant for personally whipping not only his prisoners, but other hapless souls who fall into his hands. The examples move from his vicious treatment of "guilty" adults to his outrageous treatment of innocent children. For instance, we get an account of some unlucky

Fig. 1.7. "The right Picture and true counterfeit of Boner, and his cruelty, in scourging of God's Saints in his Orchard." From Foxe, *Acts and Monuments* (1563), 1689. Courtesy of the Rare Books and Manuscripts Library of the Ohio State University Libraries.

children who happen to be bathing in the Thames as the bishop's barge crosses the river. For his amusement, the bishop has his men catch the children, "beatyng som with nettels, drawing some thorow bushes of nettels naked" (1563 ed., 1692). This is followed by the much worse account of the bishop's beating of the young son of one of his prisoners, hurting the boy so badly that the bishop decides he must release the father lest the boy die in custody. Foxe reports that "within fourtene daies after the chylde dyed, whether throughe thys cruell scourginge, or any other infirmitye, I know not" (1694).

The woodcut is not, in fact, an accurate illustration of any one of the accounts in this section; instead, it conflates details from at least two: (1) the case of John Milles, whom Bonner took to "his Orchard, there within a lyttle herbare, with his own handes beat him, first w[ith] a willow rod, that being worne well nyghe to the stumpes, then called for a burchen rodde, which a lad brought out of his chamber," and (2) Thomas Hinshaw, "a young manne, of the age of xix. or xx. yeres," who stood up so bravely to the interrogation, that in frustration the bishop was reduced to calling him a "naughty boy" afterwhich he "sent for a couple of roddes, and caused him to knele against a long bench in an arbour in his gardein, where the seide Thomas with out any enforcement of his part, offred himselfe to the beating, and did abide the fury of the said Boner" (1690–91). Here we see the seeds of several of the elements in the illustration, which nonetheless fails in several respects to adhere faithfully to the text.

The woodcut depicts the victim in a kneeling posture, his shirt raised and his breeches lowered, his back dripping with blood from the wounds he has received. However, this victim is not a 19-year-old apprentice, but a fully bearded adult — and he is not depicted kneeling willingly against a bench, but kneeling with his head immobilized between the knees of another man. This latter figure is interesting: he wears a sword, which suggests that he is an officer assisting Bonner in this scene of punishment. But he also covers his face with his hand in a gesture that indicates distress and disapproval of the proceedings. The representation of his emotion contrasts with the depiction of the two evil-visaged clerics who stand by while the torture continues. As in the illustration of Thomas Tomkyns's torture (fig. 1.4), only this attending gentleman shows any distress.

The woodcut also illustrates the bringing of more rods; however, the bearer is not a "lad," but (again) a bearded man, one of two gentlemen in the left background. Their body language is also significant. Like the two clerics in the right foreground, they appear to be discussing the scene before them. The closest figure turns his head over his shoulder to comment to his companion. It is an awkward position for depicting conversation; the man's body remains pointed forward, toward Bonner and his victim. The effect is to emphasize this gentleman's swaggering posture (chest puffed forward, codpiece prominent), suggesting his authority and willing participation. Coming forward, he carries the rods. In all parts he is the bishop's second, the secular authority lending his power to the ecclesiastical bully. He is also the antithesis of the weeping gentleman in the foreground, whose bowed shoulders and bare head mark his sympathy for the victim.

The text makes Bonner a tyrant, whose zeal for the Roman Catholic cause makes him bloodthirsty. He taunts his prisoners with threats of hell, "As truely as thou seest the bodies of them in Smithfield burn, so truely their soules do burn in hell, because they erre from the Churche" (1563 ed., 1690). To the Protestant reader, this threat is nonsense, but it is frightening nonsense. To Protestants, the bodies at Smithfield communicate two things: the sanctity of those who died and the evil of those, like Bonner, who put them to death. Foxe takes the liberty of having his Bonner acknowledge and revel in his tyrant's reputation: "They call me (saieth he) bloudye Boner. A vengeaunce on you al. I would fayn be ridde of you, but ye haue a delite in burning: but if I might haue my request, I woulde sow your mouthes and put you in sackes, & drowne you" (1690).

The woodcut, too, makes clear Bonner's relish for putting bodies to torment. It adds, however, an element the text does not choose to heighten. The illustration is deliberately sexualized, from the position of the victim to Bonner's leer to his swollen codpiece. It distills Foxe's message throughout his book of martyrs — and registers Foxe's debt to his mentor, Bale: all "Papist" clerics (whether of the English or the Roman church) are "byteshepes, tyrauntes, tormentours, termagaunts, and the deuyls slaughter menne," who devour rather than protect the souls in their cure, violators who attempt the rape of body and soul (*Epistle Exhorta-torye*, 27). For this assault, the bishop has removed his gown (it rests in a heap in the right foreground); his square cap has been cast off and lies behind him. The illustrator has removed the false lamb's wool to reveal the hidden bite-sheep: without his cap, we can see that he bears the tonsured head of a friar. The bishop is shown to be one of the "shorne sorcerers of that sodomytycall kyngedome"; the ecclesiastic's decorous robes have been cast aside to expose the sexual predator underneath (ibid., 23v).

This woodcut also disparages the bishop by appropriating the comic conventions of carnivalesque inversion common to English folk literature and popular justice. In its depiction of Bonner's grotesque figure, the illustration picks up on another strain of the text's representation of the bloody bishop, rendering him ridiculous even as it conveys his fearsomeness. The text, for instance, reports not only Bonner's violence against those he deems "heretics," but also ridicules Bonner's attempts to impose his own obviously erroneous views of Scripture and worship on discerning, Bible-reading Protestants. Foxe invites his reader "that lusteth to laugh, to se the blinde and unsauorye reasons of that Bishop which he used to perswade the ignorant . . . not to medle with matters of the scripture, but rather to beleue other mens teachinng, which hadde more skil in the same" (1563 ed., 1690). Then Foxe illustrates Bonner's "skill" by recounting the bishop's attempt to persuade John Milles of the ridiculous flaws in English translations of the Bible. The anecdote shows instead that the error rests wholly with the bishop's gross misinterpretation of the English: "If thou wert a slepe hauing a wife, wouldest thou be content thy wife to take an other man? And yet this is the scripture" (ibid., 1690). The bishop not only proves to be a poor reader of English, but a salacious misconstruer of Holy Writ.

It is with the same belittling effect in mind that the text begins its account of Thomas Hinshaw's beating with Bonner's threats, but ends it with his impotence:

> I shal handle thee wel inough, be assured: so he sent for a couple of roddes, and caused him to knele against a long bench in an arbour in his gardein, where the saide Thomas . . . did abide the fury of the said Boner, so long as the fat panched bishop could endure with breath, and till for wearinesse he was faine to cease, and geve place to his shamefull act. He had two willow roddes, but he wasted but one, and so left of. (1563 ed., 1691)

In his essay, "Robin Hood, the carnivalesque, and the rhetoric of violence," Peter Stallybrass charts a popular tradition that unmasks certain "enforcers of political orthodoxy" as oppressors and subjects them to ridicule. Not surprisingly, it appears that bishops were a favorite target of this literature of subversion and transgression. Stallybrass offers "a tentative morphology of the carnivalesque," the elements of which are highly suggestive of the techniques employed by the artist(s) who illustrated Bishop Bonner for the readers of Foxe and Daye's martyrology.[19]

The first element of the carnivalesque employed by the illustrator is what Stallybrass identifies as "the replacement of fast by feast."[20] In both of the woodcuts that offer portraits of Bonner (see figs. 1.4 and 1.7), the artist signals the bishop's worldliness and self-indulgence by emphasizing his corpulence, a sharp contrast with the temperate leanness of his victims. The text and illustration both use Bonner's body against him: the text makes him the "fat panched bishop" who tires quickly when he exerts himself beating Thomas Hinshaw. Sir John Harington corroborates this physical description of Bonner, remembering that when he was a child in Elizabethan London, the former bishop of London "was so hated, that every ill-favored fat fellow, that went in the Street, they would say it was Bonner."[21] Thus, the bishop's actual physique lent itself to an existing tradition of caricature and ridicule, linking corpulence with ill intent, unmerited self-gratulation and impotence.

The scourging woodcut is literally an exposé of the familiar figure of the bishop; it strips him of the robes that lent dignity and concealment to the bulk of his body. What we see by examining the two portraits of Bonner together is the extent to which the scourging illustration relies on the "transgression of bodily barriers" to undermine the bishop's authority. Drawing on Bakhtin, Stallybrass points out that "the carnivalesque emphasizes those parts which rupture the 'opaque surface' of the classical body: 'the open mouth, the genital organs, the breasts, the potbelly, the nose.' The head is subordinated to 'the lower bodily stratum'; the open mouth and nose are foregrounded because they are equated with the anus and the phallus."[22] Although his mouth is closed and his nose is of normal size, the bishop's head is disproportionately small with respect to his potbelly and genitals. What is remarkable about the bishop's head is the rolling fat of the neck and jowls, the smirk into which his lips are twisted, and, of course, the tonsured head and clean-shaven chin. Clearly, also, the kneeling figure of Bonner's victim fits here. The degree to which this man's dignity has been violated is key to the illustration's appeal to its viewer's sense of outrage. Not only has his skin been lacerated, but he has been forced into a submissive posture and has been compelled to expose himself to the bishop's lash and his gaze — and to our own.

What is outrageous about the events depicted in this illustration is not only its rupturing of bodily decorum, but also its "inversion of hierarchy." In carnivalesque literature, "the servant rules his master, the child rules his parents, the wife rules her husband."[23] Here, hierarchy is inverted when a gentleman is subjected to the punishment appropriate to a boy or a subordinate. It is a treatment so perverse and inappropriate that the bishop is exposed as an oppressor rather than a legitimate authority figure. From the point of view of Foxe's reformed readers, the bishop himself inverts

hierarchy by usurping temporal authority and rejecting his proper place as servant-pastor of his cure. Although inversion does
not tumble the bishop from his worldly throne into the muck
of humiliation — as it would in the ballad tradition — both
illustration and text use the bishop's unseemly bodily exertions to
link him with dirt and sweat and manual labor. The illustration
relies on its early modern readers to react strongly to its revelation
that this "lordly bishop" is no better than a base laborer. Of course,
the illustration plays to an audience that viewed the depicted scene
with the knowledge that time and events had toppled the bishop
from his see; Bonner had been humbled by the course of national
events by the time anyone read Foxe's book or saw this illustration.

While the literature of the carnivalesque habitually indulges in
"the degrading of the sacred," Protestant polemic does not target
the sacred in a general way, but attacks the ceremonies, vestures
and personnel of Roman Catholicism in order to expose them as
impostures of sanctity.[24] This is certainly one way to read the
illustrator's decision to portray Bonner disrobed; in this state of
undress, the bishop is revealed to be merely human. The clothes
that confer dignity and signify sacred office lie disregarded in the
background. Ostensibly, it is Bonner himself who casts off his robe
without concern for his or its sanctity, but of course it is the
illustrator who puts the bishop's robe and hat in the dirt precisely
to deride the pretended authority of these sartorial elements; for
the Protestant reader of this woodcut, the position of the bishop's
robes on the ground merely confirms their lack of sacred authority.

Stallybrass draws on Mary Douglas to remind us that carnival
"celebrates the triumph of 'dirt' or 'matter out of place.' . . . [In
this literature,] the boundaries of gender, class, status, the body,
the sacred, and the cultural are transgressed."[25] In addition to the
inversions of space, decorum, class, status, the body, and the sacred
detailed above, gender distortion is a key element of the woodcut.
Though I have described already the sexual enormity of Bonner's
codpiece and bodily pose, it must also be noted that the gender
coding of his figure is ambiguous. The hairless faces of Roman

Catholic clerics were habitually given a hostile reading by Protestants, who took them not as a sign of legitimate sacred devotion, but as a sign of sexual perversion, as when Bale dubs them the "shorne sorcerers of that sodomytycall kyngedome" (*Epistle exhortatorye*, 23v). Because they interpreted the priest's renunciation of adult male sexuality to be a perversion of God's creation, Protestants chose to read the shaven face as a sign that marked the priest as either sodomite or eunuch.[26] The woodcut artist offers both ways of reading Bonner: as a sexual predator or as a virtual castrato, his cheeks shorn of any mark of sexual maturity and his codpiece stuffed with padding to mock his lack. In either case, the figure's deviation from the gender codes of normative Protestant masculinity makes him grotesque. As Stallybrass writes, "In carnival, gender, like dirt, provided a concrete logic through which the subversion of deference and hierarchy could be rehearsed."[27]

The illustration also has another means of degrading the sacred, or of delegitimating Bonner's claim to sanctity: its representation of the bishop flogging the prisoner poses him less as ecclesiast than as executioner. In a study of European representations of execution and torture, Samuel Y. Edgerton Jr. traces in art and in historical records a tradition associating the role of the executioner with the devil: "Symbolically, he was regarded as the vicar of the devil, counterpart to the judge, who was the vicar of Christ. . . . [The executioner was] expected to play his vicarious devil's role to the letter. His physical appearance was anything but reticent. He was given to gaudy feathered hats, skin-tight britches with prominent codpieces, and he often stripped bare to the waist to perform his functions."[28] Edgerton argues that the executioner's villainous appearance courted a deliberate, but not wholly predictable, effect on spectators, who saw "not only a performance of temporal justice but a symbolic drama, a rehearsal of the eternal battle between the angels of God and the demons of Satan." Edgerton claims that this iconography transformed the prisoner into an image of "a pitiable soul struggling for salvation."[29] For Edgerton, this iconography explains why crowds would sometimes turn on the executioner in support of the prisoner, whom they subsequently saw not as a criminal, but as a victim. It is precisely this effect that the Bonner woodcut achieves for the Protestant viewer, who does not interpret the scene as the meting out of justice, but as the persecution of innocence.

That this tradition of visual representation influenced Protestant polemicists other than Foxe and Daye is clear in a woodcut by Lucas Cranach the Elder (fig. 1.8). Cranach debases the soldiers erecting Saint Peter's cross by distorting their facial features (scowling, hook-nosed, pockmarked), by rendering them ridiculously inept in their gestures, and by providing them with outrageously phallic weapons.[30] Cranach, like Daye's woodcut artist, relies on a pictorial tradition linking moral depravity with low social status, signaled through bodily coarseness, physical disproportion and physical exertion. But Bonner is unlike the anonymous laborers in the Saint Peter illustration; to depict him as a base and busy villain was a bold stroke on the illustrator's part.

In concert with the woodcut's representation of Bonner as base executioner, the texts collected in *Acts and Monuments* ascribe to the bishop a lack of decorum in speech, an inability to control his temper and tongue. This "transgression of the linguistic hierarchy," in which "the languages of billingsgate (oaths, curses, obscenities) are privileged over 'correct' speech" is a further characteristic of carnivalesque literature that served Protestant polemicists seeking to villify Bishop Bonner. Although Foxe does not indulge much in the language of billingsgate, he does put a curse in Bonner's mouth, making the bishop swear "a vengeaunce on you al" before announcing his desire to drown Protestants like puppies. There is an apocryphal story associated with this illustration that became an important part of the interpretation of Bonner as depicted here. Sir John Harington, in his *Supplie or Addicion to the Catalogue of Bishops* (1608), reports that this illustration was shown to Bonner while he was in prison, whereupon he exclaimed, "A vengeance of the foole, how could he get my picture drawne so right?" Harington reports that when

Fig. 1.8. *The Martyrdom of St. Peter*. From Lucas Cranach the Elder, "The Martyrdom of the Twelve Apostles" series of woodcuts. Reproduced by permission of the British Library.

the bishop was then asked "if he were not ashamed to whip a man with a beard, he laught and told him his beard had grown since, but saith he, if thou haddst bene in his case, thou wouldst have thought it a good commutacion of pennance, to have thy bumme beaten to save thy bodie from burning."[31] The bishop's pride in his deed, his linguistic tweaking of his victim's beard so long after the fact, and his refusal to honor the episode with circumspect speech were all part of the bishop's persona as constructed by his opponents both before and after Foxe and Daye took aim at him.

The woodcut itself engages in transgression of the linguistic hierarchy after a fashion.[32] The illustration contains the word "Bōno" inscribed above the bishop's right shoulder. The primary meaning of this tag, of course, is to identify the figure by name. There is, however, also a caption to accomplish this work of identification, "The ryght Picture and true counterfeyt of Boner, and his crueltye, in scourgynge of Goddes Saynctes in his Orchard," so the inscribed "Bōno" is redundant. Its secondary meaning is ironic. The bishop and his beating of God's saints is labeled "good" in the Latin of Bonner's Roman Catholic religion; thus, the illustrator scores a dual condemnation of the liturgy Bonner defends and of the cruelty with which he enforces it. From the Protestant point of view, Latin is a language that perverts the truth, rendering the good news false and inaccessible. Finally, the illustrator and caption writer indulge in a bit of bawdy double entendre at the expense of the bishop, whose name, though pronounced with a "short" vowel sound, could be spelled either with one n̲ or two according to the spelling and printing conventions of the day. (In this case the first n̲ is denoted by the macron over the o̲.) Particularly in the context of this illustration with its attention to the bishop's codpiece, the decision to spell his name with a single n̲ begs to be seen as a wink at what was then (and is now) slang for the erect penis. In all of these ways, the woodcut overturns and debases the usual, laudatory sense of "Bōno" in order to cast opprobrium on Bishop Bōner.[33]

The visual and verbal rhetorics of the carnivalesque combine to allow the Protestant woodcut illustrator, along with John Foxe and John Daye and their readers, to celebrate the defeat of Bonner and Roman Catholicism. Thus, *Acts and Monuments* musters the witness of both word and woodcut to mount a potent assault on the memory of the Marian church. The comic elements of this work seek to turn the tables on those who had abused so many Protestants, taking a measure of vengeance on them after the fact. However, even the parodic license of this text cannot erase the horror of the violence to which it witnesses. It may invite its readers to laugh at Bishop Bonner, but that does not, can not erase the sense of violation these accounts produce.

In response to this illustration and to the cumulative force of Foxe's text, the reader/viewer was prompted to acknowledge, "There but by the grace of God go I." Any Protestant could have been this bishop's victim; any Protestant might still (in Foxe's day and for generations after) fear a turn of events that would put him (or her) in that position. However, despite the work's demand that its readers empathize with the victims, it is possible to view the illustrations for the vicarious thrill of watching its spectacles of torture and execution. While the text and woodcuts construct rules for readership that make such an act decidedly transgressive, the illustrations do not and perhaps cannot exclude the prurient gaze. The voyeuristic invitation of these illustrations does not amount to an invitation to identify with the persecutors, however. The persecutors remain so insurmountably grotesque that it is diffi-cult to imagine any but the most deliberately subversive reader of the text sympathizing with Bishop Bonner and his colleagues. In-stead, as in the flogging woodcut, the illustration's openness to a voyeuristic reading increases the sexual charge of the picture for all viewers and transfers blame for it to the central figure and villain, Bonner, the defrocked bishop of London.

Foxe's *Acts and Monuments* shaped the imaginations of English Protestants for generations. Its attacks on corrupt clerics and state officials picked up where Bale and other first generation polemicists had left off, transmitting those critiques of Roman Catholicism and English ecclesiastical conservatism to a nationwide audience. The violation imagery of the work, witnessed both in word and woodcut, became ubiquitous in English culture. In 1528, William Tyndale had argued that the Roman Catholic church was responsible for infusing Christian imaginations with images of violence; paradoxically, by the turn of the seventeenth century Foxe's and Daye's work had taken over that role. Tyndale, in his *Obedience of a Christen Man*, had been responding to Catholic charges that Protestantism fomented rebellion when he took up this issue of influence, turning the Catholic accusation back on itself: "It is the bloudy doctrine of the Pope which causeth disobedience, rebelion, and insurreccion."[34] In that earliest period of the Reformation, Tyndale could still charge that the Catholic Church was the source of Christian violence, teaching believers "to kyll a Turke, to slee a Jewe, to burne an heretike, to fyght for the liberties and right of the church, as they call it": it was the Roman church which infused the culture with its understanding and expectations of violence. Had Tyndale written 35 years later, it would have been the *Acts and Monuments* rather than Roman doctrine of which he must have said, "we have sucked in soch bloudy imaginacions in to the botome of our hertes, even with oure mothers milke."[35] Tyndale, Bale, Foxe and Daye provided England with a powerful new witness to fill Protestant imaginations with visions of violence. The images were equally bloody, but were fundamentally different. These new "bloody imaginations" were not of violence the subject might perpetrate, but of violations she might suffer.

Two

"Find out this abuse"
Virgin-Violators and Sheep-Biters in
Measure for Measure

*These are not bishops but bite-sheep, tyrants, tormentors,
termagants, and the devil's slaughter-men. Christ left no such
disciples behind him to sit with cruel Caiaphas at the sessions upon
the life and death of his innocent members.*
　　— John Bale, *An Epistle exhortatorye of an Englyshe Christiane,*
fol. 27

*Duke:... Punish them even to your height of pleasure. —
　　Thou foolish friar, and thou pernicious woman,
　　Compact with her that's gone, think'st thou thy oaths,
　　Though they would swear down each particular saint,
　　Were testimonies against his worth and credit
　　That's sealed in approbation? — You, Lord Escalus,
　　Sit with my cousin; lend him your kind pains
　　To find out this abuse, whence 'tis derived.*
　　— William Shakespeare, *Measure for Measure,* 5.1.237–44

Shakespeare and Religious Controversy

Shakespeare's position with respect to religious issues has puzzled
and frustrated critics — and never more than in discussions of

Measure for Measure, a play that clearly mobilizes the imagery and rhetoric aswirl in early modern English debates over Reformation. Shakespeare frustrates these modern readers because he did not become a spokesperson for any one party and did not choose to use the stage to promote any specific theological or religio-political agenda. Shakespeare serves up characters who represent the gamut of religious opinion and politics, but it is rarely possible to say that the playwright stands squarely behind a particular character in these matters of religion. Jonathan Goldberg poses the problem this way:

> Shakespeare's relation to his culture remains difficult to summarize, not because he is apart from it, but because he assumes no fixed relationship to it. This has often made it possible to act as if Shakespeare was some timeless figure, a man for all times and yet of none. This is, palpably, erroneous. Yet opposing attempts, for instance E. M. W. Tillyard's, to moor his political and historical attitudes in a morass of Elizabethan commonplaces, have foundered. . . . The space of Shakespearean representation is, [as Stephen] Greenblatt concludes, radically unstable, a place of improvisation where all beliefs of the culture are trotted out, tried on, but where none is ultimately adopted. This is not Keatsian negative capability exactly; rather Shakespeare occupies a thoroughly theatrical space. But, we must add, his theatrical space is inscribed in a cultural theater.[1]

Shakespeare wrote plays that resonate within the theater of his culture, addressing its fantasies and anxieties, its beliefs and doubts, sometimes engaging these matters directly, but often approaching them obliquely, refusing to be reduced to agitprop or issue-drama. This is not to say that Shakespeare's plays were apolitical. As surely as they are inscribed in early modern culture, these plays are imbued with the political energies of that time and place.

It has long been a commonplace to observe that Shakespeare's plays offer something for everyone in his audiences, that his entertainments as well as his matters for thought are accessible at many levels, geared variously (and sometimes to incompatible ends) for different members of his socially heterogeneous and politically heterodox crowd. Where polemical texts (whether printed works like Foxe's *Acts and Monuments* or contemporary plays like Philip Massinger and Thomas Dekker's *The Virgin Martyr*, Dekker's *The Whore of Babylon* or Thomas Drue's *The Life of the Duchess of Suffolk*) intentionally construct a narrower ideal audience compromised of reformed and reforming believers, Shakespeare's plays allow readers and viewers to enter from many angles.[2] Preaching to the already convinced and to those whose opinions may be reshaped, polemical texts ultimately close out those who are not willing to conform themselves to the texts' perspective. In contrast, Shakespeare's plays have seemed radically open to many recent critics, who see the plays as inviting competing, politically incompatible readings by members of the same audience.[3]

In support of this argument for Shakespeare's textual openness, one might evince the range of incompatible readings critics have imposed on *Measure for Measure* over the years. The play has been interpreted variously as sympathetic to Roman Catholicism or as firmly anti-Catholic, as a celebration of Jacobean monarchy or as an attempt to subvert the king's rule, as a commentary on the sexual debauchery of London society or as an activist warning to the authorities to lay aside plans to regulate prostitution.[4] Leah Marcus has taken these divergent readings as evidence that Shakespeare's play is purposely "double written." In her view, the play has elicited so many different interpretations precisely because it was designed to produce them. These readings are symptomatic of and "inextricable from a deep division in the contemporary audience."[5]

Often these competing interpretations arise from opposing assessments of the play's attitudes toward its major characters and their actions. The duke, Isabella, Angelo and to a lesser but still important degree, Lucio, have all elicited multiple reactions from readers, viewers and critics. Is the duke a savvy manager of his subjects, a Machiavelli in the laudatory sense of that term? Or is he a Machiavelli-as-ruthless-despot, who manipulates his subjects in sinister ways and plays at barley-break with their bodies and souls? In his disguise as friar, is he to be taken as recuperating the figure of the Roman Catholic for the English stage, or does the costume draw from Protestant polemic to signal the duke's corruption? The questions surrounding Isabella are similar: is her status as novitiate meant to signal sincerity and to confirm her chastity, or is it meant to cast her as fundamentally misguided and potentially corrupt?[6] Is Angelo to be read as a "precisian" (a Puritan), or is that simply implausible given the play's Viennese setting? Does Lucio represent the voice of the people, or is he merely an anomalous trickster figure whose words are disruptive and without merit?

The play-as-text leaves these questions unanswered. The play-in-performance may choose to answer some or all of them, but may also choose to leave audiences with the uncomfortable sense that they have visited a fun-house world where character cannot be read with any confidence — a dangerous world filled with politicians and shape-shifters who use disguise guilefully. This latter view renders Shakespeare's Duke Vincentio as skilled a manipulator and con man as Jonson's Volpone, and more successful: where Jonson brings Volpone under the sway of justice at the end of his play, Shakespeare's duke controls the administration of justice at the end of *Measure for Measure*. It is my argument that by unlocking interpretive doubt about the status of its major characters, the play deliberately opens the door to this dark interpretation.

In her brilliant "local reading" of *Measure for Measure*, Marcus likens the interpretive uncertainty of the text to "a Möbius strip" where "a single twist of the fabric in the process of construction, [causes] every surface, every seemingly level plane, [to be] at the same time its own volte face." Producing an experience very like Freud's *unheimlich*, the surface of Shakespeare's play can suddenly shift so that a comfortable, familiar understanding of its action suddenly gives way to an unsettling alter-experience, in which "that which is familiar [is] rendered suddenly *other*." This shift occurred "in varying degrees depending on the strength of a given viewer's political passions."[7]

At the center of this uncanny, shifting play is the figure of the duke who costumes himself as a friar. Shakespeare invites questions about this disguise from the outset: when the duke appears in act 1, scene 3, to request Friar Thomas's help, we pick up the conversation in midstream, with the duke rebutting the friar's assumption that his secret business is an amorous one:

> No, holy father, throw away that thought.
> Believe not that the dribbling dart of love
> Can pierce a complete bosom. Why I desire thee
> To give me secret harbour hath a purpose
> More grave and wrinkled than the aims and ends
> Of burning youth.[8]

The duke denies any lascivious motives in requesting a cowl and a cell from the friar, and in this moment he reassures the audience that his motives are not base. However sacrilegious it may seem for him to don a friar's habit and to mimic a friar's office (as he does when he assists Claudio in preparing for death), Shakespeare allows the duke to contrast his actions and motivations with those of a certain character type familiar from romance, where disguise is the conventional tool of lovers. Still, there are unsettling questions. Will the duke's bosom prove "complete" and impervious to Cupid's arrows, as he boasts? It is conventional for Cupid to give the lie to such boasts and for nonlovers to fall in love as soon as they have declared their hard-heartedness. And then, why does Friar Thomas seem to have leaped to the conclusion that romance is the duke's game? Perhaps this says less about the duke than about the friar, who would countenance such shenanigans by lending the robes, cloister and authority of his monastic order to the duke. For those in Shakespeare's audience sympathetic to Protestant critiques of the hypocrisy of monastic orders, much about the duke's choice of disguise would seem unsettling and unsavory.

This tiny expository scene does two important things. First, it allows the duke to reveal to the audience what he has hidden from his courtiers: that his absence is a means of testing Angelo's character. Second, it allows Shakespeare to open the issue of the duke's own character as he uses deceit to catch corruption. Friar Thomas makes this concern uncomfortably explicit when he chastises the duke for his lax government: "It rested in your grace / To unloose this tied-up Justice when you pleased, / And it in you more dreadful would have seemed / Than in Lord Angelo" (1.3.31– 34). The qualms about the duke's methods and actions, which Shakespeare plants in this early moment, return to haunt the play most forcefully when the duke uses his disguise not only for the political and moral ends he initially admits, but also as a means of access to Isabella.[9] By the end of the play it is clear that the duke has exploited his friar's costume not only to ensnare Angelo, but to court a woman.

It is difficult to overemphasize the influence of anti-Roman Catholic propaganda in Shakespeare's England. Alongside Foxe, John Bale was the most influential among the many who developed this Protestant critique. Bale belonged to the first generation of English Protestants, making his reputation in a series of tracts protesting the repression of reformed believers during the reigns of Henry VIII and Mary I. He was dubbed "Bilious Bale" for the unrelenting, ranting prose style characteristic of his attacks on the Roman Catholic hierarchy. It was Bale's mission to show "to the worlde to theyr utter shame and confusyon" "the abhomin- able hipocresye, Idolatry, pride, and fylthynesse of those terrible termagauntes of antychristes holy housholde, those ii. horned whoremoungers, those coniurers of Egipt, & lecherouse locustes leapinge out of the smoke of the pitt bottomlesse, whiche daylye deceyueth the ignorant multytude wyth theyr sorceryes & charmes." Bale's attack on the deceptive practices and sexual hypocrisy of Roman Catholic clerics shaped Protestant rhetoric for generations.[10]

More influential still, Foxe's *Acts and Monuments* presented the history of Christianity with the intention of demonstrating that Protestantism was the surviving remnant of true doctrine and discipline, persecuted throughout time by the forces of a heretical, worldly, corrupt Roman Catholic hierarchy. The largest and most important section of the work was a documentary history of the heresy trials of Henry VIII's and Mary I's reigns. One of Foxe's key theses in the *Acts and Monuments* was his contention that state authorities had joined with Roman Catholic persecutors to hunt down and destroy true believers. As I have argued at length in chapter 1, Foxe's work underscored this assertion with a series of unforgettable illustrations, themselves every bit as effective as Foxe's text in imprinting a horror of state and church corruption in the minds of early modern English folk (see, for instance, figs. 1.5 and 1.7 in the previous chapter).[11]

Clearly, Shakespeare's deceitful friar-duke could not be a neutral figure in a culture shaped by Reformation rhetoric and politics. In this one character, Shakespeare embodies just the sort of complicitous relation between the Roman Catholic and secular hierarchies that two generations of English Protestants had been taught to fear and revile. From that perspective, the duke represents precisely the unholy alliance of prelate and aristocrat that Bale attacks:

> But whom haue you harboured (ye beastlye bellygoddes), whom haue you visited and fedde sens ye haue becomen of lowlye preachers mytred modye ydols? Not the sore and sycke, the impotent and lame, the fatherlesse and motherlesse, nor him that hath bene decayed by yll chaunces or throwne in stronge preson for the verite. No, but great lordes and ladyes, lerned menne and stowte lawers, gentylmenne, great doctours, & soche as hath fat benefices, with a bende of bolde braggers or blasphemouse swearers abought ye, to wayte upon youre tables, to holde up your tayles in the strete, to kepe youre houndes and horses, and to conueye you in the darke a pece for youre pleasur. (*Epistle Exhortatorye*, 22)

In one character, Shakespeare conflates the crafty friar and the worldly lord — or so it would seem from a Protestant point of view. Furthermore, the playwright hints that although the duke has given the impression that he is impervious to Cupid's arrows, a man "not inclined that way," he takes full advantage of his disguise to gain access to women and to play Cupid with them

(3.1.365). Certainly the duke/friar's willingness not only to meddle in, but to stage-manage such deceitful bits of sexual business as Isabella's capitulation to Angelo's proposition and Mariana's substitution in the bed trick resonates suggestively with the Protestant stereotype of friarly behavior.

"Bite-sheep, tyrants, tormentors, termagants, and the devil's slaughter-men"

The play's principle *unheimlich* moment occurs when it unmasks the friar to reveal the duke. At this moment, Angelo and Escalus have ordered the friar to be taken to prison to be interrogated with torture so that they may understand his evil intentions to the state. It has seemed clear to these two judges that their prisoner is a friar of a certain familiar sort. Escalus addresses him as "Thou unreverend and unhallowed friar," accusing him of suborning the young women to give false testimony against Angelo, who in his turn accuses the friar of committing "treasonable abuses" (5.1.299, 336). Earlier in the scene, the duke himself (then playing the role of the duke) says sarcastically of the friar that he must be "a *ghostly* father, belike," implying that he expects to find the friar quite otherwise (5.1.126; emphasis added). Of course, the audience is aware of several facts that mediate its interpretation of these characterizations of the friar. First, they have known all along that he is the duke. They also know that Angelo and Escalus are not apprised of this crucial information. Thus, when the duke casts aspersions on the friar's holiness, the audience knows that the statement is part of the duke's campaign of deliberate misinformation; he intends to mislead Angelo and the assembled people of Vienna. Still, the duke's statement calls (the audience's) attention to the fact that the friar is *not* ghostly, but a secular man in disguise. The duke's disguise becomes more uncomfortable as the audience recognizes the irony that the duke's own statement is both a sarcastic denunciation of the friar's integrity and a glance at the truth that the friar is not what he appears. The moment flickers with uncanniness, if only very briefly. The audience has been encouraged to think well of the friar, but this moment crystallizes the notion that all along he has behaved in a way not unlike the polemical stereotype.

It is Lucio, of course, who most insistently expresses the view that the friar is the very type of the false cleric. Lucio calls him variously "a meddling friar," "a saucy friar, a very scurvy fellow," "the rascal," "goodman Bald-pate" and "thou damnable fellow" (5.1.127, 135–36, 298, 321, 333). What the audience knows of Lucio suggests that he is inclined to give scandalous report. Thus, it is no surprise that when Lucio is asked if he knows "that Friar Lodowick to be a dishonest person," he responds, "*Cucullus non facit monachum*: honest in nothing but in his clothes" (257, 259–60). Lucio's Latin aphorism, which translates as, "a cowl does not make a monk," is in keeping with his other accusations that the friar is an unholy hypocrite, accusations the audience might be inclined to dismiss. In fact, his condemnation of the friar works against itself as a de facto endorsement of the duke: the audience has seen Lucio's encounters with the friar and they know he is misrepresenting what has occurred.

But there's more to this moment than Lucio's guile. "*Cucullus non facit monachum*," a cowl does not make a monk. Lucio's English witticism, "honest in nothing but in his clothes," at first seems merely a reiteration of the Latin, but his juxtaposition of the Latin and English phrases creates an ironic effect for Shakespeare's English audience, inviting them to deconstruct his assertion. The Latin words have a special and potent power. First, they divide the audience between those who can understand them and those who must take his English phrase as a translation. Latin was the provenance of the educated elite in Shakespeare's audience, which meant that the remark about the monk's cowl passed by many listeners. However, Latin was also the language of Roman Catholicism, which meant that even for those who could not discern the meaning of Lucio's first phrase, it would nonetheless have resonated as a reminder of the friar's fundamental religious error. Literal understanding was unnecessary for Lucio's statement to communicate its meaning. The play's friars, after all, would have been suspect from the outset to Protestants in the audience; the source of their suspiciousness is their Catholicism; the mark of their Catholicism is their clothes — and the alienating language of their ritual. In fact, Lucio's remark that the friar is "honest in nothing but in his clothes," would have struck Shakespeare's audience as right in tone, but precisely wrong in its particulars: the clothes of a friar were by Protestant definition dishonest.

Though it is mere tantalizing conjecture, Lucio's Latin may have received another "spin" from its audience: the phrase "*Cucullus non facit monachum*" ends with a word that might have suggested "monarch" rather than "monk" to the less educated. In the present context, where the monarch pretends to be a monk, the same mixed meaning might have registered as a pun with those who understood the Latin. Does Lucio say that the ruler is honest in nothing but his clothes? The answer, of course, is that yes, at some level, he does accuse the duke of dishonesty. Insofar as the duke *is* the friar, charges leveled against the friar adhere to the duke as well. Furthermore, the audience knows that Lucio's accusation is truer than he realizes: insofar as the duke is the friar, he is a disguising dissembler and thus dishonest. Indeed, a cowl does not make a monk, it merely disguises a duke. In the end it all comes back to the clothes (those distinctively Roman Catholic clothes): if he is honest in nothing but his clothes, and his clothes are none too honest, is the duke honest in *anything* at all? Could Lucio be right? *Unheimlich* again; the friar and the duke flicker and shift in the audience's assessment. The "old fantastical Duke of dark corners" (4.3.147) may be a product of Lucio's imagination, but his words conjure up this double for the duke. The audience indeed sees a fantastical friar who lurks in dark dungeons and arranges trysts in dark gardens. Is the friar redeemed by the shape-shifting duke, or is the duke damned by the shifty friar?

It is at this uneasy pass that act 5 comes to its crisis. The deputies order the friar to prison; he resists, and Lucio steps forward to lay hands on him. As Lucio struggles with him, he heaps invective on the friar: "Why, you bald-pated lying rascal, you must be hooded, must you? Show your knave's visage, with a pox to you! Show your sheep-biting face, and be hanged an hour!" (5.1.345–47). Of all the disparaging appellations Lucio bestows on the friar, this last one, "sheep-biting," hangs in the air. It is at this moment that the friar's cowl falls away to reveal the duke. Cleric and ruler have one face, one character, one intention, which have just been captioned for the audience: sheep-biting. Is the duke a bite-sheep?[12]

"Bite-sheep" is not a term of Lucio's (or Shakespeare's) invention. It belongs to the language of Protestant polemic and may be traced to the arch-rhetorician, John Bale, who said of Henry VIII's bishops that "these are not Byshoppes but byteshepes, tyrauntes, tormentours, termagaunts, and the deuyls slaughter menne" (*Epistle Exhortatorye*, 27). Is Lucio a militant Protestant that he speaks Bale's language? Surely not — or if so, then Shakespeare is enjoying a rich joke at the polemicist's expense. Tempting as that idea is, I think it is not so easy to dismiss the "bite-sheep" label. It captures the doubts, the uncanny queasiness that the duke elicits throughout the play. It gives a name to the way the duke's actions always seem open to double interpretation, to the way his plan to expose Angelo's hypocrisy so often threatens to turn back on itself to implicate the duke as well.

Truly double-written, the play vacillates in this moment between its various versions of the duke. Doubt and delight compete to define the moment of the duke's discovery. It must be said that the audience's first reaction to the duke's unmasking is most likely to be relief. The play had reached a crisis point where it seemed just possible that Angelo might get away with his evil deeds and that the duke might find himself trapped in his friar's costume, unable to regain command of the scene or control over the distribution of justice. The duke very nearly outsmarted himself with his own trickery. The audience reacts with relief because it has been clear all along that Angelo is the real bite-sheep, the abusive authority whose dark deeds need to be brought to light. It was Angelo who compelled Isabella to appeal her case a second time. It was Angelo who made certain that the second conference was wholly private (in contrast with their first meeting with the Provost and Lucio in attendance). It was Angelo who used that privacy to proposition Isabella, and it was Angelo who used his authority to coerce her submission to his sexual demands. Angelo is the "pernicious caitiff deputy," whose "concupiscible intemperate lust" led him to abuse Isabella. "Angelo's forsworn . . . Angelo's a murderer . . . Angelo is an adulterate thief, an hypocrite, a virgin-violator" (5.1.88, 98, 38–41).

If any character is subject to Lucio's observation that a cowl does not make a monk, it is Angelo. He is truly honest in nothing but his clothes by the end of act 2. Isabella makes the point about the disparity between Angelo's being and his seeming:

> Make not impossible
> That which but seems unlike. 'Tis not impossible
> But one, the wicked'st caitiff on the ground,
> May seem as shy, as grave, as just, as absolute,
> As Angelo; even so may Angelo,   ·
> In all his dressings, characts, titles, forms,
> Be an arch-villain. Believe it, royal prince,
> If he be less, he's nothing; but he's more,
> Had I more name for badness.
>
> (5.1.51–59)

Like the worldly, lordly ecclesiastics Bale condemns, "the Prelates in their most pompous apparel," Angelo's proud, lordly clothes cannot hide the badness within.[13] It is Angelo, who, in the style of Bale's bishops, plays the roles of "byteshepes, tyrauntes, tormentours, termagaunts, and the deuyls slaughter menne" and who "syt[s] with cruell Cayphas at the sessyons upon lyfe and deathe of [Christ's] innocent members" (*Epistle Exhortatorye*, 27). Finally, it is Angelo who has turned from his religious life of "study and fast[ing]" (1.4.60) to play a part in Shakespeare's play like the one Bishop Bonner plays in Foxe's *Acts and Monuments*.

According to this analogy, then, the duke plays Foxe and Bale's part. Certainly he could be said to take on this role when he declares to Friar Thomas that one of his reasons for disguising himself is to observe how Angelo conducts himself in office: "hence shall we see / If power change purpose, what our seemers be" (1.3.53–54). The seeming and scheming of the powerful were precisely the targets of the reformers' pens. Bale wrote at the beginning of his *Epistle exhortatorye of an Englyshe Christiane* that the searching out of such false seeming was of critical importance in a commonwealth:

> They shewe now what they haue bene, euen verye heretiques to God, trayters to theyr princes, and theues to theyr Christen commons. . . . I judge it then a bounde dewtye . . . to manifest theyr mischeues to ye universall worlde, euerye manne accordinge to his talent geuen of God: some with penne and some with tonge, so bringinge them out of theyr olde estimacyon least they shuld styll regne in the peoples consciences to theyr soules destruccyon. . . . [Christ] openlye rebuked theyr fylthye forefathers the scribes, lawers, pharisees, doctors, prestes, bisshops, and hypocrites for makinge Gods commaundementes of non effect to support theyr owne tradicions, so clerlye condempninge theyr hypocritall lyfe and doctrine. (3–3v)

Shakespeare's duke seems to think of his task in very much the same terms as those Bale laid out for Protestant resisters 60 years earlier.

The duke speaks in this polemical voice again when he announces his plan to trap Angelo in his falsehood with the bed trick, though one might wonder if his singsong verse suggests Shakespeare's contempt for such pat moralizing:

> Shame to him whose cruel striking
> Kills for faults of his own liking!
> Twice treble shame on Angelo,
> To weed my vice, and let his grow!
> O, what may man within him hide,
> Though angel on the outward side!

How may likeness made in crimes
Make my practice on the times
To draw with idle spiders' strings
Most ponderous and substantial things.

(3.1.487–96)

To fill out this portrait of the duke as righteous exposer of hypocrisy, note the duke's careful management of act 5, which strongly echoes the taunting, teasing way in which the bishop baiters draw out hidden evidence of persecution in order to call to account those who seem above the reach of the law. "Find out this abuse, whence 'tis derived" (5.1.244), commands the duke as he leaves Angelo to ensnare himself in the trap he lays for Isabella. The duke manipulates Angelo, enticing him to reenact his abuse of power in public, so the duke may then expose the deputy's fair-seeming actions as corruption. The duke holds up the light to illuminate Angelo's secrets. Shakespeare has borrowed more than the play's title from the Gospel of Luke and he owes more to Protestant polemic than a few anticlerical epithets. Echoing behind the action of this final scene is Luke, chapter 12: "There is nothing hid, that shall not be discovered, neither secret, that shall not be known. Therefore, whatsoever they have done in darkness, the same shall be known in the light." This verse served as a motto and rallying cry for Protestant reformers, among them Bale, who printed it on the title page of his *Actes of Englysh Votaryes.*

However, Shakespeare has not played fair with the polemicists. He casts Angelo as the predatory governor, then identifies him as "precise" (1.3.50). He turns the words of militant Protestantism not on the Roman Catholic figures of his play, but on the one character associated with Puritanism. In keeping with hostile stereotypes of Puritans, Angelo reportedly "stands at a guard with envy, scarce confesses / That his blood flows, or that his appetite / Is more to bread than stone" (51–53). However, Angelo's chaste behavior proves to be more like the corrupting chastity for which Bale castigated priests. It was Bale's contention that the chastity performed by priests as a work of spiritual discipline was beyond human capability and beyond God's design for human life. Thus, Bale charged that "they shall for wante of women, haue uncomely luste in their hartes, whereby they wil be giuen ouer of God to themselues. So shall they become buggerers & whoremasters."[14] As the duke's test supposes and as Protestant teaching predicted, Angelo's self-discipline and moral uprightness are found to be no match for human nature, let alone for the enticements of purpose-changing power.

Thus, Shakespeare's play might be taken as a reversal of Protestant polemic, turning its techniques back on its own party. The precisian is found to be guilty of the very corruptions and abuses that had been charged against Roman Catholics. It is not, however, a simple reversal of Balean arguments, nor a simple rejection of Foxean history. Shakespeare does not simply make heroes of the Catholics and villains of the Puritans in his play. If that were the case, Angelo's credentials as a Puritan would need some shoring up. As the play stands, Angelo's link with Puritanism rests on a single remark by the duke and relies on the audience's inference that his strictness (and ultimate hypocrisy) link him with other stage Puritans. If it were Shakespeare's intention to construct *Measure for Measure* as anti-Protestant polemic, he would surely have made his deputy more clearly Puritan, his duke and his nun more admirable, less equivocal.

In fact, Shakespeare does not seem interested in siding with one sect over another. If the play has something to say about religious side-taking, it is only that the partisans on all sides are merely human. From the play's perspective it is difficult to tell who is saved and who is damned, who belongs to Christ or to Antichrist, who is angel or devil. More to the point, the play looks beyond religion to comment on power. What *Measure for Measure* shares with Protestant polemic is not its rhetoric of doctrine, but its rhetoric of violation. Shakespeare's borrowings of Puritan catchphrases, then, refer not to Reformation theology, but to the reformers' narrative strategies for representing themselves as the victims of abusive authority.

Ravishing Subjects

Shakespeare's representation of Isabella's treatment by Angelo bears interesting and instructive similarities to one of Foxe's most famous martyr tales: "The two examinations of the worthy servaunt of God, Maistris An Askew." Foxe included Askew's account in all of the editions of his martyrology, beginning with the Latin *Rerum in ecclesia gestarum commentarii*. As the work expanded, Foxe placed Askew's tale at a key point in his narrative: it comes at the end of his account of Henry VIII's reign and serves as an important precursor to the Marian martyrdoms. Along with Jane Grey and Princess Elizabeth, Askew was one of the best known of Foxe's heroines.[15] Her case was notorious from the start: a member of Queen Katherine Parr's court, Askew was targeted as part of an organized attempt to bring an end to the queen's patronage and promotion of Protestantism.[16] The fact that Askew was tortured to induce her to name other courtiers as co-religionists shocked many in London.[17] Following her death, her writings were smuggled out of England and were published in two parts at Wesel by John Bale (1546, 1547); they then received several subsequent editions before Foxe included the narrative in his *Acts and Monuments*.[18]

In its representation of corrupt officials, Askew's narrative bears a marked similarity to *Measure for Measure*; both texts strategically manipulate gendered generic conventions to heighten the villainy of the persecutors and to denote the innocence of their victims. In her account of her handling by secular and ecclesiastical authorities in London, Askew represents herself as a vulnerable woman in the hands of men who used not only their high positions and official power to intimidate her, but also exploited their society's gender imperatives to demand her submission as a woman to their masculine superiority.[19] In the most famous section of Askew's first examination, Bishop Bonner calls her to his chambers, engineering the interview so that she will be alone with him. Askew presents this as a deliberate ploy by the bishop, who agreed that she could have several supporters accompany her, then called for her two hours before the time he had set for her friends to arrive. Thus, he was able to confront her with no witnesses present and apparently hoped to be better able to draw damaging testimony from her. Askew makes it clear that she distrusted the bishop's promise that if she confessed "the secrets of [her] hart," she need "not to fear in any point. For what so ever I did say in his house no man should hurt me for it."[20] The gendered action of this episode suggests that the bishop brings Askew to his presence alone in order to intimidate her, but then couches the interview as though he intends it as an opportunity to offer kindly counsel off the record. Bonner's promise that Askew's words will not be used against her is posed in chivalrous rhetoric: Bonner suggests that his honor and his house will protect her from hurt by any man. Askew, of course, reports the conversation in such a way that it is clear she sees through his courtly tone. She does not believe that this bishop is honorable or that the official and masculine position from which he speaks to her can imply anything but a threat of superior force.

Foxe was not the first to disseminate Anne Askew's narratives: her first editor and earliest champion was John Bale. In his editions of the *Examinations*, Bale inserted his own commentary in the midst of Askew's narrative, breaking its flow in order to reinforce her points for his readers.[21] Bale's comments on this scene applaud Askew's intuition about the bishop's untrustworthiness and underscore the gender politics she observed:

> In thys preventynge of the houre, maye the dylygent reader perceyve the gredynesse of thys Babylon Byshopp, or bloudthurstie wolfe, concernynge thys praye. . . . Christ sheweth us in the vii. chaptre of Mathew, and in other places more of the Gospell, how we shall knowe a false prophete or an hypocryte, and wylleth us to be ware of them. Their maner is as the devyls is, flatteryngly to tempt, and deceytfullye to trappe, that they maye at the lattre, most cruellye slee. Soche a won (sayth David) hath nothynge in hys tunge, but playne deceyt. He layeth in wayte for the innocent, with no lesse cruelte than the lyon for a shepe. He lurketh to ravysh up the poore. And whan he hath gotten hym into hys nette, than throweth he hym downe by hys autoryte. Psalm. 9. Thys is the thirde temptacyon of thys byshopp, that the woman shuld utter, to her owne confusyon.[22]

In this context, the conventional representation of the martyr as a sheep takes on a feminine hue in contrast with the predator images heaped on the bishop, which conform easily with Bale and Askew's gendering of murderers and abusers of authority as male. In addition to being likened to the passive and sacrificial sheep, Askew is portrayed as an "innocent" and as "prey." The general violence of the passage leads up to Bale's use of the verb "ravish," a favorite component of his polemical vocabulary. As he does here, Bale usually uses "ravish" in connection with violent beasts, meaning it in the sense of "ravening" or "ravenous" (words he also uses). Here, however, in the context of the bishop's "lurking" and "laying in wait" to "tempt" and "trap" the "innocent woman," it is difficult not to hear his intent to "ravish" as a sexual threat.

Angelo's second interview with Isabella is conducted in very similar terms, though his intention is solely to make a sexual conquest of her body. Although Bonner makes a pretense of interest in the woman's spiritual state, both texts show the men to be chiefly interested in overpowering the woman. To borrow a phrase from Bale, each seeks to throw her down by his authority. Where Askew and Bale make it clear that the bishop intends not to save her, but to kill her, it might be argued in Angelo's defense that he, at least, makes no attempt on Isabella's life. Still, Angelo does represent a mortal threat to Claudio, a threat that makes his attempt to intimidate and coerce Isabella every bit as much a life-and-death contest as Bonner's showdown with Askew.

Like Askew, Isabella suspects that Angelo is trying to entrap her with his smooth rhetoric, and, like Askew, she doubts his promises of honorable intention:

> Angelo: Plainly conceive I love you.
> Isabella: My brother did love Juliet,
>   And you tell me he shall die for it.
> Angelo: He shall not, Isabel, if you give me love.
> Isabella: I know your virtue hath a license in't,
>   Which seems a little fouler than it is,
>   To pluck on others.

Angelo: Believe me on mine honour,
        My words express my purpose.
Isabella: Ha, little honour to be much believed,
        And most pernicious purpose! Seeming, seeming!
        I will proclaim thee, Angelo; look for't.

                                        (2.4.141–51)

When Shakespeare wishes to write a play about the workings of power, a play that announces from the start that it will unfold the properties of government, his critique finds its clearest, most powerful expression not in its depiction of the law or court politics, but in its representation of abusive authority as rape. Shakespeare's play literalizes what in Askew's narrative is strictly a rhetorical device, but both works use the image to achieve the same effect.

Askew recounts that while she was in prison waiting for her interrogation by the bishop, a priest was sent to examine her on matters of doctrine. She represents this priest as a rhetorically subtle man who tries to trap her into some damaging admission. In the course of questioning her about the sacrament and about Confession, he maneuvers her into a position in which any answer she makes will compromise her. According to Askew, "he asked me, if I were shriven, I tolde him so that I might have one of these .iii. that is to say, doctor Crome, sir Gillam, or Huntington, I was contented, bycause I knew them to be men of wisdome. As for you or any other I will not dispraise, bycause I know ye not."²³ Askew's concern is that a priest chosen by the bishop would use her words in Confession as evidence in her heresy trial. If, on the other hand, she refuses to confess, that refusal will be taken as a sign of heresy in and of itself. She tries to evade the question by asking to confess to someone she knows, on the ostensible grounds that she should be able to confess to someone she knows to be wise. It is a clever ploy, but it leads her to endanger the three men she names. Thus, in avoiding one danger, she nonetheless falls into another. The priest's next question repeats the strategy, but Askew acquits herself more cleverly:

Fourthly he asked me, if the host should fall, and a beast did eate it whether the beast did receive God or no? I aunswered, Seinge ye have taken the paines to aske this question I desire you also to assoile it your selfe. For I wil not do it, bycause I perceive ye come to tempt me. And he said, it was against the order of scoles that he which asked the question should aunswere it. I told him I was but a woman and knew not the course of scoles.[24]

In a moment that has charmed modern readers, Askew surprises her interrogator by turning his tricky question back to him. Thus, she exposes the pretense that these authorities mean only to help her see her errors and to tutor her in correct ways of thinking. The priest himself does not have the answer to this question, but only means to entice her into a heresy about the nature of the host. Her plea of womanly ignorance of the rules of rhetoric taught to men in schools turns the priest's authority and his official rhetoric against him: how can he hold her guilty of heresy if, as a woman, his church and his society hold her incompetent to learn the arts of reasoning necessary to articulate the fine points of faith? If this is not a valid defense of her doctrinal "errors," it nonetheless rips the mask of decorum from these proceedings and reframes them as a straightforward matter of men bullying women.

In *Measure for Measure,* a similar contest develops between Angelo and Isabella as each tries to use the rhetoric of gender to gain advantage over the other. Isabella admits to the frailty of women, apparently conceding the usual point about women's vanity when she alludes to "the glasses where they view themselves." Her concession is a sign of humility, but it is also a powerful strategy: her concession is no sooner made than turned to advantage. Women, it seems, are frail and like their glasses, not so much in terms of moral weakness as in physical fragility. Both are easily broken — by men, as can best be seen by quoting the passage in full:

Angelo: You seemed of late to make the law a tyrant,
           And rather proved the sliding of your brother
           A merriment than a vice.

Isabella: O, pardon me, my lord. It oft falls out
　　　　　　To have what we would have, we speak not what we mean.
　　　　　　I something do excuse the thing I hate
　　　　　　For his advantage that I dearly love.
Angelo:　　We are all frail.
Isabella:　　　　　　　　Else let my brother die —
　　　　　　If not a federy, but only he,
　　　　　　Owe and succeed thy weakness.
Angelo:　　　　　　　　　Nay, women are frail too.
Isabella: Ay, as the glasses where they view themselves,
　　　　　　Which are as easy broke as they make forms.
　　　　　　Women? Help, heaven! Men their creation mar
　　　　　　In profiting by them. Nay, call us ten times frail,
　　　　　　For we are as soft as our complexions are,
　　　　　　And credulous to false prints.
Angelo:　　. . . from this testimony of your own sex,
　　　　　　Since I suppose we are made to be no stronger
　　　　　　Than faults may shake our frames, let me be bold.
　　　　　　I do arrest your words. Be that you are;
　　　　　　That is, a woman. If you be more, you're none.
　　　　　　If you be one, as you are well expressed
　　　　　　By all external warrants, show it now,
　　　　　　By putting on the destined livery.

                              (2.4.115–29, 131–38)

The effect of this scene is very much the same as in the Askew passage. When Angelo tries to use the forms of official (that is, masculine) rhetoric to hold her to account for her statements, Isabella uses her femininity to excuse herself from confronting Angelo's proposition. Her sidestepping tactic is evidence of the rhetorical skills Claudio praises in act 1, scene 2, when he says that "she hath prosperous art / When she will play with reason and discourse, / And well she can persuade" (161–63). In her, the tactic is graceful, an attempt to keep the interview focused on Claudio's sentence. In Angelo, rhetorical ropetricks backfire. When he attempts to turn her appeal to womanliness against her it merely makes a monster of him. Where he might have appeared as a lover (however unwanted), he instead cloaks himself in "a little brief authority" and becomes a tyrant (2.2.121).[25]

That Angelo is to be viewed in relation to the tyrants of Protestant literature becomes most clear in the middle of the fifth act when the duke reappears as the friar to "discover" that Isabella and Mariana's stories have not been believed and that the tables of justice have turned so the victimized women now stand accused of slander. Pitying their plight, the friar says to them, "O, poor souls, / Come you to seek the lamb here of the fox, / Good night to your redress!" (5.1.291–93). The fox, though less common in the polemical vocabulary than wolves, bears, lions and serpents, is nonetheless unmistakably drawn from that tradition. In his edition of Askew's *Examinations,* Bale cites Lamentations and Ezekiel for their pejorative fox images. However, his most significant source for the image derives from Luke 13:31–32, where, upon hearing that Herod wishes to kill him, Jesus calls that tyrant a fox.[26] Bale uses this reference to lambast Bishop Bonner for his false promise to handle Askew's case fairly: "O vengeable tyraunt and devyll. How subtyllye sekyst thu the bloude of thys innocent woman, undre a coloure of fryndelye handelynge. . . . By swearynge by thy fydelyte, thu art not all unlyke unto Herode, whom Christ for lyke practyses, . . . called also a most craftye cruell foxe, Luce 13. Thu laborest here, to have thys woman in snare."[27] Shakespeare's foxlike Angelo recalls Bale's bishops, whose exercise of worldly power reprises Herod's tyranny and whose corrupt execution of justice reiterates Caiaphas's condemnation of Christ. Shakespeare depends on his audience to hear and apply these polemical echoes as they interpret Angelo's handling of the women in act 5.

Angelo is a bite-sheep, that much is clear, but here the play flickers with uncanniness again. Even as the friar delivers this speech, which brings the weight of polemical condemnation down on Angelo, his words turn back against the duke. Condemnation of Angelo yields to condemnation of the duke for his neglect:

> O, poor souls,
> Come you to seek the lamb here of the fox,
> Good night to your redress! Is the Duke gone?
> Then is your cause gone too. The Duke's unjust

Thus to retort your manifest appeal,
And put your trial in the villain's mouth
Which here you come to accuse.

(5.1.291–97)

Although they can see that the duke is not entirely gone, the audience knows that it seems so to the two women. It must be comforting to hear the duke acknowledge what the women have felt so acutely — that the duke has been peremptory with them and not at all the figure of justice they had trusted him to be.[28] At the same time, the duke's acknowledgment only underscores that they have a right to feel abused and that the audience is correct to pity them. Furthermore, his perfectly timed reappearance as the heroic voice of righteous indignation is not likely to capture the audience's admiration: it is simply too stagey and too obviously geared toward self-promotion.[29] Thus, even in this most clear denunciation of Angelo as the play's villain, Shakespeare allows the image to shift, setting the scene for the duke's uncowling a moment later. What does Shakespeare mean his audience to make of his polemical echoes: which ruler — the duke or the deputy — is the real bite-sheep?

Executing Justice

Act 5, scene 1 of *Measure for Measure*, a scene of justice set at the city gates, presents an image not unlike the woodcut John Daye used to illustrate Foxe's account of Anne Askew's execution. That woodcut depicts the condemned prisoners bound to the stake, surrounded by a crowd of spectators, overseen by a preacher in his pulpit and by figures of authority elevated on a scaffold erected against the city wall. It offers a bird's-eye view of the event, though at such a distance that its power and immediacy are mitigated in comparison with the other, more detailed illustrations in the *Acts and Monuments* (fig. 2.1). While no single illustration offers a definitive analogue to the play's final scene, the collective imagery of the Foxe woodcuts had taught many in Shakespeare's audience

Fig. 2.1. The execution of Anne Askew. From Foxe, *Acts and Monuments* (1563). Courtesy of the Rare Books and Manuscripts Library of the Ohio State University Libraries.

how to read scenes like the one at the end of *Measure for Measure,* instructing them to identify with the victims and to see the authority figures as persecutors. In Shakespeare's play, the duke's disguise renders him an amalgam of that sinister alliance of church and state that occupied the places of authority in Foxe and Daye's work. Shakespeare borrows from Protestant polemic, but manages to empty that language of its exclusivity. In *Measure for Measure,* Shakespeare successfully transcends sectarianism. The play makes available to Protestants and Catholics of all stripes its representation of Isabella and Mariana as models of victimization.

At least for the Protestant members of Shakespeare's audience, this final scene must have resembled many of the woodcuts in *Acts and Monuments* with the assembled crowds, the cowled monks, the grim authority figures and the sympathetic victims (see figs. 1.2, 1.6). It is worth considering what makes these victims sympathetic. In the case of the woodcut illustrating the death of three Guernsey women, the lack of sympathy attributed to the crowd and officials who witness the women's suffering contributes strongly to the effect, although these minor players pale in significance beside the casual violence of the child-murdering bishop.[30] In contrast, the woodcut emphasizes the women's distress, their vulnerability, their (paradoxical) strength and their femininity to construct them as objects of compassion. The artist codes that femininity not only through the central figure's pregnancy and the rightmost figure's piety, but also through the flowing hair and exposed nape and shoulder of the left-hand figure, whose representation draws on pictorial conventions linking feminine beauty, penitence and dismay to loosened long hair.

Similar conventions are at work in Shakespeare's scene when Mariana uncloaks herself at her husband's command. I will not go so far as to insist that she bares her head in deference to authority, because the dialogue specifies only that she show her face, and her own insistence on her status as unwed "wife" makes it possible that she would deliberately keep her hair covered as a symbolic marker of her married status. If she may be thought to uncover her hair, then the iconographic similarity to the Foxe illustrations increases, but it does not depend on that detail. The key points of comparison are Mariana's distress, her femininity (coded as humility, patience, pious obedience to priestly authority and marital fidelity), and her subjection to the combined authorities of church and state. (Isabella may also unveil herself on coming forward to charge Angelo with his crimes, but there is no stage direction or dialogue to make this action certain.) The scene makes both women penitents at the duke's mercy, reducing them from accusers to accused, then transforming them to suitors for Angelo's pardon. The playwright repeatedly — and to the point of overkill — depicts their subjection to authority as the scene progresses.[31]

The women are not the play's only victims of abusive authority, and they are not the only figures we may compare usefully to Foxe. There is a third "uncowling" or unveiling in this scene of revelations, and again, the uncloaking of face and hair makes a crucial point. When the Provost "unmuffles" Claudio we see a face that contrasts the duke / friar's face in a single key respect. Claudio wears a beard. The duke does not. We know the first to be true because the play makes an explicit issue of Claudio's beardedness in two separate scenes: first, in act 4, scene 2, when the duke instructs the Provost in methods to make Barnardine's severed head appear more like Claudio's: "O, death's a great disguiser, and you may add to it. Shave the head and tie the beard" (161–62). Again in act 4, scene 3, when the Provost proposes Ragozine as a substitute for Barnardine, Claudio's beard figures as a key identifying feature: "There died this morning of a cruel fever / One Ragusine, a most notorious pirate, / A man of Claudio's years, his beard and head / Just of his colour" (62–65).

That the duke has no beard is certain from his ability to assume the friar's disguise. While the cowl or hood of his monastic garment will cover his head, making it unnecessary for him to possess the tonsured head of a friar, the cowl will not hide his face. Twice in act 5, scene 1, Lucio refers to the friar's "bald pate," extrapolating from his visible lack of facial hair to assume that beneath the cowl there will be a shaven crown. The contrast between the duke / friar's hairless face and Claudio's bearded one replicates the Protestant iconography by which the works-theology of priestly self-renunciation was made to seem a monstrous perversion of normative sexuality.

I am not suggesting here that beardedness equates to Protestantism and clean-shavenness to Catholicism; however, clean-shavenness was a crucial element in Protestant polemic's negative iconography of priestly devotion. By contrast, the masculinity and moral uprightness of Protestant martyrs inhere in the beards and hair of the victims in Protestant martyrological art. Consider, for instance, the contrast in the illustration of Tyndale's execution between the monks who lurk in the crowd and the bearded condemned man. Another striking example of this coding occurs in the illustration of Thomas Tomkyns in the presence of a room full of bald-pated clerics (see fig. 1.4 above). Shakespeare draws on this contrast when he "uncowls" Claudio's face, using the iconography of Protestant polemical art to texture his representation of Claudio, Mariana and Isabella as victims of abusive authority.

In act 5 of *Measure for Measure*, the duke stages a scene of excruciating injustice before stepping forward to set everything right. In this scene Shakespeare is neither writing nor attacking Protestant polemic, but using its grammar of victimization to comment on the state of affairs in Vienna, in England, in London: in his view, it seems, injustice is the usual order of the day. Judges and rulers and clerics have virtual impunity to be tyrannical foxes and hypocritical bite-sheep. Rarely in real life is there a duke ready or willing to play deus ex machina on behalf of the victim. Even for those in the audience who were ready to accept the duke, as Angelo does, as a "power divine," the playwright seems deliberate in constructing this ending as a too pat resolution of a very murky play.

Insofar as he figures the duke as a biblical master returned to bring his servants to reckoning (via Matthew and Luke), Shakespeare is either guilty of glaring inconsistency in his depiction of character, or means to point out the implausibly fantastic nature of an ending in which judicial corruption is unmasked in time to prevent the innocent from suffering. Where was the duke when Anne Askew was interrogated, tortured and tried? (Where, indeed, was King Henry?) Nowhere to be found, in no way willing to help. Instead, Askew found herself in the hands of men who made false promises to entrap her, who violated legal processes, bent laws and perverted justice in order to condemn and murder her. Shakespeare's play asks its audience to identify with Mariana and Isabella. For the male spectators in the early modern audience this is likely to have been a doubly unsettling experience: first the play forces them to recognize their powerlessness in the hands of authority, then it makes them recognize that it has put them in the position of women.

"Hence shall we see / If power change purpose, what our seemers be" (1.3.53–54). The duke's initial promise to expose Angelo's corruption grows more ironic as the duke's own purpose and "seeming" grow less clear. Through his uneasy portrait of the cowled duke, who is and is not a bite-sheep, Shakespeare offers a dark, almost cynical view of power and submission. All politicians, all rulers are "seemers" interested only in domination. Shakespeare shows us what these seemers really are: a collection of human beings subject to the usual desires for sexual gratification and power. Whether power changes purpose remains unclear. Certainly, it provides opportunity and confers impunity to violate at will.

THREE

"Break . . . all the bounds of manhood, noblesse and religion"
GEORGE CHAPMAN'S BUSSY D'AMBOIS

Without all dyscressyon, honestye, or manhode, he casteth of[f] hys gowne, and taketh here upon hym the most vyle offyce of an hangeman and pulleth at the racke most vyllanouslye. . . . What chaplayne of the pope hath inchaunted yow, or what devyll of helle bewytched yow to execute upon a poore condempned woman, so prodygyouse a kynde of tyrannye?
> — John Bale, "elucidating" his edition of *The Examinations of Anne Askew*

Chapman's Jacobean Henri III

If Shakespeare's *Measure for Measure* invites its audience to feel anxious and vulnerable, it makes its topical points with great care, presumably in the knowledge that playwrights were as vulnerable as any of the king's subjects. George Chapman learned this lesson early in the new reign when the king took offense at the representation of Scots in *Eastward Hoe* (1605).[1] Chapman writes from firsthand experience, then, when he has one of the characters in *Bussy D'Ambois* (c. 1607) assert that "the king's change doth breed the subject's terror."[2] Like *Measure for Measure*, Chapman's French play exposes the corrupt purposes of the powerful and explores the terrors faced by lesser subjects in the dangerous atmosphere of a royal court.

As long as he keeps his play firmly situated in France, attending to the corruptions of a foreign, Catholic court, it is in safe territory, but Chapman ventures several times onto a political terrain closer to home. Through a set of brief and carefully managed topical allusions to English concerns, Chapman establishes the domestic relevance of his nightmarish fiction. Early in the play the duke of Guise and King Henry (Henri III) debate the relative merits of French and English customs; their conversation, though set in a fictional moment a decade earlier, in fact responds to the mixture of relief and nostalgia, aspiration and jealousy with which James I's English subjects approached the new reign. Thus, when the duke of Guise disparages the Elizabethan court as "too crestfallen in all observance," his point is not that England's court ceremonies are poor, but that their splendor falls short in an absurd attempt to gloss over the plain humanity of England's aristocracy. The ceremonies are crestfallen because the Guise sees through them as a vain attempt to make "semi-gods / Of their great nobles, and of their old Queen, / An ever-young and most immortal goddess."[3] The line captures the resentment of Elizabeth that was repressed during her life, but which found expression in various ways at her death.[4] The Guise's remarks echo the sentiments of many English subjects who were truly ready for a new monarch and who had recently rejoiced to replace their old queen with a king "in the flower and strength of his years."[5]

The duke's critique does not stand unchallenged, however: King Henry counters with a defense of England through which Chapman gives voice to the nostalgia for Elizabeth which was already surfacing early in James's reign. He challenges the Guise's version of Elizabeth as the vain old woman who would allow no one to acknowledge her mortality, presenting instead a vision of

Elizabeth's "royal parts" which transcended her physical body. In King Henry's representation, she is a "great courtier," "full of majesty" and without peer. Chapman distills nostalgia for Elizabeth's personal flair and diplomatic skill, nostalgia for a virtuous court "informed" by the ample "beauty, state, and worth" of its monarch (1.2.14–24). Above all, Chapman conveys nostalgia for a monarch foreign princes admired. James had already disappointed in all of these areas. In this context, Henry's remark that "the king's change doth breed the subject's terror" must have registered as a comment on James's accession to the English throne. Although this is not, in fact, the point Henry's speech ultimately makes, it is a meaning that hovers beneath the surface of the remark.

Henry's statement, in its entirety, is actually a comment on the folly of England's emulation of French society and manners:

> Our French court
> Is a mere mirror of confusion to it.
> The king and subject, lord and every slave,
> Dance a continual hay; our rooms of state
> Kept like our stables; no place more observed
> Than a rude market-place; and though our custom
> Keep this assured deformity from our sight,
> 'Tis ne'er the less essentially unsightly,
> Which they would soon see, would they change their form
> To this of ours, and then compare them both;
> Which we must not affect, because in kingdoms
> Where the king's change doth breed the subject's terror,
> Pure innovation is more gross than error.
>
> (1.2.24–36)

Henry's picture of France is an image of disorder: in it there is both extreme social distinction and an obliteration of social boundaries: "king and subject, lord and every slave, / Dance a continual hay . . . no place more observed / Than a rude marketplace." Neil Cuddy is among the historians who have noted that James I, in fact, attempted to change the English "form," modeling his court after the French, not only in regard to the lavish entertainments for which the Jacobean court became famous, but also in the way the king prescribed its social patterns. According to Cuddy, "James in Scotland had lived in a court whose keynote, like the French court upon which it was based, was open access to and populous intimacy with the king in his Chamber. From this intimacy stemmed political influence."[6] And from this carefully orchestrated "populous intimacy" there also stemmed factional jealousy and Anglo-Scottish conflict once the Scottish court moved to England. It is in relation to James I's imposition of a new, "French" style on the English court that Chapman's characters' conversation must be understood. England in 1607 was a nation living through a change of monarch and living with the innovations wrought by its new king.

James was simultaneously dedicated to hierarchy and proud of the extraordinary "intimacy" his court fostered between king and courtier. Cuddy maintains that this paradox was systematized in the king's use of palace space. The king, indeed, allowed access to himself — if not by every slave, then at least by many degrees of subjects, but this access was rigidly hierarchized by a series of chambers in which subjects of certain levels could await their audience with the king. In order of increasing exclusivity these rooms were the Outer or Presence Chamber, the Privy Chamber, the Withdrawing Chamber and the Bedchamber. James is reported to have chastised a group of wayward and presumptuous lords, who on one occasion found their way into his Withdrawing Chamber, saying "that there was a Presence and Privy Chamber for them."[7] The fact that the Bedchamber was almost entirely a Scottish preserve occasioned extreme anxiety among English aspirants to the monarch's favor, a jealousy that intensified negative reactions to the series of favorites promoted from humble (and in many cases, Scottish) backgrounds to titles, wealth and an office in the Bedchamber.[8]

Despite this severe attention to hierarchical order and correspondent competition for place, the impression that James's court was a place of unseemly openness and mingling persisted. This impression owed less to any actual "marketplace" mixing of social classes than to two related innovations: (1) James consciously constructed his court to enforce a blending of Scottish and English subjects at each level of prestige, and (2) the levels of hierarchy had been substantially redefined by the new monarch during his infamous early program of social promotion. Chapman pointedly glosses the antagonism generated by James's wholesale creation of honors in a set of clever throwaway lines later in act 1, scene 2, where he allows a group of established courtiers to speak contemptuously of "knight[s] of the new edition" and "new denizened lord[s]" (1.2.115, 162). The sense that James was violating social "order" belonged to those (English) who found themselves excluded in favor of Scots, "new denizened lords," and other less deserving "slaves." What was, in fact, a new order appeared as an erasure of social distinction to those suffering frustrated hopes.

Thus, in the eyes of many of James's English subjects, the new court fell far short of its predecessor. This is the view captured by Chapman and placed in the mouth of his fictional king of France, who praises Elizabeth I:

> Assure you, cousin Guise, so great a courtier,
> So full of majesty and royal parts
> No queen in Christendom may boast herself.
> Her court approves it, that's a court indeed,
> Not mixed with rudeness used in common houses,
> But, as courts should be th'abstracts of their kingdoms
> In all the beauty, state, and worth they hold,
> So is hers, amply, and by her informed.
> The world is not contracted in a man
> With more proportion and expression
> Than in her court, her kingdom.
>
> (1.2.14–24)

How poignant for those in Chapman's audience feeling nostalgia for Elizabeth, that these characters speak in a moment far enough past that they can speak of the queen and her court in the present tense. In Henry's view, at least, Elizabeth's court is a model of "proportion," unsullied by "the rudeness used in common houses"; indeed, its purity owes to the very "observance" of social difference the Guise has condemned. Elizabeth's England, then, appears as a model of social order, while in France — and in Jacobean England, aristocrats compete desperately with one another for place, all the while failing to distinguish themselves from peasants. With so much at stake, this sort of competition was dangerous. To Chapman's King Henry and presumably to many in the play's audience, "innovation [was] more gross than error." Change was terrifying.

Chapman's play is a relatively early example of theatrical engagement with the issues troubling James's parliaments, and it is a good example of the cautious way in which plays voiced the rumblings of distrust.[9] By dividing its representation of royalty between the figures of Monsieur and the king, the play maintains a necessary level of ambiguity, refusing to resolve the plot's political content into direct commentary on Jacobean England. Chapman's King Henry is a deliberately slight character, which allows him to come off as a more or less "good" king. However, his credit with the audience owes mostly to his appreciative comments on the English court — and to the fact that the playwright places him in opposition to the more sinister figures of Monsieur and the Guise.

At this casual level, the king must be supposed "good" because he sides with and protects the protagonist, but this connection between the king and the protagonist is not as benign as convention might suggest. The picture of Henri III available to the English through gossip and printed accounts of French events suggested a far more disturbing character: a vain, homosexual king swayed by the flattery of favorites.[10] In this context, Chapman's representation of the king is equivocal at best, focusing as it does on his patronage of D'Ambois and his willingness to credit a favorite's critique of other flatterers. These attributes resonate not only with the most disparaging depictions of the previous king of France, but also with troubling contemporary observations about England's new king.[11]

Not Martyrs, but Victims

Chapman's *Bussy D'Ambois* is at least as challenging a play as Shakespeare's *Measure for Measure* if we are to consider the way it handles its central characters. Where Shakespeare's Viennese play has troubled critics because its ending celebrates the rule of a duke who has evaded his responsibilities, deputized a tyrant, then skulked about pretending to be a monk while his subjects suffer, one might wonder equally well what there is in the plot or characters of *Bussy D'Ambois* to inspire sympathy in early Jacobean audiences. Set in France, its "hero" is a gentleman soldier fallen on hard times who professes virtue, then accepts a salary from the prince to be his creature, buys new clothes, comes to court, seduces ladies under their husbands' noses, fights a duel in which he kills a number of other courtiers, flatters the king by disparaging flatterers, has an affair with a countess, conjures devils to try to outwit his enemies, but is killed by them anyway. The other major figures include the king, Henry III, who by Chapman's time had been the subject of hostile historiographers and was thus popularly disparaged as a homosexual and a would-be tyrant who had not held onto his throne long enough to execute his dark designs.[12] The play, however, seems to prefer him to his younger brother, Monsieur, whom it paints as a thoroughly sinister figure with an eye on the throne. Worse still, there is the duke of Guise, last of the "Guisards," whose violence in the service of Catholicism had made them the archvillains of English nightmares and stage plays.[13] Beyond these, there are only the cuckolded count of Montsurry, his adulterous wife, and her corrupt confessor to vie for the audience's sympathy. Perhaps it is a measure of Chapman's assessment of the French that the play's most appealing characters are a brash social climber, an adulteress and a corrupt friar.

Clearly Chapman realized that bad characters are more interesting than good ones, but it would be inaccurate to say that the play simply indulges in a horror tale of the gruesome misdeeds of the

French. It is tempting, but not quite true. Instead, the play asks its audience to suspend judgment and engage their concern for the protagonist and his lover. It achieves this end not by mitigating either the adultery or D'Ambois's arrogant self-promotion, but by making the bad characters so brutal, so powerfully politic, so secure in their sense of their own entitlement to an aristocratic monopoly on violence that the audience cannot help but sympathize with the lovers as underdogs.

Like *Measure for Measure*, this play works to make its audience identify with the victims, but Chapman has a more difficult task even than Shakespeare. Like Shakespeare, Chapman has linked his protagonist and heroine with some of the most widely reviled practices that Protestant polemic had associated with Roman Catholicism, but Chapman has gone several steps farther than Shakespeare. While Duke Vincentio may be charged with abusing his disguise to hear intimate confessions from Isabella and of acting as a sexual broker for Isabella and Mariana, Chapman's countess brazenly employs her confessor as a pander. Later in the play, this friar conjures devils in order to assist his lady in her attempts to keep her adultery secret from her husband. Like Shakespeare, Chapman manages to make these characters sympathetic by extrapolating and manipulating the conventions of martyrology to construct sympathy where it could not otherwise exist. While it cannot presume to make actual martyrs of its characters, it does make victims of them, victims whose suffering Chapman encodes to resonate with Jacobean audiences.

It is worth reiterating an earlier point, however: the play does not make particularly attractive figures of its central characters, nor does it excuse their adultery. Although it gives her the standard dramatic reasons for cuckolding her husband (he does not protect her from Monsieur's sexual advances, but basely tells her to put up with the prince), the play deliberately undercuts this excuse for the countess's behavior. Rather than allow the ugly scene of Monsieur's coercive proposition to speak for itself, the play prefaces it with her admission of an adulterous passion. Thus, before it gives her any reason to betray her husband, she is heard to respond to her husband's promise of a quick return with a sardonic "Would that would please me" (2.2.31–32). This sotto voce quip defines the countess as a stereotypically false woman: her lavish professions of love to her husband's face are now exposed as blatant hypocrisy. Lest this hint of trouble in the marriage be too subtle for his audience, Chapman follows the countess's aside wth a sustained soliloquy in which she lays out her inner corruption:

> I cannot cloak it . . .
> . . . of a sudden, my licentious fancy
> Riots within me. Not my name and house
> Nor my religion to this hour observed
> Can stand above it; I must utter that
> That will in parting break more strings in me
> Than death when life parts; and that holy man
> That, from my cradle, counseled for my soul,
> I now must make an agent for my blood.
> [*Enter Monsieur*]
>
> (2.2.34, 42–49)

Chapman crafts Monsieur's entrance to punctuate the countess's soliloquy. Thus, the audience knows that she is preparing to embark on an extramarital affair before it sees her struggle to fend off Monsieur's unwanted advances. When she tells Monsieur that she intends to remain a chaste wife, the audience is forced to credit Monsieur's observation that women who use "Honor and husband!" as a motto commonly utter it only to fend off men they do not fancy. While Monsieur's angry threats are frightening, it is difficult not to see this woman as the prince paints her. Chapman deliberately sets himself a challenge when he chooses this woman as his damsel in distress.

If the playwright had reordered his scenes so that the countess's disparaging remark about her husband followed his failure to defend her against the prince, or if he had delayed her revealing soliloquy until a later moment, it would be easy to see her turn of affection in a sympathetic light. Instead, Chapman insists on her culpability for her affair with D'Ambois. Declining another opportunity to mitigate her sin, Chapman introduces the friar not as a tempter who corrupts his unwitting mistress (a common stereotype in Protestant literature), but as an agent engaged by the woman: we hear her express her intention to corrupt *him*. Likewise, Chapman reminds his audience of another convention of adultery plots: the suborned waiting woman. In standard fashion, the countess finds herself alone in Monsieur's presence because the maid has made herself conveniently scarce (presumably at Monsieur's bidding). However, it is the countess herself, a short while later, who engineers Pero's convenient absence during D'Ambois's visit. There can be no thought that this is a case where a sexually cunning servant abets the seduction of a naive noble woman; there is nothing naive about the countess of Montsurry.

Still, the play insists that the audience invest its concern on this woman's behalf. The countess may be more choosy than chaste, as Monsieur suggests, but the play refuses to use this as a justification of his attempt to force himself on her. Instead, the scene capitalizes on several overlapping conventions to manipulate its audience's response to the two characters. Above all, it draws on longstanding English vilification of the French in general and of the Valois monarchy in particular to produce an expectation that Monsieur's every word and action will proceed from evil intention. The scene also assumes audience knowledge of the historical duke of Alençon and Anjou's reputation as a prince who shifted allegiance frequently without evidencing any loyalty to religious affiliation or family. A further detail about Monsieur's historical person bears on this scene: his "evil" physiognomy.[14] During the period when Elizabeth had considered marrying this Valois prince, popular report had made much of his ugliness; apparently he was quite disfigured by smallpox scarring. Like Shakespeare's Richard III, Chapman's Monsieur seems quite sensitive on this point: he angrily suggests that the countess's scruples are not moral but aesthetic. "Speak plainly, and say, 'I do not like you, sir; / Y'are an ill-favored fellow in my eye,' / And I am answered." Though she avoids insulting him in these terms (saying only, "I do not like you in that sort you like"), Monsieur remains convinced that it is his person she has rejected: "Horror of death! Could I but please your eye, / You would give me the like, ere you loose me" (2.2.85–89, 97–98). Chapman uses the character's ugliness, as Shakespeare does Richard's, both as an external marker of his evil character and as a partial explanation of his embittered psychology. At both levels, the audience is to register that this is a villain to be feared.

The scene between Monsieur and the countess also exploits the gender conventions we have seen at work in *Measure for Measure* and Askew's *Examinations*. Monsieur enters in a moment when the woman is alone and says to her things that she will not be able to prove against him should she report his behavior. In fact, like Isabella, the countess ends the scene by threatening to expose Monsieur:

> Y'are a vile fellow, and I'll tell the King
> Your occupation of dishonoring ladies,
> And of his court: a lady cannot live
> As she was born, and with that sort of pleasure
> That fits her state, but she must be defamed
> With an infamous lord's detraction.
>
> (2.2.100–5)

Her complaint seems reasonable: ladies should be able to live at court without being threatened by dissolute lords. The points it scores are gendered points: it asserts the right of women of a certain class to live in proximity to their king and in society with others of their class — as it was assumed gentlemen might expect to do. It argues for a vision of that court as a virtuous, pleasurable society and casts any disruption of that ideal as an attack on natural order — an attack mounted by sexually predatory men.

Her complaint stands in contrast to Monsieur's very different interpretation of the court and its gender politics: earlier in the scene Monsieur asserted that if she were as chaste as she claims, she would live in country retirement with her husband. Monsieur's point shifts guilt onto the woman for her choice of residence, an attitude generally in keeping with early modern English opinions regarding women's sexuality. The logic of his statement suggests that she knows the court to be licentious; thus, her decision to live there amounts to an advertisement of her sexual availability. This insinuating interpretation of the countess's behavior rings true with audience members not only because it mines cultural attitudes about women, but also because they have just heard *this* woman confess that her "licentious fancy riots within [her]" (2.2.42–43). By the end of the scene, however, the countess is able to reverse the argument because the prince has proven himself guilty of all the most vicious characteristics of his own gender. Although she is only a woman and is susceptible to all the frivolities and foibles attributed to her sex, she is no match for Monsieur — and that stands to her credit as the scene progresses.

It is a measure of Monsieur's villainy that Chapman is able to recuperate the countess in so short a space. From the start, Monsieur conducts the interview not by wooing her, but by threatening her and attempting to ensnare her with her own words. His opening tactic is to hint at the force he might use:

> Pray thee regard thine own good, if not mine,
> And cheer my love for that; you do not know
> What you may be by me, nor what without me;
> I may have the power t'advance and pull down any.

> (2.2.51–54)

The countess chooses to interpret this threat in social rather than physical terms, and professes herself to be unmoved by the prospect that this prince might reduce her husband to a "mean state." Monsieur's tone, however, increasingly hints of his capacity for real violence, rising through insinuation and belligerent questioning to mockery and sinister exclamation. But these threats remain implicit, lurking just beneath the surface of his aggressive rhetorical maneuvering.

The countess's decision to ignore his threats is a defensive strategy that exploits the reputed dimness of women as a means of avoiding direct confrontation: she pretends she doesn't understand the implications of what Monsieur has said. Like Isabella, she hopes to avert the threat by pretending to understand only the most benign level of his meaning. Chapman's character is no more successful than Shakespeare's, however, in her attempt to outmaneuver policy with politeness. Like Isabella, the countess falls prey to her antagonist's manipulation of her appeals to the conventions of womanhood. When she stands on honor, Monsieur easily deconstructs the notion of wifely "honor" as something that can be neither proved nor disproved; when she advances the security of a husband's love above the danger of placing confidence in "a dissolute friend," he counters with his argument that women who choose to live at court do so precisely to have the company of men other than their husbands. When Monsieur appears to offer her a polite exit from the conversation, she jumps to respond with the deliberately noncommital, "I do not like you in that sort you like," but this apparently benign statement proves to be a trap. To her horror, she finds that she has tacitly admitted she would accept the advances of a man she *did* like. Monsieur pounces on her with the exclamation of a duelist who senses his advantage:

> Then have at you here!
> Take with a politic hand this rope of pearl,
> And, though you be not amorous, yet be wise.
> Take me for wisdom; he that you can love
> Is ne'er the further from you.
>
> (2.2.89–93)

There are no polite ways back from this moment. The proposition has been made in unavoidable terms. She knows that she places herself in mortal danger when she rejects his gift and his proposition as "poison." The audience knows that it is merely a matter of time before Monsieur finds an opportunity to turn the "horror of death" from an exclamation into an accomplished fact. Like the wicked clerics in Askew's narrative or Shakepeare's Angelo, Chapman draws Monsieur as a man who uses his social position and his superior rhetorical skills to take advantage of a woman. In keeping with this conventional scenario, Chapman's woman earns sympathy when she bravely endures a contest in which she is so overmatched. That he ambushes her in a solitary moment, threatens her and takes advantage of her lack of rhetorical agility exposes Monsieur as a vicious bully. The play is quite clear in its demand that the audience despise Monsieur, despite any reservations its members might have about the countess of Montsurry.

Chapman draws an equally ambivalent portrait of his protagonist, D'Ambois, who is at once a grating braggart and a breath of fresh air in the formal and fetid atmosphere of the French court. Perhaps his appeal lies partly in the fact that he embodies a fantasy of social advancement which must have been shared by many in the early days of James I's reign, when the king was busy establishing his court and using knighthoods and lordships to ingratiate himself with his new subjects.[15] Furthermore, the play offers D'Ambois as an alternative to the corruption and danger of great nobles like Monsieur and the Guise. However, it must be noted that rather than assuaging their threat, D'Ambois's presence is like a spark among the tinder of these powerful men. Once he arrives at court, D'Ambois offends Monsieur by refusing to be an instrument in the prince's plots. He abruptly shifts his allegiance from Monsieur to the king and styles himself the only loyal follower of his sovereign, the only courtier who speaks truth rather than flattery or politic lies.

D'Ambois also takes seriously the king's invitation to be his "eagle," his champion to purge corruption from the kingdom. This makes him bold in his affronts to the nobles. He goes out of his way to infuriate the duke of Guise, first by courting his duchess, then by taunting him in the king's presence where neither can draw to support their words with their swords. D'Ambois even denies the Guise's social superiority when Monsieur tries to make peace between the two:

D'Ambois:	Let him peace first
	That made the first war.
Monsieur:	He's the better man.
D'Ambois:	And, therefore, may do worst?
Monsieur:	He has more titles.
D'Ambois:	So Hydra had more heads.
Monsieur:	He's greater known.
D'Ambois:	His greatness is the people's; mine's mine own.
Monsieur:	He's nobly born.
D'Ambois:	He is not; I am noble.

(3.2.71–76)

D'Ambois is arrogant and self-righteous. Certainly, the play does not suggest that he should receive the unconditional admiration of the audience. Yet his antagonists are so provoking and so much more arrogant than he that it is difficult to ignore his appeal.

When the play opens, D'Ambois is alone on the stage. His soliloquy begins as a meditation on the fact that virtue receives no reward in this corrupt world. On its face, this seems a promising place to start ("Fortune, not reason, rules the state of things"). His critique of the presumption of the great and their unacknowledged dependence on the meaner sort is a familiar one: the great politicians, like "unskillful statuaries," think that bigger is better. They believe that if they "straddle enough, strut, and look big, and gape" (like a colossal statue), speak with an "affected gravity of voice" (booming like timpani), affect "sourness of countenance, manners' cruelty, authority, wealth, and all the spawn of fortune," they will "bear all the kingdom's worth before them" (1.1.9–14). Yet he points out that this greatness is mere outward show: these "heroic forms without o'er spread, / Within are nought but mortar, flint, and lead" (16–17). Though polished and exalted on the surface, they are made from base materials. The outward show depends on much behind-the-scenes work by the little people, as when a great tall ship returns from sea and requires the towing services of "a poor staid fisherman" (26).

It is not hard to believe that this view of things was appealing to many in Chapman's audience. It seems to be the anthem of the have-nots:

> Fortune, not reason, rules the state of things,
> Reward goes backwards, honor on his head;
> Who is not poor, is monstrous; only need
> Gives form and worth to every human seed.

(1.1.1–4)

This vision of the poor as virtuous and as the foundation upon which greatness depends might suggest that D'Ambois has idealized his society. However, the vision also has a darker side that begins with the observation, "who is not poor is monstrous," and takes form in the assertion that beneath their heroic forms the stern countenanced, cruel-mannered great are composed of mortar, flint and lead. While these items might be taken in context merely as the basic materials of statuary, they must also be heard as the raw materials of war. The great and the poor do not have a wholly benign relationship according to this meditation. The "poor staid fisherman" answers to the call of the adventurers' "warning-piece," with its implicit warning that his peace depends on his cooperation. This darker texture belies the apparently harmonious picture at the end of the speech where the great must rely on the virtuous poor in order to avoid shipwreck.

But is D'Ambois a figure who speaks with the wisdom that comes through suffering, the wisdom that Shakespeare's King Lear comes to possess (if fleetingly) when he realizes the condition of the poor? Or is D'Ambois a figure like the bastard Edmund, who envies those who possess what he is denied? The courtiers who view D'Ambois's subsequent promotion with suspicious eyes think the latter, envying him his sudden change of fortune and refusing to admit him into their circle. Critics who see D'Ambois as a hero have argued for the former view, hearing him as a representative of virtue — a virtue that cannot survive the court, but which at least makes an attempt.[16] The end of his opening speech suggests that D'Ambois does not identify himself with the poor as these critics generally suppose, but that he himself has visions of greatness in which he aims to improve on the model he has critiqued:

So when *we* wander furthest through the waves
Of glassy glory and the gulfs of state,
Topped with all titles, spreading all *our* reaches,
As if each private arm would sphere the world,
We must to virtue for her guide resort.
Or *we* shall shipwreck in our safest port.

(1.1.28–33; emphasis added)

This is not a speech in which we can be confident that the speaker identifies as one whom Fortune has slighted. By the end, he speaks on behalf of those who navigate the realms of glory and of state. It is difficult to reconcile the beginning and end of this speech, but D'Ambois is not so alienated from the upper ranks of his society as some have supposed.[17] Neither is he so grand an idealist.

Although the 1641 quarto and most modern editions direct that D'Ambois enters the stage "poor," there is a difference between "the poor" and the kind of poverty D'Ambois represents.[18] D'Ambois is not "a man of inferior station," as Russell A. Fraser suggests in his introduction to the play, but "a man of spirit . . . [and] neglected worth," as Monsieur explains.[19] He is "young and haughty, apt to take / Fire at advancement, to bear state and flourish" (1.1.46–50). In other words, he is a gentleman with no means to support his rank, a man whose gentle family has fallen on hard times. This agrees with the king's ability to recognize him without introduction and the king's expectation that D'Ambois would sooner or later present himself at court. It also explains why the other courtiers are so amused when the Guise does not recognize D'Ambois in his new clothes, taking him for some truly nouveau riche "knight of the new edition" or "some new denizened lord," a commoner recently promoted to gentility (1.2.115, 162). What D'Ambois lacks is not so much rank as cash. He does not imagine himself to be like a "poor staid fisherman," except in his susceptibility to the violence of those who are greater and richer, more "colossal" than he.[20] As his opening thoughts suggest, he is meditating on how to evade these dangers and improve his fortune.

Thus it is not really so surprising that when Monsieur appears,

D'Ambois takes his appearance and his offer in stride. When invited
to live and thrive at the "wellhead," D'Ambois understands that
he is being invited to enter the courtly competition for place in
which one advances only by breaking the commandments and only
after first paying obeisance to those in higher positions. The invitation is to a court where one must

> Flatter great lords, to put them in mind
> Why they were made lords; or please portly ladies
> With a good carriage, tell them idle tales
> To make their physic work. . .
> . . . .
> To gain being forward, though you break for haste
> All the commandments ere you break your fast,
> But believe backwards, make your period
> And creed's last article, "I believe in God."
> . . . .
> 'Tis a great man's part.
>
> (1.1.91–94, 98–101, 103)

It is a court made up of great men, vain ladies and lesser souls who
aspire to greatness — men like D'Ambois who aspire to learn to
play the "great man's part." At the close of this speech he asks
Monsieur, "Shall I learn this there?" (103). D'Ambois's tone does
not imply that he will reject Monsieur's invitation, nor that he is
offended by it. It is to his credit, however, that he recognizes the
nature of the courtier culture he aims to join. Some critics have
taken these words as a promise that D'Ambois will be more
virtuous than the majority at court, but that leads only to disappointment when the character proves to be as politic as the rest.
What is clear in D'Ambois's conversation with Monsieur is that
he understands the court well enough to imagine he can manipulate it to his benefit. His tone is one of cynical and critical perception, not righteous disapproval — and what he chiefly perceives
is that Monsieur, too, has a plan for personal advancement, a plan
D'Ambois hopes to exploit.

Indeed, Monsieur has more in mind for D'Ambois than a

generous introduction to high society. As he entered the scene, Monsieur had remarked to himself (and to the audience, though not in D'Ambois's hearing) that he is implementing a plan to ready himself to take the reins of state, should that "likely fortune" result which would remove his brother and make him king. Monsieur considers that he will need a band of "resolvéd spirits about" him: men, like D'Ambois, who are "young and haughty," men who would not balk at any command, even perhaps a command for the "killing of the king" (1.1.43, 44, 49; 3.2.356). D'Ambois understands quite clearly the reasons for Monsieur's interest: "What will he send? Some crowns? It is to sow them / Upon my spirit, and make them spring a crown / Worth millions of the seed-crowns he will send" (1.1.119–21). D'Ambois listens to Monsieur's proposition with the same critical acuity he demonstrated in his opening reflections, distinguishing Monsieur's motives from his offer's courtly flourishes. Fully cognizant of the opportunity and its implications, D'Ambois accepts Monsieur's money, then shifts for himself.

"A prerogative to rack men's freedoms"

What makes Bussy D'Ambois and Tamyra, the countess of Montsurry, appealing, then, is not their virtue, but their willingness to resist the powerful and defy the base. What distinguishes the countess from her husband is that she dares imagine herself free of obligation to Monsieur. Although she is no model of chastity, she maintains her right to protect herself from unwanted advances. She imagines that there are limits to the prerogatives of princes, and she commands respect for bravely refusing to give this prince what he demands. Her husband, on the other hand, marks himself as no better than a base slave when he requires his wife to

> . . . bear with [Monsieur]:
> Thou know'st he is a bachelor and a courtier,
> Ay, and a prince; and their prerogatives
> Are to their laws, as to their pardons are

> Their reservations, after parliaments —
> One quits another: form gives all their essence.
> That prince doth high in virtue's reckoning stand
> That will entreat a vice, and not command.

(2.2.118–25)

This man who feels himself unable to challenge a prince's unjust and unreasonable assertions of prerogative was unlikely to win friends in Chapman's English audience.[21] He rests on the hope that the prince will be virtuous enough to refrain from pressing his desires. Clearly this is a vain hope, given what the audience has just seen of Monsieur, who indeed offered the countess "opportunities almost to rapes," as she reports. As the play continues, Montsurry becomes little more than putty in the hands of Monsieur and the Guise, and their contempt for him is clear. They use him for their own ends, treating him as a mere tool of convenience. The play suggests that a man who refuses to defend his rights as a subject can hardly expect to protect his property, let alone his wife. Significantly, he loses his wife's sexual favors to D'Ambois, who, although he is Montsurry's social inferior, shows more bravery in response to the predatory power of the play's noblemen: it is D'Ambois who warns the Guise not to think his "greatness" a warrant for insolence or "a prerogative / To rack men's freedoms with ruder wrongs" (3.2.121–22).

Twice in this play Chapman has D'Ambois foreshadow the violence that lies ahead: here in this reference to the rack and also in an earlier moment when, in promising to keep his lover's secret, he alludes to torture — "Sooner shall torture be the sire to pleasure / . . . Than the dear jewel of your fame in me / Be made an outcast to your infamy" 3.1.34, 36–37). The rack indeed becomes the rudest wrong practiced by the powerful on the weak in this play.[22] In the fifth act, the count of Montsurry uses the rack to interrogate his wife in a scene of sustained horror made worse by the fact that the husband acts not so much in his own interest as in the interest of the greater men who set him on. With fury supercharged by the duke's hatred for D'Ambois and Monsieur's bitterness toward the countess, Montsurry destroys the woman he loves. The husband is hardly more than a cypher for these villains. The play underscores this elision of the personal and political motivations for the countess's punishment when it employs an expressly political engine of corporal punishment. When he puts his wife on the rack, Montsurry uses for his private purposes a device that was among the most terrifying torments employed by European states for political interrogations.

The English seem to have viewed this engine with particular fear. James Heath demonstrates that the rack was often effective without actually being used: many prisoners capitulated after merely being shown or threatened with the device. Sir Thomas Smith, who served both Edward VI and Elizabeth in public office, offers this account of the English dread of torture in *De Republica Anglorum: A Discourse on the Commonwealth of England* (1583):

> Torment or question, which is used by the order of the civile law and custome of other countries, to put a malefactor to excessive paine to make him confesse of himselfe, or of his fellowes or complices, is not used in England. It is taken for servile. For how can he serve the commonwealth after as a free man who hath his bodie so haled or tormented? And if hee bee not found guilty, what amends can be made of him? And if he must dye, what crueltie is it so to torment him before! The nature of Englishmen is to neglect death, to abide no torment; and therefore hee will confesse rather to have done anything, — yea, to have killed his owne father, than to suffer torment. For death our nation doth not so much esteeme as a meere torment; in no place shall you see malefactors goe more constantly, more assuredly, and with less lamentation to their death than in England. The nature of our nation is free, stout, haulty, prodigall of life and blood; but contumely, beating, servitude, and servile torment and punishment, it will not abide.[23]

Though torture was certainly in use in England when Smith wrote (and it seems unlikely that Smith was ignorant of its use), his statement records many of the arguments against its use as a judicial instrument (that it induces false confession, that it unjustly maims the innocent, that it leaves ex-prisoners physically and socially disabled). Smith does not specifically mention the rack, but his account of suffering worse than death precisely captures the experience Chapman stages in the countess's torture.[24]

The rack was a powerful literary device: both Protestant and Roman Catholic polemicists recounted its use as a means of conveying the unrestrained brutality of their persecutors. Woodcuts illustrating this torture appear in both *Acts and Monuments* and in Richard Verstagen's Counter-Reformation treatise, *Theatrum crudelitatum haereticorum nostri temporis* (figs. 3.1 and 3.2).[25]

The most memorable narrative of a Protestant's racking is Anne Askew's description of her torture, the extraordinary ferocity of which both Foxe and Bale emphasized in their editions of Askew's *Examinations*. There, as in Chapman's play, the rack is the trump card that enables the woman to transcend all doubts about her integrity. In both works, its use reveals the evil depths of the men who employ it, while the women's perseverance through such an ordeal raises them to new heights in the audience's estimation.

What Chapman stages, then, is a spectacle out of English nightmare. It is made worse, not because he represents the sufferer as an innocent party (he does not), but because this engine of state repression is used by a man on his wife. Insofar as the Elizabethan state acknowledged its use of torture, it maintained at least a fiction of using it only for strictly controlled interrogatory purposes.[26] This play stages its use in an entirely uncontrolled and unauthorized fashion: the husband dismisses the one witness who attempts to restrain him, then unleashes his fury against his wife. From the English Protestant point of view, it is one of the play's supreme ironies that this scene makes the *friar* its spokesperson for moderation and nonviolent resolution. Montsurry so distorts the play's relative sense of evil that the friar, for all his conjuring and pandering, almost comes to seem like a "kind innocent man."[27]

Chapman wastes no opportunity to prolong or intensify the violence of this spectacular scene. First, the husband drags his wife onstage by her hair, then he supplements his own strength with increasingly powerful technologies of violence. He threatens and then stabs his wife with a knife, then stretches her on the rack. The shift of instrument from knife to rack takes time and requires the participation of several servants who apparently help to attach the countess to the device and assist in its use. Though there are no textual directions for this action aside from the entrance of the servants, it is punctuated by the woman's cries ("Oh, who is turn'd into my Lord and husband?" "Husband!" "My Lord!" "Husband, oh, help me, husband!" 5.1.143–46) and measured by its gruesome effect on her body, all of which suggests that it must be a horrible and extended bit of stage business.

Chapman also prolongs the action by means of his extravagant dialogue, supplementing the play's bloody action with the even more elaborate sufferings his characters imagine. The playwright devotes some of his most florid poetry to images of cataclysmic violence. Montsurry wails about the torments he suffers, experiencing his anger and shame as "the seven times-heat furnace of my thoughts" and as "the death / Thy tyrannies have invented in my entrails" (5.1.39, 97–98). Even before he wounds her, he imagines acting his revenge on his wife's body, literally at the site where her adultery has occurred: "In thy lap's stead, I may dig his tomb" (65). For D'Ambois he intends sudden death: "thy ruffian galley, laden for thy lust" will "dash against my rocks," but for the agent of their adultery, whose identity the wife still protects, Montsurry desires, "that I may hang him, and then cut him down, / Then cut him up, and with my soul's beams search / The cranks and caverns of his brain" (61, 60, 73–75).

The countess adds to these images of destruction with a long speech in which she begs her husband to take out his anger only on her, sparing the other actors in her crime.

> Hide in some gloomy dungeon my loathed face,
> And let condemnèd murderers let me down,
> Stopping their noses, my abhorrèd food.
> Hang me in chains, and let me eat these arms
> That have offended: bind me face to face
> To some dead woman, taken from the cart

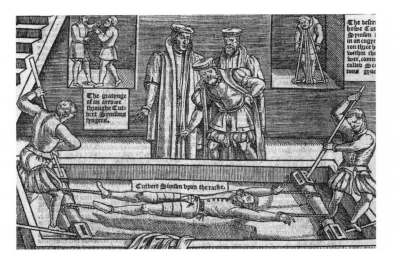

Fig. 3.1. Cutbert Simson tortured on the rack. From Foxe, *Acts and Monuments* (1563), 1651. Courtesy of the Rare Books and Manuscripts Library of the Ohio State University Libraries.

Fig. 3.2. A Roman Catholic tortured on the rack. From Richard Verstagen, *Theatrum crudelitatum* (1588), 73. Reproduced by permission of the British Library.

Of execution, till death and time
In grains of dust dissolve me.

(5.1.104–11)

In combination with the technologies of pain in evidence on his stage, Chapman's dialogue makes this scene a veritable catalog of tortures. The effect is rather like hunting quail with cannon: the violence of the scene is overwhelming; it obliterates all sense of proportion between the woman's crime and her punishment.

This scene sets the tone for the play's long final act, both in terms of its histrionic action and its reification of character.[28] In the course of the act, Chapman not only transforms Monsieur and the Guise from mere villains into neomythological embodiments of Death and Destiny, and D'Ambois, who dies standing upright, into a rival for both Vespasian and Hercules, he also metamorphoses his very human husband and wife, transforming the wronged husband into a monster and the guilty adulteress into a victim.[29] At the first moment of the scene ("Montsurry bare, unbrac't, pulling Tamyra in by the haire"), Montsurry's undress and the countess's loose hair communicate his distress and her Magdalen-like sexual guilt, but as the scene progresses, his bare, unbraced, disheveled "undress" comes more and more to recall the iconography of an executioner — a picture reminiscent of that most sensational of the *Acts and Monuments'* woodcuts, which depicted Bishop Bonner bare and unbraced, flogging his victims (see fig. 1.7).[30]

Although Montsurry mounts an argument for his right to punish his wife, the playwright makes certain that his audience judges the count's behavior beyond the pale. At the beginning of the scene, Montsurry justifies his behavior to the friar, calling it "the course I must run for my honor's sake" (5.1.21). He vows not to "pass the verge that bounds a Christian, / Nor break the limits of a man nor husband," and he insists that if she will "but disclose / Who was the hateful minister of her love, / And through what maze he served it, we are friends" (34–35, 23–25). However reasonable these professions, Montsurry is not able to keep his word. Even as he dismisses the friar, he is at the point of losing control: "Tempt not a man distracted; I am apt / To outrages that I shall ever rue!" (32–33). As soon as the friar leaves the stage, that verge is crossed with brutal consequences.

Although he continues to assert a rational basis for his actions, emphasizing his rights and her wrongdoing ("Till thou writest, / I'll write in wounds, my wrong's fit characters, / Thy right of sufferance" 124–26), the audience cannot help but perceive that there is nothing "fit" about the extremes to which he has taken his right to make her suffer. As Montsurry's violence mounts, he loses sight of the purpose of his interrogation. His idea of administering just enough pain to make his wife cooperate, though not so much as to incapacitate her, evaporates in a euphoria of bloodlust.

> Write! for it must be; by this ruthless steel,
> By this impartial torture, and the death
> Thy tyrannies have invented in my entrails,
> To quicken life in dying, and hold up
> The spirits in fainting, teaching to preserve
> Torments in ashes, that will ever last.
>
> (5.1.96–101)

In these ravings, Montsurry imagines himself no longer the interrogator, but the victim. In his flight of fancy, the countess tortures him. She is the tyrant and she is the one who is expert in the exquisite techniques by which the executioner maximizes pain without causing death.

His persecution fantasy only intensifies the audience's perception of his ruthlessness, however. Wallowing in his own misery, he delights in hers. The torture becomes an end in itself, a means of revenge-taking.

> now, torture, use
> This other engine [the rack] on th'habituate powers
> Of her thrice-damned and whorish fortitude.
> Use the most madding pains in her that ever

Thy venoms soaked through, making most of death,
That she weigh her wrongs with them, and then
Stand, Vengeance, on thy steepest rock, a victor!

(5.1.136–42)

As he puts aside his knife in favor of the rack, this apostrophe to
the abstract notion of vengeance and the all-too-concrete action
of torture reveals that Montsurry's abuse has moved far beyond its
initial, pragmatic aims. Like the practitioners of torture Elaine
Scarry discusses in *The Body in Pain*, Montsurry's torture of his
wife is really a means of reasserting his power over her, a means of
demonstrating his absolute sovereignty over the woman, who,
through her adultery, had presumed to act in defiance of his will.[31]

Montsurry's behavior in this scene also bears a striking (and
pertinent) similarity to the conduct of Lord Chancellor Wriothesley
and Richard Rich in John Bale's and Anne Askew's account of her
interrogation by members of Henry VIII's Privy Council. Askew
reports that "they ded put me on the racke bycause I confessed no
ladyes and gentyllwomen to be of my own opynyon, and theron
they kepte me a longe tyme. And bycause I laye styll and ded not
crye, my lorde Chauncellor and mastre Ryche, toke peynes to racke
me [with] their owne handes, tyll I was nygh dead."[32] Although
the two women respond differently to the pain of their torture
(Askew claims to remain unmoved by it, where Chapman's
countess capitulates to her husband's demands in order to win her
release), the men reveal the same fierce rage against the women.
The men cease to be interrogators; their professional and noble
demeanor cracks under their furious efforts to assert authority.

It is tempting to imagine that Chapman's husband, too, seizes
the levers of the rack in his own hands when his wife withstands
his servants' initial efforts. Regrettably the play fails to provide
specific stage directions for the racking, but one might read the
progression of the countess's appeals to her husband as an indication that he signifies his unwillingness to help her by adding
his hand to those administering her pain. It is mere conjecture,

but it may be that her initial cries appeal to Montsurry as he stands aloof, watching the proceedings: "Oh, who is turned into my lord and husband? / Husband! My lord!" (5.1.143–44). Her next exclamation has a different tone and represents her answer to her own question: "None but my lord and husband!" Clearly, this line registers her recognition of his unwavering resolve, but does it also register his assumption of an active role in the proceedings? "*None* but my lord and husband!" Like Askew, the countess grits her teeth and bears the pain, even adopting the rhetoric of Christian martyrdom as she prays, "Heaven, I ask thee remission of my sins, / Not of my pains" (145–46). The countess's resolve is not so firm as the martyr's, however. Her prayer ends abruptly in a desperate cry, "husband, oh, help me, husband!" Soon she begs for her release.

Although he does not presume that his audience will accept the countess of Montsurry as an actual martyr, Chapman clearly employs the techniques of martyrology in this scene. Taking cues that might have come directly from Bale, Chapman punctuates the countess's prayer with the friar's entrance and exclamation, "What rape of honor and religion! / Oh, wrack of nature!" (147–48). However ironic it may be, Chapman casts the friar in an unmistakably Balean role at this moment, making him the elucidator of the scene onstage. Bale's comment on Wriothesley and Rich's participation in Askew's racking, though lengthier, amount to precisely the same exclamation:

> Marke here an example most wonderfull, and se how madlye in their ragynge furyes, men forget themselves and lose their ryght wittes now a dayes. A kynges hygh couseller, a Judge over lyfe and deathe, yea, a lord Chauncellour of a most noble realme, is now become a most vyle slave for Antichrist, and a most cruell tormentoure. Without all dyscressyon, honestye, or manhode, he casteth of hys gowne, and taketh here upon hym the most vyle offyce of an hangeman and pulleth at the racke most vyllanouslye. O Wrisleye and Riche ii. False christianes and blasphemouse apostataes from God. What chaplayne of the pope hath inchaunted yow, or what devyll of helle bewytched yow to execute upon a poore condempned woman, so prodygyouse a kynde of tyranny?[33]

Bale embellishes Askew's account with his details about Wriothesley's removing his gown and his editorial comparison of the
lord chancellor to a hangman. It is not necessary to debate whether
the artist who created the Bonner woodcut for *Acts and Monuments* (fig. 1.7) had Bale's description of Wriothesley in mind or
whether Chapman was influenced by either of these specific
images; all three share a common strategy for villainizing the men
they portray: each strips off the constricting robes of his office and
with the robes, the constraints of "discretion, honesty, . . . manhood," or as Chapman's countess puts it, "all the bounds of manhood, nobless, and religion" (5.1.119–20). Bale's lord chancellor,
Foxe and Daye's bishop, and Chapman's count all "pass the verge
that bounds a Christian, [and] break the limits of a man [or]
husband" (23). Each becomes an executioner, filling the vile office
(and appearing in the frightening undress) of a hangman.

Chapman and Bale faced similar tasks in packaging the stories
of these two women: although many Protestants of Katherine Parr's
circle embraced Anne Askew as a godly woman, her critics charged
that she was a shameless runaway wife whose suspect moral
character complemented her heretical opinions. Askew herself
confronted and dismissed these charges directly, defending her
reasons for leaving her husband and children. Still, her circumstances were awkward for Bale, who goes out of his way to put
her behavior in a better light. Like Chapman, his chief strategy
is to present Askew as a vulnerable woman ("lyke a lambe she
laye styll wythout noyse of cryenge, and suffered your uttermost
vyolence") abused by outrageously evil men ("what devyll of helle
bewytched yow to execute upon a poore condempned woman, so
prodygyouse a kynde of tyranny?").[34] Chapman has one advantage
over Bale: because his woman is fictitious, he has authorial control
over her words and actions. Where Askew wishes to portray herself
as strong, smart and dignified, Chapman makes his woman
pathetic. Bale must "elucidate" Askew's narrative when he wishes
to achieve this effect. When Askew boasts that she did not cry
under torture, Bale transforms her resistance by likening it to the

passive suffering of a lamb, but the text remains divided between Askew's voice and Bale's.

Chapman is under no such constraints when managing his female subject. When he wishes to pull at his audience's heart-strings, he simply requires the countess to beg,

> Oh, kill me, kill me!
> Dear husband, be not crueler than death;
> You have beheld some Gorgon; feel, oh, feel
> How you are turned to stone; with my heart-blood
> Dissolve yourself again, or you will grow
> Into the image of all tyranny.

(5.1.126–31)

Still, Chapman must manage his audience's reactions. He heads off sardonic responses to this woman's appeal by placing the most obvious objection in the mouth of the scene's villain. In response to her plea, Montsurry acknowledges that he has indeed meta-morphosed into something monstrous — then claims that a similar transformation has rendered her nothing more than the embodi-ment of her sin (the image of all adultery). But he is wrong. Chap-man has accomplished something very different (and much more unlikely) — he has transformed a malefactress into a suffering woman. As Montsurry becomes more and more an image of ven-geance, she becomes increasingly human, increasingly forgiveable.

This transformation of the countess of Montsurry is crucial to Chapman's representation of Bussy D'Ambois's fate, so much so that it amounts to a structural flaw as the play allows the woman to upstage its title character. Once she commits adultery with him, the play ceases to be principally about his meteoric career at court and dedicates itself to the discovery and punishment of the woman's transgression. Along the way, it relegates D'Ambois's enemies, the Guise and Monsieur, to the sidelines (actually to the space above the stage, where they become the sinister, pseudo-supernatural puppet masters, Death and Destiny) and replaces them in the action with their factor, Montsurry. Their goal of bringing down D'Ambois for his political presumptions gives way in practice to Montsurry's revenge for his cuckolding. The sexual drama, which seems merely incidental when first introduced, swells to consume the play.

The process of this shift is worth closer consideration. In act 3, when the Guise, Monsieur and Montsurry agree that D'Ambois must be eliminated, the reasons are entirely political and pragmatic. The Guise tells Monsieur, "Y'ave stuck us up a very proper flag, / That takes more wind than we with all our sails. / . . . He must down, / Upstarts should never perch too near a crown" (3.2.132–33, 134–35). Despite all their "sails" (gold and arms and allies), these noblemen find themselves outmaneuvered by an upstart. At this point in the play it is clear that D'Ambois's aggravating political success is the reason for their animosity. His sexual activities are merely a convenient means of effecting their goal: his affair is a weakness to be exploited. "There is no such trap to catch an upstart / As a loose downfall" (143–44).

The Appeal of Women's Suffering

However, the rest of the play gives the lie to this pretense that sex is merely a means to pull down the protagonist. It is not entirely clear whether this is by deliberate design on Chapman's part or whether his plot — and his own salacious interests — simply carry him away in that direction. From this point on, all of the play's interest centers on the discovery of the lovers and on their punishment. Particularly, the play's attention shifts to the countess and the price she pays for her affair; the action keeps slipping out of the court and into the lady's private chamber. D'Ambois's death, when it finally occurs, pales in comparison with the agonies suffered by his lover. His death by gunshot is really rather anticlimactic, despite the sword fight that precedes it; both are overshadowed by the woman's torture and her continued suffering presence on the stage.

Why does the play lavish so much attention on the woman? She is, after all, merely a pawn in the men's struggle for dominance.

One reading of the play would maintain that she, like the duchess of Guise, is merely an instrument of exchange between the men.[35] In this view, the real action of the play concerns only those masculine relationships; what D'Ambois does in the woman's private chamber is simply an extension of what he has done in the king's presence chamber. As the duchess of Guise is merely a means for D'Ambois to insult the duke, so the countess of Montsurry is just another piece of aristocratic property the protagonist defiles in order to disparage her noble husband, Montsurry. By extension, D'Ambois's seduction of the countess might be read as an assault on the closed boundaries of the aristocracy, a threat to the distinction between gentleman and peer. But there is more to the play's treatment of the woman than this reading admits. If the countess were nothing more than a cypher for her husband and a vehicle for trapping D'Ambois, the play would use and dispose of her when her function was exhausted. Instead, the play almost forgets about him in its zeal to deal with her.

It is worth considering, too, that the play punishes the countess of Montsurry for a crime that Monsieur commits first. He is the one who creates D'Ambois. He is the one who admits D'Ambois to the court; he looses that disruptive force within the bowers of the aristocracy. Chapman underscores the parallels between Monsieur's and the countess's relationships with D'Ambois via his use of courtship language in Monsieur's conversations with his protégé. When he presents D'Ambois to the king and court, Monsieur calls him "sweetheart" and "my love" in an exchange in which the royal brothers liken the preferment of D'Ambois to the wooing of a mistress ("If you have wooed and won, then, brother, wear him") (1.2.55–73).

The countess's betrayal of her husband is petty compared to the betrayal of the king Monsieur purportedly has planned. But neither the characters nor the play itself punish Monsieur. He is untouchable. Throughout the play, Monsieur controls much of the action. He lurks above and behind the scenes holding the strings that make other characters do his bidding.[36] In fact, it is Monsieur who deflects the play's energies from the political sphere to the woman's transgression — a self-protective gesture on his part. At the precise moment his peers hold him accountable for promoting D'Ambois, Monsieur shifts attention from himself onto the women of the court. The deflection even carries over into the metaphors he uses to distance himself from his protégé: in the speech in which he suggests that they can overthrow D'Ambois if they discover his mistress, Monsieur likens his raising of Bussy D'Ambois to the mythological tale of Juno's creation of the giant Typhon. However, Monsieur uses his analogy in a slippery fashion: he does not occupy Juno's role for long. His aim is to cast D'Ambois as a Typhon-like disruptor wreaking havoc in the land opposed by Monsieur, the Guise and Montsurry as giant killers who, like Jove, will "strike him under th'Etna of his pride" (3.2.139). Suddenly, Monsieur is no longer the monster's creator (Juno); he is the angry god who will strike down D'Ambois. The burden of guilt remains with a woman: Juno/Tamyra, the guilty wife.

The play's vehemence in dealing with the woman is partly attributable to this scapegoating process by which Chapman distills Monsieur's treason and displaces it onto the countess's transgression. However, the play's interest in the woman is also a matter of desire. Once it has her in its sights, the play seems unable to look away until, in act 5, it keeps her on the stage — in defiance of early modern conventions of stage space — even though the action shifts from Montsurry's apartments to D'Ambois's and back.

This point has escaped critical attention, and it is a striking oddity of the play. The stage direction of the 1641 quarto describes what happens after the countess is loosed from the rack in act 5, scene 1: "Exeunt. [Montsurry] puts the Frier in the vault and follows. She raps her self in the Arras. Enter Monsieur and Guise." In this particular text, "exeunt" does not signify the exit of all onstage; rather, it announces the exit of any characters whose presence and actions do not receive separate, specific mention. Presumably this direction describes the scene's blocking in early productions. It is unusually descriptive — especially in contrast to the 1607 quarto, which includes no directions for characters to exit at this point, although it indicates the entrance of D'Ambois with two pages. In that quarto, Montsurry's speech implies his exit ("I must be messenger my selfe, / Disguis'd like this strange creature: in, Ile after, / To see what guilty light gives this cave eies"), but the text is ambiguous about the recipient of his command "in, Ile after" (59). The later quarto specifies that it is the friar's body he addresses as he shoves it through the trapdoor of the vault. The countess is clearly to remain onstage wrapped (and at least partly obscured) in an arras. The 1607 quarto, in fact, assumes that this is what the actor playing the countess has done, but it does not assist its readers in reaching this conclusion until, later in the scene, it directs that the friar's ghost should enter *to* the countess, who must already (or still) be onstage: "Intrat umbra, Comolet to the Countesse, wrapt in a Canapie" (64). In other words, the 1607 text describes a production in which the countess has wrapped herself in the bed hangings (a "canopy") and has remained onstage throughout the intervening action until the moment when the friar's ghostly reentrance through the trapdoor indicates that the action has returned from D'Ambois's chambers to the countess's.

The ghost's words to her support this reading of the directions. He enters to warn her of D'Ambois's danger and to draw her out of her passive sitting to some kind of action:

> Revive those stupid thoughts, and *sit not thus*,
> Gathering the horrors of your servants slaughter,
> (So urg'd by your hand, and so imminent)
> Into an idle fancie; but devise
> How to prevent it; watch when he shall rise,
> And with a sudden outcrie of his murther,
> Blow his retreat before he be engag'd.
>
> (Q1607, p. 64, emphasis added)

Although it would be possible to conclude that Chapman expects his audience to interpret the countess's wrapping herself into the folds of the arras/canopy as the equivalent of an exit from the stage and the space it defines (and thus, as an exit from the audience's attention), this speech suggests otherwise. Here the friar implies that the countess has been sitting on the stage in such a way that she has been able to watch the intervening scenes ("Gathering the horrors of [her] servants slaughter"). It implies that she has seen her husband deceive D'Ambois with the friar disguise and draw him toward ambush. Though it breaks the conventions of stage space, which generally hold that location changes only when all characters exit, the countess has remained rooted in her space (defined by the arras or canopy with which she wrapped herself) while the rest of the stage has shifted to represent a different location, one which she can see, but where she cannot be seen and cannot intervene. As when the friar cast a spell so the lovers could see their enemies' secret meeting, this scene also allows one character preternatural sight, but without the explanatory (if not exactly naturalizing) device of magical intervention.

The countess's presence on the stage provides a direct contrast with the entrance of the Guise and Monsieur "above" (Q1607, p. 62). Their vantage point allows them an almost omniscient view of the play's climax; in fact, the 1641 quarto adds a brief exchange between these supervillains and the assassins, which reinforces the play's suggestion that they achieve an omnipotent stature in this scene, directing all its horrors. By contrast, the countess is completely helpless, utterly unable to save either herself or her lover from disaster, despite the ghost's warning and suggested plan. Her ability to see what is happening does not give her power over her situation; instead, it forces her to see how impotent she is.

The strange staging of this act allows Chapman to emphasize how badly injured the countess is after her torture: she cannot exit when her husband and servants do. Instead, she pulls her mangled body ("her parts so disproportionate," 5.1.172) into the liminal space at the periphery of the stage and wraps herself in the meager comfort of a drapery. How much more significant if that drapery is a canopy from the marriage bed her adultery betrayed! Even if we suppose that this action might have been blocked so that the actor playing the countess withdraws into the hangings covering an inner stage, such a withdrawal may obscure the character from the view of other characters, but it explicitly draws the audience's attention. Chapman's audience knew that characters who place themselves behind an arras deserve special note. More probably, as the friar's words to her suggest, she is meant to sit where she can see — and be seen. However the scene is staged, it seems clear that Chapman has placed her so that she will remain at the edge of the audience's perception. Even as the suspenseful action moves on, her body tugs at the audience's attention.

The play has begun to pile up bodies on the stage, and does not allow them to be cleared. It is especially unwilling to relinquish the sight of this woman's battered form. The play's only departure from the practice of other tragedies which held the boards during the same period is its extraordinary tenacity in holding the woman onstage, alive, throughout the fifth act. Certainly, the vigor with which it punishes her is in keeping with what other playwrights performed on the bodies of their female characters. A desire to see women suffer and die marks many of the tragedies of the period, as the fates of Shakespeare's Lavinia and Desdemona, Middleton and Rowley's Beatrice-Joanna, the Lady of *The Second Maiden's Tragedy*, Webster's duchess of Malfi and Vittoria Corombona and Ford's Annabella variously illustrate.

The appeal of women's suffering is not only a hallmark of early modern drama, of course. It is an important feature of most of the period's literary forms from poetry to pornography — and martyrology.[37] As we have seen in the woodcuts of *Acts and Monuments*, this latter genre charted a difficult course between its celebration of the virtues of its martyrs and its emphasis on their vulnerability, a quality easily tinged with sexual overtones when a martyr was also female. The case of Anne Askew offers particularly interesting evidence of the tension these two emphases could create, because it allows us to see how two male editors shaped her material and how their attitudes about women's vulnerability shaped their perceptions of her.

Bale, particularly, has a tendency to emphasize Askew's womanly qualities: her weakness, her tenderness, and especially her youth. Consider, for instance, Bale's characterizations of her as "a gentylwoman verye yonge, dayntye, and tender" and "a woman, frayle, tendre, yonge and most delycyouslye brought up."[38] These characterizations link her gentle birth and her youth with her feminine frailty, and while they do not make explicit claims about her physical appearance, they hint that she was beautiful. (His choice of modifiers suggests early modern attributes of beauty, such as the adjectives "dainty" and "tender," not to mention the overly appreciative adverb, "deliciously," which surely does more work than necessary to describe her social or moral upbringing.) Thus, Bale borrows from literature to endow her with the features necessary to make her an appealing heroine. He can then also use her youthfulness as an indication of her innocence, as when he taunts Rich and Wriothesley with their unseemly bullying of a defenseless woman: "Ryght farre doth it passe the strength of a yonge, tendre, weake, and sycke woman (as she was at that tyme [of her torture] to your more confusyon) to abyde so vyolent handelynge, yea, or yet of the strongest man that lyveth." Bale reworks this theme when he accuses the two councillors of acting on political and material interest in Askew's case: the "wicked desperates" he calls them, who "have the voluptuouse pleasures of thys vayne worlde so dere, that they had lever to forsake God and all hys workes, than to be sequestred from them." In contrast, Askew is "thys godlye yonge woman," subjected to the predation of the two voluptuous men who not only take pleasure in worldly things, but also, Bale implies, pleasure themselves by torturing her.[39]

Bale's representation (and repackaging) of Askew styles her as an object of readerly desire. In a marginal gloss of Askew's account of being returned from the Tower (and her torture) to house arrest, "with as werye and payneful bones, as ever had paycent Job," Bale writes "sweete woman."[40] With this marginal comment, Bale guides his readers' interpretation of Askew's words. She emphasizes her fortitude and her bold refusal to be intimidated by her powerful antagonists and understates the severity of her wounds, relying on her allusion to Job to supplement her admission of weary and painful bones. Bale avoids the masculine imagery of Job, emphasizing instead her womanliness and its desirability. Furthermore, he refuses to observe the same circumspection about the bodily afflictions and acute suffering felt by Askew. In fact, he returns to describe her injuries so many times it is tempting to say that he is obsessed by his mental image of her broken body:

> 1. Lyke a lambe she laye styll without noyse of cryenge, and suffered your uttermost vyolence, tyll *the synnowes of her armes were broken, and the strynges of her eys peryshed in her heade.*
>
> 2. *For Anguysh and payne of her broken joyntes and abroused armes and eyes*, she curseth not the tyme that ever she was borne, as the maner of the unfaythfull is.
>
> 3. The martyr of Christ for her pacyent sufferaunce shall leave here behynde her a gloryouse report, where as these forsworne enemyes and pursuers of hys worde, have purchased themselves a perpetuall infamye by their cruelte and myschefe. In excuse of their madnesse, they saye, they ded it only to feare her. Is it not (thynke yow) a propre frayenge playe, whan our *armes and eyes are compelled to leave their naturall holdes*?
>
> 4. Swift eare gave Wrisleye and Ryche with their wycked affynyte to the puffed up porkelynges of the pope Gardyner, Bonner, and soch other, they folowed their cruell counsell, they enprysoned her, judged her, condempned her, and racked her at the last with their owne poluted bloudye tormentours handes, tyll *the vaynes and synnowes brast.*[41]

Certainly Bale encourages his readers to indulge their imaginations with visions of this woman's body and her suffering at the hands of these unwearying persecutors. Bale is as obsessive about revisiting the scene of Askew's racking as he is in redescribing her wounds. Each time he retells the story of Wriothesley and Rich's role, it becomes more dramatic, more outrageously violent, until, in the volume's conclusion, he tells it not once, but twice in the space of three paragraphs.

> Afore tyme hath not bene seane, soch frantyck outrage as is now,
> the judges without all sober dyscressyon, ronnynge to the racke,
> toggynge, halynge, and pullynge therat, lyke tormentours in a playe.
> . . . [They] racked her at the last with their owne poluted bloudye
> tormentours handes, tyll the vaynes and synnowes brast.[42]

Like tormentors in a play are Askew's persecutors in Bale's account — and she is like a woman in a play, a woman whose suffering
is a spectacle to be savored by the playwright and the audience
even as it is a sight to move their pity.

Foxe's editorial treatment of Askew differs from Bale's in degree,
but not in its masculine tendency to put her body on display.
Ironically, the woodcut Daye used to illustrate Askew's execution
was not one made specially for *Acts and Monuments*; instead, it
was designed to illustrate the ignominious behavior of Nicholas
Shaxton, who was arrested at the same time as Askew, but who
recanted and preached a sermon at her execution urging her to
recant as well (see fig. 2.1).[43] The illustration, then, depicts the
scene of execution as a whole and at such a distance that while it
is possible to pick out Shaxton in the pulpit, it is not possible to
identify which of the prisoners tied to the stakes might be Askew.
However, Foxe's text supplies the detail this illustration lacks:

> Hetherto we have intreated of this good woman, now it remaineth
> that we touch somwhat as touching her end and martyrdom. She
> beyng borne of such stock and kynred, that she might have lyved in
> great wealth and prosperitie, if she wold rather have folowed the
> world then Christ, but now she was so tormented, that she could
> neither live long in so great distress, neither yet by the adversaries
> be suffred to die in secret. Wherfor the daie of her execution was
> appointed, and she brought into Smithfielde in a chayre, because
> she could not go on her feete, by meanes of her great tormentes,
> when she was brought unto the stake she was tied by the middle
> with a chaine, that helde up her body. . . . Thus she being troubled
> so many maner of waies, and having passed through so many
> torments, having now ended the long course of her agonies, being
> compassed in with flames of fire, as a blessed sacrifice unto God,
> she slept in the Lorde, in An. 1546 leaving behind her a singular
> example of Christen constancie for all men to followe.[44]

Foxe's remarkable lack of detail about Askew's actual death, which he reduces to the euphemism "she slept in the Lorde," stands in sharp contrast to the detail with which he represents her bodily state leading up to the execution. Foxe includes details of which Bale was unaware: Askew was so broken by her torture that she was near death and had to be taken to her execution in a chair. Other heretics were chained to the stake, but in this case Foxe makes a special point to remark that the chain was necessary to hold her body upright. None of the three men who went with her to the stake receive any bodily description save the idealistic comment that the fire "consumed their blessed bodies in happie martyrdome."

Askew's account of her torture seems to have touched her two editors in a special way. In his early Latin martyrology, *Rerum in ecclesia gestarum commentarii*, Foxe included a Sapphic epitaph for Askew. The poem, which did not appear in any of the English versions of *Acts and Monuments*, cannot be claimed to have shaped many readers' interpretations of Askew's narrative. It does, however, open a window on John Foxe's own image of this woman. I will take the liberty of reproducing it in full along with the English translation by G. P. Goold included by Elaine Beilin in her edition of Askew's *Examinations*:

> In Annæ Askevæ Constantissimæ fœminae & martyris bustum,
> Epitaphium Sapphicum, I. F.

> Lictor incæstis manibus cruente,
> Membra quid frustra eculeis fatigas,
> Vique uirtutem laceras puellæ
>   Te melioris?

> Fortius istis pietas nitescit
> Pressa tormentis, quatitur nec ullis
> Veritas uinclis: citius sed ipsa
>   Lassa fatiscunt

> Instat immani rabidus furore
> Carnifex: ruptis iacet illa neruis
> Fœmina in neruis, socias ut edat
>   Relligionis.

Exprimit nullum tamen illa nomen,
Machinam uincit mulier tacendo.
Stant, stupent illi, furiun trahendo:
           Proficiunt nil.

Artubus luxis resoluta cedunt
Ossa iunturis, nihil in pudico
Corpore infractum est. Superat tyrannos
           Pars tamen una.

Sola enim nullis potuit moueri
Lingua rupturis: socias periclo
Dum suo soluit, iubet & quietam
           Stertere in aùrem.

Ergo quæ nullis alias reuinci
Quiuit harpastris, moribunda tandem
Soluitur flammis, cineres coronat
           Vita perennis.

Sola nequaquam potitur brabeio
Hæc tamen: partes ueniunt coronæ,
Martyres unà: Opifex, Lasellas:
           Belenianus.

Epitaph in Sapphic Verse upon the tomb of the most steadfast woman and martyr Anne Askew. I. F.

O warder, whose wicked hands are drenched in blood, why do you vainly stretch her limbs on the rack and violently tear apart a virtuous girl better far than you? Her piety shines forth the brighter for being subjected to torture; nor does she waver in truth through any fear of chains: rather do these sooner wear out and fall apart. The executioner comes forth, seething with ruthless fury: her tendons untied, the woman lies tied up to make her betray her partners in religion. But she divulges no name, and by her silence the woman proves stronger than the machine. They stand dumbstruck, and are driven mad by the delay: yet they achieve nothing. Her limbs are forced apart; her bones are broken, severed from their joints; nothing in that chaste body is left intact. Still one part of her defeats the tyrants. For her tongue alone could not be moved by any suffering: in rescuing her companions from her own peril, she bids them slumber with untroubled ears. So she who could not otherwise be overcome by instruments of torture is at last dissolved by death in the flames, and her ashes are blessed with life everlasting. Yet she is by no means alone in winning the heavenly prize: sharing the martyr's crown in company with her are a craftsman, Lassels, and Belenian.

Like Bale, Foxe envisions the scene of torture as a scene of murderous violence in which the interrogators are furious, bloody, ravening beasts. They are also predatory men. Rape imagery haunts this poem, from the first stanza's bloody-handed man who threatens the young girl to the images of her body tied to the rack, vulnerable to the fury of her tormentors. While it is true that in the fifth stanza the translator's "her limbs are forced apart" is more suggestive than Foxe's Latin lines about the breaking and disjoining of her bones, the stanza ends (in Latin as in the translation) with Foxe's suggestive riddle about the one part of her chaste body which defies the tyrants. This teasing rhetorical device renders the stanza's account of her bodily resistance sexually suggestive — if only for the moment it takes to get to the next stanza about her tongue.[45] Like Bale's elucidation, Foxe's commentary on Askew's vulnerability and suffering rewrites her narrative. Both editors see her very differently than she sees herself. Despite her insistence on her wit and strong will, both men zero in on her body: its youth, its frailty, its pain. Foxe and Bale linger over the image of Anne Askew sitting two hours on the floor after being racked, the image of her being put to bed with weary and painful bones, and the image of her being taken to her execution in a chair because she could not walk; these physical details haunt her editors. Similarly, the spectacle of a woman's racking and the continued presence of her broken body, wrapped in an arras or a bed canopy, haunt the stage in Chapman's play.

Like Bale and Foxe, Chapman places a woman's body on display to draw his audience's pity and its desirous gaze. With Foxe and Bale this amounts to an editorial slip: both intend to hold the martyr forward as a model for their readers, a fellow saint and a fellow sufferer, but both editors find that their gender difference offers them a comfortable way to distance themselves from Askew's vulnerability — and with that distance, their desire awakens. However, desire and distance are liable to collapse suddenly for Askew's readers into horrified identification with the woman who is bound to the stake by officers of the Crown, just as Chapman's spectators are liable to see themselves when they look at the woman who lies broken and subject to the malevolent power of the two great noblemen on the upper stage.

II

Ravishing the Subject's Masculinity

FOUR

"I'le want my will else"
THE RHETORIC OF RAPE AND RIGHTS

The house of every one is to him as his castle and fortress, as well for his defence against injury and violence as for his repose.
— Sir Edward Coke, *Reports*

Vermandero: An host of enemies entered my citadel
Could not amaze like this.
— Thomas Middleton and William Rowley, *The Changeling,*
5.3.147–48

Sixteenth and seventeenth century English dramatists linked women's sexual continence and their submission to the authority of their fathers and husbands not only to the well-ordering of family life, but to the preservation of social order.[1] The ideal woman could be relied upon absolutely to protect these boundaries, and the age did have a model of such feminine purity, however unrealistic she must have seemed. Lucrece, wife of Collatine, victim of Tarquin's lustful covetousness, was the English Renaissance's archetypal pattern of the violated, yet virtuous woman. Her rape, available in Ovid and Livy (and in translations of their works), was versified by Shakespeare and Middleton, dramatized by Heywood, and echoed in plays throughout the Elizabethan and Jacobean periods, including *Titus Andronicus, Valentinian* and *Appius and Virginia*.[2] Lucrece was the model wife who took her own life rather than allow any doubt that her loyalty and her children belonged solely to her husband.

English custom, which did not valorize suicide, also did not provide any clear, reassuring measure of women's purity as an alternative. Instead, the culture fed its misogynist anxieties on a steady diet of sensational tales of unchaste, quite un-Lucrece-like women who deceived their parents, their suitors and their husbands to indulge their desires. Thomas Middleton and William Rowley's *The Changeling* (1622) is just such a tale.[3] Its depiction of Beatrice-Joanna's acceptance of her role as DeFlores's whore is symptomatic of a pervasive fear of women's desire.[4]

English law treated ravishment as a crime targeted at propertied men, through a piece of their property, women. The violation of the woman in this play is shown clearly and horribly to be an assault on a man. Alonzo de Piracquo's body first and most spectacularly bears the marks of DeFlores's violence, but the play multiplies the male victims of Beatrice-Joanna's ravishment. Her father is a victim, betrayed by a trusted servant, deceived by his daughter, cheated of his heirs and the allegiances she could have provided for him through marriage. Her husband, Alsemero (who marries her when her fiancé, Alonzo, disappears) is made a cuckold before he even sleeps with his bride. DeFlores cheats him of his wedding night and mates with Beatrice-Joanna while the serving woman, Diaphanta, supplies her place as virgin in the bridal chamber. Two other gentlemen of Vermandero's household (Francisco and Antonio) very nearly become victims of the crime as well when they are apprehended for Alonzo's supposed murder. In the nightmare world of the play, no man is safe from DeFlores's lust and Beatrice-Joanna's corruption.

Not only do the victims of the ravishment multiply, but the ravishment itself doubles and redoubles crazily. The subplot chronicles the efforts of Isabella, wife of an unjustifiably jealous husband, to avoid the would-be ravishers in the household to which her husband has confined her. In the main plot, the actual rape remains hidden, while Tomazo de Piracquo chases after an imagined conspiracy between Vermandero and Alsemero to deprive Alonzo of his bride. On the day Alsemero marries Beatrice-Joanna, Tomazo first challenges Alsemero with having stolen her from Alonzo. At the end of the play, Tomazo makes his claims of ravishment explicit, demanding "a brother alive or dead: / Alive, a wife with him; if dead, for both / A recompense, for murder and adultery" (5.3.136–38). Vermandero and Alsemero are innocent of the crime Tomazo imagines; all three are lost in the funhouse mirror effect of the play, in which victims and ravishers and crimes swirl and distort.

In a culture like England's, which linked social status to property holding, it is unsurprising to find that women's vulnerability to seduction or sexual assault was a recurrent, even obsessive, concern.[5] It is a concern that intensified in the second half of the sixteenth century, when the Parliament set about to stiffen the rape statutes and the courts followed with a series of precedent-setting opinions defining the limits of this new legislation. This concern with the social ramifications of rape did not abate following the accession of James I; in fact, it seems to have been revived as James's English subjects grew increasingly anxious that the Crown was undermining their property rights. The perceived threat from above seems to have triggered a corresponding anxiety about threats from within and from below.[6]

The Coke Case

Sir Edward Coke, prominent jurist, M.P., and gentleman of wealth, was himself intimately aware of the connections between property, status and ravishment. When in 1617 Coke began to negotiate a match between his youngest daughter, Frances, and Sir John Villiers, Coke's principal motive was to save his career as a chief justice, an appointment he had lost by angering James I.[7] Sir John

Villiers was the older brother of James's powerful favorite, the duke of Buckingham. That John Villiers's important family connections were Coke's principal consideration in the proposed match is clear; as a prospective bridegroom, Villiers lacked anything else to recommend him. In fact, he was reputed to suffer from a sometimes violent mental imbalance and from recurrent, incapacitating seizures.[8] Villiers's insufficiency as a mate may have struck the daughter more forcefully than it did the father. In any case, Frances Coke refused to cooperate with her father's plan for her marriage and became the center of a protracted dispute between her wealthy parents.

Coke's wife, Lady Elizabeth Hatton, was an extraordinarily powerful woman in her own right. The daughter of Thomas Cecil, the earl of Exeter and granddaughter of William Cecil, Lord Burghley, Lady Hatton was the widow of the nephew and sole heir of Sir Christopher Hatton, Elizabeth I's wealthiest courtier. Without doubt, Coke married her for her money and connections. In his negotiations with Villiers, Coke counted on using his wife's considerable resources to provide an enticing marriage settlement. However, Lady Hatton (who continued to use that name and title despite her remarriage) was unwilling that any of her property should enlarge the Villiers family coffers, so she took her daughter into hiding outside of London in order to evade Coke's plans for Frances's marriage.

As reported by John Chamberlain in a letter to Sir Dudley Carlton dated 19 July 1617,

> These eight or ten dayes here have ben great stirres twixt the Lord Cooke and his Lady about conveying away the younger daughter, which she will no wayes consent shold match with Sir John Villers. . . . The daughter was first caried to the Lady Withipooles, from thence privilie to a house of the Lord Argiles by Hampton Court, whence her father with a warrant from Master Secretarie fetcht her; but indeed went further then his warrant and brake divers doores before he got her. His Lady was at his heeles and yf her coach had not tired in the pursuit after him there was like to be straunge tragedies. He delivered his daughter to the Lady Compton Sir Johns

mother, but the next day Edmunds clarke of the counsaile was sent with a warrant to have the custodie of her at his owne house: the next day beeing all convented before the counsaile, she was sequestred to Master Atturny and yesterday upon a palliated agreement twixt Sir Ed: Cooke and his Lady she was sent home to Hatton House, with order that Lady Compton and her sonne shold have accesse to win her and weare her.[9]

In this letter, Chamberlain captures the dramatic potential of the Cokes's tug-of-war over their daughter. Contemporaries relished the idea of the notorious curmudgeon, Coke, being dragged before the same courts from which he had recently been expelled as a justice.[10] That he was brought to that pass and thus made a fool in public by his resourceful wife compounded his disgrace. Chamberlain's account of the mother's pursuit at breakneck speed in her coach, close "at his heeles," suggests not only the tragic potential of the situation, but its rich comic aspects as well. Sir Edward Coke, England's most formidable justice, was having his beard tweaked in public by an upstart wife and daughter.

However risible the proceedings may have seemed to others, Lady Hatton's revolt against her husband's authority was entirely in earnest. The Privy Council, which heard suits filed by each parent against the other, treated the matter with complete seriousness. If the matter had not eventually been settled out of court, the case would have forced a ruling about the rights of each parent to custody of the daughter and the limitations governing the exercise of those rights.

Chamberlain reports that "the Lord Cooke was in great daunger to be committed, for disobeying the counsailes order, for abusing his warrant, and for the violence used in breaking open doores, [and that] order [had been] geven to prefer a bill against him in the Starchamber."[11] In other accounts, however, the emphasis is on the mother's usurpation of her husband's power and on her violence in stealing her daughter: "The yonge gentlewoman was stolen away by her mother; Sir Edward Cooke recovered her agayne. . . . The Ladye Hatton, as is sayed, endeavored to have taken the mayde by force frome her father, for the which she was committed prisoner to an alderman's house in London."[12]

Frances Coke's parents accused one another of "conveying away" or, more precisely, *ravishing* the young woman each from the other's custody.[13] Not only was the case sensational because of the prestige of the parties involved and because of the king's investment as a broker of the Coke-Villiers match, it was unprecedented for the vehemence and (initial) success with which mother and daughter opposed the father's will. Chamberlain wrote an epilogue to the scandal on 18 October 1617 in which he reads the affair precisely as Lady Hatton's insurrection against the proper authority of her husband:

> sure she hath done herself a greate deale of wronge, in kicking against the pricke, and by indirect courses to hinder that which lay not in her power. Her daughter was married to Sir John Villers at Hampton Court on Michaelmas day. The King himself gave the bride, and they were thrise publikely asked in the church. . . . [H]er mother's wilfulnes and animositie, together with the daunger of her continuall plottings made the busines go on the faster. She [Lady Hatton] lies still at Sir William Cravens, crasie in body and sicke in minde; there is a commission to the Lord Keper, the Lord Archbishop, Secretarie Winwod and I know not who els to examine her, of conspiracie, disobedience and many other misdemeanures.[14]

Lady Hatton's insubordination proved impotent against the will of her husband and the will of the king. When the wedding took place, the mother was still under arrest. In her absence, the father's will was enforced and the king himself, a super-father figure, gave the bride in marriage to his favorite's brother. The bride appears entirely without will in this passage; the willful mother entirely subdued by the phallic authority of the "pricke" against which she had kicked. Chamberlain pictures her incapacitated physically and mentally, completely overwhelmed by the force that quelled her rebellion, still subject to examination and judgment at the hands of both civil and ecclesiastical authority for her transgression of the normative boundaries of gender and station.

The Coke-Villiers case clearly underscores the issues of property, status and gender which were bound together in the marriage negotiations of the propertied classes — the same issues that made the crime of ravishment so threatening. Their case constituted a significant test of the patriarchalism of English law. Although in practice that system was not uniformly biased against women (there *were* individual cases in which women's rights were upheld against the claims of men), this case illustrates the way the law usually worked.[15] Lady Hatton was a woman determined to preserve intact the holdings of her late husband, despite her current husband's determination to wrest control of those lands, money and goods away from her — even despite pressure from the king himself to resolve matters in favor of the Villiers.[16] However, her ability to forestall her husband's claims on her jointure property was more a result of her family connections and of the personal antagonism that Sir Edward Coke had provoked among his peers on the bench than an indication of the property rights of women generally.[17] In the end, the king's expressed desire, reinforced by lobbying from Buckingham and Coke, swayed the authorities before whom this case was aired to rule against Lady Hatton.

If Frances Coke Villiers's story had ended with her spectacular court wedding, most contemporary observers would have agreed that her adventure had worked itself through to a solid comic resolution. But, as Chamberlain sensed, the mother's and daughter's activities threatened to turn their drama from comedy to "straunge traged[y]." In fact, Frances Coke Villiers's marriage lasted only a few years before it fell apart in a public scandal over the groom's insane fits and ostensible impotence. For her part, the bride took a lover and became pregnant with a child the Villiers family refused to accept as a legitimate heir. Though her fate was less cataclysmic than the tragedies which befell so many stage heroines in her day, the comparison is tempting to draw. Her case illustrates a crucial problem in Jacobean gender relations: although the law and popular opinion held that men had an exclusive right to control property and to make decisions for all members of their families, it was clear that women as well as men possessed wills, which prompted them to desire and to act on their own. Where in men the will was seen as the rightful expression of intention, ownership and familial authority, in women, it was associated with petulance and indulgence, especially sexual indulgence.

Rape as Social Transgression

In Jacobean England, rape was a capital offense, "for the unlawfull and carnall knowledge and abuse of any woman above the age of ten years against her will."[18] This simple definition of the crime belies a history of contest over the nature of the offense and its appropriate punishment. Beginning with the first statutes of Westminster issued early in the reign of Edward I, English law conflated two crimes: "stealing" women and forcing women to submit to sexual relations. The first crime might consist of taking poor women from their parents and pressing them into servitude against their wishes, but it also included kidnappings designed to extort money from wealthy families. An unmarried heiress might be kidnapped in order to force her parents to consent to a match between their child and a man they would not otherwise choose. Similarly, widows might be coerced into unfavorable matches under threat of violence or character assassination.

This second kind of stealing was effective because a woman's marriageability could be compromised by any doubt cast on her chastity. Her parents were forced to consider whether they could make any match for their daughter other than the match proposed by the extortioner/kidnapper once the daughter's reputation had been tarnished by her captor. A widow, of course, had a similarly unhappy decision to make for herself, as this statute from 1488 makes clear:

> [W]omen, aswel maydens as widdowes and wives, having substance, some in goods moveable, and some in landes and tenements, and some being heires apparant unto their ancesters, for the lucre of such substances beene oftentimes taken by misdoers, contrary to

their will, and after marryed to such misdoers, or to other by their assent, or defiled, to the great displeasure of God, and contrary to the Kings Lawes, and dispergement of the said women, and utter heavinesse and discomfort of their friendes, and to the evill example of all other.[19]

Sexual violation was not necessary to this crime because the possibility of its having occurred was sufficient to ruin a woman's value as a commodity in the marriage market.

The economic motive, "the lucre of such substances," was the principal concern of the statute makers. Nancy Vickers notes Lucrece's statement after the rape that she has been "robb'd and ransack'd by injurious theft."[20] English law "from the beginning of Magna Charta" was interested primarily (almost exclusively) in property rights. In a society where status and access to legal rights depended on the ownership of property, the matter of law was the settlement of property disputes.[21] Rape was no exception. Each of the pertinent statutes identifies it as a crime against family property.

The language of the Henrician statute quoted above is significant: the woman is subject to *disparagement* — the degradation and dishonor of marrying a social inferior. Her friends suffer "utter heavinesse and discomfort." Rape is not so much a physical as a social threat to women, and it is not awful because of the emotional devastation inflicted on her, but on account of the distress it causes her family and peers.[22] In general, the rape statutes redress a wrong committed against a woman's male relatives. These men, rather than the woman herself, are the victims of a rape.

Ravishment not only threatened the property of men of means, but also threatened to disrupt the divisions between different social strata. The law viewed ravishment as a crime inspired by a desire to move up the social ladder. Whether many ravishers actually succeeded in accumulating money or position from such forced alliances, the strong fear behind the language of the law was that opportunistic men could exploit women sexually to infiltrate the higher classes.[23] In *The Changeling*, Middleton and Rowley present rape in a manner that both reflects and reinforces these social fears about the crime.[24] The ravishment of Beatrice-Joanna utterly ruins her family, tainting its honor and leaving her father without heirs. The intrusion of DeFlores, a malicious servant, not only disparages the family, but annihilates it.

From the moment DeFlores forces his fingers into Beatrice-Joanna's glove — a glove he has stooped to retrieve at her father's command — the rape is coded in terms of class.[25] Although the play makes it clear that he is gentle by birth, DeFlores lives as a dependent in Vermandero's household. Gentleman or not, he is a servant. That employment absolutely defines him in the eyes of Vermandero and his potential sons-in-law, blinding them to DeFlores's intentions toward Beatrice-Joanna.

One of the principal reasons that Beatrice-Joanna herself mis-reads his actions so disastrously is that DeFlores is not socially positioned to be an object of her desire. She cannot imagine him in those terms at all. Instead, she thinks him fit only for the basest sorts of employment (murder, for instance). Beatrice-Joanna mis-takenly believes that the difference in their stations is an unbridge-able gulf. She is not unaware that he desires her, but she assumes that the desire of an inferior, far from threatening her, is a useful tool to be exploited in the form of his willing service. From her posi-tion it is unthinkable that he would make any demands on her.[26]

Beatrice-Joanna's social assumptions are not unfounded, though the audience surely knows them to be naive. The play depends on the dramatic irony of this young woman's naiveté. Although Beatrice-Joanna cannot conceive of DeFlores's plot, the play, the audience and the culture all do think and fear that men like DeFlores will do exactly what he does if given the opportunity. Like Bussy D'Ambois's affair with the countess of Montsurry, *The Changeling* presents DeFlores's act as a flagrant transgression of the boundaries of a class that seeks to exclude him.[27] He knows that he cannot satisfy his desire for Beatrice-Joanna by marrying her; that is as unthinkable to him as it is to her family. In fact, his desire for her seems to stem precisely from her untouchableness

and from his unsuitability. He understands his desire as an affront
to her family and a theft from her other suitors. It is his final boast
that he has stolen her maidenhead from her father and both her
lovers, that he has "drunk up all, left none behind / For any man
to pledge me" (5.3.170–71).

DeFlores's desire for Beatrice-Joanna is a manifestation of his
discontent with his decayed fortunes, and it is fueled by her scorn,
which he interprets as having as much to do with his inferiority as
his ill-favoredness. Early in the second act, DeFlores has a lengthy
aside in which he analyzes Beatrice-Joanna's disdain for him and
his attraction to her. He notes that uglier men succeed in attracting
women:

> I must confess my face is bad enough,
> But I know far worse has better fortune,
>
> . . . .
> Yet such a one plucks sweets without restraint,
> And has the grace of beauty to his sweet.
> Though my hard fate thrust me out to servitude,
> I tumbled into th' world a gentleman.
>
> (2.1.37–38, 46–49)

In DeFlores's mind his servitude is inseparable from his hard fate
in all other areas. His hard features and his lack of success with
women are part of an ill fortune capped by his economic misfortune.
DeFlores concludes that all of his problems are a matter of station,
a barrier he chafes against.

DeFlores indulges his desire with a fantasy of seducing and
debasing Beatrice-Joanna.

> Methinks I feel her in my arms already,
> Her wanton fingers combing out this beard,
> And, being pleasèd, praising this bad face.
> Hunger and pleasure, they'll commend sometimes
> Slovenly dishes and feed heartily on 'em;
> Nay, which is stranger, refuse daintier for 'em.
> Some women are odd feeders.
>
> (2.2.147–53)

In this vision, Beatrice-Joanna is so carried away with pleasure that she praises his most repulsive features. He imagines his passion corrupts her appetites so fully that she can no longer discern beauty from ugliness, and he imagines that she will choose to be with him when she could have her choice of better mates.

When he finally acts out his assault, and Beatrice-Joanna tries to stand on the "distance that creation / Set 'twixt thy blood and mine" to keep him at bay, DeFlores frames his act precisely in terms of the social disparagement it will mean for her. "Push," he tells her, "fly not to your birth, but settle you / In what the act has made you" (3.4.130–31, 134–35). Her horror at his presumption is the horror of social conservatism under pressure in a climate of social mobility that threatens the disparagement of some as others rise. The rape of a noble woman, for lucre and malice, was a crime that, on the seventeenth century stage, mingled social and sexual transgression in a formula calculated to touch the anxieties of that audience. DeFlores, ugly and socially inferior to Beatrice-Joanna, is every bit the "foul villain" she imagines him (3.4.140).

In this conservative view, social mobility was frightening not only because the upper classes felt themselves assailed by outsiders, but also because an undesirable match could in reality lower the status of a woman's family, leaching away their resources and humiliating them before their peers. The costs of a ravishment might include a loss of liquid assets to the interloper, a loss of expected assets and alliances from an advantageous match for the ravished daughter, and a lessening of the likelihood of subsequent lucrative matches for the other children of the family.[28] A great deal of symbolic and real capital depended upon the chastity of women.

Complicity and Consent in Ravishment Law

Women, unlike other chattel, have wills of their own. To cope with this problem, the English passed a series of increasingly complicated supplemental statutes addressing the role of women within the crime of rape. What if a woman consented to be ravished? At what age could a woman be held responsible for her consent? What if a woman were forced through violence or threats, but then consented after the fact? Her family was no less damaged. There seems to have been a widespread and continuing sentiment that the common law allowed too many women to go unpunished for their part in crimes that wreaked havoc in their families' lives.

Though it climaxed with a flurry of legal maneuvering in the second half of the sixteenth century and continued to be revived in various parliamentary bills throughout the seventeenth century, the fervor to close the loopholes in rape law began very early in English juridical history. The Westminster II statutes (1285) suspected that some cases presented as ravishment were, in fact, adultery, and added a punishment for the woman to the judgment against the ravisher. If a wife can be shown to have consented either before or after the fact, Westminster II, cap. 34 states that she can be "barred forever of action to demand her dower, that she ought to have of her husbands lands." A 1383 law extended this provision to bar from their inheritance *any* "Ladies, daughters [of noble men], and other women," who "after such rape doe consent to such ravishers" (6 Richard II, cap. 6). It is not sufficient for a woman to have resisted a rape. These laws perceive a danger that she will be seduced by the rape and that her affection and loyalty to her husband or her duty to her father may be swayed by the man who raped her. The Ricardian law states its perception that rapists in the fourteenth century were "offending more violently, and much more then they were wont," but its substance is not directed against the rapists at all. Apparently, what was of real concern was a perceived increase in the number of women who conspired to deceive and defraud their husbands and families. What was violently offensive, then, was the sexual defection of women.[29]

What we see in the statutes is a series of amendments to the common law meant to modify the sexual behavior of women. As the anonymous author of the sixteenth century treatise, *A Discourse upon the Exposicion and Understandinge of Statutes,* explained it, the function of the statutes with respect to the common law was understood to be a process of clarification and adjustment:

> The commen lawe then knowne, you shall fynde that the statute is either incresinge the commen lawe, or remedyenge a myschiefe at the commen lawe, or confyrminge the commen lawe, or making clere a doubte that was at the commen lawe, or abridginge the commen lawe, or else quyte takinge yt awaye. As for those statutes that come in encrease of the commen lawe, they shall be taken by all equytye, for synce the commen lawe is grounded upon commen reason yt is good reason that that which augmenteth commen reason shulde be augmented.[30]

The rape statutes record an ongoing effort to make clear and eliminate the doubts left by common law with respect to women's sexuality and its consequences.

English law had two contradictory responses to women. On the one hand, as we have seen, it attempted to hold them ever more closely accountable for their actions. Simultaneously, however, it viewed them as incapable of managing their own affairs. For the most part, women were not treated as autonomous individuals in the eyes of the law. Young women and married women had limited access to the legal system except through their fathers or husbands, of whom they were merely extensions. While a woman could be brought to trial for committing a crime, she could not bring suit against another on her own behalf. Furthermore, the law tended to see women as having significant moral deficiencies that made them more susceptible to error and more likely to commit crimes than men whose moral sensibilities were more highly developed. This opinion of women creeps into the language of a statute, 31 Henry VI, cap. 9, passed in 1453 to address ravishers who tricked women into becoming accessories to their own ravishment. The law singles out men who take advantage of the "innocencie and simplicitie" of women to get the women into their power and force them into marriage or into signing bonds that pay to the extortionist-ravisher. Women, though responsible for their actions, are strongly suspected of being incapable of acting responsibly.

From the earliest statute (Westminster I, passed in 1275), the law distinguished between a "damsell within age" and a woman (maid, wife or widow) who had reached the age of consent (Westminster I, cap. 14). The age of consent traditionally had been 12 for women and 14 for men, and indicated the age at which young people could officially be married. The age of consent was a legal interpretation of the age at which mind and body were fit to enter into marriage.[31] The law estimated that consummation and conception were possible for most adolescents at that age, and it was, therefore, also the age at which they were held accountable for their sexual behavior. A girl under 12 years old was assumed to be incapable of giving her consent even to relations she might think she desired, and she was believed to be too young to conceive a child even if penetration occurred.[32] As there was no threat that she would conceive a bastard child, the culture could magnanimously consider a girl "within years" to be innocent whether she had consented to her ravisher or not. After turning 12, however, she was held accountable for her sexual decisions because they could compromise her husband's or future husband's paternity and disrupt the primogenitural flow of wealth from father to child.

An act passed in 1558, the final year of Mary Tudor's reign, threw the ravishment statutes into confusion by identifying the crime as the illegal conveyance, marriage or deflowering of "any maid or woman child unmarried, being *within age of sixteen yeeres*, out of, or from the possession, custodie, or gouernance, and against the will of the father."[33] The particular target of this statute was a lesser category of ravishment in which the taking away or seduction of the woman was effected without violence, a form of the crime which may have gone unpunished because the law's existing death penalty seemed inordinately harsh.[34] Although the new law was intended to facilitate enforcement and prosecution, its actual effect was to provide the grounds for disagreement about the age or ages that affected a girl's legal position in a ravishment case.

Sir Edward Coke, whose *Institutes of the Laws of England* were the definitive Jacobean interpretations of legal theory and precedent (and whose own daughter's marriage created such a stir), suggests that age became a key issue in the Elizabethan courts' consideration of rape cases.[35] According to Coke, "the doubt that was made in 14 Elizabeth at what age a woman child might be ravished was the cause of the making of the act of 18 Elizabeth, cap.6 for plain declaration of law."[36] The statute itself declares a need for clarity: "And for plain declaration of law, be it enacted, that if any person shall unlawfully and carnally know and abuse any woman childe under the age of ten yeares, every such unlawful and carnall knowledge shall bee felony, and the offendor thereof being duely convicted, shall suffer as a felon, without allowance of Clergie."[37] What this statute plainly declares is the sternest stand against rape in the history of the English state. Ravishers could no longer invoke their benefit of clergy to avoid the death sentence for their crime, and women were on notice that they were absolutely responsible for their sexual activity from a very early age.

Common law continued to insist that a woman be 12 for her consent to a parentally endorsed marriage to be binding, but statute law now held her responsible for her decision to go with an abductor, and to marry or have sex with him, two years earlier. England's justices had been forced to consider until what age a woman could still be said to be a child. They had decided, and the Parliament enacted their decision as law, that any woman "under the age of ten yeares" was still a child. Apparently they had serious doubts whether she remained so until age 12.

Coke's *Institutes* suggests that members of the Elizabethan and Jacobean legal establishment exhibited quite serious concern over the sexual conduct of 10- and 12-year-old women. In *Aristotle's Master-Piece*, a most popular text on reproductive biology, there is a caution to parents that attests to the age's concerns about female sexuality:

> 'Tis a duty incumbent upon Parents, to be careful in bringing up their Children in the ways of Vertue; and have ever a regard that they fully not[e] their Honour and Reputation, especially the Females, and most of all the Virgins, when they grow up to be marriagable, for if through the unnatural severity of rigid Parents

they be crossed and frustrated in their love, many of them, out of a mad humour, if temptation lies in their way, throw themselves into the unchaste Arms of a subtle charming Tempter, being through the softness of good Nature, and strong Desire, to pursue their Appetites, easily induced to believe Men's Flatteries, and feigned Vows of promised Marriage, to cover the shame; and then too late the Parents find the effects of their rash Severity, which brought a lasting stain upon their Family.[38]

Rigid parents, of course, were not the only ones who feared the effects of desire on women's honor. If the prevalence of the theme in literature can be added to the great concern evidenced in these statutes, we might conclude that subtle charming Tempters lurked about the dark corners of many a father's and husband's nightmares. When *Aristotle's Master-Piece* describes "the softness of nature, and strong Desire," it pinpoints precisely those traits which the law identified as the source of women's vulnerability to rapists, the traits which made them apt to conspire in their own ravishment.

The dual nature of rape as violation and pleasure was embedded in the very terms used to identify the crime: rape and ravishment. Rape, derived from the Latin *rapere*, of which *raptus* is also a form, meant in English "the act of taking anything by force[, the] violent seizure (of goods), robbery" (*OED*). Ravishment, from the French *ravissement*, a form of the verb *ravir*, may derive from the same Latin root. Drawing on the idea of transportation, both "rape" (rapture) and "ravishment" developed the additional meaning, "to transport with delight." The conjunction of meanings embedded in these words corresponds to an ambivalence about the crime: it was simultaneously understood to be a violent theft and a sexual dalliance. The first was certainly reprehensible; the second was open to interpretation. In fact, both ravishment and rapture were terms that conspired to suggest that this kind of "stealing" might hold pleasures for the ravisher — and that the pleasure might even be experienced by the woman raped as well.

Kathryn Gravdal offers a history of the French legal and

colloquial terminology for rape.[39] She notes that in France (as in England) the legal definition of rape originally required an abduction to have taken place in order for a sexual assault to be chargeable. When, over time, the law changed to eliminate this requirement, it left the terms *ravir* and *ravissant* "free to become wholly figurative" in their popular use. It was at this point in England and in France that rapture and ravishment came to connote an emotional or sexual carrying away. Gravdal points out that "this transformation is inflected by a shift in gender coding: when *ravir* was literal, it was the male who ravished (carried away or abducted) the female. When the term soars off into the realm of the figurative, it is the female who is ravishing, who causes the male to be "carried away" and is responsible for any ensuing "acts."[40] What Gravdal notices in the language of rape was part of a larger inclination in the culture of both France and England to blame women for their own violation, as we have already seen in the statutory history of English law.

Sixteenth and seventeenth century literature is full of women who have internalized this sense of their own culpability for men's assaults on them. When Jonson's Volpone assaults Celia, she begs him,

> Feed your wrath, sir, rather than your lust,
> It is a vice comes nearer manliness,
> And punish that unhappy crime of nature,
> Which you miscall my beauty: flay my face,
> Or poison it with ointments for seducing
> Your blood to this rebellion.

> (3.7.248–53)

Likewise, at the end of Shakespeare's *Rape of Lucrece*, that chaste woman blames her beauty for Tarquin's action: "His scarlet lust came evidence to swear / That my poor beauty had purloined his eyes; / And when the judge is robb'd, the prisoner dies."[41] The legal imagery of this line underscores the gender shift in the perception of rape. Lucrece is the guilty prisoner, Tarquin the injured judge and accuser. Her beauty is a thief, a ravisher. Although we might expect that his lust would gladly perjure itself to achieve its desire, in these lines Lucrece accepts its testimony as an irrefutable truth. It is telling that in addition to being framed here as the injured party, Tarquin is also acknowledged to be the judge. He has the power of execution over Lucrece, a power these lines insist is just. Lucrece not only finds herself guilty as charged, but further condemns herself for having demonstrated poor judgment in choosing so powerful a man as her "victim."

Ultimately, Shakespeare does not intend to lay blame on Lucrece for a crime perpetrated by so obviously villainous a man. However, the logic is insidious, which inspires Lucrece — for even these few lines — to attribute Tarquin's lust to the action of female beauty. It lies beneath and eats away at the conscious attribution of responsibility for rape to the men who commit it. It says, *Yes, but had she not been beautiful, had she not been desirable, he would not have desired, he would not have raped.* The suspicion of women's complicity is so deeply embedded in the culture's language of rape and desire that even the purest women fall under its shadow.

In *The Changeling,* DeFlores, like Tarquin, finds that the thought of a woman "ravishes" (2.2.132). He seeks out Beatrice-Joanna's company in order to "please [him]self with the sight / Of her, at all opportunities" (1.1.104–5). His fantasy is that Beatrice-Joanna will be "ravished" when he rapes her, that she will find pleasure in what repulses her. "Methinks I feel . . . her wanton fingers combing out this beard, / And being pleasèd with, praising this bad face" (2.2.147–49). He imagines her an active participant in her rape. The play bears him out. Beatrice-Joanna, beautiful and desirable, is also desirous. She even comes to "love anon" what she initially "fear'st and faint'st to venture on" — DeFlores, the man she loathes (3.4.170–71). Middleton and Rowley created an archetype of the woman driven by desire in the character of Beatrice-Joanna, the traitoress who betrays her father's estate from within.

Beatrice-Joanna's Crime

The play opens at rape law's critical juncture: it introduces Beatrice-Joanna at the precise moment of her sexual awakening. Beatrice-Joanna is a young woman who previously has seen no reason to contradict, or even involve herself in, her father's arrangements for her marriage. Unfortunately for all concerned, Beatrice-Joanna meets a man who creates "a giddy turning in [her]," which makes her realize that marriage could be a sexually fulfilling union (1.1.159). This new love, Alsemero, is suitable in all respects except for his arriving on the scene five days after Beatrice-Joanna's father has completed negotiations for her marriage to Alonzo de Piracquo. The daughter knows that her father cannot honorably withdraw from the match, and that he will not entertain her objections — so she circumvents his plan and follows her heart, allowing it to lead her into a disastrous spiral of crime and corruption.

The playwrights construct the conflict of interest between Beatrice-Joanna and her father as a contest of wills.[42] Will is a term whose significance is made much of by the play. At the close of the first scene there is an exchange that foregrounds this term in order to demonstrate what is at stake in the daughter's sexuality. Boasting to Alsemero of the fine match he has made with Alonzo de Piracquo, the father, Vermandero, vows,

> He shall be bound to me
> As fast as this tie can hold him; I'll want
> My will else.
> B-J (aside):   I shall want mine if you do it.
>
> (1.1.221–23)

Beatrice-Joanna completes and confutes her father's line with her aside. Her will, that is to say her desire and her intention, conflicts with his intent for her. This daughter asserts herself as having a will separate from her father's. In order to establish Beatrice-Joanna's responsibility for her subsequent actions, Middleton and Rowley deliberately echo the language of ravishment law with its emphasis on the woman's will to have or avoid sexual activity ("with her will or against her will").

When the father speaks of his "will," the word invokes a second meaning. Here it not only refers to his immediate intentions for his daughter's marriage, but also reminds us that fathers have wills of another sort that concern their children. Her match, of course, has a material part in his will, his legal testament. Beatrice-Joanna is her father's sole heir, and her children will inherit his property. His will for the disposition of his estate requires her faithful participation, a condition Beatrice-Joanna willfully refuses.

The term "will" had a further significance in the period, which bears on this exchange in the play. "Will" also meant sexual desire, a connotation that resonates in Beatrice-Joanna's line. The independence that she asserts is specifically framed in terms of her desire. Furthermore, when DeFlores closes the scene with the promise, "Though I get nothing else, I'll have my will," his use of the term evokes the contemporary slang in which "will" was a reference to the erect penis. The intertwined sexual and legal threads of this term underscore the fundamental interconnection of this family's sexual and social welfare, both of which are undermined by Beatrice-Joanna's corruption.[43]

Beatrice-Joanna's discovery that she has a will contrary to her father's is her first step toward betraying his honor, a trespass she compounds with deceit. Beatrice-Joanna never makes her objections known, but undertakes secret steps to subvert her father's plan for her. In the moment of that first aside, her course takes shape.[44] We watch as a woman-child who once made her likes and dislikes painfully clear becomes a woman who disguises her intentions and falsifies her emotions. The aside and soliloquy become her characteristic modes of speech. Beatrice-Joanna's subsequent actions and conversations are marked increasingly by secrecy and disingenuousness.

Beatrice-Joanna has tremendous success with her program of deception, at least initially. She hides her disobedience from her father, gives Alsemero no reason to suspect her virtue, and even fools Alonzo into a false sense of her faithfulness. Tomazo de Piracquo is the first to see behind her mask. He notices her cool reception of his brother and tries to warn Alonzo, counseling him to

> Think what a torment 'tis to marry one
> Whose heart is leaped into another's bosom:
> If ever pleasure she receive from thee,
> It comes not in thy name or of thy gift;
> She lies but with another in thine arms,
> He the half-father unto all thy children
> In the conception; if he get 'em not,
> She helps to get 'em for him; and how dangerous
> And shameful her restraint may go in time to,
> It is not to be thought on without sufferings.
>
> (2.1.131–40)

How accurate Tomazo's vision is, the play reveals quickly. Beatrice-Joanna's restraint gives way to danger and shame before Alonzo has a chance to marry her, but Alonzo cannot see his danger and ignores the warning. Alsemero, too, has no inkling that anything is amiss with Beatrice-Joanna until after he has married her, although he might have recognized her love for him — and her corresponding disregard for Alonzo — as ominous signs had he considered them carefully. The fact that neither suitor picks up Beatrice-Joanna's dangerous signals is precisely the play's point. The danger of women's falseness is its subtlety, its secrecy, its ability to masquerade convincingly as virtue.

Like Tomazo, DeFlores can see what her noble lovers cannot, and he uses his knowledge to steal Beatrice-Joanna from the arms of these rivals. When he discovers Beatrice-Joanna in a secret tryst with Alsemero, DeFlores observes his advantage:

> if a woman
> Fly from one point, from him she makes a husband,
> She spreads and mounts then like arithmetic,
> One, ten, a hundred, a thousand, ten thousand,
> Proves in time sutler to an army royal.
>
> (2.2.60–64)

This is the same logic applied by Brabantio and Iago to caution Othello against trusting Desdemona's chastity in Shakespeare's play: "She has deceived her father and may thee" (1.3.289). If Desdemona is an exception to this rule, Beatrice-Joanna is not.[45] Middleton and Rowley endorse DeFlores's analysis of her susceptibility to corruption, and the play confirms the underlying conventional wisdom that a woman false to one might be false to any.

When we consider Beatrice-Joanna, we can see what the law feared. She is willful and sexual; she is deceitful and unrepentant; she does not even recognize her error as she begins her course of immorality. Ravishment law was concerned that women might lack the moral sense to conduct themselves appropriately and because their "innocencie and simplicitie" might be easily abused, women were subject to seduction and to moral error (31 Hen. IV, cap. 9). Middleton and Rowley interpret women's willfulness in much the same way the statute writers did.

As they have created her, Beatrice-Joanna is a young woman who understands her society's demand that women have sex only within marriage. Until she experiences sexual desire for the first time, she acquiesces to the match with Alonzo that her father designs for her. However, the playwrights place her in a moral dilemma when she meets and begins to desire Alsemero. When she sets about to subvert her father's plans for her marriage, Beatrice-Joanna may be attempting to find a culturally acceptable resolution to the problem she faces. If she could arrange to marry Alsemero, then she could also be an honorable wife. *Then* she would not desire anyone but her husband. She finds, however, that there is no social mechanism that will allow her to exercise her choice. She refuses to allow Alsemero to practice the one quasi-official means at his disposal to intervene in her marriage. She will not let him challenge Alonzo because she fears that the result will be either Alsemero's death or his imprisonment for murder. Finding no sanctioned means to escape a marriage she does not wish to make, Beatrice-Joanna slides easily into disreputable schemes. When DeFlores presents himself to her at the right moment, she leaps at the opportunity to allow him to kill her fiancé.

Beatrice-Joanna is both amoral and "simple." She does not hesitate to plot Alonzo's murder and apparently does not consider his death to have any moral significance. This ethical blindness also causes her to fall prey to her own "innocencie and simplicitie" in her dealings with DeFlores. She has not the faintest inkling of the kind of obligation she incurs with DeFlores through her bargain with him; she believes that he would do anything to serve her, when, in fact, his objective is sexual dominance, not submissive service. Beatrice-Joanna believes her plan will rid her of two unwanted men at once; she expects DeFlores to murder for her and then flee her father's house. She assumes that DeFlores wants only a lucrative reward for his task, but she is wrong.

> Beatrice-Joanna: Thy reward shall be precious.
> DeFlores: That I have thought on;
>   I have assured myself of that beforehand,
>   And know it will be precious; the thought *ravishes*.
>   (2.2.130–32, italics added)

Beatrice-Joanna assumes that the motive that drives men is desire for property; she overlooks DeFlores's sexual desires. Even the law, which assumes that covetousness is the principal motive for crime, does not make Beatrice-Joanna's mistake. In their anxiety over women's consent, the rape statutes always remember that sexual desire is a powerful motivator of men. Instead of taking her gold and running away, DeFlores exercises a power over Beatrice-Joanna that she neither realized she had given nor imagined he would take. She marvels that "He's bold, and I am blamed for it" (3.4.97).

In fact, Beatrice-Joanna is so unaware of her position that DeFlores must explain her predicament to her quite bluntly:

> Though thou writ'st maid, thou whore in thy affection,
> 'Twas changed from thy first love, and that's a kind
> Of whoredom in thy heart; and he's changed now,
> To bring thy second on, thy Alsemero,
> Whom by all sweets that darkness ever tasted,
> If I enjoy thee not, thou ne'er enjoy'st.
>   (3.4.142–47)

Beatrice-Joanna does not fathom her complicity in the murder, and, thus, cannot anticipate how DeFlores uses it to gain access to her: "Why, 'tis impossible thou canst be so wicked, / . . . To make his death the murderer of my honor!" (3.4.120, 122). Incredibly, she fails to recognize her responsibility for Alonzo's death.

Middleton and Rowley have designed a heroine who confirms the law's paternalistic concern for women's moral weakness.[46] Beatrice-Joanna's assumption that desire might have a meaningful place within marriage or that women might under some circumstances be sanctioned to act on desire simply does not square with Jacobean notions of marriage and sexuality. Beatrice-Joanna's project to marry the man she desires becomes a diabolic mirroring of Jacobean sexual mores. The play sees her willfulness as an all-absorbing focus on herself that threatens everyone else. This self-absorption creates the cockeyed view by which she sees herself as pursuing a logical course to an honorable marriage. "A woman dipped in blood," though she surely is, Beatrice-Joanna continues to "talk of modesty" (3.4.126).

Changelings

The law, with its straightforward statements about consent and age, its sturdy definitions of damage and disinheritance, is completely inadequate either to deter or to address the crimes in Middleton and Rowley's play. The most frightening aspect of *The Changeling* is the success with which DeFlores and Beatrice-Joanna hide Alonzo's murder and the further betrayal of their sexual alliance. Once she succumbs to DeFlores's assault, Beatrice-Joanna actively covers up the crime, hiding her incontinence and counterfeiting chastity in order to proceed with her marriage to Alsemero. In *The Changeling*'s nightmare vision, women's desire is deadly and defrauding. Middleton and Rowley play masterfully on all the legion fears about women and their traitorous sexuality to which the "consent and complicity" statutes were a reaction. With its powerful illustration of the corruptibility of women, the play confirms the validity of the statute makers' concerns, but simultaneously undermines the comfort promised by their strict penalties.

Literature and law both expressed great concern that women might falsify their sexual activity. Rape law, which sought to fix blame and to redress wrong materially, was frustrated by the near impossibility of determining whether a woman had been forced or merely seduced by her ravisher. The maddening characteristic of most rapes, of course, was that they lacked witnesses, and their facts remained obscured in the irreconcilable difference between a woman's accusation and a man's defense.[47] This dilemma drove justices to search for a test that could determine the facts of a rape with certainty.

Michael Dalton, in *The Countrey Justice* (1618), claimed to have just such a test when he advised fellow magistrates that "if the woman at the time of the supposed rape do conceive with child, by the ravisher, this is no rape, for a woman cannot conceive with child except she do consent."[48] Dalton's understanding of biology was based in the Galenic medicine still much in use. The author of *Aristotle's Master-Piece* reports the view of this branch of medical wisdom that conception occurs when the male and female seed are released during copulation — a release that had to be accompanied in both sexes by orgasm. Dalton, then, based his legal test on the assumption that if a woman conceives, she must have experienced pleasure in the act of intercourse, which in turn signifies that she consented to the act, if not beforehand, then by virtue of having enjoyed it.

The test was necessary, of course, because women lack the obvious signifiers of desire with which men are equipped. Without penises, which offer visual confirmation of arousal and satisfaction, women could easily counterfeit their experience of the sexual act. Not only did this absence of ocular proof allow women to pretend pleasure when they felt none, it also made it possible for them to conceal their pleasure when it served them to do so.

Even as Dalton was circulating his consent test, however, the medical wisdom upon which it was based was becoming obsolete. The *Master-Piece* reports Galenic opinion only to rebut it, proposing, instead, a biology of conception in which the active male seed searches out and fertilizes the passive ovum in the woman's body. Among the propositions it explicitly refutes is the Galenic belief that a woman's orgasm is produced by the ejaculation of seed.[49]

The *Master-Piece* also takes sides in another of the period's disputes over women's sexuality. It maintains that a ruptured hymen is not evidence of lack of virginity, claiming that "the Learned" affirm that

> such fracture may happen divers ways by accidents, as well as Copulation with Man, *viz.* [b]y extraordinary straining, violent coughing, immoderate sneezing, stopping of Urine, and violent motion of the Vessels, inforcibly sending down the humours, which pressing for passage break the Ligatures or Membrane, so that the intireness or fracture of this thing, commonly taken for the Virginity or Maiden-head, is no absolute sign of dishonesty.[50]

After taking away this absolute sign of a woman's falseness, the author of the *Master-Piece* offers a most interesting consolation to his readers. He will have it known that while a woman's sexual activity cannot be proved by her ruptured hymen, an intact hymen is certain proof that she remains a virgin. He illustrates the importance of this truth with a legal case in which a woman was found to have falsely accused a man of raping her. Her deceit was discovered when a gynecological exam certified that she was still a virgin. Far from offering reassurance, this illustration demonstrates the dire need for discernible proof of women's sexual status. It cautions that even when women are chaste, they may perpetrate dangerous sexual falsehoods.

The Changeling exploits its culture's anxiety about the difficulty of ascertaining the facts of women's sexuality. Alibius, the subplot's jealous husband, fears that his wife will find opportunities to cuckold him if he allows her to leave his house, so he confines her indoors in the company of the madmen and fools he treats, and entrusts her to the oversight of his wily servant. Were she so inclined, Isabella could find plenty of opportunity to betray her husband without leaving home. Certainly his unreasonable confinement of her gives her ample motive for cuckolding him, but the playwrights maintain Isabella's chastity as a counterexample to Beatrice-Joanna's falseness. The lesson of the subplot is not so much that some women are capable of chastity, but that nothing men can do will guarantee women's honesty.

In the main plot, Tomazo de Piracquo spends the entire play suspecting Beatrice-Joanna of falseness he cannot prove. Likewise, Alsemero becomes consumed by questions about his bride's chastity. The audience knows all of Beatrice-Joanna's secrets, and it waits for the other characters to realize the magnitude of her hidden sins. The plot is driven toward the moment when the truth will be revealed, but discovery is so slow in coming that it seems entirely possible that Beatrice-Joanna may get away with murder and adultery. The play, which makes its audience privy to all of the facts, builds suspense by postponing discovery until the last possible moment. It teases its audience with the specter of a woman's successful deception, withholding as long as practicable the reward of her violent punishment and her acceptance of guilt. The audience is as desperate that the truth be known as the male characters are to discover that truth.

As soon as he has married her, Alsemero begins to be troubled by hints of Beatrice-Joanna's unfaithfulness. He has, however, come to marriage prepared to deal with such doubts. Alsemero owns a medical kit that contains special preparations with which he can discover whether Beatrice-Joanna is a virgin, and if not a virgin, whether she is pregnant. Such certain tests, if they had only existed, would have been worth more to seventeenth century husbands than possession of the philosopher's stone.[51] The liquid in Glass M, which would allow a man "to know whether a woman be a maid or not," would settle once and for all the uncertainty that even a woman's body could no longer be trusted to resolve (4.1.41). Among its uses, Glass C, "to know whether a woman be with child," would have allowed Daltonite judges to resolve their cases much sooner, before a pregnancy could otherwise have been detected (4.1.26). If Beatrice-Joanna were to fail the first test, but were then to claim that she had been raped by DeFlores, Glass C might have helped to establish her guilt.

But Alsemero's science is no more successful than Michael Dalton's. Beatrice-Joanna discovers his physician's closet and reads the secret of his procedures there. With this knowledge she is able to counterfeit the signs of chastity when she is put to the test. Alsemero's medicine fails because it relies on the female body to demonstrate symptoms that will indicate the woman's condition. The play asserts what its seventeenth century audience already suspected, what the law tried so diligently to counteract: that women find it all too easy to counterfeit their reactions, to hide their deficiencies, to mask the signs that their bodies should offer as clear signals for men to read. When forced to swallow the contents of Glass M, Beatrice-Joanna gapes, sneezes, laughs and falls into melancholy just as Alsemero's text predicts a virgin will — but she is an actress, not a virgin. On her wedding night, Beatrice-Joanna supplies a body double to act her part in the darkened bridal chamber. Throughout her short marriage, Beatrice-Joanna plays the spotless bride; her act is a mask to cover the rottenness of her sin and the defilement of her body.

Women are changelings. They are changeable and interchangeable.[52] Not only are women able to counterfeit their actions, they are able to disguise themselves and substitute themselves for one another. Beatrice-Joanna capitalizes on the fact that in the darkened bedchamber women's bodies were undetectably replaceable. Alsemero is able to search his bedmate's body for signs of virginity, but cannot discern that he has the wrong woman in his bed. Beatrice-Joanna's successful evasion of his investigations testifies that women's bodies, though fleshly and material, are elusive and undecipherable.

When Alsemero at last obtains ocular proof of Beatrice-Joanna's falseness (he sees her with DeFlores in a private tryst in the garden), he realizes that instead of a wife he has married a player. He finally sees what lies behind the "visor" she has worn "O'er that cunning face" (5.3.46, 47). Her infidelity and her deception and the false testimony of her body are the characteristic untruths of actors. Women's sexuality was, indeed, a puzzle akin to the destabilized image of the transvestite player. Insofar as it was noted, the appearance of the boy beneath the woman's clothes may have been taken by early modern audiences as an image of the rotten core at the center of women, of the inauthenticity of the female sex.[53] Beatrice-Joanna is at last known to be "the changeling," a counterfeit daughter, a whore masquerading as a bride, an actor in women's clothes.

The play makes self-conscious use of this acting metaphor to call attention to what can be known and what eludes knowledge, what can be seen and what remains hidden. The final scene reenacts DeFlores's rape of Beatrice-Joanna and literalizes his "murder" of her honor, but stages this action where we cannot see it. Alsemero locks Beatrice-Joanna into a room with DeFlores, bidding them

> rehearse again
> Your scene of lust, that you may be perfect
> When you shall come to act it to the black audience
> Where howls and gnashings shall be music to you.
>
> (5.3.114–17)

From behind the closed door of the chamber come the sounds of that rehearsal, "horrid" sounds which are the climax of their relationship and of the play. This audible, but hidden, scene of lust supplies the moment of revelation for which Vermandero, Tomazo, Alsemero and their audience have yearned. But even this revelation is unclear. Beatrice-Joanna can be heard uttering ambiguous sounds, perhaps of passion, perhaps of agony. DeFlores responds with equally suggestive words, as Alsemero interprets their performance for his father-in-law and Tomazo:

> Beatrice [within]: Oh, oh, oh!
> Alsemero: Hark 'tis coming to you.

DeFlores [within]: Nay, I'll along for company.
Beatrice: Oh, oh!

(5.3.139–40)

Alsemero's remark is as much a double-entendre as the rest of the exchange. It is both a bitter taunt directed at Beatrice-Joanna, and a response to Tomazo's demand for "a recompense, for murder and adultery" (5.3.138).

Behind that closed door, DeFlores is stabbing Beatrice-Joanna, then turning the knife on himself. When he forced Beatrice-Joanna to sleep with him, DeFlores murdered her honor; now he finishes his crime with her actual murder. Her body, when DeFlores drags her out onto the stage, bears visible signs of his violation, signs that are a literalization of the violence their sexual union committed on her body and her honor and, by extension, on her family. Beatrice-Joanna makes this connection explicit when she warns her father not to touch her:

> Oh come not near me, sir; I shall defile you.
> I am that of your blood was taken from you
> For your better health; look no more upon't,
> But cast it to the ground regardlessly;
> Let the common sewer take it from distinction.

(5.3.149–53)

The daughter, of course, has already defiled her family by her actions. She understands that her body, which was vulnerable to DeFlores's assault, must be cut off from the family in order to restore it to honor. Her blood, the biological connection between father and daughter, must be shed to effect this social cure, even as seventeenth century medicine would prescribe a therapeutic bloodletting in order to remove the defiling humour from a sick patient. In this final moment, Beatrice-Joanna acknowledges the duty accepted so much more gracefully by Lucrece. She realizes that, in order to erase the shame she has cast upon her father and her husband, she must die.

The ostracism demanded by the law for seventeenth century

women guilty of consenting to their ravisher's desires is pushed to an extreme in Middleton and Rowley's play. But Beatrice-Joanna's body — bloody, dead and cast aside on the stage — is a literalization of the kind of cutting off prescribed by the law to separate a family from the daughter whose body has betrayed them. In life as on stage, honor could only be salvaged through a ritual purging of the defiled part: the woman. Once that purge is complete, Alsemero can treat the matter as closed and can encourage his father-in-law to forget it entirely:

> Let it be blotted out; let your heart lose it,
> And it can never look you in the face
> Nor tell a tale behind the back of life
> To your dishonor; justice hath so right
> The guilty hit that innocence is quit
> By proclamation and may joy again.
>
> (5.3.182–87)

When he declares, "I am satisfied, my injuries / Lie dead before me," Tomazo de Piracquo confirms the necessity and accepts the sufficiency of her death as a recompense. In this final scene, the playwrights render Beatrice-Joanna's body readable. While she lived, she was changeable and her body was a cipher. Once dead, her body's signs are clear, straightforward.

His Castle and Fortress: The Rhetoric of Rape and Rights

In drama, at least, seventeenth century Englishmen could demand justice and restitution — of property and social order. In reality things were not so simple. During the reign of James I, a new set of national circumstances revitalized and reinfused violation imagery with rhetorical potency and political currency. *The Changeling* is a representative example of the way in which the stage contributed its voices to the public discourse on national issues. While rooted in the attitudes and legalities inculcated for centuries by English statute law, the play's treatment of rape as an attack on the property of male subjects also reveals the work to have been enmeshed in a web of new concerns troubling Jacobean England.[54]

James arrived in his southern kingdom in 1603 to find his new subjects eager to embrace changes that might improve their individual circumstances, but collectively fearful that any change might deprive them of rights and possessions already theirs.[55] Thus, James's proposal that his two kingdoms should unite "as may make one Body of both Kingdoms, under me your King," was viewed by the English as a threat to their property: they feared that the poorer nation would benefit at the expense of the richer.[56] Likewise, the English were wary of their new monarch's constitutional views, coming as he did from a nation with a different distribution of power between the king and his subjects.[57]

It was observed by those who disapproved of his mounting debts that James sought to rival his European peers with his banquets, ceremonies and entertainments.[58] Furthermore, James had not been discreet in voicing his opinion that his powers should be every bit as absolute as those of other monarchs. To the French ambassador he boasted that "he and Henry IV were absolute monarchs in their dominion and in no respect dependent upon the counsels of their subjects." The Venetian ambassador reported similar claims by the English monarch: "The King is absolute now and declares that there are no ministers and no law of which he is not the master."[59] Whether or not James was sufficiently indiscreet to allow English ears to hear these opinions, the English quickly derived an accurate sense of their monarch's constitutional views. When, in 1604, James attempted to intervene in a disputed parliamentary election, the House of Commons' *official* response to his interference was that the king had misinterpreted English law or had received misinformation from his councillors; however, there were many who feared that the king was fully aware of the law and that he was trying, under the guise of ignorance, to reconstruct the constitutional division of powers. These concerns were not salved by the king's spokesman in Parliament, Francis Bacon, who, early in the debate about union, suggested that his royal master might be styled "emperor" of his newly unified realm of "Britain."[60]

Conflict between Parliament and the monarch was not new; Elizabeth had dealt with both recalcitrance and presumptuousness from M.P.s. What James found, however, was that M.P.s were afraid that a change of monarch would necessarily also mean an attempt by the monarchy to appropriate new powers. Nor was this a fear expressed only by an exceptionally vocal minority in Parliament. Qualms about the new king surfaced in private correspondence, in print and on the stage.[61] When George Chapman had his King Henry (Henri III) note that "the king's change doth breed the subject's terror, / Pure innovation is more gross than error" (*Bussy D'Ambois*, 1.2.35–36), the playwright placed in a king's mouth the warning that James's subjects hoped their new king would heed. Until they found him to be content with the kingdom's current state, they preferred to fear the worst of him than prove themselves too trusting to their own cost.

Within the first two weeks of his first parliamentary session in 1604, James had alarmed members of the House of Commons with statements suggesting that he understood Parliament to exist only at his will and subjects' rights to exist only at his pleasure. Specifically, he had said that members of the House of Commons "derived all matters of privilege from him and by his grant."[62] Although this statement did not elicit an immediate or hysterical response from the Commons, it was remembered when, at the end of the session, the Commons drafted a defense of their unproductive term in a document tentatively called "The Form of Apology and Satisfaction." The document alleges that the king's "assertions . . . tend directly . . . to the utter overthrow of the very fundamental privileges of our House *and therein of the rights and liberties of the whole commons* of your realm of England, which they and their ancestors from time immemorial have undoubtedly enjoyed under your Majesty's most noble progenitors."[63] The chief liberties that were being claimed by Parliament in this document were (1) that the members of Parliament be freely elected without interference in the electoral process by the Crown, the Privy Council or other governmental bodies; (2) that "the persons chosen, during the time of the Parliament . . . be free from restraint, arrest and imprisonment"; (3) that members "may speak freely their consciences without check or controlment."[64] In addition to a fundamental argument about the division of power and rights within the English state, this document and its authors were concerned with a very immediate practical issue: whether members of Parliament were free to debate and express their concerns and opinions or whether they would be constrained by fear of arbitrary arrest for speaking in opposition to the king's will. It was customary for the monarch to grant these freedoms at the beginning of each parliamentary session, and it was customarily held that these privileges protected all but the seditious from fearing that their speech in Parliament would be charged against them after the session ended, but James's subjects had come to fear that these freedoms would not be maintained by their new king.

This is the fear glossed by Chapman in *Bussy D'Ambois*, when Montsurry advises his wife to

> bear with [Monsieur]:
> Thou know'st he is a bachelor and a courtier,
> Ay, and a prince; and their prerogatives
> Are to their laws, as to their pardons are
> Their reservations, after parliaments —
> One quits another: form gives all their essence:
> That prince doth high in virtue's reckoning stand
> That will entreat a vice, and not command.
> So far bear with him; should another man
> Trust to his privilege, he should trust to death.
>
> (2.2.118–27)[65]

From start to finish this is an unflattering picture of princes. A "good" prince is merely one who does not forcibly abuse his subjects, one who attempts seduction, but stops short of rape. Monsieur's attempt at sexual abuse becomes a metaphor that opens out onto a variety of princely practices in this passage, a variety of practices specifically linked to James I, the prince who reportedly thought himself the master of all laws.

If we untangle its syntax, Chapman's analogy is this: Princes' prerogatives are to their laws as their reservations are to their pardons. Princes reserve the right to arrest M.P.s after the dissolution of Parliament; thus, the reservation nullifies the freedom implied by the ceremonial pardon granted at the opening of the session. This is a specific and topical complaint. The prior claim, being more general, is more disturbing: the king's prerogative nullifies the protective effects of the nation's laws. This, too, evokes real concerns actively voiced in early Jacobean England, where their prince seemed intent on exploring the full extent of his powers and was quick to claim that any action objected to by the Commons was a power due to the prerogative of the Crown. For their part, the Commons complained of and sought to challenge the king's right to grant monopoly patents or to levy impositions, which amounted to taxation without parliamentary consent. There was also vigorous resistance to James's attempts to extend the jurisdiction of prerogative courts, where a subject could have no appeal to the civil law.

At the heart of the 1604 "Apology" is the observation that "the prerogatives of princes may easily and do daily grow. The privileges of the subject are for the most part at an everlasting stand."[66] Prerogative and privilege: these key words resonate between Montsurry's statement and the rhetoric of these English M.P.s. Princes' "*prerogatives* are to their laws as to their pardons are their reservations . . . one quits another. . . . So far bear with him; should another trust to his *privilege*, he should trust to death." To the writers of the "Apology" and, apparently, to Jacobean theater audiences, it seemed that their king felt nothing could stand in the way of prerogative powers — and it was coming to seem that the privileges of the people (in Parliament and beyond) were no certain safeguard for their lives.

Although the fear for life and limb was mostly rhetorical (the standard politician's ploy of pressing an argument to its extreme), there *were* real concerns at the heart of the subject's rights debate. In the parliamentary arena, where M.P.s were accustomed to thinking of issues in legal terms, the question of subjects' rights boiled down to the issue of whether English law truly allowed English subjects to own private property, or whether they held it merely as feudal villeins at the will (and whim) of their lord. Were they "tenants of right" or merely "tenants at will"? James's assertions of his prerogative suggested the latter. M.P.s looked to English legal history, especially to the Magna Carta, to assert the inviolability of property rights.

In 1610, for instance, William Hakewill argued not only that the king should be prevented from levying any sort of imposition between parliamentary sessions in peacetime, but that this prohibition should extend to wartime as well. Hakewill's fear was that if such a prerogative power were admitted, there would then be no way to control or limit it in the event it were abused: "Who shall judge between the king and his people of this occasion? Can it be tried by any legal course in our law? It cannot. If then, the king himself must be the sole judge in this case, will it not follow that the king may levy a tax at his own pleasure, seeing his pleasure cannot be bounded by law?"[67] "If the king could thus seize the property of his subjects at his pleasure they could not then be said really to hold their own property *except* at his pleasure, as tenants at [the king's] will."[68]

When Hakewill warned that the king's "pleasure cannot be bounded by law," he chose a more inflammatory synonym for "will." Both "will" and "pleasure" could be neutral legal terms, but, as we have seen, both terms also carried connotations of sexual desire and sexual abuse — in legal usage and in casual speech. Hakewill chose the less subtle of the two terms to make his point that the king's impositions amounted to a seizure or *ravishment* of subjects' property against their will — a violation.[69]

The shared concern for property between the language of English rape law and the Jacobean discourse of subjects' rights quite logically extended to a shared concern for inheritance. The M.P.s who drafted the 1604 *Apology* make their claims "in the name of the whole commons of the realm of England, with uniform consent for ourselves and our posterity."[70] The *Apology* never made its way out of Parliament, but its language did: in 1610, John Chamberlain, who was not an M.P., reported on the extra-parliamentary reaction to a speech in which James had expounded his prerogative and had cautioned M.P.s that even if he were a tyrant, they could have no recourse against his exercise of his proper powers. Writing to Ralph Winwood, Chamberlain says, "I hear it bred generally much discomfort, to see our monarchical power and regal prerogative strained so high and made so transcendent every way, that if the practice should follow the positions, *we are not like to leave our successors that freedom we received from our forefathers, nor make account of anything we have longer than they list that govern.*"[71] Similar rhetoric appears in parliamentary materials from 1628, when the particular issues between Charles I and his Parliament were fresh versions of old concerns: taxation without consent, imprisonment without cause shown, the use of martial law to try people in courts outside the common law system (which eliminated the possibility of appeal). In debating these issues and constructing what came to be the Petition of Right, M.P.s were still using this rhetoric of property, rights and heirs violated. Sir Edward Coke declared that when the king had been forced to assent to the petition, Coke would "leave it to my child as his greatest inheritance."[72] When it became clear that Charles would not respond to the petition without equivocation, Coke characterized the king's behavior as "a violation of the liberties of the subject," and recalled the saying that "whosoever violates laws does not hurt certain citizens, but goes about to overthrow the whole commonwealth." The king's unacceptable response was, to Coke's mind, "the greatest violation that ever was."[73] As Coke's repetitious iteration of the term suggests, in the late 1620s violation remained a powerful metaphor although it had long since become a rhetorical commonplace.

The connection between the subjects' rights debate and ravishment law was more than a matter of the former coopting the latter for use as a rhetorically potent metaphor.[74] In addition to the legislative measures designed to address threats to the collective property rights of English subjects from the encroachment of royal prerogative, there were also proposals for a number of new ravishment bills to protect individual men's property from rapists and seducers (and from the rebellious, licentious women who might abet them). For instance, a series of documents describing bills that were under consideration for introduction in the House of Commons during the first Jacobean Parliament survive from 1603–04. Along with proposed bills against purveyance, monopolies, corrupt enforcement of the penal laws and a bill seeking to protect landowners from claims that property they long had considered theirs was actually the possession of the Crown, there is a proposal for legislation against secret marriages without the consent of parents or guardians.[75] Thus, property owners were seeking protection both from the Crown and from their impressionable daughters' unscrupulous suitors.

Ravishment and royal prerogative were again linked in James's second Parliament. The boldly stated Petition of Grievance (1610) expressed dismay over James's appointments to the ecclesiastical commission and his attempts to broaden that court's jurisdiction. The Crown could then use its puppets on the commission to suppress opposition through seizure and execution of any subject the king might target. Potentially this was a threat striking the very heart of subjects' liberty: their "lives, lands, bodies, [and] goods."[76] If one pursues the reasoning of this petition to its conclusion, however, it becomes apparent that the immediate irritation motivating the Commons was neither so broad nor so grand as its rhetoric suggests. The present abuse cited against the ecclesiastical commission is that it encourages women to be disobedient to their husbands by ordering husbands to support their estranged spouses.[77]

In 1614, the House of Commons considered "an act to prevent the elopement and willful departure of wives from their husbands."[78]

According to this bill, wives who left their husbands "to live with the adulterers shall be disabled of their jointures."[79] This legislation, like most of the other bills introduced in 1614, fell by the wayside as M.P.s focused their energies on crafting a bill against taxes and impositions levied by the king without parliamentary approval. One member declared that "if the King may impose by his absolute power then no man [is] certain what he has, for it shall be subject to the King's pleasure. . . . Let us not leave our posterity in worse case than our ancestors have left us."[80] Thus, Parliament again turned its attention from lesser issues of property to the central property threat posed by the Crown.

The Changeling is evidence that the link between ravishment and rights was as much on the minds of playwrights of the period as it was of Jacobean M.P.s. While it would be difficult to count the number of works that presented sexual violation in direct connection with abusive rule (we need think only of the proliferation of Lucrece literature to see this point), there were a number of plays that directly engaged the discourse on subjects' rights. In retrospect, the most obvious of these plays may be Francis Beaumont and John Fletcher's *The Maid's Tragedy* (1610–11), which links sexual predation with royal usurpation of subject's rights. The play's king forces a nobleman, Amintor, to abandon his troth-plight wife in order to marry a woman the king has chosen for him. On his wedding night, Amintor finds that his bride refuses to consummate the marriage — *not* because she is frozen by conventional maiden fear, but because she is the king's mistress. The king requires the young man to acquiesce to an arrangement where his bride is never to be his own. Not only has the king "violated" Amintor's wife, he has violated the young man's right to marry a woman of his own choosing (idealized by the play as a woman he loves) and his right to pass his property to children of his own begetting. In essence, though unbeknownst to any but the principals, the king's arrangement amounts to a seizure of Amintor's estate: Amintor's family line will die out and his property will pass to the king's offspring. The play runs inevitably toward a tragic conclusion which includes the king's murder and the death of nearly every other major character. At its end, the heir to the throne offers this pat moral:

> May this a fair example be to me
> To rule with temper, for on lustful kings
> Unlooked-for sudden deaths from God are sent;
> But curs'd is he that is their instrument.
>
> (5.3.292–94)

The play does not go out of its way to be topical; to have done so might well have been impossible. This, after all, is a play that stages the murder of a king. To link that king overtly with King James would have been treasonous. Indeed, the play keeps its emphasis on the king's lustfulness, as the moral makes clear. It is the king's mistress who murders him, tying him to the bedposts, then stabbing him. The erotic content of this scene keeps the murder focused as a revenge for his lust rather than for his other violations.

A second play, *Appius and Virginia*, which was probably written during the second decade of James's reign, explores another aspect of ravishment's connection with subjects' property rights.[81] Although this play displaces its critique from kings to judges, it is still clearly a representation of abusive power. When the daughter of a prominent citizen refuses his advances, the villainous judge, Appius, uses his position to seize her from her father. Claiming that she is, in fact, a bondwoman, the judge is able to use a legal maneuver to nullify her father's claim to the young woman. This play does not romanticize love or familial relationships: the father sees the issue less in terms of his daughter's distress than in terms of his family honor and his family's property. Rather than lose ownership of her to the judge, the father kills her. The judge's ingenious legal proceeding has special significance. We have seen that in the parliamentary debates about the rights of subjects, the issue turned around the legal distinction of whether subjects' property was held "of right" or "at will." If "of right," then the subject owned his property. If "at will," then the king owned all property and granted use of it to tenants or villeins through a feudal relationship. The latter circumstance was clearly repugnant to English subjects for economic reasons, but the issue was about more than wealth. The issue extended beyond the property rights of English men to the status of their own persons. If they were merely "tenants at will," then they were not freemen, but bondservants, who by definition could own no property.[82] The play strikes at the emotional core of the national discourse of prerogative and rights when Webster's judge succeeds in alienating the father's property in his daughter by reclassifying her as a bondwoman.

While *The Changeling* is less overtly topical than *Appius and Virginia*, it is no less engaged with the issues of subjects' rights. Where *Appius and Virginia* and *The Maid's Tragedy* treat the abuse of power in scenarios easily seen as analogous to the abuses of prerogative charged against James I, *The Changeling*'s rape plot is clearly different. Where the other plays may be said to fear a threat from "above," this play sees a threat of violation from "below" and "within." The father, Vermandero, initially believes that he and his daughter have been slighted by her noble fiancé, which, if it were true, might be construed as another version of abuse from "above." However, the audience knows all along and the father eventually learns that it is the gentleman servant, DeFlores, who has joined with his daughter to dishonor the family. Vermandero's response reveals how surprising he finds such an assault from within and below: "an host of enemies entered my citadel / Could not amaze like this" (5.3.147).

When *The Changeling* came to the stage, the English people were confronting the serious prospect that their king intended to match the heir to the throne with the Spanish infanta. By the 1620s James I's reign appeared to have been an endless series of skirmishes between the Crown and its English subjects. Now it seemed that the king, whose attempts to encroach on subjects' rights had been more or less held in check through persistence and vigilance, might trump all of these efforts in a single blow.

With its proven reputation as an enemy to Protestantism and its history of attempts to seize England for territorial and religious conquest, Spain was the great "enemy without," which had been held at bay for 70 years. Here was the appalling prospect that the king might open the door to his citadel to admit Spanish, Papist invaders. The enemy "without" was about to become the enemy "within." The fate of English Protestants seemed likely to be entrusted to a Spanish Catholic princess who would mother the next heir to the throne. The dangers posed by women to their husbands' estates was, in 1621–22, not merely a threat to private domestic relations, but to the "domestic" estate of the nation.

Protestant polemicists were quick to combine invasion imagery with the rhetoric of violation in their responses to the Spanish match. In *Vox Populi; or, Newes from Spayne* (1620), Thomas Scott depicts King Philip as a would-be ravisher who imagines "so incircling Europe at one instant, and infolding it in our armes."[83] In an equally pointed manner, *An Experimental Discoverie of Spanish Practices* (1623) likens King James to a foolish captain who lets the enemy into the fortress: his dealings with the Spanish, a "manifest knowne enemy to the State," are marked by "carelessness and improvidence."[84] This confluence of imagery found its most direct expression on the stage in Middleton's daringly topical *A Game at Chess* (1624). The induction to that play brings Ignatius Loyola onto the stage to boast of Spain's intention to rape England. The action of the play itself repeatedly figures Spanish Catholic figures as seducers and ravishers. The audience and the white pawn are told that "the Black King's blood burns for thy prostitution . . . / He dies upon a pleurisy of luxury / If he deflower thee not" (4.4.64–68).

Although *The Changeling* seems devoid of any but the most oblique acknowledgments of the political resonances of its treatment of a Spanish bride's betrayal of her father, her fiancé and her husband, these concerns are what Zara Bruzzi and A. A. Bromham call a "central absence" in the play.[85] Rape, then, is both the literal and the repressed matter of this play. It is in relation to this super saturation of significance that the play's distinctly un-satisfying conclusion can be understood.

Middleton and Rowley give their play an improbably "happy" ending. What began as a nightmarish vision of the consequences of a woman's desire and of her inadequate defense of her honor, ends like a fairy tale. In this fictional world, the truth comes to light and justice holds the guilty parties to account. Death com-pensates death, and the innocent survivors can see that they will "joy again." The family reconstitutes itself as a male circle, no longer vulnerable to the vagaries of women. Alsemero reminds Vermandero that he has "yet a son's duty living" (5.3.216). Despite Beatrice-Joanna's betrayal, Vermandero accomplishes the alliances he sought to forge with the Piracquo brothers and with Alse-mero — and those bonds are more fast now that there is no further danger to be feared from her. These men, her survivors, frame Beatrice-Joanna's death as the necessary prerequisite to their for-mation of a more perfect family, an all-male family.

It might be noted that the surviving characters are also protected from that other threat to male rights, the monarch, by virtue of the fact that the play wholly represses this figure. *The Changeling* is one of the rare early modern tragedies with no ruler represented in the plot. Some critics have been intent on reading Vermandero as a figure for James I — and some of the connections they have drawn are suggestive, but I would argue that brief allusive moments aside, the overriding effect of this play derives from its refusal to include any royal figures in its dramatis personae.[86] (None even receives mention in the dialogue.) The idealized scene at the end depicts men conducting their own affairs, settling their own estates, exercising their rights as subjects in the absence of any interference from "above." If these characters are like kings, it is in the sense of having sovereign rights over their own property and inherit-ance. They are lords of their own property in the sense evoked by Sir Edward Coke when he wrote that "the house of every one is to him as his castle and fortress, as well for his defense against injury and violence as for his repose."[87] But the personal "sovereignty" of a man over his goods and chattel was a fortress under siege in Jacobean England, as Coke knew well from his years championing subjects' rights in Parliament and from his long tenure in offices appointed (and revoked) by the Crown — not to mention the knowledge he had gained through his experience as a husband and father.

Despite its valiant effort to invoke closure and wholeness, the play's idealized community of male subjects feels less like a castle than a house of cards able to stand only as long as the threats — from above and below and within — can be repressed. The barrenness of this resolution is readily apparent. The "happy" ending betrays its own artificiality, with its rhymed couplets and self-referential theatricality — and, of course, it doesn't feel happy at all. It offers a manifestly fictional resolution to problems that defy such simplistic treatment.

Only on stage could the fifth act be depended upon to supply a full confession and a complete recompense to the victims of a ravishment. Of course, the law also sought to supply such a recompense. Ample evidence of the failure of the legal establishment to redress the damage of rape is available in the history of Parliament's perpetual tightening of and tinkering with the statutes and in the continued wrangling of judicial authorities over the interpretation and application of those laws. For all of its efforts to define women and to proscribe their sexual behavior, the law found them to be changelings whose complicity eluded detection. Middleton and Rowley's play tries to manage what the law could not when it exposes the falseness of a woman for all to see, but it is ultimately no more successful than the law in allaying the fear that a woman might succeed in deceiving her family and friends. It was a fear fed rather than eased by stories like this one. This fear required, but could not be satisfied with, the bloodied bodies of women like Lucrece and Beatrice-Joanna. Its loathing of the vulnerability of the female body demanded scenes of retribution and blame like this one in *The Changeling*. But the self-condemning, willing death Beatrice-Joanna dies could only increase the anxiety of a culture that set women as the sentinels to guard familial honor.

FIVE

Arbella Stuart Seymour

"THIS UNADVISED YOUNG WOMAN . . .

SO WILFULLY BENT"

Yf your Majestie had vouchsafed to tell me your mynd and accepte that free will offeringe of my obedience I would not have offended your Majestie Of whose gratious goodnes I presume so much that, if itt weare as convenient in A worldlie respect as mallice may make itt seeme to seperate us whom God hath joyned, your Majestie would not doe evill that good might come thereof, nor make me that have the honour to be so neare your Majesty in bloud the first presedent that ever was, thoughe our Princes maie have lefte some as litle imitable for so good and gratious a King as your Majestie as David's dealinge with Uriah.

— Letter from Arbella Stuart Seymour to King James

When George Chapman published his *Homer Prince of Poets* in 1609, he addressed one of 14 presentation verses prefacing his volume to Arbella Stuart, whom Chapman described as "our English Athenia, Chaste Arbitress of virtue and learning."[1] Stuart was the king's cousin and his dependent. As a member of the royal family, she occupied a place of importance in James's court, but as a potential rival for his throne, James kept her on a pension small enough to limit her independence. The learning for which

Chapman praises her was the result of an education designed to prepare the young woman for the throne she might one day occupy. The chastity he praises was also due to her position: as a potential royal claimant, Stuart's marriage was a political tool exploited first by Queen Elizabeth and then by James, who found it more advantageous to consider matches for her than to arrange one. In 1610, when Stuart committed what amounted to treason by eloping with William Seymour, another potential royal claimant, she was arrested and imprisoned. Separated from her husband, held in close confinement and threatened with banishment to the north of England, Stuart was not only subject to her monarch's lasting displeasure, but also to the laughter of ungenerous contemporaries, who quipped about the "hot blood" that had spurred her to so risky a marriage.[2] No longer the arbitress of virtue and no longer in a position to bestow patronage, Stuart receives no mention in the second edition of Chapman's *Homer* published in 1611; thus, the poet expunged the politically awkward presence of a woman who had fallen into disgrace.

For most of her life Arbella Stuart fought to avoid political, social and familial erasure. To the end, she refused to play the self-abnegating role of a Beatrice-Joanna; neither to Elizabeth nor to James would she confess herself to be "that of your blood . . . taken from you / For your better health" (*The Changeling*, 5.3.149–50). Indeed, Stuart persistently reasserted the rights of blood and place of which both monarchs sought to deprive her. Stuart's literary remains, her letters, record her struggle against the royal relatives who despoiled her estate and sought to deprive her of the opportunity to marry and have children. Stuart was not a woman who could fit her society's pattern for feminine behavior. She had not been raised to be feminine in the usual early modern sense of that role: she had been raised to be a queen. This, of course, was the untenable paradox of her position: she was raised to exercise sovereignty, but remained a subject. Thus, while Arbella Stuart may seem to be so exceptional a case as to have little in common with ordinary women, her contemporaries viewed her in familiar gendered terms as the willful woman in conflict with seventeenth century English society. In the context of this study of the gendered discourses of subjects' rights and royal prerogative, Stuart is an interesting anomaly because of her paradoxical positioning as woman and property owner, princess and subject.

Stuart was the great-great-granddaughter of Henry VII, born in 1575 to Charles Stuart, the earl of Lennox, and Elizabeth Cavendish, daughter of the formidable Elizabeth Talbot, countess of Shrewsbury, by her second husband.[3] Lady Arbella's Tudor and Stuart heritage made her a rival to her cousin, James VI of Scotland, in his bid to succeed Elizabeth I on the English throne. According to the conventions of succession, Arbella stood below James in order of inheritance, but she had been born and raised on English soil, though her father held a Scottish title and owned Scottish as well as English estates. James's Scottish birth and foreign parentage might have been used to debar him from the English succession; thus, Stuart posed a credible threat to James even after he became king of England. In fact, both Elizabeth and James had reason to fear that with the right factional backing Stuart could have usurped the throne.

As the object of suspicion by both of the monarchs under whom she lived, Stuart's personal circumstances were particularly unfortunate. When her father died within a year of her birth, she should have inherited both his estates and his title, which had been granted to him outright and should have passed to his heir, irrespective of gender. The Scottish regent, however, seized the estates and refused to confer the title.[4] In 1578, when she was three, Stuart's situation worsened when her paternal grandmother died deeply in debt to the English Crown, which seized her jointure properties, the English Lennox estates, in payment of the debt.[5] What ensued was a squabble between the English and Scottish crowns in which Stuart's patrimony was wholly consumed. First, James demanded the English properties, and when Elizabeth replied that nothing remained after payment of debts and fees, James revoked the Lennox title and conferred it on his favorite, Esmé

Stuart. At that point the family jewels, which had been in Arbella's grandmother's possession at her death, were all that remained of the vast Lennox wealth. These jewels were entrusted to Margaret Stuart's personal secretary to keep for Arbella; instead, they ended up in the possession of the Scottish king (*Letters,* 16). It was with good reason, then, that Arbella Stuart felt she had been mistreated by both her royal cousins; her life's work was a long and ultimately futile effort to recover her estates and to produce an heir to perpetuate her line.

Although Stuart's maternal grandmother was granted wardship of the child when Elizabeth Cavendish died in 1582, the queen insisted on the exclusive right to negotiate for her marriage.[6] In acknowledgment of her position in the line of succession and in compensation for the loss of her inheritance, Elizabeth gave Stuart a token pension of £200, leaving the wealthy countess of Shrewsbury to shoulder the cost of educating, feeding, clothing and providing an appropriate entourage for a princess royal. The grandmother simultaneously instilled in Stuart a strong sense of entitlement to the title and property of which she had been deprived and a profound sense of the unjust burden her dependence placed on her extended family. Clearly the latter reinforced Stuart's sense of grievance for the loss of her inheritance and lent urgency to her ambition to marry well in order to repair her own fortunes and to repay her family's investment in her upbringing.

This twinned sense of entitlement and familial obligation runs throughout Stuart's letters, but is especially pronounced in those letters dating from two periods of crisis in her life: the first following a failed attempt to arrange her own marriage in 1602, the second following her elopement with William Seymour in 1610. In both instances, Stuart took great risks to take her life's course into her own hands; in both instances, she acted when she ceased to have faith in the efforts of her relatives and her monarch with regard to her marriage and her property. It is unsurprising, then, that in both instances Stuart's self-justifications are based on elaborations of her sense of injury and loss, her sense that she had no choice but to act in her own interest when no one else seemed mindful of her welfare or respectful of her rights.

Throughout her life, Stuart used the means at her disposal to maneuver for advantage with the monarchs who kept her in their thrall. When she did not have direct access to her monarch, as she did not in the two most critical junctures of her life, she turned to writing to court forgiveness, indulgence, approval, favor. While she did not enjoy success, her letters demonstrate a mastery of the conventions of courtly petitioning: Arbella possessed great facility with the modes of flattery, self-promotion, strategic misdirection and appeal. However, her letters also reveal a willingness to break convention, to replace the codes of courtiership with a rhetoric of abuse borrowed from parliamentary debates over property rights and from Protestant martyrological literature.

Carving for Herself

Stuart twice attempted to negotiate marriage with sons of the Seymour family, whose royal descent represented the next most credible claim to the throne after Stuart's own. Stuart's strategy in seeking this alliance drew inspiration from a precedent set in the previous generation when Edward Seymour, earl of Hertford consolidated two royal lines by marrying Catherine Grey against the queen's wishes early in Elizabeth's reign.[7] If that match was daring, what Stuart attempted in the last months of the queen's life was an audacious bid for succession. Though there is more disinformation than candid confession in the documents that survive from this affair, it seems that during Stuart's youth there had been cautious talk between the two families about the possibility of a match between Lady Arbella and one of the earl of Hertford's heirs, though both sides knew that if the queen learned of it, she would certainly oppose such an alliance in order to prevent a consolidation of the rival claims. Based on these speculative discussions (and perhaps on a more recent and more solid proposal she claimed had come from the earl himself), Stuart had reason to believe that the Seymours would be open to such a match if she communicated her willing readiness, so she sent a messenger during the 1602 Christmas holidays to open negotiations with the earl of Hertford.[8]

What followed was not well managed on at least one side: the messenger Stuart sent was a mere servant, and it seems that when he requested a private audience with the earl, Hertford became alarmed and refused to hear the man's message without others present. Once the subject was announced before witnesses, the earl had no choice but to renounce any participation and to turn the servant and his letter over to the Crown.[9] An alternative interpretation of events, one to which Stuart seemed to subscribe, suggests that the earl had set her up, leading her to commit herself to negotiation and then exposing her, presumably to damage her chances of succession and to promote his own family's place in the rivalry for Elizabeth's throne.[10] During her interrogation, Stuart offered a third scenario to explain what had transpired with the earl of Hertford: he had suggested the proposition, but she had no wish to involve herself in so disloyal a conspiracy, so she sent a messenger with whom the earl could not meet privately; thus, she had forced his exposure of his own plot and had done "even the best service that ever Lady did hir Souveraigne and Mistresse" (*Letters*, 131).

In phrases like this addressed to Sir Henry Brounker, the court investigator, and to her grandmother, Stuart represents her motives for taking such unprecedented action on her own behalf. She claims a most unconventional desire to "be my owne woman," and to "enter into somm great action to winne my selfe reputation, try hir Majesties love to me . . . try what my frends would do for me, and how I could imploy my frends and servants, and make strangers to me effect my desires without being beholden to them" (*Letters*, 168, 131). These desires for autonomy, authority and renown sound very much like aspirations to royal prerogative. In any case, they are fantasies of a kind of self-assertion generally denied early modern women. Stuart seems, however, to imagine herself in terms which transcend her gender. "I should have adjudged my selfe unworthy of life," she wrote to Queen Elizabeth by way of justification, "if I had degenerated from the most renowned stocke whearof it is my greatest honour to be a branch, so for truth and not ostentation sake I protest I have endeavoured to contribut my myte to the treasure of honour long heaped up by the most worthy" (*Letters*, 126). She conceives of herself not only as sole heir of an important family, but as its champion, a hero worthy of standing in the company of the most renowned. Certainly she views herself as the only one willing to take the action necessary to preserve that family line from oblivion: if she does not assert herself, no one else will act on her behalf.

At the age of 27, Arbella Stuart seems to have reached a point when the ambiguity of her situation was no longer tolerable. Her behavior at this juncture amounts to what Frank Whigham describes as a "seizure of the will," a term he uses to describe "certain moments of self-construction or identification": "I deploy this phrase as a programmatic pun, with multiple elements. I mean to point both to appropriation, the act of grasping, of taking, of violating, of seizing control, and to ecstasy, the thrill or spasm or fit of emotion, of transcendent feeling, that often accompanies the gesture in the plays of early modern England." The term touches not only Stuart's deliberate effort at self-fashioning, her attempt to seize control of her person, her estate and her social/political position, but also gets at the less voluntary aspects of her behavior, "the spasm or fit of emotion" that accompanies her efforts at self-determination.[11] What Whigham does not describe, but which seems clearly a part of Stuart's experience, is the uncontrolled, seizurelike reaction that accompanies her *failure* to grasp the social advancement she risked so much to achieve.[12] Contemporaries perceived her actions and subsequent words of explanation as erratic, impulsive, even mad. Her unaccountably misjudged embassage of marriage, her subsequent rash attempt to escape her grandmother's house with the help of an armed escort, and her fancifully bizarre written explanations of her motives suggest that the episode might be seen as a seizurelike spasm in the usually well-ordered existence of an intelligent woman who reached the limits of her tolerance for the uncertainties of her position.

That Stuart should have reached such a pass in the months between December 1602 and March 1603 is no wonder. Even in Derbyshire the tension and sense of anxiety that accompanied the last months of Elizabeth's reign must have been palpable. Clearly the extended Stuart/Talbot/Cavendish family (no doubt the Seymour family, as well) felt themselves to be at the epicenter of speculation during these liminal months when Elizabeth's continued refusal to settle the succession combined with her poorly concealed ill health to keep the nation on tenterhooks anticipating a moment that could not be postponed indefinitely. That Arbella Stuart, who stood to gain or lose most, could not bear to wait on fate or the machinations of others to determine her future, seems perfectly understandable. Even after the failure of her elopement and the foiling of her planned escape from Hardwick Hall, Stuart continued to fight for recognition from Elizabeth with the only weapon she had to wield: her pen. Thus, she wrote to Brounker in March, threatening to make her mistreatment publicly known:

> I can beare it as long as I thinck Good to convince them that impose it of hardnesse of hart, and shake it off when I thinck good to take my Christian liberty, which either shall be apparently denied me and the whole world made judge upon what cause, or colour, or how justly given or taken and by whom. or must be prevented by a reflux of hir Majesties favour to me in greater measure then I have hitherto found. which I do not doubt of if it would please hir Majesty to take that course, which hir Royall inclination would take with those of hir owne bloud, if it weare not to my great astonishment diverted from them, to those 2. counsellers [Cecil's and Stanhope's] kinred. they favour theyr kinred against hir Majesties, hir Majesty defendeth not hir innocent, unstained bloud against theyr mallice.
> (*Letters*, 159)

Several simultaneous frustrations run together here, welling up in a single tirade. In what follows, Stuart asserts the unfairness of her treatment when the earl of Hertford has not been investigated for his role in the marriage scheme. She points out that she has received no thanks for her willingness to delay pressing her suit against the king of Scotland. She demands a reconsideration of the reasonableness of the match she attempted to make for herself and reminds her readers why she might feel that the time had long passed for waiting patiently on others to act on her behalf: "have I stained hir Majesties bloud with unworthy or doubtfull marriage? have I claimed my land these .ii. years though I had hir Majesties promise I should have it?" (*Letters*, 160).

In the letters to Sir Henry Brounker, Stuart articulates a strong sense of grievance for wrongs of omission and commission on the part of Queen Elizabeth, who, to Stuart's mind, seems to have deemed her "unworthy of [her] Princely care and love" (*Letters*, 124). Most bitter is her sense of the ease with which Elizabeth could have helped her regain her patrimony, had the queen chosen to wield "the great seale of England by which I might have recovered a little land, which a most noble great great uncle of mine gave his neece, when he bestowed hir of a noble exiled gentleman" (*Letters*, 151). In another document, Stuart bluntly accuses Elizabeth of neglecting her rights and abetting James in his theft of her property: "it was the Kinge of Scottes whome her highnes favoured so much as for fere of offendinge him she [Arbella] mighte not be allowed the libertye of the lawe to sew, nor to sende into Scotlande to clayme an Earledome or the [lands] or recompense for them" (*Letters*, 141).[13] "It seems her Majesty careth not for knowing any thing concerning me," Stuart asserts, "but to breake my just desires" (*Letters*, 160).

Key to Stuart's grievance is her assumption that she possesses rights that have been transgressed, rights that the law would necessarily uphold were she allowed the "liberty of the law to sue" those who have wrongfully seized what was hers. Stuart believes she has been denied a legal right inherent in English citizenship, the right to own property and to seek redress through the courts if that property is stolen, damaged or wrongfully seized.

Stuart's sense of grievance extended beyond the loss of her property, however. She was also frustrated by the strictures placed on her personal freedom. At 27 years of age, she was still expected to sleep in the same bedchamber with her grandmother, not allowed to walk outdoors unattended, not allowed to choose her own companions, tutors or pastimes. In a letter to Brounker, she complains that Queen Elizabeth has denied her "that liberty . . . which many Infants have" and has bound Stuart "within straiter bonds then the duties of a most dutifull subject and servant" (*Letters*, 135–36).

Stuart employs the language of subjects' rights to articulate her sense that she has been extraordinarily abused:

> When it shall please hir Majesty to afford me those ordinary rightes which other subjectes cannot be debarred of justly, I shall endevour to receive them as thanckfully now as if they had binne in due time offred, though the best part of my time be past whearin (my hart being not so seasoned with sorrow as it is) comfort should have binne wellcomm and better bestowed because my hart was not then so over-worne with . . . unkindnesse and sorrow. (*Letters*, 158)

Stuart was, in fact, being debarred of liberties that other subjects (without a royal pedigree) could expect. Her sense of the injustice of this situation never waned and she tirelessly articulates the rights she believes are her due as a subject. After her elopement in 1610, she returns to this same line of argument when she appeals to the chief justices of the realm to intercede for her on the grounds of habeas corpus when James insists that she should be exiled to Durham without trial or due process.[14] In both cases, her appeals to the rhetoric and theory of subjects' rights failed to win Stuart the liberty she desired, and her contemporaries seem to have been largely unimpressed with her claims to deserve such rights.

In fact, Stuart was not an ordinary subject. She might be debarred such rights on the grounds that she was a woman and might be expected to concede to the needs, wishes and property of male subjects. These were the unstated grounds on which her lawsuits to regain her property were denied despite their merit: the property and title had been conferred elsewhere, to others whose proprietary claims were no better, but nonetheless weighed more than Stuart's. She was also debarred of "ordinary rights" on the grounds that she was a royal princess, who was subject to similar limitations to those Shakespeare identifies as constraints on Hamlet,

> His greatness weighed, his will is not his own,
> For he himself is subject to his birth.
> He may not, as unvalued persons do,
> Carve for himself, for on his choice depends
> The sanity and health of this whole state;
> And therefore must his choice be circumscribed
> Unto the voice and yielding of that body
> Whereof he is the head.
>
> (1.3.17–24)

Like Hamlet, Stuart was subject to her birth. Raised to be a queen, she remained a subject. Educated and trained to rule, she was asked to put her life on hold in case the queen should need to use her. Bred to aspire to a throne, she was expected to sacrifice any personal ambitions she might have to the will of a ruler who seemed only to require her absence and self-effacement. In effect, Elizabeth expected Stuart to be so entirely chaste, silent and obedient as to be a nonentity.

Shakespeare's insight into Hamlet's untenable position suggests that he and his audience were sympathetic to the personal tragedy suffered by those great enough to stand in the line of succession, but far enough from the throne to be subject to the extraordinary obligations of royalty without its benefits. Hamlet's inability to carve for himself in marriage costs him his relationship with Ophelia and, arguably, costs Ophelia her life. Sympathy for Hamlet's plight does not, however, suggest that Shakespeare disputes the need for one in Hamlet's position to subject his will to the demands of the state. Neither did Arbella Stuart's contemporaries dispute the actions of the two monarchs who held her virtually captive to their wishes, though there were sympathetic assessments of her unhappy plight. The Venetian ambassador, for instance, offered an apt reading of Stuart's situation in 1607:

> The nearest relative the King has is Madame Arbella. . . . She is twenty-eight years old; not very beautiful, but highly accomplished, for besides being of most refined manners she speaks fluently Latin, Italian, French, Spanish, reads Greek and Hebrew, and is always studying. She is not very rich, for the late Queen was jealous of everyone, and especially of those who had a claim on the throne, and so she took from her the larger part of her income, and the poor lady cannot live as magnificently nor reward her attendants as liberally as she would. The King professes to love her and to hold her in high esteem. She is allowed to come to Court, and the King promised, when he ascended the throne, that he would restore her property, but he has not done so yet, saying she shall have it all and more on her marriage, but so far the husband has not been found, and she remains without a mate and without estate.[15]

However much her contemporaries may have regretted the cynical dealings of the monarchs who promised marriage and dowry for Stuart without any intention of honoring those promises, their pity did not extend to affirmation when Stuart tried to carve for herself. Her struggles for self-determination were condemned as willful, first and most forcefully by her exasperated grandmother, who wrote to the queen requesting that "this unadvised young woman," so "wilfully bent," be moved to some other guardian's custody so she might "learn to be more considerate."[16] She was expected to know that "[her] will was not [her] own," doubly so because she was a woman and should have deferred to those with authority over her. Of course, when she did not acquiesce to this expectation, she was condemned not only as a rebel against the royal will, but as a woman who had indulged in what the culture held to be the most predictable of women's sins: willful pursuit of sexual fulfillment.

The ideology governing the role of women within the institution of aristocratic marriage demanded that those women subjugate themselves to the dynastic good of the family. Frank Whigham formulates the ideological imperative for early modern aristocratic women in this way:

> A woman's fullest achievement of legitimate self-hood, by this logic, ought to be the full self-willed subordination or gift of herself and her capacities, her agency, to this *telos* of familial reiteration, seen as extending back and forward in time in a maximally coercive way (in obligations to ancestors and descendants alike). . . . Her family's attempted management of her sexual life is precisely a *denial*, of her *will*.[17]

This is precisely the ideology to which Stuart committed herself in her pursuit of a marriage that would restore her family line and produce heirs to extend that line into perpetuity. The early modern "noble woman's ideal devotion to dynastic ends is seen as, supposedly felt as collective self-abnegating, an abnegation proposed from without, summoned from within."[18] Ironically, Arbella Stuart's devotion to dynastic ends summoned not self-abnegation from her, but a supreme act of self-assertion. Of course, what was at play in Stuart's case was a conflict of dynastic loyalty: Queen Elizabeth demanded that Stuart submit herself to the good of a larger dynastic unit which would subordinate her line; she refused. In her defense, Stuart constructs herself as a chaste woman, obedient to the ideological demands of her culture that she marry an appropriate husband; then she attempts to insinuate herself into Elizabeth's dynastic plan:

> If it please your Majesty to examine the whole course of my life your Majesty shall finde Gods grace hath mightily wrought in me poore silly infant and wretch that how soever others have taken wiser wayes, I have had as great care and have with more and in truth meere innocence preserved your Majesties most royall linage from any blott as any whosoever. and as I should have adjudged my selfe unworthy of life if I had degenerated from the most renowned stocke whearof it is my greatest honour to be a branch, so for truth and not ostentation sake I protest I have endeavoured to contribut my myte to the treasure of honour long heaped up by the most worthy and with out comparison of all Europe most worthy Princes

> whose great measure of worthinesse, renowne, and felicity your
> Majesty with out comparison exceedes, and that you long and ever
> may do so is and at all times hath binne my dayly and fervent prayer
> to the Almighty and ever shall be to my lifes ende. (*Letters*, 126)

Stuart makes a complex rhetorical maneuver here, praising
Elizabeth's lineage and inserting herself into it, while casting her
own marital endeavor not as a challenge to Elizabeth (whose long
life is Stuart's fervent prayer), but her contribution to the preservation and promotion of that royal stock whereof she and Elizabeth
are mutually descended. Stuart's strategy is to finesse the demand
for self-abnegation into an opportunity for self-promotion.[19]

The language and strategies of this particular letter are most
interesting. It is the second letter Stuart wrote to Queen Elizabeth
following the failed elopement, and it marks a shift in Stuart's
attitude about the affair and its aftermath. Her first letter to the
queen was a very brief acknowledgment of her deed and appeal for
forgiveness, which emphasizes Stuart's humility and reliance on
the queen's grace: "I humbly prostrate my selfe at your Majesties
feete craving pardon for what is passed" (*Letters*, 122). The second
letter is far more daring. It attempts to "spin" what had passed,
implying that the self-abnegation demanded of Stuart by the queen
has nearly produced a much more extreme form of self-erasure,
moving her to "willingly yeld to griefe as I have donne heartofore
and that very lately to almost my utter overthrow both of body
and minde" (*Letters*, 124). In this formulation, the required sur-
render of will becomes tantamount to a demand for Stuart's suicide.

However desperate she may wish to sound, the self constructed
by this letter is a willful, active self full of resentment for the harsh
treatment Stuart has received at her grandmother's hands. She can
not resist gloating about the "very many things" she has done
"without hir [the grandmother's] knowledge." Meanwhile, the
letter suppresses Stuart's actual offense (the attempted marriage)
and asserts that her only desire and the end of all her recent behavior
has been to win a recall to Elizabeth's presence: "I have not dealt
rashly in so important a matter but [have taken] advise of all the

frends I have how I might attaine your Majesties presence." Stuart writes herself into such a sense of self-righteousness that she attempts to coerce the queen into aiding her, first by playing to sympathy, then by means of a veiled threat of rebellion, albeit one attributed to others and ostensibly rejected by Stuart:

> And as I have forborne till now to impart thus much unto your most Excellent Majesty lest it might diminish your Majesties good opinion of me and increase [my grandmother's] severity so I have all the other wayes I could devise not by way of complaint but mone disclosed my most distressed state to your Majesty of whom onely I have expected and with silent and stolne teares implored and expected reliefe. and have utterly neglected or rejected all other meanes how well liked of others soever.

The breathless quality of this complaint and its extremes of emotion (pathos to anger, boastfulness to pious deference) lend the letter the quality of a tantrum of frustrated self-assertion by a woman who felt herself opposed on every side (*Letters*, 124–26).

"I can rule my tongue": Stuart's Rhetorical Craft

Indeed, as her captivity dragged on, Stuart envisioned herself as one embroiled in a contest of wills and had the temerity to challenge those who sought to impose on her. In one of her letters to Brounker, Stuart chides him, saying

> Sir Henry I cannot but wonder at your light beleefe when great ones tell you incredible tales, and incredulity when you have the word and oth of a Puritan [her description of herself], for a certeine truth. if your commission be not to examine such great ones as I presume to accuse in matters of truth, alas what a dwarfe am I thought at Court. . . . Truly I can tell, and I will tell you truly, even as I told you; even as I would have it; for if I do not or rather have not since I saw you broken somm of your good frends of theyr will I am greatly deceived. (*Letters*, 149)

Here she reveals that she sees her predicament as a power struggle in which certain courtiers have tried to manipulate her and have assumed they could control her circumstances. Clearly she has been frustrated by the lack of credibility accorded her accusations. In response, she tries to correct the balance of power by pulling rank: she presumes that she should be taken seriously as a straightforward matter of course because of who she is. It stings her that her stature is not what she expected. "Alas, what a dwarfe am I thought at Court" asserts that they have misjudged her and mistaken the degree of deference due to her. It records her embarrassment at being so undervalued, but there is also an implied threat in this passage. She intimates that courtiers would do well to hedge their bets and not burn their bridges with a woman who might one day be their queen — however unlikely that might seem at the moment. Stuart constructs herself here as a woman who prefers to be seen as willful, even in the face of all the damning gendered associations of that judgment, rather than have others perceive her as pathetic in her impotence to enforce her will.

Ironically, this effort to control how others will perceive her is precisely the point at which Stuart fails in this letter. The pride and self-assertion of the passage disregard the realities of her situation as she writes: she rails at those who hold her captive. Throughout the passage she seems careless of her tone and the effect it will undoubtedly have on her intended reader. In fact, the passage seems ill conceived from start to finish, beginning as it does with arrogance and proceeding through an erratic tirade of boastful posturing. The phrasing bears the marks of hasty, impulsive composition. Particularly when she reaches the business about truth and telling, she seems to be borne on by the sound rather than the sense of her language: "Truly I can tell, and I will tell you truly, even as I told you; even as I would have it." In this and other passages, Stuart seems to give vent to an overwhelming urge to scold and excoriate her captors and interrogators. When he added it to his files, Robert Cecil noted at the top of this letter: "by this Time you see I think she hath some strange vapours to her braine."[20] The posturing and the rage and the impossibility of either having any effect on the Court officials who were intercepting and filing these epistles made Stuart seem quite mad in Cecil's opinion.

To recent critics, however, Stuart has seemed far from mad. Though Stuart had failed to render the world or her life as she "would have it," she continued in the aftermath of that failure to assert herself in the only medium she had at her command: the letters she knew were destined for Cecil's file. Barbara Kiefer Lewalski argues that in her letters to Sir Henry Brounker, Stuart practices "a rhetoric of disguise" and "concealment."[21] Once she realizes the seriousness with which the court has imposed surveillance on her, she converts her letter writing into a tool to assert her will against those charged with handling her: if she is to pay such a price, she will monopolize their time and attention until they tire of attending to her. "I can rule my tongue howsoever I be overruled otherwise," she boasts to Brounker, who will have to scrutinize, process, and investigate each assertion in the letters Stuart sends him, letters densely and playfully packed with classical and biblical allusions and riddled with word games, vague affirmations and veiled accusations (*Letters*, 150).

Perhaps Stuart's best known device in the letters of 1602–3 is her creation of a "secret lover" to help defer the danger she had incurred with the Seymour affair. At its most straightforward level, she intends her revelation that she has a secret paramour to corroborate her assertion that she never had any serious plan to marry Hertford's grandson; at a deeper level it seems that she is replacing one love entanglement in which she played a scandalously forward role with another in which she proves herself a more acceptably feminine beloved. Steen has pointed out that Stuart's description of the lover is wholly conventional: his one fault is jealousy; he trusts her "with more then I would have him even the secretest thought of his heart"; he has "never requested any thing but was more for my good and honour than his owne" (*Letters*, 33–34, 130, 129). For her part, Stuart casts herself in equally conventional terms: she has tested his love by pretending to spurn him, but she loves him "too well (even since I could love) to hide any thought, word, or deede of mine from him unless it weare to aw him a little" (*Letters*, 130). However, at the same time that she is creating this chivalrous, protective beloved who has coached her in all that she has done so far (another dodge from responsibility for her own assertiveness), she also fills the letter with pride and relish for her own bravado and cleverness.

> I am more desirous hir Majesty should understand every part and parcell of the devise, every Acctor, every action, every word and sillable . . . then your Ladyship is, because I know more then your Ladyship doth or shall (because it is most for your Ladyships honour and good it should be so) till hir Majesty be acquainted and fully satisfied that I have donne nothing foolishly, rashly, or falsely, or unworthy of my selfe (*Letters*, 131).

If she intended this letter to baffle her tormentors, it may well have had that effect. Certainly it gave Sir Henry Brounker something else to be concerned with than the abortive Seymour affair. In fact, it drew him back to Hardwick Hall for another bout of interrogation for which he came equipped with a detailed set of questions based on Stuart's suggestive phrases in the letter.

In the interview that followed, Stuart proves herself a master of irony and rhetorical manipulation. In fact, she runs rings around the man sent to pin her down on the fine points of her many assertions and insinuations. The results of this session survive in a document in which Brounker recorded Stuart's answers to each of his queries. Whatever Stuart actually imagined the phrases about a beloved to mean when she wrote her letter, under Brounker's questioning she transforms each phrase into an opportunity to cast insinuations upon the earl of Hertford, to hurl insults against her grandmother, and to expound on the deceitful, ignoble practices of King James. This last ploy was too subtle by far for poor Sir Henry Brounker, who came away with the impression that Stuart suffered from some overwrought virgin's fantasy about a love affair with her married, homosexual cousin, the king of Scotland. However, it seems more likely that Stuart was having her way with Sir Henry, offering deliberately fey answers to the questions in order to frustrate her questioner and perhaps to underscore in her own mind the bitter grievance she actually harbored against her cousin. For instance, when asked "who it was that she had loved so well ever sohens she could love as she coulde never hyde any thoughte from him unles it were to awe him a little and to make him werye of his Jelousye," Stuart answered, the King of Scots (*Letters*, 142). "The King of Scots" was also her answer when asked "who he was that was so famous for his secrecye, and had more vertewes then any subjecte or forreyne prince" (a set of attributes which are only partly complimentary) and again when asked "what this gentleman was with whome she hath delte so unkyndly, shreudly, and proudly, whome she hath tryed as goulde in the fire and hath alredye accepted him and confirmed it, and will never repent nor deny him whatsoever befall her" (ibid.). These answers explain how Sir Henry came to his conclusion that she suffered from romantic delusions, but the possibility seems never to have crossed Brounker's mind that Stuart was enjoying a sardonic laugh at this cousin who was so far from being her beloved or she his that he had bestowed her property on a homosexual favorite and left her penniless. She would never repent or deny him, indeed!

When Stuart declares that the King of Scots is he "whose councell she hath kepte thes many yeres and will do whilst she live if the disclosing therof will be hurtfull to him or his and . . . [he] whose name she longeth to discover to her majestie, and who dareth not see her nor sende but by stelth," it is possible, as Lewalski suggests, that she names James primarily because his is the one name that can be named without harming the named man.[22] However, it is also likely that Stuart speaks ironically here and indeed relishes naming James not as one whose reputation she longs to protect, but as one whose name she thrills to engage in such a risible context. A small revenge, perhaps, but a pointed one.

Several of the statements beg for an ironic reading because they are so clearly indictments of James's self-serving mistreatment of Arbella. "Beinge demaunded what the noble gentleman was that taught her to pretende one arrande, and to deliver another with a safe conscience, to speake riddles to her friends and to try the truth of offered love she sayde that she lerned these lessons out of the Bible by the King of Scotlandes example who proveth all things by Scripture," and is, therefore, by Stuart's measure both a savvy politician and a great hypocrite. Brounker reports that "Being demanded who the gentleman is that woulde forsake her rather then offende her majestie never so little she constantly affermeth that it is the Kinge of Scottes" (*Letters*, 142, 144). The vehemence of her affirmation on this point measures her sense that James has ruined her in his pursuit of Elizabeth's crown. It is poignant that Stuart's bureaucratic interrogators could not appreciate the sarcasm of her answers, but chose instead to think her pathetic, vain and deeply delusional.

Remembrance of Persecutions Past: Stuart's Rhetoric of Will Violated

In response to the condescension and contempt with which those in power treat her, Stuart seems to hunker down into a defensive posture from which she refuses to give direct answers about her actions or her motives. She treats her writing not as an opportunity to represent the "truth" about herself, but as a means of protecting herself by offering so many competing versions of herself and her actions that her handlers will not be able to sort them all out.[23] Putting on and casting aside these various guises, she appears alternately suicidal and resolved, fretful and patient; she is the heroic lover protecting a beloved from discovery, then the smart, sardonic misanthrope with special malice for her cousin, James VI, but she is also a Puritan moralist and a Protestant martyr by turns. Stuart's facility at representing herself in diverse ways is an inspired form of resistance.

Lewalski compares the "madness" of Stuart's manic, imaginative, muddled prose to the antic masks adopted by certain of Shakespeare's characters: "As with Hamlet or Poor Tom, apparent madness offers a cover for otherwise unspeakable defiance of authority."[24] On the contrary, defiance is the one *explicit* component in most of Stuart's responses to authority during this period. "Have I conceiled this matter thus long from frends, servants, kinsfolkes, all the world to reveale it now . . . [I have been] so injuriously intreated that they who have either occasioned executed furthered or suffred such vigour [rigor?] to light on me and so long to continue may thanck them selves if they have lost all the interest of voluntary obedience they had in me" (*Letters*, 160–61). Another apt dramatic analog for Stuart's behavior is the one she invokes when she models herself after Kyd's "mad" Hieronymo, the much abused good man at the heart of *The Spanish Tragedy*. "For myself," Stuart declares, "I will rather spitt my tongue in my Examiner or Torturers face, then it shall be said to the dishonour of her Majesties abused authority and bloud an extorted truth came out of my lippes" (*Letters*, 161). Although a direct criticism of the queen is indeed unspeakable here, Stuart's defiance could not be more explicit.

The predominant strategy in Stuart's writing during the crisis of 1602–3 is an effort to transpose the register of "will" rhetoric in order to reframe herself not as the willful woman whose reputation has been impugned, not as the politic plotter who has been publicly exposed in her effort to court a suitor and a dynasty, not as the desirous, ambitious and (worst of all) foolish woman who sought marriage with a family that spurned her and turned her over to the authorities, but instead as a brave victim of others' impositions of will:

> [I] might be condemned by all the world for a credulous foole if I could beleeve any thing but what I finde and that is unkindenesse and rigour, or a faintharted foole which weare farre worse if I should yeild to power which hath already spent it selfe against my unyeilding hart, which will rather burst then utter

one thought by constraint of any and the greater the threatnings and the more violently it is assaulted the greater will the Victory be. (*Letters*, 165)

Her only foolishness would be to believe the false promises of her captors or to give in to their violence. Her only admission of willfulness is her proud refusal to bow to those powerful imposers who would "breake my just desires" (*Letters*, 160).

Again and again she deploys the rhetoric of abuse, drawing models from her wide reading (from the classics to the Bible to martyrology and polemic) to represent herself as the patient sufferer who cannot be daunted by her oppressors. Sometimes she emphasizes her vulnerability, as when she writes "Let me live like an Owle in the wildernesse since my Pallas will not protect me with hir shield" (*Letters*, 162). At other moments she underscores her fortitude and resolution in the face of violence and treachery:

> Unregarded menaces I assure you shall neither daunt me, nor the worst that any mortall creature can do unto an other shall not extort a thought out of my mouth, fairer meanes might have laden you home with that treasure you camme for without acquittance but now I have no more to say to you but I will say no more, thinck, say, or do what you list.
> Hardwick this Friday.   *Damnata iam luce ferox*
> > > > Arbella Stuart. (*Letters*, 155)

In this instance, Stuart reinforces her representation of herself as the prisoner who cannot be made to confess with a quotation from Lucan's *Pharsalia*: "Damnata iam luce ferox" [furious by daylight having been condemned] describes the resolve with which a band of warriors fought, though they knew their position was hopeless.[25] Lucan reports that after fighting heroically for two days, this doomed band committed suicide rather than accept dishonorable defeat. Stuart's use of the phrase ends a letter in which she reports how dismal and disrespectful her treatment has been at her grandmother's hands. In her choice of allusion, she represents herself as a besieged captive aware of the mortal threat posed by her enemies and heroically ready to withstand their violence. She manipulates this scenario to shame her captors into better treatment of her, freighting her complaint not only with an unflattering representation of their behavior, but also with an implied threat that she might kill herself rather than continue living in such circumstances.

In a similar vein, she taunts Brounker, vowing that "seeke and examine and torture whom you list," he will never learn the "concealed truth" she refuses to divulge (*Letters*, 169). This reference to torture and interrogation is one of several phrases in her letters which suggest that Stuart was reading Foxe's *Acts and Monuments* during her months of captivity, particularly the sections describing the arrests and ill treatment of Anne Askew, Jane Grey and Princess Elizabeth. For instance, "seek and examine and torture whom you list," seems to echo a moment near the beginning of Foxe's account of Elizabeth's imprisonment in the Tower, where he hints that extraordinary efforts were made to find or manufacture evidence to implicate the princess in the Wyatt uprising: "It would make a pitiful and a strange story, here by the way to touch and recite what examinations and rackings of poor men there were to find out that knife that should cut her throat."[26] Again, when Stuart asks, "Will you not use me as well as Traitours are used who am not guilty of thought word or deede which rightly interpreted can be the least offensive to hir Majesty and can be racked to no greater than a sinne of silence?" she not only reiterates Foxe's general theme that Princess Elizabeth was treated more harshly by the Tower authorities than convicted traitors would have been, she also echoes a phrase he uses repeatedly to assert Elizabeth's innocence of any offense against Mary either by "thought, worde, or dede."[27] I will concede that the formulation "thought, word or deed" was a common one and its appearance in both texts might be the result merely of similar circumstance; however, Stuart's statement leads her not only to echo Foxe's account of Elizabeth's unjust detainment, but also to recall Anne Askew's torture, the key element of which was her refusal to answer her interrogators even when racked. Askew reports that "they did put me on the rack, because I confessed no ladies or Gentlewomen to be of my opinion, and thereon they kept me a long time. And because I lay still and did not cry, my Lord Chancellor and Master Rich, took pains to rack me with their own hands, till I was nigh dead."[28] Stuart follows her boast that she can only be racked to "a sin of silence" with a description of her patience in suffering, which she promises to maintain with an Askewlike stillness and silence: "But remember if I endure these greevous wounds without striving or speaking it is because I have recommended my selfe to the Lord of Hostes whose Angelles have lifted my soule from my afflicted body higher then they are able to reach that exceede hir Majesties commission and torture the condemned to exile with expectation."[29] Likely, she has Askew in mind again when she pledges not to cooperate despite "all the commandements and threatnings and wrongs and torments all the Counsell, Rackmasters and all the ministers of hir Majesties indignation, can poure on me" (*Letters*, 172). Her conflation of councillors and "Rackmasters" evokes that shocking moment of Askew's account in which the two Privy Councillors take it upon them to tighten the rack "with their own hands."[30]

Such reading could not help but feed the melancholy apprehensions Stuart suffered during these weeks of uncertainty. Undoubtedly it shaped her sense of her own position and offered her models for representing herself. In her long letter to Brounker written on Ash Wednesday, 9 March, which she cites as the liturgical anniversary of the earl of Essex's execution, Stuart seems close to a nervous breakdown. She fears the sinister machinations of powerful courtiers and the strain makes her appeal for her fate to be made certain:

> For the passion of God lett me comm to my triall in this my prison instantly. . . . Thearfore lay the Axe to the roote of the tree in time, and let me loose my head which for lesse cause and upon no ground but my frends faults her Majesty hath threatned to take as I told

you, whilest nobody will hinder it, and I shall joyfully and thanckfully receive as God receive my soule. (*Letters*, 163)

This sense that her death has been designed by others and would be opposed by none takes shape in a further passage in which she again echoes the rhetoric of violation familiar from Protestant polemic:

> my Lord of Herford will lend his helping hand and the .2. Counsellors for his sake or what other privat or publick respect so ever makes them deale thus sinisterly with me who would presume to have and take the upper hand of the best of them but for hir Majesties knowne pleasure of derogating from my due many wayes, to write their bloudy pleasure in hir Majesties name. (Ibid.)

"Their bloody pleasure" resonates powerfully with echoes of Bale and Foxe, and though such phrases appear in so many of their texts it is impossible to say that Stuart is remembering it from any one, a particularly noteworthy instance of this sort of blood-thirst imagery occurs in the account of Princess Elizabeth's imprisonment in *Acts and Monuments*, where Foxe asserts that there was an inordinate "gaping among my Lords of the Clergy, to see the day wherein they might wash their goodly white rochets in her innocent blood."[31] Of course, if Stuart is modeling herself after Elizabeth in her famous past sufferings, she is also placing Elizabeth in the tyrant's role once played by Queen Mary, and in this particular passage Stuart is not the least subtle in doing so. Her reiteration of the word "pleasure," which links the queen's disparagement of Stuart with her bloodthirsty minions' eagerness to strike off Stuart's head, gives a sardonic twist to an old polemical strategy in which a writer blames the monarch while appearing to blame only the evil councillors. While technically observing this rule of decorum, Stuart leaves no doubt that she intends to accuse Elizabeth of encouraging the ill treatment she has received.

Although Stuart did not face torture during her interrogations, and thus may seem to exaggerate her apprehensions and her suffering in these letters, her danger was real. She was familiar not only with the precedents of Protestant martyrology, which seem remote from her circumstances, but also with the much more apt precedents in Tudor history, which led her to fear that she, like the earl of Essex (her friend), Mary Queen of Scots (her aunt), and Jane Grey (the earl of Hertford's sister-in-law), might face execution for treason in attempting to maneuver toward possession/inheritance of the throne. She is not hysterical in her fears. However, she announces her fears strategically in order to cast herself as victim and impotent nonthreat in these letters where she chooses rather to sound paranoid, distracted or mentally unhinged than to sound in any way competent of the ends of which she is suspected.

Puritan Poses

In certain letters that followed her abortive attempt at marriage in 1602–3 and again in the aftermath of her marriage to William Seymour in 1610, Stuart dons the guise and rhetoric of a "Puritan." The label requires some clarification as it is one she applies to herself and by which she means several things at once. Interestingly, it is a label she used throughout her adult life, in joking, self-deprecating ways when she wished to distance herself from her peers. Usually Stuart adopts the role with a tongue-in-cheek playfulness as she does in the letter to her favorite uncle, Gilbert Talbot, earl of Shrewsbury, whom she thanks for sending her instructions about her behavior at court, which she promises to follow "as farre forth as they are Puritanlike. . . . I trust you shall see in me the good effects of your prayer, to your great glory for reforming my untowardly resolutions and mirth (for great shall the melancholy be that shall appeare in my letters to you)" (*Letters*, 180). In this and other letters, she laughs at her own Puritan sensibilities, presenting herself as the odd moral soul at a court given to frivolity and immorality. Here she pretends that the role of Puritan will require her to be sober and melancholy when she is naturally mirthful, but she is, in fact, entirely mirthful in assuming the pose of youthful deference to a wise, strict uncle, who, her sly characterization suggests, was more mirthful than Puritanlike himself. In her letters to her aunt and uncle Talbot, Stuart constructs herself as a detached, bemused and reluctant participant in the activities of life at court. The self-deprecation with which she mediates her "Puritan" pose allowed her to lighten her censure of her contemporaries by acknowledging how obnoxious and self-righteous such criticism could appear. Used to describe others, the term "Puritan" was a derogatory epithet; when Stuart applies it to herself it is both a concession of her awkward outsider's status at court and a claim of moral high ground.

It is to claim moral superiority that Stuart uses the term and the pose in her letters to Sir Henry Brounker, whom she chastises for disbelieving her when she has given him "the word and oth of a Puritan" to support her claims (*Letters*, 149). The phrase appears in the letter in which she goes on to note "what a dwarfe am I thought at Court." In this instance, her use of "Puritan" to describe herself suggests an awareness of the condescension and contempt with which courtiers viewed the conventicling godly folk of the middling sort, who were so easily dismissed with the sneering label of "Puritan," and implies some kindred feeling with that scorned group.

What degree of identification Stuart felt with actual Puritans is unclear in this or other instances where she invokes the term; however, she clearly uses the term to position herself in opposition to those who condemn and harass her. It is a posture she adopts to signify both her veracity and her sense of persecution:

> sure I am it is neither for hir Majesties honour, nor your creditt I should be thus dealt with all. Your will be donne. I recommend my innocent cause . . . to your consideration, and Gods holy protection, to whom onely be ascribed all honour praise and glory for now and for ever Amen. for all men are liers. Theare is no trust in man whose breath is in his nosthrilles. And the day will comm when they thatt judge shall be judged, and he that now keepeth theyr counsell and

seemeth to winke at iniquity, and suffer it to prosper like the greene
bay tree, will roote out deeprooted pride and mallice, and make his
righteousnesse shine like the noone day. *I was half a Puritan before*
and Mr. Holford who is one whatsoever I be, hath shorthned your
letter and will shorten the time more then you all. . . . Your poor
friend Arbella Stuart. (*Letters*, 157; emphasis added)

Her technique of aligning herself with known Puritans (here, Mr.
Holford) has the effect of borrowing their devotion and credibility
and of flanking herself with a group of supporters at a time when
she felt very much alone and exposed. Stuart repeats this gesture
in another letter by summoning up the ghost of Mr. Starkey, a
clergyman who had been questioned regarding his involvement in
Stuart's schemes, who had ended his captivity by committing
suicide. "You saw what a despair the greatness of my enemies and
the hard measure I have received (and my fortune is not yet bettered)
drave innocent discreet learned and godly Mr. Starkey into," she
writes Brounker. "Will you be guilty of yet more bloud?" (*Letters*,
162). In this case, the gesture emphasizes her isolation, while
appropriating the rhetorical and moral power of martyrology for
her cause.

Stuart's facility in wielding the Bible as a weapon, as she does
in her pseudoliturgical riff to Brounker quoted above, is a key
element in her arsenal of Puritan rhetoric. She begins by mocking
him, saying, "Your will be done," a formula that insinuates Brounker's ungodliness. She proceeds by paraphrasing texts from Isaiah,
Psalms and the gospels of Matthew and Luke in her attack on men
"whose breath is in [their] nosthrilles," whose iniquities "prosper
like the greene bay tree," and who can expect their comeupance
on the day "when they thatt judge shall be judged."[32] With this
biblical outpouring, Stuart advances the fatalistic tone of the letters
in which she indicates her readiness to die; here, death is not only
welcome, it promises the righting of wrongs that this life has heaped
upon her. For while human judges may fail her and may abuse
their authority to hurt her, the divine judge will bring her persecutors to justice. That justice is inescapable however distant it

may seem; the man whose breath is in his nostrils has only a tenuous grasp on life, which is as frail and fleeting as the man's trustworthiness.

Bale's favorite motto, drawn from Luke, chapter 12, is a similarly effective verse about the certainty of judgment, which he wielded against the hypocrites and persecutors of his day: "there is nothing hid, that shall not be dyscouered, neither secreate, that shall not be knowne. Therefore, what so euer they haue done in darknesse, the same shall be known in the light."[33] This biblical material is the mainstay of Protestant polemic; it is a weapon Stuart uses infrequently, but to great effect.

David's Dealing with Uriah

During the period of her imprisonment following her marriage, Stuart (now Arbella Stuart Seymour) wrote a series of letters to King James in hopes that he would set aside his anger and release her to live with her husband. These letters are much more controlled in their tone and rhetoric than the angry letters she wrote in 1602–3. For these letters, there survive multiple drafts indicating the care with which Stuart crafted and honed her presentation of her case. Her situation was more serious than it had been in the earlier instance when she had failed to achieve her marital aim. James, from whom Stuart once claimed to have learned her use of the Bible as a rhetorical tool, is reported to have said of her marriage that she "had etne of the forbidne trie," an indication that he saw her action as an unforgivable sin.[34] Indeed, months passed and James did not relent.

In December 1610, after six months in custody, Stuart despaired of courtesy and returned to the rhetoric of abuse that had been her tool in the earlier crisis. Now she wrote a blunt letter to James complaining of his harshness and his perversity in taking offense at her marriage when he should have arranged a marriage for her years earlier. She elaborates on James's neglect and his arbitrariness in objecting to her action, saying it was impossible for me to ymagine itt could be offensive unto your Majestie havinge fewe Dayes before geven me your Royall consent to bestowe my selfe on anie Subject of your Majesties (which likewise your Majestie had done longe since) Besides never having ben either prohibited any or spoken to for anie in this land by your Majestie these 7 yeares that I have lived in your Majesties house I could not conceive that your Majestie regarded my Mariage att all.[35]

At the heart of this letter is Stuart's assertion that although James may look to English history and find precedents for monarchical meddling in the marriages of other, subsidiary royals, there is no precedent for separating those "whom God hath joined." (She conveniently forgets the obvious precedent of Queen Elizabeth's annulment of Catherine Grey's marriage to Edward Seymour, her husband's grandfather, whose actions were, in fact, a model for her own.) She asserts that such precedents as James may find in previous cases are templates for tyranny rather than models appropriate for "so good and gracious a king as your Majesty." Then, at the zenith of her argument, Stuart likens such tyrannical interference to "Davids dealinge with Uriah."[36]

Her suggestion that James's actions are like "David's dealing with Uriah" characterizes his behavior as a kind of sexual abuse. It is an interesting and awkward allusion in that Stuart seems to liken herself to Uriah, the murdered husband of Bathsheba. Certainly she is not suggesting that James has intervened in her marriage because he has lascivious designs on her (as David did because he desired Bathsheba); instead, she plays freely with the gendering of her allusion. Whether she means to suggest to James that she suspects he has lascivious designs on her young husband is anyone's guess; however, as a subject whose spouse has been taken away, Stuart's situation is reminiscent of Uriah's, and insofar as she may have feared that her imprisonment would lead to her death, the analogy reminds James how deeply David regretted his selfish and sinful treatment of Uriah.[37]

It is worth noting — for the light it sheds both on James's reasons for recalcitrance in Stuart's case and for the context in which it puts her sense of herself as having been abused — that in 1610 James was wrangling with his Parliament, assuring them that even if he were a tyrant, they could have no recourse against his exercise of royal prerogative. It is the same year in which the M. P. William Hakewill warned that the king believed that "his pleasure cannot be bounded by law" and John Chamberlain wrote to Ralph Winwood that in view of James's usurpations of subjects' rights, "we are not like to leave our successors that freedom we received from our forefathers, nor make account of anything we have longer than they list that govern."[38]

Stuart's case, though extraordinary, is exemplary of the gendered rhetoric of abuse with which both the monarch and his subjects habitually describe their outrage at the misconduct of the other: from James's point of view, Stuart is just such a woman as ravishment law declared should be punished for acting on her own caprice to the detriment of her family's reputation and estate. James, in fact, maintained that Stuart's elopement was an "Indignitie" and an attack on his honor.[39] James claimed the right to intervene in Stuart's marriage on the grounds that she was his ward (legally, she was not) and that she had no right to marry "without acquainting his Majesty; which had been a neglect even to a mean parent."[40] James's assumption of parental rights in this case is of a piece with the patriarchal posture he attempted to construct for himself in relation to the nation as a whole, and his reaction to Stuart's insubordination was similar to his furious reaction to the recalcitrance of his parliaments. The Venetian ambassador reports that James declared that he would not tolerate Stuart's attempt to "rule her life after her own caprice" and Lady Jane Drummond wrote to Stuart to inform her that, in response to her petition for mercy, James had likened her action to Eve's eating the apple (*Letters*, 71, 292).

For her part, Stuart maintains that James is the willful, capricious one, who has deprived her of the ordinary rights due any subject, rights to property and progeny, and that in doing this James has ravished her possessions in the same way that David ravished life and wife from Uriah the Hittite. Stuart's use of this cross-gendered allusion illustrates her perception of herself as an aristocratic subject entitled to act on her own behalf in the protection and advancement of her estate, a self-perception that defies the limitations of gender usually imposed by seventeenth century English culture. Stuart uses this device to signify her sense of victimization as a subject whose property, spouse and prospect for progeny have all been ravished from her by her monarch. Steen has written of Stuart that although she

> may never have fully reconciled what Mary Beth Rose describes in women's autobiographies as "the felt conflict between self-effacement and self-assertion, between private and public life, and between individual personality and social role," cultural expectations did not altogether color what Stuart thought of herself. In the unrevised drafts and marginal notes of the court letters, even of these tumultuous years, we hear a voice that did not speak as humble woman or subject. Stuart chafed at the role. Her creation of a deferential self [in those letters where she does so] was an attempt to exploit the patriarchal models and use the language of flattery and obedience as an indirect means of achieving power when overt power was unavailable. (*Letters*, 81)

As we have seen, her creation of a deferential self was an imperfect achievement. Arbella Stuart Seymour viewed herself first as an aristocrat and a royal, and only secondarily as a woman and a subject; yet, during the years when she writes from imprisonment, she writes as one who has been forced to recognize her powerlessness as a subject in the thrall of an oppressive regime. Her use of the rhetoric of abuse, drawn from the religious and political discourses in play about her, throws into sharper relief the gender dynamics operative in the figurative language of violation that was applied to problems of property and subjecthood by so many of her contemporaries.

Six

"This sight doth shake all that is man within me"
Sexual Violation and the Rhetoric of Dissent in *The Cardinal*

How much are kings abused by those they take
To royal grace! Whom, when they cherish most
By nice indulgence, they do often arm
Against themselves; from whence this maxim springs,
None have more need of perspectives than kings.
— *The Cardinal*, 5.3.293–97

Tyrannizing Lordly Prelates

In 1637, William Laud, archbishop of Canterbury, brought suit in the Court of Star Chamber against John Bastwick, Henry Burton and William Prynne as seditious libelers for pamphlets in which they attacked state institutions, particularly the Church of England and the bishops who served it. Prynne, who was the best known of the three, a lawyer and sometime member of Parliament, was accused of having (pseudonymously) authored a tract, *Newes from Ipswich* (1636), which appealed to the king to curb his bishops:

223

> O our most pious King *Charles*, as thou hast in two severall Declarations, protested before God, to all thy loving Subjects, that thou wilt never give way to the licensing or authorizing of any thing whereby any innovation in the least degree, may creep into our Church; nor never connive at any *Backsliding into Popery.* . . . So now behold these desperate innovations, purgations, and Romish practices of thy Prelates.

In this tract, Prynne sees the Protestant religion, its faithful ministers and its believers suffering in "the jawes of these devouring Wolves, [the] tyrannizing Lordly Prelates." He seeks to move the king to side with the people against the bishops, who, he says, are "trampling all thy lawes and subjects liberties like Cob-webs, thy subjects like Dogges and dirt under their tyrannicall feet." Prynne essentially throws down the gauntlet and dares the king to take it up, declaring that Charles must

> now or never shew thy selfe (as wee all hope, beleeve and pray thou wilt) a Prince more worthy of this glorious Title, then any of thy Royall progenitors, by rooting all Popery, Superstition, Idolatry, Errours, Innovations, out of this Church and Kingdome, by restoring the preaching, the Preachers of Gods Word, and purity of his Worship, and taking vengeance on these perfidious Prelates.[1]

Newes from Ipswich is an attack on Matthew Wren, bishop of Norwich, and, by extension, an attack on Laud, who had used his archbishopric and his sway with the other bishops to institute changes in the Book of Common Prayer, to reposition the Communion table to the extreme east end of the church, and to reintroduce altar railings and crucifixes.[2] Prynne's tract objects on theological grounds to these changes that he feared were part of a Counter Reformation intended by Laud to reunite the English with the church of Rome.

Prynne understands, however, that there are constitutional issues at stake as well. Charles I was the titular head of the Anglican Church and in that capacity had made several proclamations declaring his commitment to maintain (though not to extend) the Protestant character of the church and of the nation. Without Charles's approval, Laud could not have proceeded with his "innovations." The tract uses its pretense of addressing the king to point out that Charles had made a practice of saying one thing in his public proclamations while tacitly endorsing Laud's program by not opposing its implementation. Prynne's assertion that the civil liberties of the nation's subjects were being infringed by the activities of the "tyrannical" bishops, then, was tantamount to calling Charles himself a tyrant.

Prynne's cause was a political movement seeking further Protestant reform of the Anglican Church. Termed "Puritans" by their detractors, these activists, who preferred to refer to themselves as the godly party, understood that there was a direct correlation between Laud's autocratic government of the church and Charles's insistence on ruling the nation without calling a Parliament, the people's representative voice in the government.[3] The increasingly literate and persuasive nature of the propaganda published by the godly party convinced Laud to make examples of Prynne and the other two men. All three were well educated and well connected (Burton was a clergyman and Bastwick a physician), and it was clearly Laud's hope that he could disparage them, robbing their movement of credibility and cutting into its support.

At the end of a highly publicized trial in which the three defendants were not allowed to speak in their own defense, Prynne, Bastwick and Burton were convicted and sentenced to serve life terms in prison, to pay fines of £5,000 each, and to have their ears clipped in the public pillory. Prynne had already suffered ear-clipping and imprisonment for libeling the queen with his antitheatrical tract *Histriomastix* (1632). For this new offense he was sentenced to lose the remainder of his ears and to be branded on each cheek with the initials S. L., designating his crime of seditious libel. The disfigurements of the three pamphleteers were carried out as a public spectacle before the miscreants were sent to remote prisons to serve out their sentences.

Laud miscalculated badly. He had counted on the social position of the defendants to command the attention of the press and to frighten the godly party into submissiveness by demonstrating his willingness to punish not only the minor figures, but the ringleaders as well. Indeed, the affair riveted the attention of the capital, but the effect was not at all what Laud had hoped. The particular punishments inflicted on the men were shocking, not because dismemberment and branding were unusual, but because they were penalties of a harshness usually reserved for an inferior class of offenders.[4] With this sentence, the state seems to have violated the delicate balance of public executions: the spectacle it created raised pity rather than revulsion in the public, and instead of shaming the criminals, it made heroes of them.[5] While Laud's political allies reported the episode with glee, he neither converted his opponents to his point of view, nor silenced their criticism for long. In fact, it seems that more than any other single incident in the years before the outbreak of the English civil wars, the disfigurement of Prynne, Burton and Bastwick solidified resistance to the government of Charles I. The three writers became martyrs for English Protestantism.

The godly party saw this affair as a confirmation of the claims the three men had made in their writings. Bastwick's observation in *The Letany of John Bastwick* (1637) that, "It seeme they would faine be at their old occupation againe, a butchering of vs at smithfield; and that is the thing indeed which their feirce and bloud-thirsty ambition aspires to," seemed prophetic in the aftermath of his punishment.[6] Prynne's use of a graphic language of physical abuse to depict the "wounds" inflicted by the "trampling," "devouring" prelates was justified by his treatment in the pillory, where the figurative wounds he had described in print were reproduced and literalized on his face.

The horror of this spectacle entered the national consciousness and colored the political rhetoric of the critical half-decade before fighting broke out between the forces of the Parliament and the king. In 1640, Captain Audley Mervin evoked its memory as an illustration of the government's contempt for the legal rights of the English people when he urged the Irish Parliament to "surveigh the liberties of the Subjects, every prison spues out illegall attachments and commitments, every pillory is dyed with the forced blood of the Subjects, and hath eares, though *not* to heare, yet to witnesse this complaint." Mervin deliberately echoes the biblical injunction that all with ears should hear, to call attention to pillories where ears have been used not for hearing, but as witnesses to abuse. Later in the same tract Mervin compares Job's suffering at Satan's hands to the mutilation suffered by English subjects under sentence of ecclesiastical justice: "when he proceeds to infringe Iobs liberty, [Satan] doth not pillory him, nor cut off his ears, nor bore him through the tongue; he onely spots him with some ulcers; here Sathan staines, when these persons by their trayterous combinations, envie the very bloud that runs unspilt in our veines."[7] William Smith, M. P. for Winchelsea, used the image as a hook to demonstrate the interrelatedness of religious and civil oppression:

> Honour and Riches have been set up for gods, in competition with [God], Idolatry and Superstition have bin introduced, even into his House, the Church, and He expulsed . . . and those who would not tremble thus to dishonour God, would not scruple to doe it to their Parents, or injure their Neighbors, eyther by murther of themselves; or names; or by Adultery, *Davids great Crimes*: they have not onely rob'd God of his Honour, but men of their Estates, and of part of themselves, Members and Eares have bin set to sale, even to the deforming of that Creature, whom God had honoured with his owne Image, that they might colour this their wickednesse . . . and all this proceeded out of an inordinate desire of that which was their Neighbors.[8]

In these speeches, Prynne, Burton and Bastwick's wounds become the wounds of the populace, inflicted on them by the archbishop, the courts and (as Smith reminds us through his allusion to David) the king.

By 1640 the nation, stressed by a severe depression, became polarized over the twin issues of civil and ecclesiastical reform.[9]

This deadlock was broken when economic necessity forced Charles to end his 11 years of "personal rule" and call a parliament. In November, the Long Parliament assembled at Westminster to address the grievances of the nation. When on 5 July 1641 Parliament abolished the Court of Star Chamber, it was striking out at the institution that had martyred Bastwick, Burton and Prynne, an institution that had long been a symbol of the arbitrary powers of the king's prerogative and the archbishop's will. By abolishing the Star Chamber, the act also removed the instrument of press censorship, effectively neutralizing the government's control over what was printed in the nation. This new freedom of the press was celebrated on the title page of a tract published in London in 1643, which claimed to reveal "One Argument More Against the Cavaliers . . . Printed in the Yeare When Men Think What They List and Speake and Write What They Think."

With the loosening of controls on the press, London was flooded with pamphlets alleging and analyzing the abuses of monarchy, the tyranny of bishops and the many infringements of the rights of England's subjects.[10] In addition to the partisan sermons and speeches of politicians like Mervin and Smith, the presses were opened to the writers of tracts and treatises expressing any opinion that would sell copy. Cheaply printed scurrilous attacks on the archbishop reignited popular outrage against him. *Archy's Dream*, a pamphlet ostensibly written by the king's jester who had been "exiled the Court by Canterburies malice," opens with a jest about a nobleman who had sons "he knew not well what to doe with; he would gladly make S[c]hollers of them, but that he feared the Arch-Bishop would cut off their eares." *A New Play Called Canterburie His Change of Diot*, a dialogue not intended to be acted, opens with a scene in which the "Bishop of Canterbury" sits at table with a Doctor of Physicke, a Lawyer and a Divine and is not pleased with the fine meal they offer him. Instead, he demands "Carbonadoed cheek," and when they cannot satisfy him, he calls in a troop of armed bishops who seize the three hosts. The archbishop cuts off their ears, declaring that they will make a fine

"little dish for rarity." "This I doe," he says, "to make you examples, / That others may be more carefull to please my palate."
Laud had indeed made an example of Prynne, Bastwick and Burton,
an example that mobilized the nation to dissent.[11]

The Cardinal and Partisan Politics

In the winter of 1641, the King's Men produced James Shirley's
play about a weak king manipulated by his favorite, an ambitious
and dangerous prelate. As the chief playwright for the company,
Shirley's plays were the featured productions at each end of the
Blackfriars season: one in the winter, another in the spring.[12] That
theatrical season saw the tension between Charles and Parliament
escalate. *The Cardinal* was the next to last play of Shirley's to be
produced before the theaters were closed by order of Parliament.
Licensed on 25 November, it played during the tumultuous month
of December when conflict and fear reached a peak in the City.
First, there was open unrest among citizens: shopkeepers and
apprentices neglected their businesses to muster in the streets and
about Westminster demanding the ouster of the bishops from the
House of Lords. Londoners were maintaining a state of armed
readiness against an expected attempt by the king's cavaliers to
suppress political opposition.[13] Like accelerant poured onto a
smoldering fire, London's presses were full of daily reports of Irish
Catholic rebellion, raising fears that English Catholics, too, might
rise to slaughter their Protestant neighbors — and that such a
massacre might be encouraged by church and Crown, whose
political purposes it would serve. By January 1642, the king felt it
necessary to leave Westminster for his safety, and in August Charles
declared open war at Nottingham.[14] In the midst of the civil
upheavals of 1641–42, *The Cardinal* played to audiences in a
metropolis preoccupied with the very issues of monarchy, religion
and civil rights that are the play's central concern.

Shirley was a royalist and possibly a Catholic.[15] The fact that he
wrote for the theater in itself marked him as an enemy of the

reformist aims of the godly party. However, rather than being an obviously royalist vehicle, *The Cardinal* is a play that seems ambivalent about the king and his policies. Oddly enough, its criticism of meddling monarchy and clerical coercion echoes the grievances expressed by the godly in their tracts, reminding us that in the early 1640s, Charles I faced a crisis of support even among those who eventually supported him in his war against the Parliament.[16] Party lines were not as clearly drawn as they came to be later in the decade and they never cut clearly along class lines. Despite the fact that the theater played to an elitist audience in the 1630s and 1640s and despite the antagonism of the godly party to theatergoing, neither the audience at theaters nor the playwrights who entertained them can be assumed to have been in the king's pocket.[17]

The play presents the story of a young widow, the Duchess Rosaura, who has fallen in love with, and promised to marry, the Count D'Alvarez. Before the play begins, however, the king has interposed in her plans and insisted that she marry Columbo, nephew to the powerful cardinal. When we see the duchess she is still contemplating what she will do in the face of this imposed match. Although she has initially acquiesced, she decides that she cannot break her vows to Alvarez. She writes a deceptive letter to Columbo, asking him to renounce his claim to her, which he does, believing that it is a coy test of his love. When Columbo returns from war, he finds that the duchess has married Alvarez with the king's blessing. Enraged, he interrupts their wedding feast and murders the bridegroom. The king sentences Columbo to death, but in the interval between the third and fourth acts, Columbo is released for reasons that baffle not only the audience, but the courtiers on stage. The duchess then conspires with Hernando (a soldier with private reasons to hate both Columbo and the cardinal) to revenge Alvarez's death with Columbo's murder. Hernando accomplishes the murder while, to conceal her part in it, the duchess feigns madness. The cardinal, who nonetheless suspects her, convinces the king to appoint him guardian for the (apparently) incapacitated duchess. The cardinal attempts to rape the duchess and is prevented by Hernando. Though foiled in this first objective, the cardinal succeeds in poisoning her before dying himself. Only then does the king take charge, marveling at the villainy of his favorite and resolving that kings ought to be more aware of what is happening in their courts.

For Shirley, as for his audience, the play was part of the public discourse on present events in the capital. Dramatists routinely used plots centering on sexual coercion and violation as mechanisms for commentary on political power. This convention did not operate merely at a subconscious level, but was an acknowledged technique understood by audiences. Ben Jonson, for instance, complained in his introduction to *Volpone* that the habit of looking for the political relevance of plots was so popular that it got a great many dramatists into trouble:

> Application is grown a trade with many, and there are [those] that profess to have a key for the deciphering of everything; but let wise and noble persons take heed how they be too credulous, or give leave to these invading interpreters to be overfamiliar with their fames, who cunningly, and often, utter their own virulent malice under other men's simplest meanings.[18]

Jonson's contention is that malicious persons were reading sedition into innocent plays. His "poor playwright" tone reveals Jonson's sensitivity and defensiveness in this matter: he had himself been in trouble on more than one occasion for plots that were none too innocent.[19]

The most interesting aspect of Jonson's remark is the witness it offers to the existence of a taste for "deciphering" political meanings from apparently apolitical plots. Lois Potter, in *Secret Rites and Secret Writings*, maintains that during the Interregnum, royalist writers used romance literature as a medium for encoding subversive political commentary. She documents a tradition among English readers of looking for coded meanings in such texts, citing as an early example the 1628 English language edition of Barclay's

Argenis, which included a key to its hidden meanings. Potter also points out that William Dugard's 1655 edition of *Arcadia* made the case that Sidney had intentionally constructed his text as a decipherable allegory, "shadowing moral and politick results under the plain and easie emblems of Lovers."[20] In 1656, William D'Avenant made clear in his dedication of *The Siege of Rhodes* to Edward Hyde, earl of Clarendon, that he intended his readers to perceive a correspondence between the fictional siege of Rhodes and the persecution of the royalist party in the 1650s:

> I have brought *Solyman* [emperor of the Turks] to be arraign'd at your Tribunal, where you are Censor of his civility & magnificence. Dramatick Poetry meets with the same persecutions now, from such who esteem themselves the most refin'd and civil, as it ever did from the Barbarous. And yet whilst those vertuous Enemies deny *heroique Plays* to the Gentry, they entertain the People with a Seditious *Farce* of their own counterfeit Gravity. . . . My Lord, it proceeds from the same mind not to be pleas'd with Princes on the Stage, and not to affect them in the Throne; for those are ever most inclin'd to break the Mirrour who are unwilling to see the Images of such as have just authority over their guilt.[21]

D'Avenant's audience was to find Solyman's Turkish heathens reminiscent of the "civil," "vertuous" and "seditious" parliamentarians who had executed the king and closed the theaters.

Shirley's audience, then, had a marked predisposition to mine texts for their topical allusions. *The Cardinal* rewards this taste with coy references to "the short-haired men" and to the king's "prerogative." It is not, however, an easily decoded royalist allegory of the kind D'Avenant later produced in *The Siege of Rhodes. The Cardinal*'s focus on the victimization of the duchess turns the critical edge of the play back on the king and his counselors. Indeed, had any of the godly party set aside their aversion to the stage long enough to attend a performance of *The Cardinal*, they would surely have been amused and pleased to have witnessed their best arguments against episcopacy and monarchy coming from the mouths and embodied in the actions of Shirley's characters.

In the most general terms, the play might be understood as a sympathetic observer's warning against the wrongheaded policies that were leading Charles toward a war that would tear the nation apart.[22] But its sympathy is strained in places, and the emphasis is heavily on the king's wrongheadedness. Shirley audaciously assigns lines to "the King" which acknowledge that his use of his prerogative has infringed on the rights of his subjects. In the middle of the play, the king admits to the duchess that it "did exceed the office of a king / To exercise dominion over hearts, / That owe to the prerogative of heaven / Their choice" (3.2.185–88). Finally, the king closes the play with a further admission of his limitations:

> How much are kings abused by those they take
> To royal grace! Whom, when they cherish most
> By nice indulgence, they do often arm
> Against themselves; from whence this maxim springs,
> *None have more need of perspectives than kings.*
>
> (5.3.293–97)

Shirley has created a "king" who confesses precisely those things that Charles refused to concede: that his policies have been short-sighted and that he has allowed the rights of his subjects to be abused.

The Cardinal and the Duchess: Violating the Body Politic

The Cardinal's sympathetic portrait of the duchess, whose sexual autonomy is restricted and then assaulted, stages a critique of Archbishop Laud in terms very similar to those employed by the godly party. These tracts often describe the church as a woman sexually imperiled by powerful representatives of the Anglican hierarchy. For instance, in a speech to the House of Commons, published in 1641, Viscount Faulkland insisted that "some Bishops and their adherents . . . have defiled our Church."[23] William Prynne used characteristically colorful language to paint the same picture in an attack on the Anglican cleric John Cosin (1628): "Go on therefore, you Christian Heroes, and valiant worthies of the Lord, to vindicate the cause, and Doctrines of our Church, against those *Cozening*, treacherous and rebellious Sons (if Sons) of hers, who have betrayed her with a kisse and *wounded her with one hand, whiles they seemingly imbrace her with the other.*"[24] In a similar vein, a tract explaining *The Principal duty of Parliament Men* (1641) uses an Old Testament analogy to illustrate the necessity of Parliament's "punishing those publicke offenses, which either have been scandalous, and perillous unto the Church, or pernicious and noxious unto the Commonwealth, as the children of *Israel* joyned themselves together, as one man, to revenge upon the Benjamites, the wickednesse committed by them, unto the Levites wife."[25] These passages reveal dismay as well as disgust in their presentation of the abuses committed by Anglican churchmen. The sexual imagery is not only a strategy here, not merely a rhetorical tool, it is also an expression of how deeply threatened and how intimately wounded the writers feel. The church in these images has been raped (by her own sons, in the case of Prynne's attack on Cosin), and the readers are called to feel that assault as a personal affront, to internalize the insult. It is true, however, that both of these illustrations allow their readers a comfortably male position with which to identify. The church is female, but the reformists are called to be like the men of Israel and to revenge her injury.

Other tracts omit the revenger role (though possibly it is still implied), leaving the reader to identify himself with the victimized church, the violated woman.[26] Archbishop Laud frequently appears as the ravisher in such tracts: "he brought innovations into the Church, making her of a pure Virgin a very Strumpet." In another pamphlet, Laud is "the Orcke of Canterbury, that great Monster, [who kept away] the Church of England from Christ her spouse, and . . . polluted her with Popery." It is not just the church, but the nation as a whole and each citizen individually, whom Laud assaults in *The Times Dissected*, which concludes that his corruption of Charles led directly to "the rapine and spoile of subjects" (9).[27]

The gender-crossing required of male readers of these images is reminiscent of the gender blurring in the imagery we have seen employed by Captain Audley Mervin when he told Parliament that "every pillory is dyed with the forced blood of the Subjects," where "forced blood" is evocative of rape even though his allusion is clearly to the punishment of three men (Burton, Bastwick and Prynne).[28] The writers of these complaints construct an audience of male readers who feel emasculated by the powerful figures governing the nation: emasculated, feminized, then raped.

Indeed, the rape imagery of the tracts is joined with another cluster of images depicting the castration of England's subjects. In *Newes from Ipswich*, Prynne appealed to the king against "these perfidious Prelates, who have thus gelded thy Fast-booke . . . [and] openly abused thy onely Sister; and her Children."[29] Taking Prynne's lead, and with his punishment specifically in mind, a number of writers likened the experience of living under Charles and Laud to dismemberment. The author of *A Rent in the Lawne Sleeves; or, Episcopacy Eclypsed*, creates a Laud-like bishop who explains to a Jesuit his methods of enforcing conformity: "For all those whom favour nor promotion could not perswade; although against their consciences, to admit our ceremonies, which were as so many introductions, to the confirmation of the Catholique Religion in this land, wee constrain'd some by whipping and scourging, others by dismembering and strict imprisonment." William Smith (whom I quote at greater length above) bemoaned those who "have not onely rob'd God of his Honour, but men of their Estates, and of part of themselves, *Members and* Eares."[30]

Reinforcing all this figurative talk of violation and dismemberment were a series of prosecutions and a corresponding explosion of tracts detailing real sexual misconduct on the part of Anglican clerics. Among them, John Gwin, vicar of Cople, was charged with numerous adulteries and an attempted rape.[31] *The Petition and Articles Exhibited in Parliament Against Dr. Fuller, Deane of Ely, and Vicar of St. Giles Cripplegate with the Petition Exhibited in Parliament Against Timothy Hutton, Curate of the*

Said Parish, by the Parishioners of St. Giles contains similar charges.[32] By listing the official titles and offices of the two clergymen, this pamphlet emphasizes the height from which they are being toppled and illustrates the gulf of antagonism between the clerics and their "humble" parishioners. Another case that received particular attention was the trial of John Atherton, the Irish bishop of Waterford and Lysmore, who was executed for sodomizing another cleric. The popular press took great glee in "outing" the secret sexual sinners among the Anglican clergy.[33]

The pamphlets use their sexually violent imagery to appeal to their readers at two levels. These metaphors and examples of violation blacken the Anglican Church and the state that supports it, making it seem that no reasonable, right-thinking Christian could consider aligning with any cause but that of the godly party. At the same time, these tracts are calculated to raise alarm, to play on fears that cast reason aside and draw London's reading public into a posture of defense against the abuses of Laud and Charles and the cavaliers of his army: all of them agents of authoritarian rule and anti-Christian conspiracy. The language and images of sexual violence infuse these texts with an intimate menace, striking where the reader/victim feels most exposed, reducing men to womanly vulnerability.

This same sort of mechanism is at work in Shirley's play which requires its audience to identify with a woman's plight and to override the gender boundaries that separate her experience from that of the men in the audience. The lords, who stand about the court during each act, provide the model for the audience's consideration of her as they comment on the king's actions ("This is the age of wonders," "Wondrous mischiefs," 4.1.1), the cardinal's intrigues ("He wants no plot," 2.3.12), and the duchess's misfortunes ("that most oppressèd lady," 5.1.10). As the king and cardinal subject the duchess to their political maneuverings, these two lords lead the audience to see her as a figure for the oppression of all subjects in the realm under the unjust rule of this weak king and his self-aggrandizing favorite.

The violence in *The Cardinal* does not confirm the powerful masculinity of its audience; rather, it works on their insecurities, fears and sense of emasculation at the hands of a corrupt monarchy and church. In the pamphlet literature, this unsettling effect was not only a response to the social pressures under which the London population struggled, it was also a strategy of the pamphleteers to galvanize this unrest into a political movement. We have no information to illuminate the playwright's and theater company's political intentions, nor do we have evidence of the effect of Shirley's play on its audience, which is unfortunate, because theater offered resources to manipulate its audience's emotions that the print medium lacked. Certainly the play takes advantage of the stage to give flesh to the fearfulness of its villains and the vulnerability of its victim in ways that may have made it quite effective politically.

The play stages a series of escalating confrontations between the duchess and the cardinal. In the first of them, she is a formidable adversary, railing at him for his "crimes" and telling him to his face what others grumble behind his back but dare not say directly. The duchess paints his arrogant trespasses in precisely the language of the tracts attacking Laud:

> What giants would your pride and surfeit seem!
> How gross your avarice, eating up whole families!
> How vast are your corruptions and abuse
> Of the king's ear! At which you hang a pendant,
> Not to adorn, but ulcerate.
>
> (2.3.143–47)

She leaves him almost speechless in the face of her attack. Amidst the rush of her accusing words, he can only manage to ask, "Will you now take breath?" and to warn, "I'll have you chid into a blush for this." In addition to charging him with corrupting the king, the duchess examines the cardinal's abuse of his clerical office, urging him,

> Leave, leave, my lord, these usurpations,
> And be what you were meant, a man to cure,
> Not let in agues to religion;
> Look on the church's wounds.
>
> (2.3.152–55)

She extends her play on the idea of the cardinal as a "curate" who does not cure, but wounds his charge when she proceeds to accuse him of violating the church:

> 'tis your
> Ambition and scarlet sins that rob
> Her altar of the glory, and leave wounds
> Upon her brow; which fetches grief and paleness
> Into her cheeks; making her troubled bosom
> Pant with her groans, and shroud her holy blushes
> Within your reverend purples.
>
> (2.3.157–63)

The passage is reminiscent of Prynne's attack on Cosin and of the many tracts in which Laud is depicted as the church's ravisher. Her paleness, panting, groaning and blushing are all conventional representations of the physiological signs of a ravished woman's shame.

The duchess is not yet in the desperate position her imagery describes. She is not yet the cardinal's victim, but his adversary. Like the "short-haired men" who, she warns the cardinal, will "crowd and call for justice," she has the strength of her words and a formidable presence with which to protest his wickedness. Like the godly party she invokes, though, she sees the danger the cardinal represents, and she articulates the tyrannical possibilities of his power. Her words, of course, prefigure the direction Shirley's tragedy will take. Generic formulas combine with the topical allusion she has invoked (Laud's persecution of the godly) to prepare the audience to expect the duchess's fate.

The second round of this sparring match between the duchess and the cardinal occurs in act 4, after the duchess has been stricken by the death of Alvarez. When the cardinal tells her of Columbo's pardon and release from prison, her response revives the specter of rape in order to measure the injustice:

> In my poor understanding, 'tis the crown
> Of virtue to proceed in its own tract,
> Not deviate from honour; if you acquit
> A man of murder 'cause he has done brave
> Things in the war, you will bring down his valour
> To a crime, nay to a bawd, if it secure
> A rape.
>
> (4.2.237–43)

In these two scenes with the cardinal, the duchess raises the chief grievances of the London populace and calls these impositions rape, just as the tract writers did. She objects to the juggling of justice that results from collusion between armed men and corrupt enforcement of law. She even implicates the king, whose judgment is infected by the whisperings of his flattering favorite. Shirley coyly invokes the king in this second speech, when the duchess insists that it is the "*crown* of virtue to . . . not deviate from honour." Shirley points to the king's crown through an ostensibly neutral metaphor about virtue, but it is a coy phrase that unravels easily to accuse the Crown of deviating from honorable courses.

In this second scene, however, her attack is indirect, and it is aimed at Columbo rather than the cardinal himself. The duchess no longer has the forcefulness she possessed in the earlier scene. Now she must be politic with the cardinal, couching her criticism in self-deprecating phrases ("in my poor understanding") and turning fair-seeming words sour with sarcasm rather than speaking her mind directly ("we may meet again, and yet be friends"). She insists on her right to demand justice for Columbo's crime, but she must then suffer the cardinal's account and justification of Columbo's pardon.

The actual rape scene, when it comes in act 5, draws to its logical conclusion the play's vision that the men (king, cleric, and soldier), whose position is ostensibly to uphold virtue and to protect order, have fallen to licentiousness and predation. The cardinal perverts his responsibility as the duchess's guardian when he attempts to seduce her. Shirley stages the scene in the duchess's bedchamber, where she has hidden Hernando in the hope that he will find an opportunity to murder the cardinal. Hernando (and the audience with him) eavesdrops on the duchess and the cardinal, who are at dinner in the adjoining room offstage. Hernando interprets the action in the other room, which he can partly see, though the audience cannot. When music begins offstage, Hernando signals that something is amiss. The duet which can be heard is not appropriate accompaniment for a celibate priest with his ward: it is an amorous ballad between a shepherd and his mistress. Hernando notes acerbicly, "'tis not / church music, and the air's wanton, and no anthem / Sung to 't, but some strange ode of love and kisses" (5.3.119–21).

The cardinal behaves even less like a churchman when he ushers the duchess into her chamber and dismisses her attendants. Clothed in his clerical robes, the cardinal appears vested with all the trust and responsibility of his office, then proceeds to transgress all bounds of propriety, first embracing the duchess and then struggling with her when she resists his advances. Hernando's continued presence, though hidden from view behind an arras, further underscores the violation taking place in the room: a guilty act, which the cardinal has tried to hide from all eyes. Supposing himself to be private with his victim, the cardinal casts aside all of his fair words and steps from behind the masquer's robes — his churchman's dress — to reveal the monstrous truth of his evil intentions.

The cardinal's robes were a sign overloaded with meaning in London in 1641. The tract writers had made the garments of the Anglican clergy (and of Catholic priests, whose garb Anglican vestments closely resembled) symbolic of all the enormity of sin and theological error that the godly attributed to the established church. The pamphleteers cleverly undermined the power and authority conveyed by clerical dress by suggesting that the robes were unnaturally feminine. To these writers, a bishop's apparel was "the smocke of the whore of Rome."[34] "The surplice, which as some say, in the former time was the smocke of Pope Joan, . . . was made wide, by reason she had a great belly."[35] In their vestments, the bishops with their "curled locke[s] of Antichrist" were likened by sneering pamphleteers to "comely Matrons."[36]

The tracts charged churchmen with effeminacy not to tame the image of the Anglican clergy, but to increase its monstrosity. That the "Orcke of Canterbury" wore the "smocke of the whore of Rome" made him all the more terrifying. Crypto-Catholicism, sexual sin, effeminacy and hypocrisy all hid beneath churchmen's robes. Combined with a long-established English literary and theatrical tradition of Catholic priests who abused their social and moral authority to commit heinous crimes and indulge in sexual immorality, this renewed attention to the perverse symbolism of clerical dress lends Shirley's rape scene an ugliness and political immediacy unprecedented in English theater.

The cardinal's transformation in act 5 from formidable politician to sexual predator, though not unexpected, is horrible to witness. In fact, the most appalling thing about this final confrontation is the fact that although the duchess is aware of the cardinal's intentions and has her feigned madness as a weapon to keep him aloof, she is unable to outmaneuver him. Although she pretends surprise at his behavior ("How came you by that cloven foot?"), she and the audience have known all along that the cardinal is rotten with hypocrisy. The scene reaches its peak of horror when he overpowers her despite all of her preparations to hold him at bay. His capacity for evil far exceeds her ability to combat — or even to evade — his malicious designs. In the end, she is at his mercy; neither she nor her several rescuers has any power to prevent him from killing her. The dramatic intensity of this staged rape/murder lends a power to its political critique that mere pamphlets could not achieve.

Class and Gender: Ambiguity and Anxiety

The political crisis facing the nation was inflected not only by religious factionalism, but also by class hostility. The pamphleteers who wrote as the mouthpieces of the godly party attacked the "lordly prelates" and the secular nobility for their place in the established social and religious hierarchies. The social chauvinism of this literature is never far beneath the surface and is often unabashedly open, yet it was a discourse designed to obscure the heterogeneity of the adherents of various religious and political factions in order to rally support from the middling sort. The reformist tracts of the early 1640s portray their readers as a group of upstanding citizens constituting a Protestant minority threatened from above and below by Arminian bishops, by popish plotters, and by unseen masses of Catholics at large in the country, who would deprive beleaguered Protestants of their property, honor, and even life in the process of handing the English nation over to the pope and the Catholic powers of Europe.[37]

The godly opponents of Anglicanism shrewdly supplemented their theological arguments with appeals to the class prejudices of their readers. Thus, they insinuated that several powerful bishops had risen from very humble backgrounds to their positions of power. The bishop of Ross was said to be the son of a "Peddler in Poland," and Bishop Wren was purportedly "born in Cheap-side, his father a Haberdasher of small wares." William Laud's roots as the son of a Reading clothier were also thrown up as evidence of his unfitness for his archbishopric of Canterbury.[38]

This anti-Anglican propaganda cut both ways with its social critique. In addition to belittling bishops with humble social origins, it damned the group by associating them with a corrupt and overpowerful nobility, together with whom they oppressed their inferiors.[39] Prynne was chief among the pamphleteers using this strategy as he attacked the "Lordly" prelates. Embedded in Prynne's oft-repeated tag, "Lordly," was an allusion to the secular power wielded by the bishops in the upper house of Parliament where they held seats and constituted an important voting block.[40] Prynne's rhetorical use of the term sought to convert long-standing social antagonism between the classes into immediate political action on the part of his middle-class readers.

The tracts also capitalized on stereotypes about the Catholicism of the nobility. There was a widespread suspicion in the City that the wealthy residents of the Strand (the nobility and greater gentry who could afford to maintain fashionable London residences) were largely a population of Catholics.[41] The author of *The Black Box of Rome opened*, for instance, declares, "I am sure the Strand, Covent-Garden, Drury-lane, St. Giles, and Holborn, are so replenished with Priests and their people, that they openly call one another to go to Mass (in other places) or to Somerset house, as familiarly as one neighbor will call another to go to one of our Churches."[42] The hostility in this tract is directed as much at the class to which these suspected Catholics belonged as at their religious practice. The emphasis is on the difference between "neighbors" and the residents of these specially named districts whose households are so "replenished" that even their priests have servants.

Similar attacks were aimed at the cavaliers, army officers who, after the failed war with Scotland, returned to London to lobby Parliament for their unpaid and grievously overdue wages. These idle men became notorious as scoundrels who ate and drank on credit (or on threat of violence), caroused and vandalized and treated the law-abiding citizens as inferiors to be cheated and abused at whim.[43] A contemporary broadside, complete with an engraving showing two cavaliers smoking, drinking and gambling, said of them:

> Here sits the prodigal Children, the younger brothers (Luk. 15.12) Acting the parts of hot-spur Cavaliers. . . . With the debauched Gallants of these lascivious and loose-living times, he draws his Patrimony through his throat. . . . [H]e daily haunts Taverns. . . .

> [H]e is enraged unto blood, and most damnable resolutions and designs, terminated in the death and destruction of the next man he meets, that never did, neither thought him harm. . . . These are children of spiritual fornication, such as go a Whoring from God after the idols of their own brains: Hos. 1.2 such are superstitious Romanists.[44]

The cavaliers depicted in the illustration on this broadside are clearly upper-class men: their long curls, jaunty clothing and swords mark their social station. Furthermore, the clothes and the curls were taken as signs of their "effeminacy," their womanish vanity and self-indulgence.[45] Sexually debauched, murderous, and a Papist, the cavalier was a character possessed of all the traits necessary to become a bugbear for the godly of London who heard not only actual reports, but also hearsay and fiction to lend evidence of his criminality.

The tracts of the London propagandists depicted the king's party as a uniformly corrupt group of Catholic cavaliers and debt-ridden grandees. *The Cardinal* is not so harsh in its characterization. Where the pamphleteers see only corruption at the court, Shirley paints a more complex picture of a monarch's circle. These finer distinctions are possible, in part, because the play ignores the class tensions of the pamphlet literature by ignoring the larger world outside of the court.[46] Looking at the court without the religious and class antagonisms that animate the tracts, Shirley sees the court as a microcosm of the larger nation. He reveals that even within the court, power pools in the hands of the politic few and works to their advantage without scruple for the injuries incurred by the powerless. Shirley provides figures with whom his audience may identify (or at least sympathize) within the play's court, an affinity the pamphleteers could never feel. Hernando, Alvarez, the duchess, and the anonymous lords are all sympathetic in their struggles to survive the impositions and injuries inflicted on them by the cardinal. Even Columbo, who plays a doubly awkward role as the cardinal's nephew and the duchess's undesired extra fiancé, is by all accounts a worthy and honorable man.

Shirley does not, however, allow the process of identification to be a simple one. The compromises of life at court tarnish these characters. The play has reservations about each and every one of them, and this conflict dominates the drama. Shirley, who couches his political observations in the guise of a story of matrimonial negotiation, expresses his ambivalence toward his characters through his presentation not of their conduct in matters of state, but of their gendered behavior. Interestingly, it is in regard to the men that the play has most difficulty, and this concern reveals itself as a destabilizing doubt about the characteristics that adhere to normal, appropriate masculinity.

Whereas Jacobean tragedies tended to displace angst onto women, whom they scapegoated as violators of social order, this play focuses its sense of crisis on the excesses and failures of its aristocratic men. In the earlier plays men represented an order and hegemony threatened, but not destroyed, by social change precipitated by the weakness of women. In the face of civil war, no such order seemed sure to London theater audiences. The crisis of masculinity expressed in the pamphlet literature and also in Shirley's play reflects the depth to which social certainties had been shaken. In the tracts we have witnessed a deep sense of emasculation, and in this play about the court we find a profound destabilization of confidence in aristocratic manliness. Columbo's hyper-masculinity threatens the peace, and Alvarez's insufficient masculinity is not a viable alternative. Balance seems to elude all of the principal men in *The Cardinal.*

The play particularly problematizes the Count D'Alvarez, Duchess Rosaura's true love. That he is the duchess's choice speaks in his favor, and the audience is further encouraged to approve of him because the evil cardinal's schemes injure him. When Alvarez appears, briefly, he seems to be an honorable, reasonable, altogether sympathetic fellow, but he is hardly given enough time onstage to solidify this impression. In fact, other characters are allowed much more time to discuss him than he is given to speak for himself. Before he ever steps out on stage, other figures comment extensively about his person and character. The lords, for instance, deem him an appropriate mate for the duchess both in birth and in temperament, but they are disturbed by his acquiescence in the face of her forced match to Columbo. They can not determine whether Alvarez's inaction is a sign of his politic wariness of the cardinal or simply of cowardice. The second lord wavers, finally saying, "If wisdom, not inborn fear, make him compose, / I like it" (1.1.43–44). Still, it seems to them that any man of spirit would challenge Columbo's presumption to the duchess.

There is also something troubling about the similarity that the lords observe between Alvarez and the duchess.

> 1 Lord: She has a sweet and noble nature.
> 2 Lord: That
> Commends Alvarez, Hymen cannot tie
> A knot of two more equal hearts and blood
>
> (1.1.50–53)

Although, in the lords' estimation, Alvarez's kinship to the duchess's sweet and noble nature seems to be an endorsement of his best qualities, the play turns this praise into a liability. It soon seems that Alvarez is too much like her. When the duchess's maids of honor are given their turn to pass judgment on Alvarez, they remark more than once on his "sweetness":

> Valeria: Were I a princess, I should think Count D'Alvarez
> Had a sweetness to deserve me from the world.
>
>   . . . .
> He's young and active, and composed most sweetly.
> Duchess: I have seen a face more tempting.
> Valeria: It had then
>   Too much of woman in't; his eyes speak movingly,
>   Which may excuse his voice, and lead away
>   All female pride his captive; his hair black,
>   Which naturally falling into curls —
>
> (1.2.34–35, 37–42)

This description illustrates a crux in what early modern England identified as effeminacy in men: Alvarez appeals to women because he is like them in beauty (his curls, his eyes), even like them in voice, and seems to enjoy their company and feel at ease with them. These traits which may endear him to women like Valeria and the duchess make him seem unmanly to other men. His effeminacy in early modern terms is not then simply a function of his feminine appearance and is not an indication of homosexuality, but is an indication that he is a woman's man, deemed too much like a woman because he does not separate himself sufficiently from women to establish his masculinity.[47]

If Valeria's description suggests Alvarez's effeminacy, Celinda's preference for Columbo's martial masculinity and superior intelligence makes the play's attention to Alvarez's deficiencies more clear. The inference and innuendo of these comments about Alvarez are damaging, and Shirley adds to them, giving Columbo and the cardinal opportunities to record their hostile opinions of Alvarez's womanishness later in the play. The cardinal denigrates the duchess's attraction to Alvarez:

> Because Alvarez has a softer cheek,
> Can like a woman trim his wanton hair,
> Spend half a day with looking in the glass
> To find a posture to present himself,
> And bring more effeminacy than man
> Or honour to your bed; must he supplant [Columbo]?
>
> (2.3.109–14)

For his part, Columbo contents himself with calling Alvarez "her curlèd minion" (3.2.137).

Presumably, the actor playing Alvarez confirms his character's youthful sweetness with a physical presence that is boyish or at least slight of physique. In his introduction to the Revels edition of the play, E. M. Yearling notes that a cast list from an early Restoration revival of the play suggests that the actor assigned to this role was young enough to have only recently graduated from women's parts. The fact that Alvarez has few lines and does not (is not trusted to?) die on stage may suggest that the King's Men cast the role in this way in the original production. If, indeed, the character were assigned to a young man familiar to the audience from previous women's roles, Alvarez's womanishness could only have been further underscored.

Despite the fact that three of the speakers who belittle him are biased against him, the weight of suggestion lies heavily with their assessment that Alvarez is rather too feminine. In this attribute, he follows a well-established stereotype of courtiers. Eight years after *The Cardinal*'s debut, Milton warned against a settlement with Charles II, a man "bred up, not in the soft effeminacies of the court only, but in the rugged and more boisterous license of undisciplined Camps and Garrisons." Here, Milton links effeminacy with courtly pastimes in the company of women and contrasts it to the homosocial (and, in his opinion, equally objectionable) fellowship of military pursuits — precisely the contrast made in the play between Alvarez and the soldierly Columbo.[48]

The effeminacy and debauchery of court life became a chief element in attacks on the Stuart monarchy in the 1640s and 1650s. At the center of the court and at the heart of all of the furor over its womanish men, was the king, whose chief failing, in the opinion of these critics, was his relationship with his wife. Charles I was widely criticized for subservience to the wishes and policies of Henrietta Maria. In the later years of the war and throughout the Interregnum, accounts of his uxoriousness were retailed to discredit his cause and his son's. Lois Potter offers an account of the parliamentary seizure in 1644 of the contents of a ship that ran aground on the south coast of England. Among the items taken was a painting headed for Spain, which purportedly depicted Charles I offering a scepter to Henrietta Maria, who "declines it and offers it to the Pope . . . [by which means the] Pope and Queen share the Scepter of England between them."[49] Potter reports that the painting, which was read as a depiction of Henrietta Maria's domination of her husband, was made available for public viewing in the Court of Star Chamber. This choice of exhibition space was a masterful stroke of vengeance on the part of Parliament. Charles's image was thus traduced in the place most associated with his government's (abuse of) power.

In the years before war broke out, however, criticisms of Charles were possible only in veiled terms. Parliamentarians, guided by the protocols of political rhetoric, and even the less restrained pamphleteers, avoided any direct criticism of the king, focusing instead on his domineering wife, his "evil counselors," and on the archbishop, pretending that these advisers were bullying the king into following their "malignant" plans.[50] To have acknowledged that Charles was responsible for the policies of the Crown would have been to acknowledge that Parliament and the nation were pushing for a constitutional reform abolishing the monarchy.[51] This indirect criticism was doubly effective: it not only attacked the king's policies, but also denigrated the king's competence by pretending that he was not responsible for his own actions.

Also practicing this strategy of indirection were a number of critics who focused their condemnation not on the current regime, but on the court of James I. By shifting their aim to a previous generation and by prefacing their work with disclaimers noting that Charles I did not condone the libertinism of his father's court, these writers were able to find a safe channel for their anti-Stuart views. In her account of her husband's life, Lucy Hutchinson describes James's court as a place of "lust and excesses" where people were softened and seduced to debauchery by the lavish entertainments and opulent lifestyle: "To keep the people in their deplorable security till vengeance overtook them, they were entertained with masks, stage plays, and sorts of ruder sports. Then began Murder, incest, Adultery, drunkenness, swearing, fornication and all sort of ribaldry."[52] In histories like Hutchinson's the characterization of courtiers centers on unflattering portraits of particularly notorious men, especially on George Villiers, duke of Buckingham, the great favorite of both James and Charles.

Shirley's portrait of Alvarez as the duchess's "curlèd minion" resonates darkly with the depiction of Villiers in these anti-Stuart tomes. When Hutchinson mentions the "Catamites" of James's court she has Villiers foremost in her mind. He was "raised from a knight's fourth son to that pitch of glory, and enjoy[ed] great possessions acquired by the favour of the king upon no merit but that of his beauty and prostitution."[53] A tract from 1641 less than favorably comparing the duke of Buckingham to Elizabeth's favorite, Robert Devereux, earl of Essex, concluded that Villiers's chief recommendations were "the daintiness of his leg and foot," his "very pleasant and vacant face," and his "sweet and attractive manner." This sweetness was echoed by Bishop Godfrey Goodman, who thought Villiers "the handsomest bodied man in England, his limbs were so well compacted, and his conversation so pleasing, and of so sweet a disposition."[54] Although Shirley does not imply that Alvarez is anything but an appropriate heterosexual mate for the duchess, his effeminacy and "sweetness" of character and the actor's youth (and possible reputation as a transvestite player) combine with Alvarez's easy subjection to the cardinal's interference, to the duchess's will, and ultimately to Columbo's blade, to problematize him as a figure for the audience's sympathy.[55]

Effeminate decadence was one side of a schizophrenic characterization of the courtiers who surrounded Charles I. The propaganda flooding London in 1641, and presumably the readers of those tracts, saw courtiers simultaneously as effete and violent. "Cavalier," which became the preferred term for the gentlemen who surrounded Charles, alternately conjured up images of richly dressed courtiers or of armed soldiers. The cavalier of Charles's court was both: his station and education afforded him with tastes for leisured pursuits as well as training in military discipline and the arms to exercise those skills.

Shirley's play divides the two sides of this aristocratic figure into two separate characters: Alvarez, who personifies "courtliness" to a fault, and Columbo, whose military prowess is both attractive and frightening. In praise of Columbo, the lords call him "a gallant gentleman" and "a man of daring / And most exalted spirit; pride in him / Dwells like an ornament, where so much honour / Secures his praise" (1.1.22, 24–27). Celinda finds him to have "person, and a bravery beyond / All men that I observe" (1.2.52–53). To Valeria, however, these qualities are not virtues:

> He is a soldier,
> A rough-hewn man, and may show well at a distance;
> His talk will fright a lady; war and grim-
> Faced honour are his mistresses; he raves
> To hear a lute; Love meant him not his priest.
>
> (1.2.53–57)

The two ladies who keep company with the duchess and comment on her suitors offer the audience clues as to how their opinions should be weighed and how the men they champion should be viewed. Valeria, whose name is almost an anagram of Alvarez's, is as honorable and sensitive as the man she endorses. Valeria's approval of Alvarez, combined with the duchess's love for him, is a strong recommendation. Celinda, who is linked to Columbo through the alliteration of their names as well as by her preference for his person, shares his haughtiness and self-centeredness. She further prejudices herself and the credibility of her opinion by compromising her honor with Columbo, with the result that she becomes an object of scorn at court and must marry beneath her station in order to repair her reputation. His connection with this unpleasant lady tarnishes Columbo's credit with the audience.

For his own part, Columbo appears to be a strict upholder of military honor in the scene in the camp where his strategy conflicts with Hernando's. Although the other officers indicate that he has been too harsh with Hernando, the worst that can be said of Columbo at this point is that he has no fear of battle and will not tolerate any suggestion of cowardice from his troops. When he returns from the war, however, Columbo confirms Valeria's assessment of his faults, revealing the extent of his haughty pride and the force of his fury. There is an especially uncomfortable moment when Columbo presumes to remind the king that soldiers secure the kingdoms of monarchs.

> [W]here is honour?
> And gratitude of kings, when they forget
> Whose hand secured their greatness?
> . . . .
>   [S]oldiers are
> Your valiant fools, whom when your own securities
> Are bleeding you can cherish, but when once
> Your state and nerves are knit, not thinking when
> To use their surgery again, you cast
> Them off, and let them hang in dusty armouries,
> Or make it death to ask for pay.
>   (3.2.220–22, 228–34)

The allusion to England's army impatiently waiting to collect its back pay cites a real injustice, but it also associates Columbo with the trouble caused by those unemployed soldiers. Furthermore, his reminder that his sword has secured the state also implies the opposite: his force can be destructive when he feels he has been injured.

The duchess and Alvarez bear the brunt of his angry discontent. Although his first imposition on the duchess's sexual autonomy was merely as an innocent pawn in the cardinal's plans, Columbo becomes as much a tyrant as his uncle. While he has given up any intention of marrying her, he intends to exercise complete control over the duchess's sexuality:

>   do not fear
> I come to court you, madam, y'are not worth
> The humblest of my kinder thoughts; I come
> To show you the man you have provoked and lost,
> And tell you what remains of my revenge.
> Live, but never presume again to marry,
> I'll kill the next at th'altar, and quench all
> The smiling tapers with his blood; if after
> You dare provoke the priest and heaven so much,

To take another, in thy bed I'll cut him from
Thy warm embrace, and throw his heart to ravens.

(4.2.63–73)

Certainly Columbo has been provoked by the duchess, who first let him believe she was content to marry him and then changed her plans, making him look foolish. His rage, however, is overwhelming and bloody; it is out of proportion with the injury he suffered, particularly when he knew in advance that she loved Alvarez.

The play is uncomfortable with its courtiers. The privilege and power of the life they lead taints them all. Shirley's play depicts an aristocracy in decline, consuming itself with its own violence. At the wedding feast in act 3, Alvarez allows the mysterious masquers to lead him away to his death, an absolutely passive victim of Columbo's plot. When Columbo returns to stand over the dead body of this poor rival, calling all in the theater to be "spectators in my act," what they see is a deed that has assailed not only the body of the aristocracy, but the substance of monarchy. Shirley brazenly points toward England's king and his reputed lack of manliness, when his fictional king of Navarre can manage only this most undignified response: "This sight doth shake / All that is man within me" (3.2.99–100).

Because Columbo's act has shown the vulnerability of the monarch (both physical and emotional), it threatens to unravel the intangible aura of majesty that justifies the king's position and power. The king recognizes this danger, concluding that Columbo's affront "That with such boldness struck at me," "bids me punish it / Or be no king" (3.2.208, 204–5). Shirley ends this scene with a nasty bit of irony: with Alvarez still bleeding at their feet (150 lines later), the king finally works his anger to a height sufficient to sentence Columbo to death, an act the duchess concludes "shows like justice" (3.2.248). If the play's explication of the falseness of "shows" (the deadly masque, the duchess's letter trick, the king's hollow majesty) were not enough to undercut the assurance of this final line, we have only to wait for the fourth act to open to find that the king's justice is as frail as his manhood.

The peculiar concern of Shirley's play with the masculinity of its male characters, like the monstrously mixed sexuality of the cavaliers, courtiers and prelates in the pamphlet literature, suggests that the issue for both the play and the godly was not the sexual behavior of men like Laud, or Buckingham, or Alvarez, or Columbo; rather, it was the political influence and social station of these men that were of real concern and were the source of tremendous jealousy, fear and loathing.

This vehement response reflects a realization of the gravity of the national crisis in 1641. Insofar as the play complains of the same abuses that the pamphlets fought and shares the imagery and the sexual obsessions of those tracts, it makes their case with a persuasive force that they could not approach; yet, Shirley takes great pains to distance his play from the political aims of London's godly party. When the duchess speaks of the church's "altar" (2.3.159), she uses a critical word in the language of religious affiliation of Shirley's day. Calvinists within and without the Anglican Church held as their principal grievance Laud's repositioning of the Communion table so that it served as, and was called, an altar. Altars were a feature of Catholic churches where the sacrament was distanced from the people and only partly shared with them. The Anglican church, under the influence of Calvinist bishops from the 1570s until Laud's ascendancy in 1633, had brought the Communion table forward and offered the wine as well as the bread to congregants. Laud pushed the table back to the east end of the church and set up rails about it.[56]

Shirley, then, is not positioning the duchess as a champion of reformed theology against the cardinal's innovations. Instead, she adopts a pragmatic approach that seeks ecclesiastical reform in order to save prelacy from its critics. To this end, the duchess urges the cardinal to reform himself:

> [It is my] hope, my lord, you will behold yourself
> In a true glass, and see those injust acts

That so deform you, and by timely cure
Prevent a shame, before the short-haired men
Do crowd and call for justice.

(2.3.164–68)

The duchess's characterization of the "short-haired men" as a mob that protests in crowds (which they did repeatedly at the end of 1641) clearly marks the duchess and Shirley — and probably a large block of his audience, as well — as members of a party that disparaged the aims and methods of the "roundheads."

Brian Manning details the formation of such a party in the Parliament during the course of 1641. What he calls the "party of order" was a coalition of religious and social moderates who constituted a "party" only in the loosest sense of that term. They did not agree on all issues, and most did not align themselves with Charles, yet they came together in order to restrain the radicalism of some of his opponents.[57] This party worked to appease the godly so that real reform (both in church and state) could be avoided. The difficult position of this party of order was expressed by Edmund Waller in a speech to his fellow members of the House of Commons on 3 July 1641:

> I see some are moved with a number of hands against the Bishops, which I confess, rather inclines me to their defence, for I look upon Episcopacy, as a Counter-scarf, or outwork, which if it be taken by this assault of the people, and withall this Mysterie once revealed, that we must deny them nothing when they aske it thus in troopes, we may in the next place, have as hard a taske to defend our propriety, as we have lately had to recover it from the prerogative.[58]

Waller sees that Parliament could become a hostage to the will of the London masses if they reward the mobs demonstrating outside Parliament by granting their demands for religious reform. He is no more anxious to submit his vote and his property to the will of the people than he is to submit to the will of the king. Again, class chauvinism is at work. The party of order formed to protect the interests of rich merchants and the greater gentry from infringement by M.P.s with a constituency of the middle class and their dependents, who, it was feared, might target the property and power of their social "betters" once they had successfully eliminated their superiors in the church.[59]

The party of order stood in an uneasy position between Charles and his fiercest opponents. Fearing war, they hoped to broker a peace by urging reform on the king and the church while frustrating the parliamentary maneuvers and mass demonstrations of the godly party, which sought to force more thorough change. Shirley's play demonstrates a similar conflict. Its allegiance seems to be first with its aristocratic characters, yet it sees their flaws magnified to unbearable proportions and portrays their abuses so feelingly that its strongest impression is of their corruption.

In *The Subject of Tragedy*, Catherine Belsey describes the tension between Shirley's ostensibly royalist ideology and the play's critical presentation of its monarch. In Belsey's view, this tension owes to a "contradiction between the ideological project and the requirements of the story."[60] It is her contention that the narrative requirements of the plot dictate a need for conflict, which Shirley could only supply by making his king acquiesce to the cardinal until the final act when the monarch reasserts himself to return order to the stage and to the fictional kingdom: a stronger king would have ruined Shirley's plot. She observes the odd disappearance of the king from the action for the bulk of the fourth and fifth acts, during which time his sentence against Columbo is reversed and the command of the court seems wholly to be in the cardinal's power. Belsey concludes: "If the king's promise had stood uncontradicted and Columbo been executed, the play would have ended with act III. It is only the otherwise unaccountable absence of the sovereign which makes revenge imperative and sustains the narrative for another two acts. The effect, of course, is that the royalist project is severely undermined." Belsey observes the deep ambivalence at the heart of Shirley's play, but I think we need not write off his certifiably odd characterization of the king of Navarre to narrative necessity.

Alternatively, the king's absence from acts 4 and 5 may be read as Shirley's effort to isolate the king from the action that occurs in his absence. The king's absence allows the cardinal to plot and plan unhindered. It allows the audience to focus on the duchess's abuse by Columbo and the cardinal, and to focus their emotional response on these tyrants. It allows the duchess's counterstrategy to seem like the only course available to her in a world where justice is abortive and where there is no final authority to hear her appeal. More to the point, it allows the king to avoid implication in the violence and ugliness of the court, which his presence would either deter or direct.

Shirley is aware that his protection of the king is a poor compromise at best: the king acknowledges his failing in the final moment of the play when he exclaims,

> How much are kings abused by those they take
> To royal grace! Whom, when they cherish most
> By nice indulgence, they do often arm
> Against themselves; from whence this maxim springs,
> *None have more need of perspectives then kings.*
>
> (5.3.293–97)

The king concedes his own implication in the deeds of his favorite, and names his great weakness: he lacks proper vision. He has not seen what was happening in his court, and he has not been able to judge the character of those who were closest to him. This confession is a good thing. In the end, Shirley's king recognizes his failings and takes charge of his country. However, the cumulative picture of monarchy offered by the play is deeply unstable. The conflicted characterization of this monarch is underscored by the structural instability of the play, which centers on the king.

Belsey is absolutely right that the problem in *The Cardinal* is one of ideology, but not of ideology in conflict with other, more formal demands on the dramatist. The play, and particularly its presentation of monarchy, is the site of ideological stress, of a conflicted, contested, as yet unsolidified ideology-in-the-making.

In 1641 royalism was not yet a well-formulated notion. It was not yet even associated with a true political party. Few of Charles's subjects were comfortable with his vision of monarchy; he faced critics of all religious persuasions and from across the social strata. As we have seen, the moderate members of Parliament were more likely to object to Charles's policies than to align themselves with the king's interests. It was not until later in the decade when parliamentary opposition to Charles came to be associated with "Puritan" extremism and antimonarchism that a "royalist ideology" jelled, which tied religious moderation to efforts to restore Charles to the kingship he effectively lost in 1642. Embedded in the text of Shirley's play and enacted on the Blackfriars' stage, was the ambivalence of a nation not yet ready to contemplate the abolition of monarchy, but in desperate hopes of reforming the monarchy and the monarch it had.

III

Renegotiating the Rhetoric of Abusive Sexuality

SEVEN

Margaret Cavendish and the Regicidal Historiographers
CHASTIZING THE ROYAL WILL

Paint last the King, and a dead shade of night
Only dispers'd by a weak taper's light,
And those bright gleams that dart along and glare
From his clear eyes, yet these too dark with care.
There, as in the calm horror all alone
He wakes, and muses of the uneasy throne;
Raise up a sudden shape with virgin's face,
(Though ill agree her posture, hour, or place),
Naked as born, and her round arms behind
With her own tresses, interwove and twined;
Her mouth locked up, a blind before her eyes,
Yet from beneath the veil her blushes rise,
And silent tears her secret anguish speak;
Her heart throbs and with very shame would break.
The object strange in him no terror moved:
He wondered first, then pitied, then he loved,
And with kind hand does the coy vision press
(Whose beauty greater seemed by her distress),
But soon shrunk back, chilled with her touch so cold,
And the airy picture vanished from his hold.
In his deep thoughts the wonder did increase,
And he divined 'twas England or the Peace.

— from "Last Instructions to a Painter. London, 4 September 1667"

Within days of Charles I's execution at Whitehall on 30 January 1649, advance copies of a book purporting to be the king's memoirs were selling as quickly as they could be supplied. *Eikon Basilike: The Portraiture of His Sacred Majesty in His Solitudes and Sufferings* ran through two issues before its official release in bookshops on 9 February. In its first year of publication, the work went through 35 editions in England, several English editions published abroad, and a number of foreign language editions printed both in England and on the Continent.[1] In the *Eikon*, Charles (actually a ghostwriter claiming to be the king) presents the rationale for his actions before and during the civil wars.[2] His task is to justify the ways of monarchy to the common citizens who approved of or acquiesced to the king's conviction for treason against the state. This posthumous apology is a pointedly political document seeking to raise pity and remorse among the people of England and intending to exploit the trauma of Charles's execution in order to turn the tide of public opinion to royalist advantage.[3] In each successive chapter of the *Eikon*, the king represents himself as reasonable and patient beyond measure in the face of "the evil machinations" of the Parliament and "the madness of the people."[4] The "King's Book," as the *Eikon* came to be known, succeeded in using the popular press to revise the depiction of Charles as a tyrant promoted in parliamentarian propaganda throughout the 1640s.

In order to dampen the wild popularity of the *Eikon Basilike*, the Council of State enlisted John Milton to write a rebuttal. *Eikonoklastes*, designed as a scrupulous line-by-line contradiction of Charles's work, deconstructs the King's Book, exposing the class chauvinism and self-interest of its author:

> [The king] alleges, that *the cause of forbearing to convene Parlaments, was the sparkes which some mens distempers there studied to kindle.* They were indeed not temper'd to his temper; for it neither was the Law, nor the rule by which all other tempers were to bee try'd; but they were esteem'd and chos'n for the fittest men in thir several Counties, to allay and quench those distempers which his own inordinate doings had inflam'd.[5]

In italics, Milton cites Charles's stated reason for not calling Parliament during the eleven years of his "personal rule" and then alleges the mendacity of the royal writer who would have his readers believe that he, the king, was the sole bastion of reason in the nation. It is Milton's project throughout *Eikonoklastes* to turn the king's words in on themselves in order to demonstrate that Charles was by nature an intemperate man who believed himself beyond the law, and who was singlehandedly responsible for pushing the nation into armed conflict. Milton, in fact, paraphrases rather than quotes Charles's statement, streamlining it to better focus on the points he intends to attack.[6] In the passage as he renders it, Milton makes much of Charles's accusation that "some men" (that is, the leaders of the godly party) were the instigators of dissent. His play on the word "temper" turns its sense against Charles, so that in Milton's usage the parliamentarians were "tempered" and reasonable in their dealings with the king, who is seen here as ill-tempered (willful and peevish), *un*tempered or unruly (not conducting himself according to the legal rules of his kingdom), and himself the instigator of those civil "distempers" that tore the nation apart.

Milton further teases out of Charles's writing the king's disdain for England's common subjects and the arrogance (as Milton interprets it) that allowed Charles to think of his own interest as outweighing any other. Milton (accurately) cites Charles as saying, "Hee hoped by his freedom and their moderation to prevent misunder-standings," but asks, "And wherfore not by their freedom and his moderation?" (356). Milton challenges the king's assumptions about the roles appropriate to the monarch and his subjects, cutting to the heart of the constitutional debate that developed during the course of the civil wars. Milton draws out of Charles's formulation its basic interpretation of the relationship between kings and subjects:

> But freedom he thought too high a word for them; and moderation too mean a word for himself: this was not the way to prevent misunderstandings. He still *fear'd passion and prejudice in other*

> *men;* not in himself: *and doubted not by the weight of his* own
> *reason, to counterpoyse any action;* it being easie for him, and so
> frequent, to call his obstinacy, Reason, and other mens reason, action.
> Wee in the mean while must beleive [sic], that wisdom and all reason
> came to him by Title, with his Crown; Passion, Prejudice, and action
> came to others by being Subjects. (356)

As Milton discerns, over and over throughout the *Eikon Basilike*,
Charles positions himself as the only possessor of reason in the
midst of a chaotic nation. Charles contrasts his own "reason and
conscience" to the "popular heat," the "passion and prejudice" and
the "desires of those that were factiously discontented."[7] *Eikono-*
klastes undercuts the king's claims to reason and reconciliation
not only by showing Charles to have juggled the historical record
in his book, but by emphasizing the condescension and belittle-
ment in Charles's account of his subjects' behavior. The tone Charles
adopts in order to seem a wise and authoritative figure, Milton
reads as an insult and a sign of the king's innate lack of judgment.

Vigorous sales of the *Eikon Basilike* suggested that its senti-
mental appeal was persuading English readers to readopt the
mythology of monarchy worn thin by partisan propaganda and the
ugliness of war. According to Milton's account, the Council of
State feared "the cunning drift of a factious and defeated Party, to
make the same advantage of [the king's] Book, which they did before
of his Regal Name and Authority," and sensed that the publishers
of the book "intend[ed] it not so much a defense of his former
actions, as the promoting of thir own future designes" (338).[8] In
other words, the Parliament feared losing the support of the
population in whose name they had ostensibly won a war against
monarchy. It had been relatively easy to destroy the king's mortal
body, but the ideology that underlay the throne was proving far
less easy to eradicate. It was Milton's urgent task to reach the
Eikon's readers and distance them from the seductive nostalgia of
the royalist text.[9] Thus, he claims that he labors

> [F]or their sakes who through custom, simplicitie, or want of better
> teaching, have not more seriously considered Kings, then in the

gaudy name of Majesty, and admire them and thir doings, as if they breath'd not the same breath with other mortal men, I shall make no scruple to take up (for it seems to be the challenge both of him and all his party) to take up this Gauntlet, though a Kings, in the behalf of Libertie, and the Common-wealth. (338)

If the success of the *Eikon Basilike* measures the residual strength of royalist ideology, Milton's job was to deprogram and re-educate a population apparently returning to the familiar ideological patterns the wars had interrupted.

Milton's *Eikonoklastes* was the first in a series of partisan historical works published during the Interregnum with the express purpose of discrediting the institution of monarchy and, particularly, the Stuart kings, James I and Charles I. The goal of these texts was to render it impossible for Charles II to make good his claim to the English throne. Although they ultimately failed in this aim, these writers did succeed in planting a durable skepticism toward monarchs and cavaliers. When the Restoration finally took place, Charles II and his royalist supporters found it necessary to recreate the mythology of kingship to serve as the ideological base on which the new king's reign would rest. This project required royalists to counteract the work of Interregnum historians in order to reestablish a credible and appealing pattern for Stuart monarchy.[10]

First in the ranks of these Stuart champions was John Dryden, who eventually received the title poet laureate for his enthusiastic efforts at royal mythmaking. During the first decade after the Restoration, Dryden emerged as the master of heroic drama, a spectacular genre in which lavishly costumed kings and aristocratic heroes fought boldly in battle and in love. In both of these endeavors, Dryden's heroes sought to reshape the public's opinion of aristocratic men, offering to replace the twinned images of overbearing braggart and rapacious villain, which had come to characterize the cavalier in anti-Stuart literature, with a new image of dashing, enviable masculinity.

Though Dryden was indisputably the most prolific Stuart

champion of Restoration letters, he was beaten to the pen by another royalist, the marchioness (later duchess) of Newcastle, Margaret Cavendish, who, in the midst of the Interregnum, returned from exile to London, publishing three volumes of poems, fiction and philosophical reflection. It is truly remarkable that she, the wife of the nation's most renowned war criminal, was able to publish these works during a period when the government continued to feel insecure in its victory over the royalist forces, a period when many London presses were churning out anti-Stuart polemic, which clearly feared that the ideological work of undermining monarchy had not yet been fully accomplished. Perhaps it was clear to the authorities that they did not need to worry about Cavendish's works becoming best-sellers; however, the books did make something of a splash. People read them, if only to speak knowingly and dismissively of them.[11] Paradoxically, Cavendish's reputation for eccentricity — and her gender — may have served her well in her publishing endeavors, making her work appear relatively harmless.

An alternative explanation for Cavendish's freedom to publish rests in the works themselves: the fictions she produced may have seemed to do more damage than good to the royalist cause because of their deeply conflicted representations of royal and aristocratic men. Throughout her writing life, Cavendish found it necessary to engage the stereotypes of aristocratic excess and abuse that were so much a part of the antimonarchical literature of the war years and the Interregnum, yet she had more difficulty redressing those stereotypes than Dryden did. As one whose family had suffered grave losses of property and life during the wars, as a former gentlewoman-in-waiting in Henrietta Maria's service, and as the wife of a royalist commander, Cavendish had reason to uphold the symbols of the royalist cause, but as a woman she seems to have held a deep distrust for the central symbol of that cause: the aristocratic man. This issue is a problem in a number of Cavendish's works of fiction and drama, most notably in the novellas, *The Contract* and *Assaulted and Pursued Chastity*, which appeared in her 1656 collection, *Nature's Pictures drawn by Fancy's Pencil to the Life*, and in plays like *The Sociable Companions; or, The Female Wits* and *The Convent of Pleasure*, both published after the Restoration in the volume *Plays, never before Printed* (1668). In these works, Cavendish sounds astonishingly like her contemporaries of the opposite party when she employs a rhetoric of violation in which the villains are royal and royalist men.[12]

Regicidal Historians and the King's Willpower

A vigorous group of Interregnum historians joined Milton in his effort to bury Stuart monarchy in the muck of notoriety. Designing accounts of the events of the civil wars and of the reign and execution of Charles I that emphasized his failures as a man and as a monarch, these histories learned from the success of earlier propagandists to link political malfeasance with sexual transgression as a way to cast opprobrium on the monarchy. The propaganda published by the godly party in the early 1640s encouraged readers to fear that Charles intended to extend his prerogative and encroach on the property rights of English citizens. By depicting the alleged impositions of the Crown as rapes and mutilations committed on the common citizens, these tracts made inflammatory appeals to their readers' prejudice and fears.[13]

A decade later, regicidal historians revived that language and imagery in order to recapture the anxiety generated by wartime propaganda and convert it to a settled disgust for the institution of monarchy. For instance, in his preface, the author of *The Life and Reigne of King Charls, or the Pseudo-Martyr discovered* (1651) asserts that Charles deserved to die "by the high hand of Justice, not for common faults and frailties (incident to human nature) but presumptuous sins, sins of blood, perfidy, cruelty, rapine, wilfully perpetrated in the face of God and man." Later, the same text likens Charles to Tarquin, the Roman tyrant famous for raping Lucrece, noting that "his Posterity" were expelled from Rome "for lesse Tyranny" than Charles committed in England.[14]

The principal assertion of the antimonarchists was that the Stuart kings intended to establish an absolute monarchy and abolish the representative institution of Parliament. In a letter addressed to the Parliament, which served as the preface to his book, *Monarchy No Creature of Gods Making* (1652), John Cook warns against tyrants and their councillors who make "their will a Law," a phrase that recurs throughout the genre. For instance, *The Pseudo-Martyr discovered* repeats the phrase as a more explicit reference to Charles's years of personal rule, when he "rule[d] alone without other Law than his own Will."[15] M[ary] Cary also echoes this idea in *The Little Horns Doom and Downfall; or, A Scripture-Prophesie of King James, and King Charles, and of this present Parliament unfolded* (1651), which claims that Charles, "thought to have changed those Laws, which had been by preceding Princes made for the privileges of the people, in civil, and spiritual respects; and to have imposed laws destructive to the peoples freedom and liberty, and to have ruled all by his own will, and made the people slaves thereunto."[16] Likewise, the author of *The Pseudo-Martyr discovered* asks, "[W]ith what expense of blood and treasure did this King labor to enslave the English Nation, and to reduce the poor people (as naturalized vassals) under the bondage of his lawless will and lust?" In his *History of the Parliament of England* (1647), Thomas May characterizes Charles's will in the same way. Of Charles's action in dissolving his second Parliament, May says, "the King acted over the same things, which formerly he had done; and that grant, instead of fortifying the Kingdom's Liberty, made it appear to be more defenseless then before, that Laws themselves were no bar against the Kings will."[17]

These writers stress the gross unfairness of a system in which the will of a single human overrides the needs and concerns of the rest of a nation. For "millions of people to be subject to the Arbitrary lusts of one man," Cook writes, "Reason abhors it, and God approves it not though he permits it to be."[18] Cook and his companions make deliberate and strategic use of the secondary sexual connotations of the term "will," converting the king's political impositions into sexual demands.

These antimonarchist writers set out to prove that Charles was a tyrant by pointing to the arbitrariness of his will, which, they insinuated, was not only a will to power, but also a will to pleasure irrational and boundless in its desires. Milton, for instance, wrote of the "soft effeminacies of [Charles's] Court" and remarked

> how voluptuously, how idly raigning in the hands of other men, [Charles I] either tyranniz'd or trifl'd away those seventeen yeares of peace, without care, or thought, as if to be King had bin nothing els in his apprehension, but to eat and drink, and have his will, and take his pleasure. . . . This then we might have then foreseen, that he who spent his leisure so remissly and so corruptly to his own pleasing, would one day or other be wors busied and imployd to our sorrow. (571, 570)

Milton labels Charles I "voluptuous," which is precisely to say, willful and pleasure-seeking.[19] The word also hints at the king's sexual indulgence, as does Milton's use of the phrases "have his will" and "take his pleasure," which were conventional euphemisms for intercourse emphasizing the imposition of male desire. The corrupt pleasures of Charles's leisure are left to the reader's imagination, but Milton has suggested an interpretation with his sexually loaded language. Milton clearly understood that the easiest way to deflate "the gaudy name of Majesty" was to expose the king's abusive indulgences.

In a work provocatively titled, *The Divine Catastrophe of the Kingly Family of the House of Stuarts; or, A Short History of the Rife, Reign, and Ruine Thereof. Wherein the most secret and Chamber-abominations of the two last Kings are discovered, Divine Justice in King Charles his overthrow vindicated, and the Parliaments proceedings against him clearly justified* (1652), Sir Edward Peyton also describes Charles I as "willful," adding his own rhetorical embellishments to what was becoming a stock characterization of the late king. Charles, Peyton asserts, "made his Sycophants of the Council-Table, Judges of the Right of his people, [and] the Star-Chamber the Executioners of his unbridled will."[20] Peyton charges the king with "most wicked Oppression" of his people and with seeking to exercise an "unbridled power"

(6–7). These same words reappear when Peyton describes Charles's intention of abolishing Parliament: "this wilful Prince with an inconsiderate fury; [was] inflamed with that fire, to settle to himself and his successors an unbridled power of dominion; which hurried him on with the whirlwind of passion" (3).

Peyton correlates Charles's authority with his lust when he couples the words "unbridled" and "power." Repeatedly, Peyton selects adjectives habitually paired with the words "lust," "passion" or "desire," then couples them instead with "power" and "will" in order to evoke a sexual connotation in those words. Thus, he denigrates Charles's power by associating it with rape. This is Peyton's strategy when he tells his readers that "[Charles] plotted with his wicked Council . . . [that] every one [who] denied to give him money, or that would not subscribe to his endless will and easeless power, [be] hurried to Prison. . . . This unjust resolution he took upon him, unless they yeelded to his unsatiable desires" (5). Here Peyton's closing metaphor casts Charles's exercise of political power as rape. In his representation of Charles, Peyton uses the most conventional language for lust ("inflamed with desire," "whirlwind of passion," "yeelded to his unsatiable desires") to reinterpret Charles's political desires as sexual crimes and to render him monstrous to readers.

Peyton's rhetoric makes a highly charged and carefully calculated emotional appeal to its audience, an appeal echoed by several of his peers. *The Pseudo-Martyr discovered* denounces Charles's "restless appetites" and "the raging malady of his ambition . . . wherein his will and lust had predominance over his reason" (40). In rhetoric suggestive of rape, that same text depicts the English nation held captive "under the bondage of [the king's] lawless will and lust" (23). Another text reports the attack of an M.P. on Charles's innovative methods of taxation: "it is a Record wherein every man might read himself a slave that reads it, having nothing he can call his own, all prostitute to the will of another."[21] In this M.P.'s nightmarish vision, Charles claims a proprietary interest in all parts of his subjects' estates, not only their property, but also their persons. According to this assessment, no aspect of an English subject's life can be considered safe from royal encroachment; this inflammatory statement makes its point by piling the threat of sexual servitude, prostitution, on top of the rhetorical red flag of slavery.

Each of these texts equates the king's will with his desires; each uses suggestive language to imply sexual malfeasance. Lack of documentation does not stop some of them from making broadly scurrilous claims about the royal family. Peyton's title page, for instance, announces that his volume will reveal the "most secret and chamber-abominations of the last two kings," and his text insinuates such unsubstantiated gossip as the speculation that James I, Prince Henry, Charles I and Charles II all were bastards. Trumping Peyton, Anthony Weldon's *A Brief History of the Kings of England* chronicles the alleged sexual misdeeds and extramarital adventures of all the English monarchs. To explain his obsession with the topic, Weldon writes, "[I]f any Man ask why I make such mention of their Bastards? I answer, only to let the World see what Foundation these six and twenty Bastards have laid for Honorable, Noble and Right Worshipful Families of a long Continuance, which have been maintained by the Blood and Treasure of this oppressed Nation."[22]

Weldon's formulation gives the lie to the honor and birthright of England's royal house and, perhaps, of the nobility as a whole. In each of these antimonarchical texts, the author makes the case that the extravagance of the court and the king constituted an unbearable cost (of both blood and treasure) to the nation's citizens. The author of *Britania Triumphalis* (1654), though he finds little in Charles's own sexual conduct to criticize, casts plenty of blame on the court:

> Another principal Cause [of the wars] was the lamentable corruptions of the Court, not inferior in vice to the most infamous Court in Europe, not excelling in any thing that might be called virtuous, but inured themselves to a soft and luxurious life, abounding in all manner of voluptuous and effeminate pleasures . . . but still wanting

fuel for the fire of their prodigality, daily invented some new and
indirect courses and ways to torment the people.[23]

Peyton hones the specificity of this argument and sharpens its
appeal to the anxieties of his male readers when he charges the
aristocrats of Charles's court with cuckolding the nation's husbands, recalling "the fashion of Charles his reign, how sin was
hatched from an egg to a Dragon, to devour holiness of life; insomuch that the Masks and Plays at Whitehall were used only
for Incentives to lust; therefore the Courtiers invited Citizens wives
to those shows, on purpose to defile them in such sort" (47).
Whether casting Stuart monarchy as a sexual threat to the masculine reader or as a cuckolding seducer of readers' wives, these
texts use their sexual rhetoric to raise anger, indignation and
visceral repugnance in ways that reasoned debate of political theory
never could.

The antimonarchist historians did not restrict their attack to
the most recent monarch. Any king would do. When they wanted
evidence of the corruption of kings and their courts, the historians
turned to the reign of James I for the plentiful examples of sexual
license it provided them. Lucy Hutchinson, for instance, offers this
pithy depiction of James's court:

> The Court of this king was a nursery of lust and intemperance; he
> had brought in with him a company of hunger-starved poore Scotts,
> who comming into this plentiful kingdome surfetted with riot and
> debaucheries. . . . The generallity of the gentry of the land soon
> learnt the Court fashion, and every greate house in the country
> became a sty of uncleannesse. To keepe the people in their deplorable
> security till vengeance overtooke them, they were entertain'd with
> masks, stage playes, and sorts of ruder sports. Then began Murther,
> incest, Adultery, drunkennesse, swearing, fornication and all sort
> of ribaldry to be no conceal'd but countenanced vices.[24]

Here Hutchinson alludes to the series of highly publicized scandals
involving major figures within the Jacobean court: the Essex divorce
and its corollary, the Overbury murder; the Roos/Lake scandal
which brought down the secretary of state when he and his wife

were found to have conspired with his daughter to falsely accuse her husband of incest; Frances (Coke) Villiers's notorious adultery with Robert Howard. However, although she comments on "the King and Queene['s] lust and excesses," Hutchinson only glancingly touches on the behavior which other antimonarchist historians made most of: James I's same-sex liaisons.[25]

Peyton acquaints his readers with the fact that "King James [was] more addicted to love males than females, though for complement he visited Queen Anne, yet never lodged with her a night in many years" (29). Peyton's comment on the duke of Buckingham, that "the king sold his affections to Sir George Villiers, whom he would tumble and kiss as a Mistress," doubly undermines James by alleging the aberrance of his sexual behavior, then casting it as a kind of prostitution in which James's affections (not Buckingham's) are the wares for sale (31).

Francis Osborne is another who has a great deal to say about James's favorites. In his *Traditionall Memoyres on the Raigne of King James* (1658) Osborne writes of Philip Herbert, that he was "a man caressed by King James for his handsome face." "Caressed" is a mild euphemism that might be overlooked or underread, if it were not the case that, later in the work, Osborne becomes much more specific in his explication of James's behavior with his favorites. These favorites lay in James's

> bosome, a place reserved for younger men of more indeering Countenances: And these went under the appellation of his Favorites or Minions. . . . Now as no other reason appeared in favour of their choyce but handsomnesse, so the love the King shewed was as amorously convayed as if he had mistaken their Sex, and thought them Ladies. Which I have seene Somerset and Buckingham labour to resemble, in the effeminatenesse of their dressings. Though in w[horish] lookes and wanton gestures they exceeded any part of woman kind my Conversation did ever cope withall.[26]

In his *Court and Character of King James* (1650), Anthony Weldon, too, focuses on the gender-bending quality of James's relationship with Buckingham, using it as a way to convey his contempt for

James. "The King," Weldon writes, "was more impatient, then any woman to enjoy her love."[27] Weldon goes farther than his peers, rendering the king himself physically grotesque:

> His tongue too large for his mouth, which ever made him speak full in the mouth, and made him drink very uncomely, as if eating his drink . . . ; his skin was as soft as taffeta sarsnet, which felt so, because he never washed his hands . . . ; his legs were very weak, having had (as was thought) some foul play in his youth, or rather before he was born, that he was not able to stand at seven years of age, that weakness made him ever leaning on other mens shoulders; his walk was ever circular, his fingers ever in that walk fiddling about his cod-piece.[28]

The emphasis here rests not only on James's unseemly posture and untoward behaviors, but also on the very feel of his skin, requiring readers to imagine themselves in intimate contact with James's unpleasant person, to imagine themselves the objects of his unwelcome intimacies.

In these descriptions, the king's sexuality is excessive and extravagant, his person deformed and ill-carried, but in none of them is it rendered so palpably disgusting as in *The None-such Charles* (1651), which embellishes on Weldon, railing against James, "who could not contract his horrid filthinesse within his Bed, his Ganimedes Pallet, or his Closets. . . . He must have the Publique to be witnesse of his lascivious tongue licking of his Favourites lips, and his hands must (as his Court and Character mentions) bee seen in a continual lascivious action."[29] At the same time that it complains about the publicness of James's sexuality, this history seeks a new, wider audience before which to display James's lasciviousness.

As we have seen in earlier chapters, throughout the seventeenth century the English populace (or the writers who addressed them) expressed a great anxiety about what kings did in private, what policies and plans they hatched in Privy Council, what conspiracies might be bred in the interstices of the court. Jonathan Goldberg has cautioned that there was no real privacy for early modern monarchs, almost no concept of privacy for such persons:

> When persons are in private they are unobserved, withdrawn, invisible. Such a situation is almost unimaginable. The king, so fully a public person, scarcely even had such a moment to himself; his most intimate bodily functions, his dressing, undressing, and going to bed, were attended, public events. . . . We therefore need to get over the shock of James asking Frederick about his wedding night, or the *frisson* that Anthony Weldon's portrait of the king, playing with his codpiece, leaning on his favorites, inevitably produces.[30]

However true Goldberg's observation may be as a gauge of James's experience and expectations, the frisson created by Weldon's portrait of the king is not merely a product of our modern expectations and prudishness. Weldon quite clearly intends to create a stir. His portrait of James censures the king for his lack of decorum, if not his breaking of the boundaries between private and public behavior. The obsession of these histories with the "chamber abominations"[31] of England's monarchs appears time and again as an opening of what was closed, an exposure of what was hidden, a revealing of what was not previously visible — to those who do not have access to a monarch's privy chambers. The frisson is the thrill of exposing not what is private in the usual sense, but of exposing what has hitherto been privileged, behaviors previously presented only for an aristocratic audience. The veil Weldon pulls aside for his readers' titillation protected the mysteries of class privilege as much as the mysteries of sexual indulgence.

These texts all seek to present their readers with a textual equivalent of "ocular proof" of the menace of monarchy. Thus *The Kings Cabinet opened*, which revealed Charles I's private letters in order to demonstrate the king's falseness in his negotiations with Parliament, likens its unveiling of the king's secrets to the lifting of a theater curtain: "now by Gods good providence the traverse Curtain is drawn, and the King writing to Ormond, and the Queen, what they must not disclose, is presented upon the stage."[32]

The sexual aberrations of James and Charles which these histories detail with such interest are presented as violations — of the minion's body, of gender boundaries, of Christian mores, but also of the public purse, of private property and of the nation's security. Their secret passions and their treacherous plans were "presented upon the stage" of these texts for all to see. Readers of these histories "saw" both a titillating display of sexual transgression and evidence of their own violation at the hands of the kings who had ruled over them. However, in their exposure of the sexual monstrosity of the Stuarts, these works return violation for violation. The details of James's patronage of Buckingham or Charles's collusion with the French were not retold merely to make readers feel ill treated, but to do violence to the monarchs' reputations, to destroy any residual strength their memories might have held. These texts draw "the traverse Curtain" to reveal both a tyrant Charles and a puppet Charles manipulated by his wife, while also exposing a womanish sodomite in the role of James.

Despite the aversion most of the antimonarchist writers felt for the stage, such theater metaphors are common in the histories because they provide such an apt visual analogue for the textual exposure in which they engage.[33] Osborne, for one, uses a theatrical metaphor precisely to focus on what could and could not be known about James I, what could and could not be seen:

> Nor was his Love, or what else posterity will please to call it (who must be the Judges of all that History shall informe), carried on with a discretion sufficient to cover a lesse scandalous behavior; for the kings kissing [his favorites] after so lascivious a mode in publick, and upon the Theater as it were of the world, prompted many to Imagine some things done in the Tyring-house, that exceed my expressions no lesse than they do my experience.[34]

Contemptuous as he is of the publicity of James's behavior, Osborne seeks to spread knowledge of James's conduct to new audiences. The impulse to expose the king's secrets, however, only emphasizes how much remains hidden. The king's very public lasciviousness suggests still more outrageous actions committed in private, actions so shocking they cannot be performed publicly and so outlandish they defy description. Because it is beyond the ability of language to describe, this behavior begs to be seen, yet remains tantalizingly obscured from view. The writer is shocked and yet strains to see or to imagine these secret and scandalous actions.

Margaret Cavendish: The Rhetoric of Ravenous and Beastly Desire

The peopling of Restoration comedy with debauched cavalier rakes amounts to a royalist thumbing of the nose at the stereotypes that had once so effectively damaged their cause; equally, the superabundance of these characters may be seen as a sort of inoculation against the stereotype's future potency as an opposition resource. A separate explanation must be offered for the debauched cavalier rakes of Margaret Cavendish's Interregnum fictions: given their timing and context, they hold an entirely different significance. These works were published while the royalist cause was at its lowest ebb, while William Cavendish, Charles II and many others remained in exile. Certainly she does the cause of these exiles no favor when she peoples her stories with rapacious aristocrats and overbearing princes. Margaret Cavendish's royalism was a conflicted and inconsistent affiliation.

Janet Todd has noted that Cavendish's fiction creates a "fantastic, wish-fulfilling, compensatory world" in which she is able to order life as she would have it.[35] Certainly, her own life was not as she would have had it during the Interregnum. Though she and her husband were able to live a relatively luxurious life in Antwerp in a house built by the painter Peter Paul Rubens, it was a life lived at the mercy of creditors who periodically pressured them for payment and sometimes threatened to let them starve.[36] In 1653, Margaret Cavendish and her brother-in-law, Charles, returned to London where Margaret published the first of her works, *Poems and Fancies* and *Philosophical Fancies*, but where their first order of business was one of economic necessity: the Cavendishes had returned in order to compound with Parliament for their estates. Though her brother-in-law had some success, the state would not countenance Margaret's petition for a wife's portion of her husband's property. In the prefaces to her first work, *Poems and Fancies* (1653), Cavendish describes the distress that has marked the nine-month gestation of her work from conception to publication, "my rest being broke with discontented Thoughts, because I was from my Lord, and Husband, knowing him to be in great Wants, and my self in the same Condition. . . . I shall nor cannot be much Poorer."[37] Cavendish repeatedly intimates in her prefaces and glancingly hints through her fictions that she and her husband have paid what she considers an inordinately high price for his loyal service to the Crown.[38]

Margaret Cavendish's literary works were entered into a marketplace dominated by those who were hostile to her person and party. It seems unlikely that her publications were designed to repair the family's finances; instead, it appears that she imagined her work to be a tool for restoring the Cavendish reputation and for saving the Cavendish name from oblivion in "this Iron Age" of "Hard Hearts."[39] William's prefatory tributes to Margaret, which had become a standard feature of her publications, served in the Interregnum works as a vehicle to carry his voice where his body could not go, as when he addresses the readers of *Nature's Pictures* (1656), wishing them well in their "soft Beds, [where] Sleep seize you with delight, / So Noble Friends, I bid you all good night. W. Newcastle."[40] If these works yearn for a restoration, it is the restoration of the marquis and marchioness of Newcastle to their rightful places and to their wonted wealth. As for a restoration of the monarchy, Cavendish undoubtedly assumes that this is the larger political agenda, but she does not necessarily take it as part of her project. Furthermore, while she seems to support royalism on principle, she has many reservations about aristocratic ascendancy in practice.[41]

Despite her ambivalence about royalism, there can be no doubt

regarding Cavendish's sentiments toward the Interregnum government: she disparages the Parliament, belittling its politicians as
the basest of commoners.[42] Although Cavendish assumes a careful
posture of nonengagement in "Politics of State," claiming that her
texts are "harmless, modest, and honest," the claim is disingen-
uous. When she asserts that she would not presume "to busy
[her]self out of the Sphere of [her] Sex, as in Politics of State, or to
Preach false Doctrine in a Tub, or to entertain my self in harkening
to vain Flatteries, or to the incitements of evil persuasions," she
distances her work from political pretensions by naturalizing her
reticence as a characteristic of her gender.[43] Her statement,
however, suggests the political agenda she would forward were
she to busy herself beyond the sphere of her sex: she has a royalist's
disdain for the preaching of "false doctrine in a tub," an allusion
to a phrase popularized by John Taylor, "the water poet," in the
pamphlet titled, "A Tale in a Tub" (1642), which sparked a veritable
flurry of "tub" pamphlets variously supporting or ridiculing
sectarian preaching, especially by members of the lower classes,
the radically political and the feminine sex.[44] The none-too-subtle
subtext of Cavendish's disavowal of political purpose is an assertion
that the politics of the current state amounts to vain flatteries,
incitements of evil persuasions, and the false doctrine of tub-
preachers.[45] In another passage from the same prefatory letter,
Cavendish asserts the "simplicity" of her work by contrasting it
to a number of things she takes to be truly blameworthy:

> For though my Ambition's great, my designs are harmless, and my
> ways are plain Honesty. . . . Neither am I ashamed of my simplicity,
> for Nature tempers not every Braine alike; but tis a shame to deny
> the Principles of their Religion, to break the Laws of a well-governed
> Kingdom, to disturb Peace, to be unnatural, to break the Union and
> Amity of honest Friends, for a Man to be a Coward, for a Woman to
> be a Whore; and by these actions, they are not only to be cast out of
> all Civil society, but to be blotted out of the Roll of Mankind. And
> the reason why I summon up these Vices, is, to let my Friends know,
> or rather to remember them, that my Book is none of them. (*Poems
> and Fancies*, A4v)

What Cavendish takes to be unnatural and uncivil becomes a litany of royalist charges against the cowardly, unlawful, irreligious war waged by the Parliament against the king of a well-governed kingdom and his honest friends.

Cavendish is more complex — less simple and far less plain — than she pretends in these prefatory letters. Despite her assertion that "heroic actions, public Employments, powerful Governments, and eloquent Pleadings are denied our Sex in this Age," when Margaret Cavendish takes up the pen, she engages the public and political discourses of her day.[46] She works carefully and with apparent indirection through the guise of fiction writing; however, fiction was an accepted medium for political engagement, especially among royalists.[47] Even as she constructs a veil of womanly modesty through her claims to restrict herself to apolitical genres/subjects and through her inclusion of William's supportive, husbandly prefaces, Cavendish emerges from behind these screens in the garb of a heroic champion.[48] She appears as the creator of witty, able heroines who fight bravely for the cause of right rule, who restore peace to shattered kingdoms, who redesign the governments of flawed states, and who plead eloquently for justice, amity and virtue. However harmless Cavendish may wish her work to be thought, it amounts to a taking up of the gauntlet thrown down by Milton and his antimonarchist peers. It amounts to a challenge of the Interregnum government in whose capital city she published her work.

In fact, when she finally ventures to write an openly political text, her 1667 memoir of her husband's participation in the civil wars, Cavendish quite explicitly opposes her work with the partisan texts of the opposite party: "those Arch-Rebels never wanted Astrologers to foretell them good success in all their Enterprises, nor Poets to sing their Praises, nor Orators for Panegyrics; nay, which is worse, nor Historians neither, to record their Valour in fighting, and Wisdom in Governing."[49] Nevertheless, when she writes the "Romancical Tales" of *Nature's Pictures* (and later, *The Blazing World*), she ventures into a highly politicized royalist genre with the intention of critiquing both the conventions of that genre and the symbols of her own party's cause. In a preface to *Natures Pictures*, Cavendish criticizes the content of most romances, "wherein little is writ which ought to be practiced, but rather shunned as foolish Amorosities, and desperate Follies . . . an unprofitable study, which neither instructs, directs, or delights."[50] Here, Cavendish echoes the standard moral attack on secular literature, the same attack that Philip Stubbes and Stephen Gosson mounted against plays at the end of the sixteenth century. More importantly, though, it is the same attack mounted by William Prynne and his peers against the decadent literary genres, which with Prynne's help came to be associated so indelibly with royalism: plays and romances.

> If I could think that any of my writings should create Amorous thoughts in idle brains, I would make blots instead of letters; but I hope this work of mine will rather quench Amorous passions, than inflame them, and beget chaste Thoughts, nourish love of Virtue, kindle human Pity, warm Charity, increase Civility, strengthen fainting patience, encourage noble Industry, crown Merit, instruct Life; and recreate Time, Also I hope it will damn vices, kill follies, prevent Errors, forewarn youth, and arm the life against misfortunes: Likewise to admonish, instruct, direct, and persuade to that which is good and best.[51]

Thus, when Cavendish writes her "harmless," virtuously feminine tales, she damns the vices, follies and errors most associated with the party she ostensibly supports. Particularly, she assails the failures of virtue, pity, charity and civility, the unchaste thoughts and amorous passions of the aristocratic men of the romance genre and the royalist cause.

Cavendish places herself in an awkwardly ironic relation with those same arch-rebels, the regicidal historians and propagandists, whose work she deplores, when she echoes their insinuating representations of debauchery as an essential characteristic of aristocracy. Cavendish joins her political opponents in taking up a well-established strategy from earlier opposition literature. A brief survey of pamphlet titles from the 1640s will suffice to illustrate the point: *The Brothers of the Blade: Answerable to the Sisters of the Scaberd; or, A Dialogue betweene two Hot-spurres of the Times, Serjeant Slice-man, alias Smell-smock of Coney-Court in Chicklane, and Corporall Dam-mee of Bell-alley neere Pick-hatch. At their first meeting in the walkes in Moorefields, upon the Returne of the one from the Leaguer in the Low-Countries, and the late comming to London of the other from the Campe in the North, at the disbanding of the Army* (1641); *The Unfaithfulnesse of the Cavaliers* (1643); *The Just Reward of a Debauched Cavalier* (1643); *The Insolency and Cruelty of the Cavaliers* (1643) and, most damning of all, *Prince Ruperts Burning Love to England: Discovered in Birminghams Flames* (1643), which makes the cavalier-as-rapist characterization most directly.

As these titles illustrate, the opposition practice of insinuating the sexual indulgence of cavaliers was of a piece with a larger strategy of presentation in which royal and royalist men appear as rapacious, violent abusers of the innocent citizens of the English nation. As earlier chapters have illustrated, that strategy was an old one. For our present purposes, we need only trace it back to the opposition literature of the late 1630s, when godly writers like Henry Burton wrote of Charles's court that it was home to "Parasites and Court Gnathoes," "seducing the King" with their "sycophants' tongue[s]." Such men (bishops in "collusion with Courtiers") Burton describes as "blind watchmen, dumb dogs, plagues of souls, false Prophets, ravening wolves, thieves and robbers of souls" who turn the king against his "most loyal, loving, dutiful, faithful, obedient peaceable subjects."[52] Similar passages occur frequently in tracts ascribed to William Prynne, who casts the godly people and their ministers as innocent prey subject to the "will and rapine of these beastly ravening Lordly Wolves," as he terms the Arminian bishops of his day.[53]

Given the ubiquity and political effectiveness of this representation of royal and royalist men as ravening beasts driven to extremes of violence and perversion by the unchecked bidding of their wills, how are we to understand the work of Margaret Cavendish, whose representations of aristocratic men use precisely these same devastating stereotypes to indict their behavior? Can we avoid the conclusion that she colluded with the regicides when she peopled her tales and plays with debauched cavaliers and lustful princes? There are nearly as many examples of this pattern as there are works in Cavendish's oeuvre. There are, for instance, the reprehensible brothers of *The Sociable Companions*, who drink away their remaining money while their sisters go hungry and who raise their glasses to the Seven Deadly Sins, the Furies and Death, but reject proposed healths to wisdom, honesty, chastity, virtue, the Muses and the Graces. Cavendish treats with more seriousness the action of *The Convent of Pleasure*, which turns on the deceit and sinister devices of a prince who contrives to rob Lady Happy of her name, her happiness and her freedom when he coerces her to marry him. "The Contract," a short story, similarly highlights the debauchery and unfaithfulness of a duke who learns to regret his mistreatment of the woman his father arranged for him to marry, while the novella, *Assaulted and Pursued Chastity*, centers on a virtuous young lady pursued and serially assaulted by just such another licentious prince. In fact, this latter tale contains not one, but two lustful princes, the second being the King of Amour who wages a war of territorial and sexual conquest against the Queen of Amity in the final segment of the story.

Several objections to this reading of Cavendish's politically awkward gender politics bear consideration. First, it is certainly true that not every aristocratic male character within the *Nature's Pictures* collection is a villain. Indeed, there are stories of true love wherein honorable princes and young gentlemen would rather die than betray the beautiful young noblewomen with whom they are in love. Perhaps it is merely for variety of plot that Cavendish produces the lust-driven, bloodthirsty abusers of such tales as "A Description of Love and Courage" or "Assaulted and Pursued Chastity"; certainly, she strives to tell all manner of love stories she can devise. Second, it is true that not all of the bad men in

Cavendish's works are aristocrats: counterexamples occur in *The Blazing World*, where the story opens with a rape committed by a merchant, and in *The Convent of Pleasure*, in which a series of playlettes-within-the-play depict working husbands as well as gentlemen and lords as spendthrift louts and drunken abusers.

Third, it might be argued that what we see in these representations has more to do with Cavendish's ambivalence about marriage and about her culture's sexual double standard than with her politics. Famously, Lady Happy remarks that

> Men are the only troublers of Women; for they only cross and oppose their sweet delights, and peaceable life; they cause their pains, but not their pleasures. Wherefore those Women that are poor, and have not means to buy delights, and maintain pleasures, are only fit for Men; for having not means to please themselves, they must serve only to please others; but those Women, where Fortune, Nature, and the gods are joined to make them happy, were mad to live with Men, who make the Female sex their slaves.[54]

Lady Happy's complaint does not single out aristocratic men, though it does make a point about social hierarchy: poor women lack the resources to avoid subordination to men. Her assumption, however, is that the men of lower station with whom such women will be obliged to mate will be as great "troublers of Women" as their social superiors. As critics have thoroughly documented, Cavendish's ambivalence about marriage shows up throughout her work, in her letters as well as her fiction and her plays.[55] Although this ambivalence bubbles up again and again in her representations of masculinity, it surfaces most often (and with special vehemence) in her representations of aristocratic masculinity.

A notable instance of this linkage between aristocracy, masculinity and sexual abusiveness occurs in *Assaulted and Pursued Chastity*, where Cavendish refuses to mitigate the prince's behavior. He is not only a brothel keeper, a whore-master, a rapist and a pirate, he is (like *The Contract*'s duke) an adulterer. At his first introduction to the young heroine of the tale, this prince expects that he will be able to purchase her sexual services; when she resists this arrangement, he offers to rape her. When her resourcefulness enables her to evade his aggression (she shoots him), the prince reforms his expressions of desire, now aiming to seduce rather than to compel her. He explains that he would gladly make her his bride were he not already married. Like the calculating suitor in her later play, *The Sociable Companions*, who says of his courtship of Old Lady Riches, "I would have her live till I am married to her, and then let her die as soon as she will," the prince argues that young Miseria should not concern herself with compassion for his wife, nor should she let a technicality like his marriage stop them from consummating their relationship: "He told her they were both young, and his wife old, almost ripe enough for death, sith a little time more would cut her down; wherefore, said he, let us enjoy ourselves in the meantime, and when she is dead, we will marry."[56] Such cold disregard for women (especially for wives) recurs in men throughout Cavendish's oeuvre and does not sit well with her heroines, who are quite capable of seeing that the men who would seduce them — even the men who would marry them — have only self-serving interests at heart. While it is true that Cavendish notes the coarseness and brutality of men of other classes, her works are most concerned with the behavior of well-born men and the collateral damage suffered by well-born women.

Finally, it might be objected that for Cavendish rape is merely a plot device rather than an issue of serious magnitude. It is true that in *The Blazing World* and in "Assaulted and Pursued Chastity," rape is a vehicle for spurring the central female character to heroic action, a device that makes it possible for her to do what no woman could otherwise attempt. Thus, in *The Blazing World*, it is the instigating action which sets in motion the young Lady's adventure, and in "Assaulted and Pursued Chastity" it allows "Travellia" (a pseudonym Miseria adopts) to travel, to explore new worlds, to lead armies and (along the way) to conquer the affections of characters of both sexes. Certainly, the "ravishment" in *The Blazing World* is a device: the rapist is a foreigner and a merchant who is so far "beneath her in birth and wealth" that he steals the young lady because "he could have but little hopes of obtaining his desire" (125). As an expendable lower caste figure, he is dead within the first paragraph, having done no more than launch the lady on her adventure. Cavendish uses him without scruple and casts him aside like so much chaff once he has saved the young lady from her respectable and comfortable, but dreary existence "gathering shells" near her father's house.

In "Assaulted and Pursued Chastity," however, the threat of rape is more complicated and far more serious both in terms of its place within the plot and its bearing on the representation of aristocratic masculinity. In this instance, rape is not the device that frees the young Lady from the usual course of a woman's life: the war in her home country and her (un)fortunate shipwreck achieve that end. Although it is the spur which makes Travellia move on from one episode of her story to the next, and thus may be seen as the gateway to adventure for Cavendish's heroines in both of these works, in "Assaulted and Pursued Chastity," Cavendish treats rape as an occasion of terror and as a fate worse than death. Furthermore, in this story, the rape is perpetrated not by an easily dismissed, ultimately unimportant merchant, but by a prince, whose lust the story treats as an ugly side effect of his expectation that all things, including all humans, lie within his prerogative rights. Cavendish makes this point when she first introduces the character, "a subject Prince" of the kingdom of Sensuality, whom she describes as "a grand monopolizer of young virgins" (50). This mention of monopoly specifically links him with one of the chief abuses attributed to monarchy by its mid-seventeenth century opponents.

The prince in question is not only a regular patron of whores, he controls the sex trade in his kingdom. First, the narrator identifies the prince's "chief officer" in the town in which the action occurs as the old bawd who holds the young heroine captive. The narrator then reveals that the prince himself owns the brothel within which the heroine finds herself imprisoned. His first act is to inquire of the bawd "how his customers increased"; his second act is to sample the newest merchandise.

When the young lady meets her prince for the first time, she endures his appreciative assessment of her person, attends while he bargains with the bawd, then attempts "briefly and wittily" to fend off his "light questions," telling him (ah, so naively) that she hopes "by [his] noble and civil usage . . . [he will not] rob [her] of that which Nature gave." As she characterizes it, the ravishment he threatens resonates not only as a sexual crime against her person, but as an unjust seizure of a subject's property. Cavendish puts in the young lady's mouth the familiar language of protest used against Stuart monarchs from the beginning of the century. "It is an injustice to take goods from the right owners without their consent; and an injustice is an act that all noble minds hate; and all noble minds *usually* dwell in honourable persons," says the young Lady, "such as you seem to be; and none but base or cruel tyrants will lay unreasonable commands, or require wicked demands to the powerless, or virtuous" (52). Clearly, Cavendish knows her readers will hear this speech with an ear for its dramatic irony. The reader knows the prince means to have his way with her, and knows that while aristocratic ideology teaches that "noble minds *usually* dwell in honourable persons," this fellow will prove to be a disappointment.

The young lady appeals to his honor and his nobility in vain. Cavendish could hardly have done a better job working in the key themes of parliamentary propaganda had she been tutored by Milton himself. "Most noble sir," says her heroine, "show yourself a *master of passion*, a *king* of clemency, a god of pity and compassion, and *prove not yourself a beast to appetite*, a *tyrant to innocence*, a devil to chastity, virtue and piety" (52). Master, king and god. However noble this prince's birth, his character does not contain the honor, pity, innocence, compassion, chastity, virtue and piety that Cavendish's young lady expects to find as the natural attributes of aristocracy. Rather than god, king or master, she finds him to be a devil, a tyrant, a beast.

The second time Cavendish's young lady meets her prince (after he recovers from the gunshot wound she delivered the first time), she is his prisoner. Their interview goes somewhat differently this time, in part because he has been impressed with her courage in defending herself and in part because he now knows she is a lady, a fact that has a chastening effect on him as her "birth made him doubt she would not be so easily corrupted, as he had hoped before" (57). Cavendish appeals to her readers' expectation that noble *ladies* are inherently chaste, a fact she does not call into question in her narrative. In the same sentence, however, she appeals to her readers' knowledge that the chastity of noble *men* is not to be depended upon. Again, her heroine hopes in vain that his birth will have created in him a compassion that will lead him to spare her: "knowing his birth gave her more hopes of honourable usage" (57). Poor thing. It takes her less than two paragraphs to realize her optimistic error. "O what a torment will this be, said she [reflecting on her captivity], to be frighted every day with this ravenous lion!" (57).[57] In sum, Cavendish accepts the proposition that noblemen, like beasts, are ruled by their desires.

The picture Cavendish conjures up of a prince aroused by a captive maiden upon whom he intends to prey, is not far removed from the image of England bound and subject in Charles II's lascivious bed concocted a decade later in "Last Instructions to a Painter. London, 4 September 1667," a poem attributed to Andrew Marvell:

> Paint last the King, and a dead shade of night
> Only dispers'd by a weak taper's light,
> And those bright gleams that dart along and glare
> From his clear eyes, yet these too dark with care.
> There, as in the calm horror all alone
> He wakes, and muses of the uneasy throne;
> Raise up a sudden shape with virgin's face,
> (Though ill agree her posture, hour, or place),
> Naked as born, and her round arms behind
> With her own tresses, interwove and twined;
> Her mouth locked up, a blind before her eyes,
> Yet from beneath the veil her blushes rise,
> And silent tears her secret anguish speak;

Her heart throbs and with very shame would break.
The object strange in him no terror moved:
He wondered first, then pitied, then he loved,
And with kind hand does the coy vision press
(Whose beauty greater seemed by her distress),
But soon shrunk back, chilled with her touch so cold,
And the airy picture vanished from his hold.
In his deep thoughts the wonder did increase,
And he divined 'twas England or the Peace.[58]

Cavendish's heroine, too, spills tears with similar results: they only arouse the villain further. "With that, tears flowing from her eyes, as humble petitioners to beg her release from his barbarous intention, but he, by those tears, like drink to those that are poisoned, grows more dry, so did his passions more violent, who told her no rhetoric could alter his affections" (52). Like Marvell's Charles, Cavendish's prince finds the lady's distress arousing, although he, too, shrinks back upon finding her cold and resistant; the difference is that Cavendish's young lady requires first a pistol, then a vial of poison (self-inflicted) to deflate the interest of her prince. Marvell's prince's interest shrivels perhaps because he finds England and peace not as seductive and yielding as he had dreamed, perhaps because to Marvell's mind, the prince is not as potent as he might wish others to believe him, or because the prince is not so potent in political matters as in his renowned bedchamber.

Where Marvell allegorizes early Restoration politics in the guise of the king's sexual fantasy, Cavendish often does the reverse, elaborating her male characters' offensive sexual behaviors through allusions to monarchical abuse. Three examples should serve to illustrate the point. Cavendish embeds one of these moments at the climax of *The Contract*, a convoluted tale of a duke who has married a woman he now despises, despite having agreed to a precontract that should have obligated him to marry the story's heroine many years before. As the story reaches its turning point, the duke, who has met and fallen hopelessly in love with the heroine, threatens her that if she marries the man her guardian has chosen for her, he will murder this husband on their wedding day. The duke further promises that he will pursue her even from beyond the grave to keep her from enjoying any other lover or husband. The heroine objects to this violent warning as "an unheard of malice to me, or an impudent and vainglorious pride in you." The duke responds by invoking his precontract with the heroine, a contract he deliberately transgressed when he married, but which he now wishes to use to annul his marriage in order to possess the woman of his dreams:

> Said the Duke, you cannot want an owner whilst I live, for I had, nor have no more power to resign the interest I have in you, than Kings to resign their crown that comes by succession, for the right lies in the crown, not in the man, and though I have played the tyrant, and deserved to be uncrowned, yet none ought to take it off my head, but death, nor have I power to throw it from myself, death only must make way for a successor.[59]

This uncomfortable conceit ostensibly uses the divine ordination of kings to illustrate the unbreakable obligation forged by marriage contracts, but the duke's double transgression of marriage (the one he was contracted to make and the one he actually made, but wishes to break) rebounds against the first term within the metaphor to illustrate the bad faith of tyrants who indeed deserve to be uncrowned. This is precisely the conjunction of sexual imagery and political rhetoric used to vilify Stuart kings by their godly and parliamentary opponents in the 1640s and by regicidal historiographers in the 1650s. Cavendish's political ideology may promote the doctrine that even tyrants must be obeyed by their subjects, but her metaphor and her tale as a whole undercut this doctrine by illustrating its most unpleasant consequences.[60] Though the tale ends "well" with the young lady's successful appeal to the law to annul the duke's marriage in favor of her precontract with him, this ending does not pretend to heal or compensate for the unpleasantness sowed by the duke's early misbehavior. The lady may have him, but one wonders if Cavendish means her readers to ask the question posed by another of her heroines: "Since there is so much folly, vanity and falsehood in Men, why should Women trouble and vex themselves for their sake"?[61] And having asked that, might not her readers likewise think themselves prompted to ask why, given the folly, vanity and falsehood of kings, subjects should trouble themselves for monarchs' sake?

A second instance of Cavendish's use of antimonarchist rhetoric to critique masculine behavior may be found in *The Contract*, when Cavendish allows her young heroine to offer a wise and wary assessment of the hidden evils of aristocratic marriages, a conversation which again turns on the ills of monarchy. The young lady's uncle says,

> [H]ere is a great match propounded to me for you, the like I could not have hoped for, which is the Viceroy, he is rich.
> Yet, said she, he may be a fool.
> O, he is wise and discreet, said he.
> Said she, I have heard he is ill natured, and froward.
> Answered her uncle, he is in great power and authority.
> He may be, said she, never the honester for that.
> He is, said he, in great favor with the King.
> Sir, said she, princes and monarchs do not always favour the most deserving, nor do they always advance men for merit, but most commonly otherwise, the unworthiest are advanced highest; besides, bribery, partiality, and flattery, rule princes and states. (22)

The uncle warns her "not to use rhetoric against yourself, and overthrow a good fortune, in refusing such a husband," a statement that seems ironic under the circumstances. Cavendish does not heed the warning implicit in the remark; instead, she uses the uncle to develop a picture of the alternative aristocratic marriage his niece might make if she rejects marriage to an old man in favor of marriage to a young, dissolute one (22).[62] "I perceive that you would marry some young, fantastical, prodigal fellow, who will give you only diseases, and spend your estate, and his own too, amongst his whores, bawds, and sycophants; whilst you sit mourning at home, he will be reveling abroad, and then disturb your rest, coming home at unseasonable times" (23). The niece's portrait of corrupt, jealous, rich, old men echoes in the mouths of characters throughout Cavendish's works as does the uncle's portrait of the aristocrat as a young man, the latter an apparently accurate portrait of the duke whom the niece would prefer to marry. From Cavendish's point of view, it would seem that no aristocrat is likely to be much of a catch — either for the women who marry them — or, as the niece points out, for the kings who employ their services as councillors and companions.

A third instance of Cavendish's use of antimonarchist imagery to trouble her representations of aristocratic men occurs near the end of *Assaulted and Pursued Chastity*. As she describes the distasteful alliance of the Prince of Sensuality with the King of Amour in their tyrannical efforts to coerce sexual submission from the women they love, Cavendish offers this image of the two men fawning on one another: "The Prince in the meantime was in high favour with the King, who asked and took his counsel in everything; and sending for him one day, . . . when he came, he hung about his neck, as was his custom" (94). This is not a generic image of sycophantic behavior meant merely to demonstrate this king's lack of wisdom in depending on such a flatterer. Instead, the image of a king hanging on the neck of his favorite, or more generally, of one man *leaning* on the neck and shoulders of another, belongs to an early modern tradition of gestural codes signifying homo-erotic attachment. Compare, for instance, this description from the Baines libel, a document collected by investigators seeking evidence against Christopher Marlowe: "St. John the Evangelist was bedfellow to C[hrist] and leaned always in his bosom, . . . he used him as the sinners of Sodoma."[63] Cavendish's image bears close similarity to a libel of another generation: Anthony Weldon's infamous description of James I "ever leaning on other men's shoulders."[64] In *Assaulted and Pursued Chastity*, Cavendish uses the image to load her representation of two violently heterosexual characters with the residual reprehension which clung to King James and his minions in the years following the fall of the house of Stuart.

When we consider Cavendish as a royalist writer taking up the gauntlet thrown down by Milton and his fellows, we see at best an awkward gesture. While we do not have any reason to suppose that she was ambivalent about the royalist cause, her characterizations of aristocratic men create an uncomfortable paradox. Even in those works where Cavendish offers a partial antidote to the problem created by her unflattering depictions of cavalier men, the restorative effect is imperfect. In *The Sociable Companions*, for instance, Cavendish differentiates herself from antimonarchists by insisting that it was the war itself that caused England's surviving cavaliers to grow fierce and dissipated. In that play, a female character suggests that "the Civil War hath made those sorts of Men like Vultures, after a Battle, that feed on the Dead, or dying Corpse" (34). When another character asserts, "I find that the Cavaliers are the best deceivers," he is answered, "They have been so oft deceived themselves, that they have learned by their misfortunes" (58).[65] In the preponderance of her works, however, she offers no such excuse for the ill conduct of royal and aristocratic men.

Indeed in *Assaulted and Pursued Chastity*, Cavendish constructs a uniquely awkward version of royalist mythology. Near the end of her tale, she has the prince tell his story of exile in a way obviously meant to be topical. But how different does this account of exile sound under Cavendish's pen than under the hand of other royalist writers! When asked by his friend, the King of Amity, for advice about how to win the affections of an unresponsive lady, the prince replies, "Alas . . . I have had so ill success in love, that what I doted on most did hate me worst; which is the cause I have left my country, friends, and estate, lost the peace of mind, the joy of mirth, the sweets of pleasures, the comfort of life, hating myself because she doth not like nor love me; . . . I wish her dead, because none should enjoy her but myself" (95). Doubtless, William Cavendish might have characterized his feelings for England as a love unappreciated by those upon whom he and his king had tried to bestow their care, but the violence of this fictional prince's expression of his affection and the deadly jealousy he describes here make Margaret Cavendish's exile narrative sound much closer to *Prince Ruperts Burning Love to England: Discovered in Birminghams Flames.*

Curiously, improbably, *awkwardly*, Margaret Cavendish brings closure to her novella by recuperating her prince. In the end, Cavendish treats him as something more than a villain. In the course of events, the Lady Miseria/Travellia falls in love with her would-be ravisher, so when his old, unloved first wife conveniently dies, his beloved agrees to marry him. What redeems the prince as a suitable mate for the heroine is his unflagging love for her.[66] Paradoxically, his insatiate desire for the young lady and his unrelenting pursuit of her maidenhead become testimonials to his faithful love of her. That he has left home and kingdom, risked his life and suffered economic hardship on her account, finally trumps his violence and his irreverence toward marriage. The work closes with a suitably royalist resolution: the King of Amour marries a newly willing Queen of Amity, who agrees to live with him in his realm on the condition that in her stead, the kingdom of Amity be ruled by the Lady Travellia and her new husband, the Prince of Sensuality:

> The next day they caused their councils to meet, where they concluded the marriage of the King and Queen; and that the Queen should live with their King in the Kingdom of Amours, and that her first son should be heir to the crown, and her second should be heir to the Kingdom of Amity; but in case there were no sons, or but one, then daughters should inherit.
>
> In the meantime, the Prince, and his Princess that was to be, should be Viceroy, or rather she should rule, who was so beloved of the people, as if she had not only been a native born, but as if she had been born from the royal stock. (114)

To this arrangement, the common people of both kingdoms offer rousing attestations of their love and acceptance. The resolution of this troubled Interregnum fiction, then, is a fantasy of Restoration.

Despite her reliance on the rhetoric of ravenous and beastly desire, despite her affinities with the harshest critics of monarchy and cavalier masculinity, Margaret Cavendish finds aristocratic men to be necessary, even desirable. Despite the misery and travail they cause women, noble men receive the qualified endorsement of the duchess of Newcastle. Likewise, Cavendish endorses monarchy, though in her works she consistently argues that monarchs rule best when they themselves are ruled by their wives.[67] In fact, this is the key to the optimistic resolution of "Assaulted and Pursued Chastity." While in Cavendish's assessment, lustful men are as "perjured, murd'rous, bloody, full of blame, savage, extreme, rude, cruel, not to trust" as Shakespeare's Sonnet 129 famously asserts, women constitute the strong, reliable, moderating influence in Cavendish's vision of social relations. Cavendish rejects her culture's denigration of women as the weaker vessel and, instead, insists that women offer the salving, saving antidote to masculine rule. Certainly this is the vision of Cavendish's Interregnum novellas, and it is central to the utopian vision of *The Blazing World* (1666), where the protagonist voyages to a new world, marries its emperor and is made ruling empress by her spouse. When this empress desires to consult on matters of policy, she turns not to her husband, but summons the duchess of Newcastle to the Blazing World, where the duchess graciously provides the wise counsel necessary.

Cavendish was not always so optimistic that women's wisdom would be entertained in a masculine world, however. Though *The Blazing World* confirms that Cavendish's utopian vision of women's wise rule survived the Restoration, it is tempting to see in her work from the 1660s, especially in the plays, a contrast to the optimistic tableaus of political and marital restoration which give closure to her Interregnum novellas. The obvious case in point is the troubled ending of *The Convent of Pleasure*, where she makes no effort to recuperate its prince from the negative impression created by his bald seizure of power, of property and of Lady Happy's person.

Although she concedes that men are desirable to women (Lady Happy exhibits all the symptoms of lovesickness for the prince[ss]: sleeplessness, yearning, physical wasting and bodily passion),

Cavendish nonetheless supports Lady Happy's initial assertion that men "are Obstructors" of women's happiness: "[I]nstead of increasing Pleasure, they produce Pain, and instead of giving Content, they increase Trouble; instead of making the Female-Sex Happy, they make them Miserable" (2.1, p. 223). The male figures in the play uniformly bear this out: the dissipated would-be suitors convince us absolutely that Lady Happy has made the right choice when she cloisters herself; the debauched, drunken, violent, violating men in the play-within-the-play offer further witness to the various means men use to exploit, bully and brutalize women; finally, the prince, though an attentive lover, causes Lady Happy to grow "melancholy," "pale and lean," even suicidal as she expresses a preference for death over love (4.1, pp. 239, 240).

If there is any mitigation of the prince's usurpation of Lady Happy's rule, it comes through his initial willingness to enter her cloister and spend time in female guise. However, it is difficult to argue that Cavendish makes his period of feminine masquerade a learning experience. In fact, the prince spends little time in women's apparel before receiving permission to dress in masculine garb to play the role of "servant" lover to Lady Happy (a role we are told other women play within the convent's ostensibly single-gender society). Furthermore, the prince's lack of sympathy toward the women whose marital woes are the subject of the play-within-the-play suggests that the prince does not learn compassion or deep sympathy for women during his sojourn as "princess."

In the end, Cavendish makes no apology for the prince when he threatens to ravish Lady Happy if her government does not agree to allow him to marry her. "[G]o from me to the Councellors of this State, and inform them of my being here, as also the reason, and that I ask their leave I may marry this Lady; otherwise, tell them I will have her by force of Arms" (5.1, p. 244). Perhaps Cavendish envisions that the prince softens his military and sexual threat with an amorous embrace, making a pun of "arms," but the threat remains (and there is no stage direction to specify the mitigating gesture). The prince's maneuver is not only a hostile political action, it deliberately circumvents Lady Happy's legal autonomy by negotiating with her sovereign for possession of her. He does not propose to her; her consent is not required.

The best that may be said is that in his appropriation of Lady Happy, the prince demonstrates his ability to command and to rule; the play, however, refuses to endorse this as a joyful conclusion. Rather than restoration (of harmony, of fruitfulness, of right rule), it remains a coup. The prince, who in fact has been justly criticized for neglecting his kingdom, now displays the more sinister behaviors associated with monarchy as he asserts royal prerogative to seize on Lady Happy.[68] It is an unbridled and aggressive assertion of royal will equal to anything the antimonarchists devised in their treatises. The final insult comes when the prince dismantles the convent without even acknowledging that this is what he has done: he gives the convent to the fool, Mimic, without a thought either for Lady Happy's wishes or for the fates of the other women cloistered there.[69]

Lady Happy's sheltered convent provides all of the luxuries and entertainments of a royal court. Madam Mediator aptly describes the attractions of Lady Happy's resort: "for my part, I had rather be one in the *Convent of Pleasure* then Emperess of the whole World; for every Lady there enjoyeth as much Pleasure as any absolute Monarch can do, without the Troubles and Cares, that wait on Royalty; besides, none can enjoy those Pleasures They have, unless they live such a retired or retreated life free from the Worlds vexations" (2.3, p. 226). During his sojourn the prince enjoys the convent's pseudocourtly pleasures, including its relief from all of the labors and responsibilities of rule, but his presence subverts the chief benefit the convent offers to its female residents: freedom from the demands of the aristocratic marital economy and the dangers of courtly sexual dalliance. His presence exposes the untenable paradox of Cavendish's attempted recuperation of aristocracy and masculinity: though she admires the pleasures and power of aristocracy, she sees that those pleasures and that power cannot be separated from the indulgence and violence with which they are habitually expressed.[70] The retreated, idealized life Lady Happy creates in the convent cannot be maintained in a real world. At the end of *The Convent of Pleasure*, Cavendish relinquishes the play's fantasy that women might eschew men and still enjoy the perquisites of wealth and status. She even forgoes the optimistic fantasy expressed in the other works that women might rule their royal husbands. It is tempting to see in the discontents of Cavendish's Restoration plays an intensification of her apprehensions about privileged masculinity. However, what the ending of *The Convent of Pleasure* makes most clear is that Cavendish values aristocracy despite her distrust of aristocratic men: despite the unresolved tensions and disappointments of this play, the author remains willing to match her heroines to her dashing, rakish, unreformed princes. Cavendish's commitment to the ideology of aristocratic privilege outweighs her misgivings about the men who exercise that privilege.

EIGHT

Boiling Passions, Bloody Hearts, Horrid Spectacle

DRYDEN'S CONQUEST OF ENGLAND FOR THE STUARTS

Honour burns in me, not so fiercely bright;
But pale as fires when master'd by the light.
Ev'n while I speak and look, I change yet more;
And now am nothing that I was before.
I'm numm'd, and fix'd and scarce my eyeballs move;
I fear it is the Lethargy of Love!
'Tis he; I feel him now in every part:
Like a new Lord he vaunts about my Heart,
Surveys in state each corner of my Brest,
While poor fierce I, that was, am dispossest.
　　　　　　— John Dryden, *The Conquest of Granada*, Part 1, 3.1.332–41

Staging the Restoration

On 2 September 1642, Parliament outlawed playacting, charging that plays were "Spectacles of Pleasure, too commonly expressing lascivious Mirth and Levity."[1] According to this view, London's professional theater was a danger to the Commonwealth, both because it was a distraction from the more serious endeavors of prayer and preparation for war, and because of its strong associations with the sort of indulgent behavior parliamentarians attributed to courtiers and cavaliers. Theater had come to be seen as a strongly royalist institution, and the connection was not merely symbolic. Theater was linked to the court because of the Crown's patronage of the professional companies and because of the lavish dramatic entertainments mounted at the Stuart courts. In their writings, the antimonarchists insistently link theater with licentiousness and scandalous behavior, rendering it a kind of shorthand diagnosis of what ailed the nation during the reigns of James I and Charles I. Thus, when Sir Edward Peyton wishes to denounce James's favorite, Robert Carr, earl of Somerset, he reveals that Carr's taste in literature was limited almost exclusively to plays: "This Somerset being elected of the Council, furnished his Library only with twenty Play-books and wanton Romances; and had no other in his Study. A Lord very likely to give wise counsel!"[2] Likewise, Lucy Hutchinson determines that theatrical entertainment was a key element of the "lust and intemperance" of the Stuart court, and, further, that it was an opiate for the masses: "to keep the people in their deplorable security till vengeance overtook them, they were entertained with masks, stage plays, and sorts of ruder sports."[3]

After the Restoration, Charles II cultivated both official and unofficial connections between the court and the stage. Charles granted royal patents for two new companies, then treated the public theater as the public wing of his court. Princes and courtiers wrote plays and patronized professional writers; they invested money and lent properties and clothing for use on stage; they socialized with the players and playwrights.[4] Most importantly, they attended plays with an unprecedented frequency, lending the playhouses the additional allure of being places where average citizens could mingle with aristocracy.[5] The theater became a principal part of the new pageantry of the restored monarchy and a key institution for the production of neomonarchist ideology.

Heroic drama became the showpiece genre of this theatrical revival. Big productions with innovative sets and dazzling costumes dressed up these tragicomedies about love and war, personal rivalry and political upheaval. For all of its exotic trappings and foreign settings, heroic drama was a celebration of the English Restoration, of nobility and of true kingship.[6] It addressed itself to real concerns that troubled the nation with the restoration of the king. Were subjects obliged to obey tyrants? Were kings not merely mortal men swayed by the same desires as others, but presented with far more temptation and opportunity? The answers offered by this genre complimented the king and soothed a populace that had been divided by the wars, reassuring the English that although their king had been exiled and chaos had prevailed, they could now reconcile all of their differences by rallying around the new monarchy.

In her study of Restoration drama and culture, Susan Staves notes that the protagonists of heroic dramas

> always behave well and always preserve honor intact under kaleidos-copically shifting circumstances — and are thus quite unlike the vast majority of real royalists who endured the Civil War, com-pounding for their estates when given a chance in the forties, desert-ing the cause by taking the Covenant and Negative Oath, and accepting the inevitability of Cromwell's rule in the fifties. Charac-ters like Boyle's Mustapha behave as their creators and their audi-ences would like to have behaved, but, for the most part did not.[7]

For the Restoration to succeed, the English needed to rewrite history, to misremember their participation in events. Heroic drama contributed to this effort a prettified and mythologized version of England's recent past in which the heroes were loyal, honorable, well-bred royalists who, after long suffering and years spent in obscurity, finally triumphed and led their country to the threshold of a new golden age.

Heroic drama was wish-fulfillment literature with a political motive, and it was flattery of the highest kind aimed at the Stuart court. In the wondrous beauty and virtue of its heroines and the amazing bravery and achievement of its heroes, the court was meant to see itself, and the citizenry were meant to feel pride in their newly restored monarchy. These plays undertook to promulgate a shiny new vision of social hierarchy, presenting the restoration of kings to their thrones as the salvation of nations torn apart by civil strife or beset by enemies from without.

The heroic plays of this period, however, seem to belie their political applications by foregrounding their heroes' love interests and allowing government and war to seem merely a backdrop for more personal concerns. These plays displace the anxieties and dangers of civil upheaval onto the sexual conflicts that trouble their characters. To some critics, heroic drama's displacement of conflict away from a political plot onto the domestic relations of the plays has seemed to be an avoidance strategy.[8] It is true that the wounds of civil strife were still fresh in England and were still dangerous as well as painful to probe.

However, there is more at work in heroic drama than a rechanneling of painful political issues into safe sexual plots. Because criticism of the sexual conduct of England's nobility and kings was an essential element of the parliamentarian attack on monarchy, these plays about the love lives of nobles and princes could hardly be apolitical. Kings — especially Stuart kings — had been shown to be unsuitable because they did not check their desires. Antimonarchist propaganda of the war and Interregnum years forcefully and effectively claimed that it was the indulgence of desire that led monarchs to oppress their subjects.

Armed with their painstaking (and sometimes painfully tedious) exposition of Passion's assault on Reason and Honor's struggle to control Passion, heroic plays directly confronted the negative portrait of the monarchy as presented in the Interregnum press. These plays treat sexual violence as a *psychomachia* in which desire and honor wage a dangerous conflict for control of the heroes' souls. Resolving the conflict in favor of honor, heroic plays confirm their heroes' conviction that honor "is the Conscience of an act well done: / Which gives us pow'r our desires to shun. / The strong and secret curb of headlong Will."[9] The love plots of these plays constitute the centerpiece of heroic drama's revisionist project as they attempt to reconstruct the sexual stereotype of aristocratic and kingly character.

The Lethargy of Love

John Dryden, playwright to the King's Company, was among the most prolific writers of heroic plays. One of his last endeavors in the genre, the two-part *Conquest of Granada by the Spaniards*, was performed in December 1670 and January 1671 at the height of heroic drama's popularity.[10] As the title suggests, the play recounts a story of the fifteenth century war for control of Granada, but it is a story less concerned with the battles between the Spanish and the Moors than with the internal factionalism that split the Moors and contributed to their defeat. It is the story of a nation divided by religious disagreements, ruled by a king, Boabdellin, who cannot quell the dissension between the rival parties. Clearly, the outlines of the play's political situation bore a marked resemblance to England's own past.

At the level at which Dryden may be said to have devised a political allegory, he supplies his play with a mysterious hero, Almanzor, whose prowess in battle and whose private code of honor hint at a hidden noble pedigree, which comes to light only at the end of ten acts of drama. Almanzor proves to be the long lost cousin of King Ferdinand of Spain: his royal blood and Christian ancestry explain why he has been the only man able to transcend the infighting of the Moorish Granadans. The play closes with the comforting suggestion that Almanzor is perfectly qualified to govern Granada; he will be the one man able to reconcile the Granadans to one another and to their new position as subjects of the King of Spain.

All of the business of war and faction, however, drops into the background in the face of the play's real interest: the love affair between Almanzor and Almahide, bride of Boabdellin, the king of Granada. This love drives the play through its long ten acts. There is no real suspense in the political plot, of course, as history records the Spanish victory. What drew audiences to the second night of Dryden's play was their desire to know whether Almanzor and Almahide ever overcome the obstacle her marriage to Boabdellin presents. How the couple's seemingly impossible love will work out provides most of the play's interest — and there are other lovers to be concerned about as well. There is the hopeless rivalry of two moderately principled men, Prince Abdalla and his friend, Abdelmelech, for the love of a scheming, evil woman, Lyndaraxa. There is also the much opposed union of the play's Romeo and Juliet figures, Ozmyn and Benzayda. While the title on the cover of the play proclaims its subject to be war, the first page of text suggests an alternative title better suited to the priorities of its plot: there Dryden calls it *Almanzor and Almahide; or, The Conquest of Granada.*[11]

In Dryden's conception, "Love" recapitulates the violence inherent in the wars which provide the backdrop for his action. Mobilizing all of the conventional imagery by which literature cast war as a metaphor for love, Dryden presents the romantic entanglements of his characters as a war within a war.[12] The link between love and war becomes explicit in several scenes where Dryden presents battle as an aphrodisiac and arousal as a military strategy. When *The Conquest* opens, Boabdellin describes a tournament he has sponsored to celebrate his approaching marriage to Almahide. The young Moorish soldiers have spent the day fighting stylized combats for the pleasure of his bride and the other ladies. The whole event is an elaborate courtship ritual designed to make the men more attractive to their lovers and to raise Almahide's admiration and desire for her fiancé, the king. Later in the play, women involve themselves in real battles in hopes of influencing the outcome. Lyndaraxa makes use of her sex appeal to spur her forces to success when she appears on the parapets of her tower at the height of battle. The Spanish employ a similar strategy in the last act of the sequel, when the Spanish queen and her ladies appear on the battlefield, spurring Spain's soldiers to victory.

Dryden extends the "love is war" metaphor and literalizes it for the stage through his presentation of women besieged and men made captives of love. In the second part of the play, when Hamet and Zulema attempt to rape Almahide, their lust is a manifestation of their factional hatred; in this assault, sexual violation recapitulates political violence. In another episode, Benzayda falls in love with Ozmyn when her family insists that she kill him. Ozmyn's bondage functions at two levels: as an aphrodisiac for Benzayda, and as a metaphor for his reciprocal love, which enslaves him to her. Dryden again enacts the link between love and war in the scene where Lyndaraxa refuses to yield her control of the Albayzin fortress, much less her virginity, to either of her suitors. In like fashion, when the fortified tower, within which Almahide had been protected, falls to Almanzor's forces, her capture coincides with their falling in love. In both of these cases, Dryden draws on the longstanding tradition likening women's chastity to a fortress under siege and their seduction or rape to a fortress penetrated by enemy forces.[13]

The play most fully elaborates its representation of lovers as adversaries through Almanzor's romance with Almahide. These lovers conduct their courtship as though it were a sparring match. She protects her honor and he challenges it. Almanzor presses her to admit that she loves him; she rejects each argument he puts forward. When he makes no progress against her refusals, Almanzor becomes increasingly aggressive. Almahide experiences his persistence as a threat, objecting that since he has given her freedom, he must honor her refusal of his suit:

> Almahide: Cease, cease a Suit
> So vain to you and troublesome to me,
> If you will have me think that I am free.
> If I am yet a Slave my bonds I'le bear,
> But what I cannot grant, I will not hear.
>
> Almanzor: You wonnot hear! you must both Hear and grant;
> For, Madam, there's an impudence in want.
>
> Almahide: Your way is somewhat strange to ask Relief;
> You ask with threatning, like a begging Thief.
> Once more Almanzor, tell me, am I free?

> Almanzor: Madam, you are from all the World — but me.
>
> . . . .
>
> Almahide: Nay now you use me just as Pyrats do:
>
> You free me; but expect a ransome too.[14]

Although he does not physically threaten Almahide, Almanzor's verbal "impudence" increases until he proposes a most horrifying violation. He tells her:

> If not a Subject then a Ghost I'le be;
> And from a Ghost, you know, no place is free.
> Asleep, Awake, I'le haunt you every where;
> From my white shrowd, groan Love into your Ear.
> When in your Lovers Arms you sleep at night,
> I'le glide in cold betwixt, and seize my Right.
>
> (Part 1, 4.2.418–23)[15]

The suggestion of rape is strong in Almanzor's macabre words and this is not the only occasion on which his importuning of Almahide moves toward violence. In two later scenes (one in part 1, 5.1, and another in part 2, 4.3), Almanzor pushes Almahide to the point where she imagines death for one or both of them as the only alternative to his demands. In the second part of *The Conquest*, Almanzor corners her in a secluded place and pressures Almahide until, all other means of rebuffing him having failed, she wields a dagger and threatens to kill herself.

Dryden constructs Almanzor's relationship with Almahide as an impossible passion: there is no honorable way for them to act on their desires. Almahide is engaged to be married to (and, by part 2, actually does marry) King Boabdellin. Her love for Almanzor and his love for her, then, is something they must struggle to control in order to behave honorably. Although they cannot choose not to love, these characters recognize that they can choose how they will act on that love. Almahide resolves, for instance, that "my Love I will, by Vertue, square; / My Heart's not mine; but all my actions are" (part 2, 1.2.219–20). The struggle between them is largely a struggle in which Almanzor presses Almahide to consummate their passion while she reminds him of their duty and helps him to remain firm in his commitment to the honorable course they have decided to follow.

In spite of these scenes in which Almanzor aggressively pursues Almahide, Dryden does not portray him as a rake. Indeed, the point of Almanzor's portrayal seems to be that he is a man of such strong character that he can control himself in spite of his overwhelming desire for Almahide. Dryden offers a new twist on the conventional presentation of love-as-war by demonstrating that men as well as women, Almanzor as well as Almahide, experience desire as an assault. In heroic dramas like *The Conquest of Granada*, Love is a force that overtakes the unwilling and the unaware. Dryden always accords it a capital L, underscoring his depiction of Love as an independent entity at work in his play.[16] This formidable Love does battle on men and women, taking possession of them.

The men who fall in love experience the process as an attack on their honor and on their independence — on their will. Warriors, who can turn the tide of battles with the sheer strength of their persons and personalities, find themselves suddenly acting against their own interests and against their stated intentions. Love turns out to be a greater force than the greatest warrior can resist. Dryden has his hero complain of physical pain as a symptom of his desire: "I'me pleas'd and pain'd since first her eyes I saw, / As I were stung with some *Tarantula*" (part 1, 3.1.328–29). He cannot resist this force which he describes as a conquering enemy:

> Honour burns in me, not so fiercely bright;
> But pale as fires when master'd by the light.
> Ev'n while I speak and look, I change yet more;
> And now am nothing that I was before.
> I'm numm'd, and fix'd and scarce my eyeballs move;
> I fear it is the Lethargy of Love!
> 'Tis he; I feel him now in every part:
> Like a new Lord he vaunts about my Heart,
> Surveys in state each corner of my Brest,
> While poor fierce I, that was, am dispossest.

> (Part 1, 3.1.332–41)

Almanzor, who has been able to subdue armed mobs and win battles against all odds, announces himself "master'd" and "dispossest" by a Love personified as a conqueror surveying his new territories and his captives.

The numbing and lethargy Almanzor describes are typical of Dryden's construction of Love in his heroic plays. The experience of Love emasculates this hero, whose name proclaims him to be all man.[17] Once he loves, he can no longer exercise the liberty characteristic of masculinity, and he no longer feels his usual attraction to "armes and the dusty field" (330). In early modern parlance, Almanzor has been made "effeminate," emasculated by a desire to spend his hours in the presence of women. Love has weakened his affinity for masculine pastimes and companions. Like Almanzor, Prince Abdalla finds to his dismay that

> Love like a Lethargy has seiz'd my Will.
> I'm not my self, since from her sight I went;
> I lean my Trunck that way; and there stand bent.
> As one, who in some frightful Dream, would shun
> His pressing Foe, labours in vain to run;
> And his own slowness in his sleep bemoans,
> With thick short Sighs, weak Cries, and tender Groans.
>
> (75–81)[18]

Dryden's description is strangely contradictory. Love at once mans and unmans Abdalla, causing him to desire in a traditionally masculine fashion (his phallic "trunk" strains in the direction of his beloved), yet disabling him from any action. His trunk "stands" not erect, but "bent." The "thick short Sighs, weak Cries, and tender Groans" he describes could well be the sounds of lovemaking, but in Abdalla's comparison they are signs of helplessness emitted by an impotent dreamer caught in the snare of a terrifying nightmare.

When Dryden represents the emasculating effect of love on aristocratic men, he enters a politically fraught territory. Among the most damaging weapons in the arsenal of the antimonarchist historians was their assertion of Charles I's effeminacy. As he could not be charged with homosexual behavior as his father had been, and as he was neither a rapist nor an adulterer, Charles did not supply his detractors with much specific material on which to ground their efforts at tarring monarchy with the brush of sexual enormity.[19] His life did, however, provide one sexual "aberration" to attack, and the historians seized on it. They sought to render Charles contemptible by insinuating a special sort of effeminacy in his character: in their hands, he appears as a weak husband overruled by his overbearing (and secretly promiscuous) wife.

The godly party had made much of Charles's uxoriousness in their propaganda before and during the wars because it served a dual purpose: it portrayed him as an unfit monarch and allowed them to play on fears of Charles's softness toward Papists. Queen Henrietta Maria, sister of the king of France, was indeed the chief champion of England's Catholics. The godly insinuated that her influence over Charles was strong enough to have made him a secret convert to Rome.

A 1641 tract purporting to publish a secret letter between the queen's confessor and a conspirator in France provides a particularly good illustration of this godly party strategy. In the letter, "Father Philips" reveals that he thinks little of Charles's manhood, writing, "God knows the King is much dejected. The Lords much affrighted, which makes the Citizens, and house of Commons show their heads; some have braved little less than to overthrow his Majesty, who if he had but an ordinary spirit, might easily quash and suppress these people."[20] According to this reporter (ostensibly one of the king's own allies), Charles is weak, weak enough to fear the common citizens. He is, however, not the author of his own policies: his advisors (his wife and her Catholic priests) believe he should put down the godly by force. The tract encourages its readership to despise the king for his effeminate fearfulness, but also to expect that he will be led to take violent action against London's citizens by his pernicious Catholic wife.[21] The brilliance of this tract is that it claims to be private, treasonous correspondence within the king's party. Therefore, its critique of the king is to be taken by the tract's readers as truth for several reasons: the truth it records of the king's weakness is something the writer laments, something "Father Philips" would never admit to any but his most trusted allies. Likewise, the tone of contempt and malice the writer reserves for "these people," the citizens and Commons, is not meant for public consumption. The tract's revelation of the private attitudes, intentions, strategies and struggles of the king's party is a major coup. The letter's seizure and its exposure in Parliament by William Prynne — and its subsequent publication — attest to the superior organization and cleverness of the opposition, while underscoring the need for such opposition to so base, so craven, so dangerous a monarchy.

After the publication of the king's private correspondence seized by parliamentary forces during the battle at Naseby in 1645, the antimonarchists were supplied with additional fuel for their characterization of Charles as a man debilitated by his inordinate love for his wife.[22] The letters show him to have sought Henrietta Maria's approval on a wide range of matters from military strategy to the makeup of Prince Charles's household. The publication's introductory material implies that this evidence shows the king to be incapable of even the simplest independent decision-making. The king had deputized his wife to buy arms and negotiate in Europe for foreign aid, leading one member of Parliament to observe, "she marcheth in the head of an Army, and calls herself the Generalissima; you may see further in her Letters, the great interest she hath in the Kings Counsels, no Office or Place can be disposed of without her."[23] When the letters were published, the editor pointed out that "It is plaine, here, first, that the Kings Counsels are wholly managed by the Queen."[24]

The queen's strength and the king's weakness were, then, prepackaged themes of contempt ready for use by the antimonarchist historians.[25] The author of *Britania Triumphalis*, for instance, insinuates that Charles was entirely ruled by his privy councillors and implies that the king was too weak a character to have executed the malicious plans attributed to him: "And though the King was judged to be the Patron of those many innovations and miscarriages that befell the Church and Commonwealth, yet I am fully persuaded they proceeded not from the depravedness of his will, but the flexibility of his nature, overwhelm'd by his pernicious Counsel, by which he seem'd of a lesser magnitude than otherwise he would have done."[26] Not his will, but his weakness was Charles's fault according to this tract's view. It is an ingenious and doubly damning argument. The passage cleverly reasserts the depravity of the king's will while also alleging his incapacity to direct a serious or complex governmental agenda. The particular depravity of *this* king is an indulgent weakness that abdicates the business of rule to "pernicious" others.

The Life and Reigne of King Charls, or the Pseudo-Martyr discovered takes a both / and view of Charles's willfulness, holding that both Charles's "natural obduracy" and his deference to his wife were to blame for England's troubles. The text drips with sarcasm when it considers Henrietta Maria:

> were we not all of us of the English Nation, a happy people to see our King governed by the directions and documents of a woman, a strong Papist; and of the house of *Medicis* by the Mother, a most Emperious and dangerous generation of women, and fatal to all places wheresoever they came? a wife its true she was, but such a one as ruled and over-ruled that stiffness of his constellation, and effected more with him than either himself could doe, or the inward of his Council of State durst attempt.[27]

The text depicts Henrietta Maria as sexually dominant, "rul[ing] and over-rul[ing] that stiffness," rousing or rendering Charles impotent as it serves her purposes. Quite unlike the Charles of the previous tracts, *this* Charles has the ability to frighten his councillors into ineffective silence. This is the old willful Charles familiar from Milton, Peyton, Cook and the authors of such anonymous tracts as *The None-such Charles His Character*. Clearly, antimonarchists found in Charles a malleable target, who could be charged simultaneously with a boundless lust for power (using the rhetoric of hypermasculinity and ravishment) and with uxoriousness (using the language of effeminacy). There was no need to reconcile the contradiction of these attributes. The writers' aim was to make Charles appear monstrous; the more outrageous their claims, the better.

Thus, when Dryden crafts a prince who falls helplessly in love with an evil, power-hungry seductress, he revisits this particularly damaging characterization of Charles I. Prince Abdalla's testimony that "Love like a Lethargy has seiz'd my Will," invokes both of the antimonarchists' most effective negative representations of Charles: his willfulness and his vassalage to the evil, power-hungry seductress he had married. "I'm not myself, since from her sight I went; / I lean my Trunk that way, and there stand bent" (part 1.3.1.75–77) complains the prince, echoing the complaint of parliamentary propagandists against Henrietta Maria's ability to rule and overrule "that stiffness of [Charles's] constellation," which should have ruled himself and his nation.

Central to Abdalla's speech is Dryden's peculiar construction of the "will." As he formulates it in this play, the will is the seat of reason, the source of his characters' honorable intentions. When his heroes fall in love, their wills are "seiz'd," overtaken and possessed by passion. Dryden portrays Love as an external, alien force. In this conception, the playwright breaks with conventional configurations of desire that equated it with the will and assumed that humans willfully seek gratification of their desires. In Dryden's play, however, desire does not originate in the will; if his characters are "willful" in their pursuit of desire, it is because their wills have been taken hostage and have lost their normal ability to resist Love.[28] When Almanzor and Abdalla (and Almahide) love, it is *against* their wills.

Dryden's effort to reinvent the relationship between desire and the will is particularly important to the royalist project of *The Conquest.* Dryden's work is clearly on display in an exchange (part 1, 3.1) between Abdelmelech and Abdalla, two friends who find themselves rivals for Lyndaraxa's love.

Abdelmel:	Think, brave Abdalla, what it is you do:
	Your Quiet, Honour, and our Friendship too,
	All for a fickle Beauty you foregoe.
	Think, and turn back before it be too late;
	Behold, in me th'example of your Fate.
	I am your Sea-mark, and though wrack'd and lost,
	My Ruines stand to warn you from the Coast.
Abdalla:	Your Councels, noble Abdelmelech, move
	My reason to accept 'em; not my Love.
	Ah, why did Heav'n leave Man so weak defence
	To trust his frail reason with the rule of Sence?
	'Tis overpois'd and kick'd up in the Air,
	While sence weighs down the Scale; and keeps it there.
	Or like a Captive King, 'tis born away:
	And forc'd to countenance its own Rebels sway.
Abdelmel:	No, no; our Reason was not vainly lent;
	Nor is a slave but by its own consent.
	If Reason on his Subjects Triumph wait,
	An easie King deserves no better Fate.
Abdalla:	You speak too late; my Empire's lost too far,
	I cannot fight.

(46–69)

In response to Abdelmelech's futile effort to persuade him not to love Lyndaraxa, Abdalla describes the contest between "sence" (desire) and reason as a lopsided battle in which reason, "like a Captive King, 'tis born away: / And forc'd to count'nance its own Rebels sway" (62–63). To a sympathetic audience, this line alludes to Charles I's captivity, coloring with additional poignancy Dryden's depiction of desire as an ungovernable force. It adds a second layer of displacement to Dryden's treatment of Love. Here, as elsewhere in the play, the playwright externalizes Love in order to shift blame for his characters' actions onto it. In this particular speech, however, Dryden goes a step further, demonstrating how foreign this unruly Love is to his aristocratic characters by allying it, instead, with the parliamentary "Rebels" who overwhelmed the late, lamented King Charles. The allusion signals Dryden's effort throughout the play to counteract the antimonarchist vision of kings and courtiers as intentionally (willfully) decadent.

Dryden's use of Abdalla as the speaker of these lines complicates his refutation of the antimonarchists. It is a choice that very nearly undermines the scene's royalist credentials, as Abdalla proves himself a most awkward vessel for allusion to Charles. Dryden's strategy seems at first glance to involve deferring blame for aristocratic lust by demonstrating Love's power to overwhelm both honor and reason, even in good men — and Abdalla is a clear example of this. Abdalla does not want to betray his friendship with Abdelmelech by loving Lyndaraxa (already beloved by the other man), and he does not want to do the dishonorable things she has commanded him to do, but he finds his love overwhelming. When Dryden casts Abdalla's love as an internal rebellion analogous to civil rebellion, he adds the emotional, nostalgic appeal to the lost royalist cause and its royal martyr. But the prince, who speaks of himself as a "captive king," soon proves himself to be no more than a rebel, usurping his brother's throne in order to impress Lyndaraxa. In Love's thrall, Abdalla commits treason against a brother he has no reason to resent; he does it to gain a throne he does not covet. However eloquent he may be in his own defense, Abdalla's actions make him the very type of the lustful aristocrat at the heart of antimonarchist critiques. Just as Dryden appears to have established his agenda for recuperating Stuart monarchy, he quite deliberately shifts from the rhetoric of royal martyrdom to the deconstructive mode of *The Pseudo-Martyr discovered*. The nostalgic mythos of the "Captive King" seems once again to have been given the lie, and this time by one of the monarchy's strongest supporters.

Against this scoundrel prince, Dryden presents Abdelmelech, a far more sympathetic and infinitely more honorable character, an aristocratic male, who though equally captive to his love, maintains a clear sense of conscience and honor. In another highly paradoxical move, Dryden places lines in *this* character's mouth which echo the characteristic critiques of aristocratic behavior leveled by the antimonarchists. In response to Abdalla's assertion that Love holds him captive, for instance, Abdelmelech insists on humans' responsibility for their actions, even in love,

No, no; our Reason was not vainly lent;
Nor is a slave but by its own consent.
If Reason on his Subjects Triumph wait,
An easie King deserves no better Fate.

(64–67)

"An *easie King* deserves no better Fate"? If we needed a reminder that Dryden was not writing a simple political allegory, this is it. How are we to interpret Dryden's apparent advancement of anti-monarchist views? Abdelmelech, the speaker of such inflammatory thoughts, is an honorable man, while Abdalla, promoter of nostalgia and rationalizations, proves himself to be suggestible and easily swayed. Abdalla is, in fact, the embodiment of the weak king whom Abdelmelech here and antimonarchists elsewhere portrayed as a slave to his passions unfit to govern other men. (Abdalla concludes later in the scene, "I cannot, will not; nay I would not fly; / I'le love; be blind, be cousen'd till I dye," 100–1.)

Dryden uses this scene to establish a tricky balance in his depiction of Love and his representation of aristocratic behavior. In fact, he uses Abdelmelech not as a figure for antimonarchists nor as a mouthpiece for their views, but as a means of co-opting a portion of their critique for his own argument. We can see Dryden at work here, constructing a new model for Restoration conduct, which claims to hold up a higher standard. Abdalla is necessary to Dryden's argument in order to give force, even by negative example, to his contention that Love is a formidable opponent with a power not to be taken lightly. Dryden uses this scene and these two men to define the difficulties and the requirements of honor in what he would have his audience conceive as a new age.

Dryden does not, in fact, propose either Abdalla or Abdelmelech as an ideal man. Instead, it is Almanzor who serves as Dryden's model of nobility. Almanzor is the one man truly fit to govern Granada because he is the one man able to maintain his honor and his military valor, while also maintaining control of his will — in spite of Love.

Gaps in the Defense

Dryden's heroic drama had only mixed success redressing the
sexual slanders of the Interregnum histories. Dryden adopts a
problematic defensive posture in the play, accepting the dangers
and tyrannies of desire proposed by antimonarchists, but claiming
that his superhuman Almanzor, though sorely tested by desire, is
able to overcome it. Dryden does not always convincingly negotiate
his argument that desire and will are separate things. His attempt
to separate monarchy into two categories, bad and good, is another
defensive move. Dryden accepts that *some* kings are tyrants in
order to claim that others are paragons of virtue.

In this strategy, Dryden is like Arthur Wilson, who in 1654
published his *History of Great Britain*, a work with carefully muted
royalist sympathies. Of monarchs, Wilson wrote: "So *Princes* should
always shine in *Glory*, and a *Noble Soul*, that loathes to soil it self
in sordid things, is the true *splendor* of it. But when they grovel
here for trash and trumpery, and trade away that gallant stock of
Love housed in their *Peoples Hearts*, for some false *Coin*, minted
by *Passion*, mutable *Affection*, or mis-led *Reason*, they do degrade
themselves."[29] Wilson associates the base passions of princes with
their political corruption, but still holds to an ideal of kingship as
an institution of "splendor" and of kings as men of "Noble Soul,"
who "shine in Glory" and whom their subjects love. Neither
Wilson nor Dryden doubt that princes sometimes err gravely. When
Wilson casts the downfall of princes in terms of sexual debasement
(and the ideal of kingship in terms of a noble love between prince
and people), he is like Dryden in accepting the essential critique
of the antimonarchists, but both the playwright and this historian
maintain a vision of a good prince who will disdain the sordid and
refuse to debase himself with passion.

In Dryden's heroic plays, there are frequently tyrants who have
all of the monstrous sexual appetites that the antimonarchists
assigned to Charles I's will, and there are also occasionally weak
kings who are unable to manage their kingdoms by themselves.

Boabdellin, in Dryden's *Conquest*, falls into this latter category, and the similarities between his characterization and the depiction of the uxorious Charles in the Interregnum histories seem to have made some in Dryden's audience uncomfortable.

Dryden was criticized for creating a hero who spoke "insolently" of monarchy. Particularly offensive, it seems, was the scene in which Almanzor settles the dispute between Granada's rival factions when Boabdellin cannot. Almanzor insists that subjects must obey their kings (although he holds himself, because he is not a subject of Granada, exempt from any duty to Boabdellin). However, when Boabdellin asks the two obstinate parties to drop their arms because, "A King intreats you," Almanzor lets his disdain show and takes matters into his own hands: "What Subjects will precarious Kings regard: / A Beggar speaks too softly to be heard. / Lay down your Armes; 'tis I command you now" (part 1, 1.1.274–77). Almanzor rebukes Boabdellin's weakness, then displays his own strength to effect what the king's will cannot; this would perhaps be excusable as timely aid, except that Almanzor exercises command in a manner that clearly usurps the king's authority.

In "Of Heroique Playes: An Essay," with which Dryden prefaced the 1672 edition of *The Conquest*, he responds to the criticism "that [Almanzor] is a contemner of Kings": "I must therefore avow, in the first place, from whence I took the Character. The first image I had of him, was from the Achilles of Homer . . . who, in strength and courage, surpass'd the rest of the Grecian Army: but, withall, of so fiery a temper, so impatient of an injury, even from his King, . . . he not only disobey'd [Agamemnon]; but return'd him an answer full of contumely." Dryden reports that his critics also took offense because Almanzor does not remain constant to the Moorish king's cause, but shifts his allegiance from one faction to another. Dryden objects that Almanzor has no obligation to the king of Granada, "He is not born their Subject, whom he serves: and he is injur'd by them to a very high degree. He threatens them, and speaks insolently of Sovereign Power: but so do Achilles and Rinaldo."[30]

Dryden might have defended Almanzor more persuasively if he had pointed out that Boabdellin is not only *not* Almanzor's sovereign, he is also *not* the legitimate king of Granada. The play itself makes this point repeatedly, insisting that the Christian Spanish have the only true claim to rule Granada and that Boabdellin is a usurper who has been false to his vow to turn power over to the Spanish king. No doubt these complaints are the reason that Dryden makes such an effort to remove any doubt about Almanzor's respect for monarchy at the end of the second part of *The Conquest*. There, Almanzor willingly subjects himself to King Ferdinand of Spain, declaring:

> I bring a heart which homage never knew;
> Yet it finds something of itself in you:
> Something so kingly, that my haughty mind
> Is drawn to yours; because 'tis of a kind.
>
> (Part 2, 5.3.282–85)

If the audience has been anxious about Almanzor's treatment of a monarch, Dryden reminds them that true sovereignty draws obedience even from the proudest heroes.

Dryden's strategy of distinguishing good kings from bad ones, legitimate rulers from usurpers, does not really settle the issue that disturbed Almanzor's critics. Dryden's play suggests that a *good* king is the salvation of a nation torn apart by war and faction, and in the amazing revelation of Almanzor's true identity, he provides an analog for the return of Charles II from obscurity. The neomonarchist project of the play denies the necessity of convincing its audience that every monarch is a fit ruler. In this way, it avoids the necessity of reconciling the conflicting pictures of Charles I, the martyr and the tyrant. Instead, the play celebrates Charles II as the nation's dashing young king: a warrior and a man of honor.

I do not mean to suggest that Dryden intended a simple identification of Almanzor with Charles II. The play is decidedly not a simple political allegory in which we should be able to equate particular characters with particular historical figures. The royal figures of this play are slippery indeed if we attempt such a project. There are, in fact, reasons to read Almanzor not as a figure for Charles, but for his brother, James, duke of York (later James II), not the least of which is Dryden's dedication of the play to James when the two parts were published in 1672. In that dedication, Dryden specifically compares James to his stage hero, suggesting that "if at any time [Almanzor] fulfils the parts of personal Vallour and of conduct, of a Souldier, and of a General; or, if I could yet give him a Character more advantagious than what he has; of the most unshaken friend, the greatest of Subjects, and the best of Masters, I shou'd then draw to all the world, a true resemblance of your worth and vertues."[31]

We must remember, however, that this dedication followed the production of the play by two years, and as Alan Roper points out in his commentary on the play, "the association of James and Almanzor . . . exists in the dedication, not in the play."[32] This dedication, then, may have been another facet of Dryden's response to the unanticipated criticisms his characterization of Almanzor had elicited from theater audiences. The continued failure of Charles and his wife, Catherine, to produce legitimate heirs to the throne, in combination with James's increasingly open Catholicism (with all of its political implications and intimations of trouble ahead), may have led many of the play's viewers to see the Stuart brothers in the play's royal siblings, Boabdellin and Abdalla. That identification would have rendered the play an ominous study in the potential splintering of the English royal family into rival factions. Dryden's dedication to James defuses this reading of his play and may also be read as a public relations treatise in James's favor as it reminds readers of his good and faithful service for his country and his brother's throne.

With the publication of his dedication, Dryden flatters the heir-apparent of that throne and argues again for the legitimacy of Stuart monarchy. Nancy Klein Maguire reads Dryden's connection of James with Almanzor as an attempt "to recapture the euphoria of the Restoration for James."[33] I have been arguing that the images of monarchy are multivalent in this play and are not reducible to allegorical equations of a single person with a single character, but it seems to me that Maguire is absolutely right in identifying the principal mode of the play as nostalgia and "mythography." Whether James or Charles (or sometimes one and then the other) were taken by audiences and readers to be represented in Dryden's characterization of Almanzor, the play works hard to recapture the glory and the freshness of Charles's Restoration.

By 1670–71 when *The Conquest* appeared on the stage, this picture of the monarchy was decidedly more myth than substance. Ten years into his reign, Charles had proved himself to be an expensive dependent on the national purse, and he had spent his waning youth (he was, by then, 40 years old) cultivating his glamorous image rather than proving himself to be a statesman of substance.[34] Perhaps when the first heroic plays were written, their authors genuinely hoped that life would imitate art, that the new king would model himself after the virtuous heroes who cut such a glorious figure on the stage.[35] Probably even then the high ideals expressed by these texts were politic flattery salted with a tacit acknowledgment of the gap between text and reality, between prince and stage-hero.

The task of recreating a viable monarchist ideology was at least as problematic in 1670 as it had been in 1660, perhaps more so. The energetic mythography of Dryden's plays not only works against the obvious disparity between stage ideal and royal fact, but draws attention to Charles's divergence from that ideal. Charles was not interested in being an honor-bound hero. His strategy for reviving the Crown was to defy rather than reply to the antimonarchists.

By the time *The Conquest* was written, heroic drama had developed a structure that made this gap between Charles's defiant behavior and the defensive rhetoric of heroic virtue an integral part of the play. Nowhere is this more clear than in the plays' treatment of sex. For all of their rhetoric about honor and strength of will, heroic dramas were designed to titillate their audiences. In the tradition of marriage comedies, heroic dramas defer the consummation of their lovers' relationships until after the fifth act closes, but these Restoration plays take the whole matter of courtship several steps beyond comic treatments of the subject. Restoration comedy, of course, is known for the frankness of its lovers and the bluntness of their wooing. As we have seen, heroic drama shares this directness of expression and adds several doses of histrionic poetry to make Love seem more potent and more dangerous. *The Conquest of Granada*, particularly, outdoes all comic plays for its deferral of gratification and its exploitation of the titillating potential of that structure. Almanzor and the audience must wait ten acts for Almahide to accept his advances, though he comes achingly close to seducing her several times. Dryden closes the play with a sly acknowledgment of the game he has played in teasing his hero and his audience: Almahide accepts Almanzor's proposal only to deny him again. She insists on observing a "year of Widdowhood," mourning for the husband she did not love before she will allow Almanzor, whom she loves passionately, to marry her (part 2, 5.3.337).

There seems to have been an almost "camp" quality to these plays, and the adherence of characters like Almahide to such excruciatingly strict codes of honor is one aspect of their over-the-top absurdity. The spectacle Almahide presented as she expresses her chaste determination to avoid all impropriety must also have been an open joke to Restoration audiences. The actress who created the role of Almahide was Nell Gwyn, who returned to the stage especially for this role after having the first of her children by the king.[36] That the theatrical companies doubled as escort services for the aristocracy was no secret, and the king's penchant for taking actresses as his mistresses was well known.[37] Nell Gwyn was the most famous of these women. She was a favorite of audiences, best known for her roles in romantic comedies, and her relationship with the king was lamented by theatergoers who were loath to lose her from the stage.[38] Gwyn's appearance, then, in

Dryden's play drew audiences who came especially to pay homage to their favorite starlet — a fact that could not help but have influenced the way those audiences interpreted Almahide and her dedication to chastity.[39]

The gap between the professions of virtue in these plays and their sexual appeal to their audiences is also evident in the musical interludes of bawdy song and dance interspersed within the action. The first of these interludes in *The Conquest* is presented as an entertainment designed by Almahide to please her fiancé. It consists of a "Zambra Dance" and a song sung by a young man about an erotic dream in which he consummates his love for a virgin, who in waking life will not yield to his desire. The song displays all of the most conventional seventeenth century literary euphemisms for sex ("she came my flames to meet," "my heart did fire," "how long can you my bliss and yours deny?"), spinning out a racy tale laced in double entendre:

> No, let me dye, she said,
> Rather than loose the spotless name of Maid:
> Faintly me thought she spoke, for all the while
> She bid me not believe her, with a smile.
> Then dye, said I. She still deny'd:
> And is it thus, thus, thus she cry'd
> You use a harmless Maid? And so she dy'd!
>   I wak'd, and straight I knew
> I loved so well it made my dream prove true:
> Fancy, the kinder Mistress of the two,
> Fancy had done what Phillis wou'd not do!
> Ah, Cruel Nymph, cease your disdain,
> While I can dream you scorn in vain;
> Asleep or waking you must ease my pain.

(Part 1, 3.1.219–32)[40]

This song employs the same bullying tone that Almanzor resorts to in his moments of highest frustration with Almahide's virtue, but here it is more clearly a masculine joke. Although strikingly violent ("Dye then, said I . . . and so she dy'd"), this song is a masculine fantasy of mutual enjoyment. Apparently, the woman's "death" is what she desires, the reason for her smile. And, of course, the final joke is that men can derive pleasure with or without their lovers' cooperation, the "rape" (with which the woman is fully complicit, though she feigns objection) need not really be enacted since men are so skilled at constructing masturbatory fantasies to satisfy themselves. The play's pretense that this entertainment was designed by proper Almahide gives way in light of the obviously gratuitous function of the song as a brief erotic bonus with which Dryden rewards his audience for enduring all of the play's heavier moments of moralizing.

Even those pretentious moral speeches are frequently spiced with innuendo. The most entertaining of these occurs when Ozmyn and Benzayda, the play's young and ostensibly inexperienced lovers, first meet. Benzayda's father orders her to kill Ozmyn, but when she lays eyes on him she falls in love. She pleads for his life, and Ozmyn begs for death at her hands:

Benzayda: You see I tremble when I touch a sword.

         . . . .

Ozmyn: I'le guide the hand which must my death convay;
       My leaping heart shall meet it half the way.

        . . . .

       Defer not, fair Benzaida, my death;
       Looking on you —
       I should but live to sigh away my breath.
       My eyes have done the work they had to do;
       I take your Image with me; which they drew;
       And when they close, I shall dye full of you.

        . . . .

       Haste, Madam, to fulfill his hard Commands:
       And rescue me from their ignoble Hands.
       Let me kiss yours, before my wound you make;
       Then, easie Death I shall with pleasure take.
             (Part 1, 4.2.258, 261–62, 277–82, 314–17)

Dryden twists the sex and death puns of this scene so that Benzayda, wielding her phallic sword, has the aggressor's role, and Ozmyn plays the "feminine" part, willingly waiting to be "wounded" by

Benzayda's blade and wishing to die "full of [her]." This scene rewards its sexually sophisticated audience with more than the usual diet of double entendre, making the most of the ironic gap between what these young lovers mean to say and what their words mean to their auditors.

Dryden employs a similar brand of sophisticated innuendo in an exchange between Almanzor and the Spaniard, Arcos, when, during a pause in the fighting, they declare their admiration for one another:

> Arcos: The hatred of the brave, with battails, ends:
> And Foes, who fought for Honour, then, are Friends.
> I love thee, brave Almanzor, and am proud
> To have one hour, when Love may be allowed.
> . . . .
> Almanzor: The Man, who dares, like you, in fields appear,
> And meet my Sword, shall be my Mistriss here.
>
> (Part 2, 3.3.1–4, 7–8)

Dryden does not ask us to presume that these warriors (who later turn out to be father and son) intend their exchange as homoerotic flirtation, but he constructs their words to have that ring nonetheless.

Thus, *The Conquest of Granada* is, in equal doses, archly lascivious and overearnest as Dryden's characters alternate between titillating, bawdy talk and overwrought, histrionic speech-making. In the former mode, they tease their audiences with suggestions of activity reserved for the "tyring house" and the royal bed-chamber. In the latter, they fret about their "boyling passions," bewail the violence done their wounded, "bloody hearts," and quake before the "horrid Spectacle" of desire's war on honor (part 1, 2.1.179, 3.1.73, 4.2.229). As it is pulled and strained by these two irreconcilable modes of action, Dryden's play enacts the inconsistent, conflicted state of royalist ideology a decade after the Restoration.

NINE

"Willing rape is all the fashion"
PARTISAN POLITICS AND UNRULY SEXUALITY IN
APHRA BEHN'S *THE CITY HEIRESS*

Ladies . . . love to be ravisht of a Kindness. Why, your willing Rape is all the Fashion.
— From Aphra Behn, *The City Heiress*

. . . Women pardon force, because they find
The Violence of Love is still most kind:
Just like the Plots of well built Comedies,
Which then please most, when most they do surprize.
— From John Dryden, *The Rival Ladies*

Violating the King

In June 1680, the earl of Shaftesbury, leader of the Whig party, brought two cases before the grand jury at Westminster.[1] The first was a charge of recusancy against James, the duke of York.[2] The second was a charge of "High Treason and other High Crimes and Misdemeanors" against Louise de Kéroualle, the duchess of Portsmouth. Together, these charges constituted a bold attack against two of the most highly placed Roman Catholics in the nation: the king's brother and the king's lover.

325

The 22 articles against de Kéroualle accuse her of promoting Roman Catholicism, of wielding influence with the king for the purpose of promoting Papists to high office, of receiving lavish gifts from the king at the nation's expense, of attempting to convert Charles II to Catholicism, of giving "Popish Priests" access to the king's person, and of hiring Catholic cooks and allowing them opportunity to poison the king.

The first and most inflammatory of the charges accuses the duchess of endangering Charles's life in a more direct way:

> I. *Imprimis*, That the said Dutchess hath and still doth cohabit and keep company with the King, having had foul, nauseous and contagious Distempers; which once possessing her Blood, can never admit of a perfect Cure; to the manifest Danger and Hazard of the King's Person, in whose Preservation is bound up the Weal and Happiness of the Protestant Religion, our Lives, Liberties and Properties, and those of our Posterity for ever.[3]

Historians seem to have found these charges ludicrous; they uniformly pass over this incident with little more than a sly nod to the substance of the articles as though the whole event were no more than an off-color joke in rather poor taste.[4] Though they are hysterically exaggerated, like most of the other accusations made against principals in the largely fictional "Popish Plot," the charges against de Kéroualle are hardly frivolous. Like Henrietta Maria and Catherine of Braganza, the Roman Catholic wives of Charles I and Charles II, the duchess of Portsmouth was "suspected of translating erotic intimacy into political influence," and was charged with treasonous abuses against the monarch and his country.[5]

In fact, the charges against the duchess are entirely typical of the Whig strategy in that emergent party's campaign to limit the prerogative powers of the Crown and to pass a bill excluding James from the royal succession. The charges against de Kéroualle were partly a political ploy to gain her cooperation in the Whig efforts to force an exclusion bill on the king, but they were not sham charges. The prosecution would most certainly have gone ahead if an indictment could have been obtained, and she might well have been convicted if she had been brought to trial.[6] De Kéroualle must have known that this prosecution was in deadly earnest, coming as it did at the height of the Popish Plot crisis, when juries were heavily weighted with Whig sympathizers and public prejudice against Roman Catholicism had been deliberately aggravated by Whig propaganda. The previous year, five of the nation's most highly placed Roman Catholic nobles had been arrested in relation to the plot, and in January 1680, William Howard, viscount Stafford, had been executed for his supposed role.[7]

The charges against de Kéroualle were, themselves, a brilliant propaganda vehicle for the Whigs. While they had nothing new to reveal about the king's extramarital dalliances, they did provide an opportunity to publicly deride his most important mistress as a pocky whore, while maintaining the appearance of legal propriety. This attack functioned at two levels simultaneously. First, it was a serious threat to the duchess, whose presence evoked deep anger in some of the king's subjects. The famous anecdote about Nell Gwyn's being mistaken for de Kéroualle attests to the vehemence of feeling directed at the French woman. Surrounded by a hostile crowd, Gwyn emerged from her carriage to appease her attackers with the witticism, "Pray, good people, be civil; I am the Protestant whore."[8] At the same time, the real object of this legal action and the propaganda it inspired was not the king's Catholic whore, but the king himself.[9] In order to pass an exclusion bill, the Whigs either had to convince Charles to capitulate to their design or force him to do so by overwhelming him with popular (and electoral) support for the bill. This particular assault not only appealed to popular fears of Catholic designs against the monarch, it damaged the king's standing with his people.

In the time-honored antimonarchist tradition of striking a blow against the king in the name of his best interest and personal safety, the Whig charges against de Kéroualle took very public aim at the king's lasciviousness. The first article charges her with attempting to murder the king by infecting him with syphilis, a disease she was as likely to have contracted *from* him as to have passed *to* him. The king's sexual activity and sexual health were of secondary concern to his political opponents, of course, but they were more likely to sway public opinion than a well-reasoned argument of the issues.

The real concern of the Whigs was not that Louise de Kéroualle would corrupt the king's body with her sexual diseases (or that she would poison him or allow him to be murdered), but that she would influence his policies and his choice of advisers. The poet John Wilmot, earl of Rochester, articulated this sentiment in a dialogue poem circulated privately in Whig circles:

> King: When on Portsmouth's lap I lay my head,
>   And Knight does sing her bawdy song,
>   I envy not George Porter's bed,
>   Nor the delights of Madam Long.
> People: Now heavens preserve our faith's defender
>   From Paris plots and Roman cunt;
>   From Mazarin, that new pretender,
>   And from that *politique*, Grammont.[10]

A more prosaic statement of the same concern appeared in a contemporary newsletter circulated in Northamptonshire, which suggested that de Kéroualle, "with a Cabinet Caball of a few such others had the management and conduct of all the greatest affaires of the Nation." Sir James Johnson conveyed a similar opinion of the distribution of royal power when he observed that "The King off france could whore well & governe well, our King could whore well, but not governe."[11]

There is more to Johnson's bon mot than a suggestion that Charles was too busy pursuing his own pleasures to bother with government. The comparison of Charles II to Louis XIV echoes the commonplace assertion that the English court sought to imitate the French in all things: in dress, art, religion and political style. It seemed to some of his detractors that Charles's court was merely an annex of the French court. Furthermore, it was taken for granted that Louise de Kéroualle and her rival, Hortense Mancini, the duchess of Mazarin, were agents of the French king, or were at the very least a pipeline of information and influence for the French. The thought that Louis XIV controlled Charles's favorite mistresses and that he might, in fact, control Charles through their manipulation seems to have occurred to many in England, including Sir James Johnson and the disaffected court wit, Wilmot. In this context it was little comfort that the king had Protestant whores as well as Catholic ones.

The Whigs, who sought to enhance representative government in the nation and to contain the power of the Crown, had good cause to suspect that Charles would prefer to rule the nation singlehandedly (as Louis XIV did in France) if he could find a way to finance his government without recourse to parliamentary supply.[12] Sir Henry Capel summed up Whig concerns about French influences on Charles when he asserted that "From popery comes the notion of a standing army and arbitrary power."[13] Where "royal prerogative" was the catchphrase used to convey the odiousness of perceived Jacobean monarchical overreaching, and "will" was the Caroline propagandists' ubiquitous term, "arbitrary power" was the rallying cry of the exclusionist Whigs.

The idea that the duchess of Portsmouth posed a threat of sexual violation to the body of the king and to the body politic came to the framers of her indictment directly out of the language and imagery of Whig exclusion propaganda. In his study of the politics of London's commoners, *London Crowds in the Reign of Charles II*, Tim Harris describes one such publication, *A Scheme of Popish Cruelties*, which "contained a number of prints illustrative of its title: jesuits, monks and friars ravishing and abusing women; popish villains beating the brains out of tender infants and putting their mothers to the sword; and bloody papists cutting the throats of protestants or burning 'Martyrs for the True Religion.'"[14] Another tract reminded its readers of the martyrdoms suffered by Protestants during the reign of Mary Tudor, warning that "the last time popery reigned amongst us our divines were butchered by the name of heretic dogs, our houses plundered, our wives and daughters ravished."[15] Ravishment — not of the king, but of the unprotected populace — was the propagandist's best tool and the Protestant subject's worst nightmare.

As the godly party had used sensational accounts of horrific violence perpetrated by the rebellious Irish to convince the English citizenry of the dangers of Roman Catholicism in the years leading up to the civil wars, so during the exclusion crisis the Whigs reported Catholic war atrocities from the Thirty Years' war on the continent. *England's Calamity Foreshewn in Germanie's Miserie* focuses on the rapes, tortures and savage murder of Protestant believers. In one instance, the tract claimed, Catholics "tied burning matches to the tongue, noses, eyes, cheeks, breasts and legs: Yea! And the privy parts of women they stuffed with gunpowder and fired!"[16] The exclamation marks underscore the zeal with which this pamphlet exploits its salacious imagery to storm its readers' imaginations. The same pamphlet includes two woodcuts of a sort similar to those that accompanied the *Scheme of Popish Cruelties* (the genre had become heavily formulaic in the hundred years since the publication of Foxe's *Acts and Monuments*). What is striking about the woodcuts in *England's Calamity* is not the scenes they depict (Protestants burning, women ravished and children slaughtered), but the language with which they are captioned: "Your wives and daughters ravished . . . together with little children's brains dashed against the walls."[17] *Your* wives and daughters ravished. More directly than usual, this tract makes the argument that the royal court's sexual libertinism and its indulgence of Roman Catholicism were direct threats to the metaphorical body of the political nation and the material bodies of the nation's individual subjects. The tracts imply that the threat was very real and very personal: any and every subject stood to suffer.

John Dryden twists the rhetoric of violation in yet another direction in his anti-Whig allegory of the exclusion crisis, *Absalom and Achitophel*. The work seeks to derail Whig efforts to promote Charles II's oldest son, James Scott, duke of Monmouth, as an alternative heir. His supporters, a significant faction within the Whig party, were willing to disregard Scott's bastardy in view of his Protestantism. Dryden's biblical allegory equates Charles with King David, Scott with the concubine's son, Absalom, and the Whig leader Anthony Ashley Cooper, earl of Shaftesbury, with the wicked councillor, Achitophel. The allegory also implies Dryden's position: Absalom's attempt to seize his father's throne does not end well, after all. However, despite his committed Tory loyalty, Dryden is not blind to the king's weaknesses, and the work is as much a word of caution to the Crown as it is a denunciation of the opposition.

At a key moment in the poem's buildup to rebellion, Achitophel counsels Absalom that, all indications to the contrary aside, his father really desires Absalom to be his heir, but needs Absalom to seize the initiative:

> And who can sound the depth of *David's* soul?
> Perhaps his fear, his kindness may Controul.
> He fears his Brother, though he loves his Son,
> For plighted Vows too late to be undone.
> If so, by Force he wishes to be gain'd,
> Like women's Leachery, to seem Constrain'd:
> Doubt not, but when he most affects the Frown,
> Commit a pleasing Rape upon the Crown.
>
> (467–74)

This section of the poem reveals Dryden's ambivalence: it depicts the rebels as ravishers, particularly marking the Achitophelian Shaftesbury as a dangerously clever manipulator; however, it also diminishes the king by equating him with duplicitous, lustful women. This characterization not only acknowledges Charles's appetite for lecherous women, but suggests that the king's character is no more refined than that of a wanton woman. Of course, Dryden places these words in Achitophel's mouth, a device that enables the author to criticize the king's character and policies without being overtly disloyal. In this way, the poet demonstrates how Charles's weaknesses play into his enemies' hands, making it difficult for his supporters to counter opposition attacks.

This passage suggests another level of concern beneath the de Kéroualle indictment. Where the articles accuse the duchess of perpetrating a sexual assault against the innocent king, no one really thought the king innocent. His complicity with the French and with the Roman Catholic church was assumed in the same way that the culture assumed the complicity of women with their rapists, believing that women wish "to seem Constrain'd" as a cover for their willingness to be seduced. In fact, it seems that Dryden and the Tories, no less than their Whiggish contemporaries, feared that Charles might give way on points he pretended to cherish as dearly as a woman her honor. The Whigs' fear, of course, was that Charles would convert to Catholicism or subvert the Parliament. The Tories feared the possibility that Charles might eventually give way on the points on which "the loyal party" had staked their reputations and careers.[18] Specifically, they feared what Dryden's Achitophel urges: that Charles wanted to exclude James, but wished to appear to have been forced to do so.

Partisan Representations of Sexuality on Stage

By virtue of generic convention, Restoration comedy celebrates and critiques human behavior, especially the social rivalries and romantic entanglements that complicate, but inevitably enable, marriages. Like the heroic drama, Restoration comedy also reveled in the presence of actresses, who lent their real feminine flesh to roles that once would have been impersonated by cross-dressed boys. As with the heroic drama, this novelty encouraged playwrights to stuff their plots with physical stage business to display those feminine bodies in the most alluring, most intriguing, most provocative situations. In comedy, the predictable result is a good measure of farcical hide-and-seek (what Janet Todd has called the stage business "of darkness and doors"), a generous serving of cross-dress and exotic disguise, and a savory side of sexual situations including a sizeable portion of threatened ravishments.[19]

It was once in fashion for critics to argue that all of this tasty, tantalizing titillation was merely escapist distraction for theater audiences seeking to avoid the concerns of their real lives in a politically unsettled country. Then critics awoke to the obvious: sex and theater may have been the stuff of fantasy, but not escapist fantasy in a capital city where sex was relentlessly politicized. Michael Neill comments on the political astuteness of Restoration comedy, "which takes account of the political sensitivity of its patrons." He observes that Restoration comedy commented on topical issues, weaving these insights into the urbane banter of its lovers and their compatriots. He remarks that "the dramatists are often able to endow the most seemingly frivolous material with surprising and impudent suggestiveness, turning the dizzying round of sexual competition, erotic combat, and parental oppression into a figure for more serious forms of power struggle." In fact, the turbulent sexual impulses represented on stage were more than merely "figure[s] for more serious forms of power struggle," more than merely signifiers pointing toward actions of real political significance beyond the playhouse: each performance of these plays was a political act in its own right.[20]

As we have seen, depictions of unruly sexuality had long been put to partisan use by those who struggled for power in the political nation. Thus, during the Exclusion Crisis the king's sexual shenanigans and the erotic escapades of his courtiers were exhibited in opposition propaganda as evidence of his and their unfitness for the serious business of government. The representation of extravagant, uncontrolled sexuality as characteristic of aristocratic or royal figures onstage continued to be an activity inflected with partisan significance.[21] Likewise, the representation of London aldermen as hypocritical lechers was designed to raise an equal and opposite partisan reaction.[22]

Whig theater ranged from Shadwell's comic denunciations of lewd Tory rakes and Nathaniel Lee's tragic representation of the rape of Lucrece, the founding event of Roman republicanism, in

Lucius Junius Brutus, to popular entertainments like *The Coronation of Queen Elizabeth*.[23] This last was a vehemently anti-Catholic play staged at both the Bartholomew and Southwark fairs in 1680, which, in the tradition of Middleton's *A Game at Chess*, caricatured Roman Catholic figures as sexually monstrous: in this play the pope seduces and impregnates a nun, signifying the fertility of Roman Catholic corruption.[24] Tory plays answered by making sexual abuse a feature of rebellion as it is in Otway's *Venice Preserv'd* and Ravenscroft's revision of *Titus Andronicus*, where the rape of Lavinia is framed as "an Invasion on a Princes right."[25] As Susan J. Owen points out, "for Whig dramatists, rape is a trope of tyranny and of popery, and women's resistance a symbol of the subject's resistance to tyrannical government."[26] For Tory playwrights, rape signals the anarchic energies of dissent, and *attempted* rape derides the inability of opposition leaders to control their movement or to execute their designs. With regard to the failed rapes in Tory comedies, Arlen Feldwick suggests that the fact that women are able to resist the advances of Whiggish would-be ravishers (and feeble City husbands) illustrates Whig incapacity to govern: "Whigs are made *so* incompetent and contemptible that women can fool and control them. This reflects a clear inversion of the 'proper' order, according to which women are subservient to men. In [the Tory dramatist's] view, the Whigs are *deserving* of manipulation at the hands of women, because they pretend to an authority on which they have no valid claim."[27] Tory artists punish their Whig characters with the humiliation of being outsmarted by mere women.

An interesting case in point is Aphra Behn's *The City Heiress*, which debuted in April 1682. Firmly embedded in the sexual intrigues of its plot is a Tory celebration of the king's recent triumph over the Whig party. In the character of Sir Timothy Treat-all, "an old seditious Knight, that keeps open House for Commonwealthsmen and true blue Protestants" (203), Behn serves up a stinging satire of the once powerful, but recently defeated Whig leader, the earl of Shaftesbury.

Shaftesbury's power had been broken when Charles dissolved the Oxford Parliament in March 1681 and arrested a number of Whig conspirators. Shaftesbury had been tried for treason. His acquittal by a London jury packed with Whig partisans had not repaired his grip on power, and within the year Shaftesbury was forced to flee to Holland.[28] To the delight of all in Behn's play, the Shaftesbury character, Treat-all, is first duped into believing that he has been elected king of Poland, then robbed by his nephew, who uses treasonous documents found in the robbery to blackmail his uncle. Finally, Treat-all marries a woman he supposes to be a rich heiress, only to find that she is his nephew's cast mistress.[29]

Behn depicts the Tory victory over the Whigs as a triumph of wit and sexual prowess over foolishness, hypocrisy and impotence.[30] Treat-all fancies himself "young enough to marry" and potent enough to disinherit his nephew by fathering "a Son and Heir of my own begetting, and so forth" (1.1, p. 207). To this end, Treat-all pays court to Lady Galliard, a wealthy young widow. Furthermore, when his nephew, Wilding, asks Treat-all to shelter an heiress he plans to marry, the older man proposes to her immediately. Lucre and lechery equally motivate the aging Treat-all.

Of course, all of Treat-all's greedy matrimonial plans go awry. He loses the widow, Lady Galliard, to his nephew's friend, Sir Charles Meriwill, who owes his success with her to the coaching of his beneficent, raucous "Tory-rory" uncle, Sir Anthony Meriwill (1.1, p. 212). Furthermore, Treat-all learns too late that the young "heiress" he has married is not Charlot Gett-all, but Wilding's kept mistress, Diana. Janet Todd has observed of Behn's belittling treatment of the parliamentarians in *The Roundheads*, another of her Exclusion Crisis plays, that "in Behn's formulation, cavalier against roundhead becomes the common plot of youth outwitting age and taking its women. Politics falls into sexual struggle and government is reduced to bedroom farce."[31] Indeed, Behn's method is to reduce the opposition through farce from formidable authorities to impotent fools. In Treat-all, Behn converts the conventional role of blocking character to political allegory. The foolish old uncle outmaneuvered by a potent young nephew figures Whiggism as out-of-date, unfashionable and lacking either substance or credibility.[32]

Behn gives Treat-all the vocabulary and opinions of a stereotypical London alderman, an old-style parliamentarian, and attributes to him the political agenda of Whiggism. Describing his own merits, Treat-all announces that "My Integrity has been known ever since Forty one; I bought three Thousand a year in Bishops Lands, as 'tis well known, and lost it at the King's return; for which I'm honour'd in the City" (1.1, p. 207). Those he opposes are "Tarmagant Tories . . . the very Vermin of a young Heir," in his opinion, a group of "leud and vitious" young men, who "keep their Wenches, Coaches, rich Liveries, and so forth, who live upon Charity, and the Sins of the Nation" (1.1, p. 205). When Treat-all meets Sir Anthony Meriwill, he derides Meriwill's churchgoing: "You are for the Surplice still, old Orthodox you; the Times cannot mend you, I see" (1.1, p. 210). Aversion to the vestments and ceremonies of the state church remained a central theme of opposition treatises, as for instance when Andrew Marvell enumerates the errors of Roman Catholicism, among them "Vestments, Consecrations, Exorcisms, Whisperings, Sprinklings, Censings, and Fantastical Rites, Gesticulations, and Removals so unbeseeming a Christian Office, that it represents rather the pranks and ceremonies of Jugglers and Conjurers."[33] Behn makes Treat-all brag that his own churchgoing is merely "to save my Bacon, as they say, once a Month, and that too after the Porridge is serv'd up"; in other words, Treat-all attends only to avoid the recusancy laws, managing his attendance to avoid taking Communion.[34] In short, Treat-all is a representative Whig, one who "talks gravely in the City, speaks scandalously against the Government, and rails most abominably against the Pope and the French King" (1.1, p. 206).[35]

The Whig trait Behn attacks with most vehemence is the stance of moral superiority adopted by City politicians and partisan propagandists, who attacked court licentiousness and presumed to speak as the moral voice of the nation. The play opens with Sir Timothy scolding his nephew for his vices:

[I] have had ye out of all the Bayliffs, Serjeants, and Constables Clutches about Town, Sir; have brought you out of all the Surgeons, Apothecaries, and pocky Doctors Hands, that ever pretended to cure incurable Diseases; and have crost ye out of the Books of all the Mercers, Silk-man, Exchange-men, Taylors, Shoemakers, and Sempstresses; with all the rest of the unconscionable City-tribe of the long Bill, that had but Faith enough to trust, and thought me Fool enough to pay. (1.1, p. 204)

Treat-all is not, himself, free of vices, nor does he expect others to be — as long as they share his politics. Behn takes brilliant revenge on the Whigs through this character who unwittingly reveals his own hypocrisies, as when he weeps crocodile tears over the nephew he is casting off:

[Weeping.] Before he fell to Toryism, he was a sober, civil Youth, and had some Religion in him, wou'd read ye Prayers Night and Morning with a laudable Voice, and cry *Amen* to 'em; 'twou'd have done one's Heart good to have heard him — wore decent Clothes, was drunk but on Sundays and Holidays; and then I had Hopes of him. [Still weeping.] (1.1, p. 205)

The night of the robbery, Wilding and his fellow bandits flush Mrs. Sensure, the housekeeper, out of Treat-all's bedchamber, where the two have been reading seditious Protestant sermons together: a copy of "A Sermon preacht by Richard Baxter, Divine" drops out of Mrs. Sensure's "bosom" (5.1, p. 279). The comedy of this scene in which the poor, embarrassed woman strives to put a fine face on her compromising circumstances turns upon the equally devastating possibilities that the ostensibly upstanding Treat-all has been fornicating with his housemaid or that he is incapable of the deed and has satisfied himself with the titillation of having sermons read to him by a woman in her nightdress.

Treat-all's advances toward the miss-in-disguise-as-heiress, Diana, are a further exposure of his false morality:

> Diana: But I have given my Faith and Troth to Wilding.
> Treat-all: Faith and Troth! We stand upon neither Faith nor Troth
>   in the City, Lady. . . . Nay, had you married my
>   ungracious Nephew, we might by this our *Magna
>   Charta* have hang'd him for a Rape.
> Diana: What, though he had my Consent?
> Treat-all: That's nothing, he had not ours.
> Diana: Then shou'd I marry you by stealth, the Danger wou'd
>   be the same.
> Treat-all: No, no, Madam, we never accuse one another; 'tis the
>   poor Rogues, the Tory Rascals we always hang. Let 'em
>   accuse me if they please; alas, I come off handsmooth
>   with *Ignoramus*. (3.1, p. 246).

Whig assertions that the king's arbitrary government would rob them of their property and of the legal rights guaranteed by "Magna Charta," are seen here to cover their illegal schemes to appropriate the property of others. Treat-all's reference to the "Ignoramus" verdicts of Whig-packed London juries was a reminder of the trials in which a number of Catholic (Tory) men were executed for treason as conspirators in the Popish Plot, while Shaftesbury, when he came to be tried, was acquitted by a verdict of ignoramus, or lack of evidence. In this scene and its topical reference, the audience sees that the real ravisher and traitor is the Whig, Sir Timothy Treat-all.

While Whig propaganda sought to speak with moral authority, the stance articulated by Behn through the play's Tory men denies the relevance of morality or at least of moralistic posturing. Where Treat-all accuses Sir Anthony Meriwill of Acountenanc[ing] Sin and Expences," the play seconds Meriwill's denial of both charges: "What Sin, what Expences?" The Tory position holds that the pleasures, pastimes and personal indulgences of the monied fuel the national economy to the benefit of those City-dwelling moralists who condemn the Tory while taking his money. "What Sin, what Expences?" asks Sir Anthony with regard to his nephew's characteristic Tory behavior. "He wears good Clothes, why, Tradesmen get the more by him; he keeps his Coach, 'tis for his Ease; a

Mistress, 'tis for his Pleasure; he games, 'tis for his Diversion: And where's the harm of this?" (1.1, pp. 211–12). According to this argument, desire (for goods, for entertainment, for sex) is natural to all and is, therefore, not a negative character trait. In a characteristic satiric gesture, Behn "proves" the truth of this Tory proposition by having a Whig admit its truth. Treat-all concedes the point when he recalls a Commonwealth law against boasting: "Oh, that crying Sin of Boasting! Well fare, I say, the Days of old Oliver; he by a wholesom act made it death to boast; so that then a Man might whore his Heart out, and no body the wiser" (1.1, p. 206). In Treat-all's mock-Whig logic, it is not licentiousness which is to be condemned, but the appearance of licentiousness.[36] Behn's scrutiny reveals Whig morality to be a sham, while maintaining that Tory immorality is unabashed human nature.

In contrast to Whig moralizing, the Tory stance amounts to a bold-faced — and strategic — acknowledgment of sexuality. Dryden's *Absalom and Achitophel* begins with just such a declaration:

> In pious times, e'r Priest-craft did begin,
> Before *Polygamy* was made a sin;
> When man, on many, multiply'd his kind,
> E'r one to one was, cursedly, confind:
> When Nature prompted, and no law deny'd
> Promiscuous use of Concubine and Bride;
> Then, *Israel's* Monarch, after Heaven's own heart,
> His vigorous warmth did, variously, impart
> To Wives and Slaves: And, wide as his Command,
> Scatter'd his Maker's Image through the Land.

(1–10)

Dryden's tone is complex. Partly tongue-in-cheek, partly serious, he claims scriptural precedent to remind his readers that morality shifts with time and that the God of the Bible did not always condemn promiscuity.[37] Comparing Charles II with David (and Solomon, who outdid his father for wives and concubines), Dryden claims for his king divine right to rule and to procreate. With good

Tory humor, the poet proposes that Charles's sexual capacity is heroic in proportion. Dryden neither hides Charles's promiscuity, nor apologizes for it; instead, he makes a virtue of it, a characteristic Tory move.

Susan J. Owen notes that "Whig criticism of royal and court libertinism is countered by Tories with a combination of indulgence and erasure, and refocusing the charge upon the opposition."[38] If sexual intemperance is an unfortunate feature of royal and court behavior, the Tories argue, it is equally common among — and much more dangerous when practiced by — Whig citizens. Thus, Tory propaganda regularly offered "news" of unruly citizens, especially those stirred to violence by the frenetic Whig bonfires and street protests. Tim Harris describes a representative example of this sort of Tory publication:

> On 4 September 1682, according to Nathaniel Thompson [a Tory propagandist], a "Holding-forth Brother," returning home drunk that night, staggered into the path of a coach which only narrowly missed him. He therefore struck the horses and the coachman, crying out "Tory, Arbitrary Power." This prompted a crowd to gather, who proceeded to break the windows of the coach, and we are told that a cobbler shouted to the passenger, a "Lady of Honour," that he was as good or better a man than her husband.[39]

We are a long way here from the inept citizen cuckolds of Tory comedy; however, both representations of Whig sexuality work in the same way. The social presumption of the cobbler in this news report and his sexual threat to the "Lady of Honour" suggest the social and political pretensions of men, who, from the Tory perspective, were both dangerously unworthy of political power and absurdly incapable of perceiving their own limitations.

The audacity with which Tory writers acknowledged the libertinism complained of by their Whig detractors and the zeal with which they attacked the sexuality of the opposite party is a function of the smug class chauvinism that leads them to depict the Whigs as mere citizens and, more condescendingly, as rabble. "Each cobbler's [a] statesman grown, and the bold Rabble / Convert each Alehouse Board to Council-Table," asserts one Tory tract; another warned of the leveling pretensions of exclusionists who would "teach the Nobles how to bow / And Keep their Gentry down / . . . The name of Lord shall be abhorr'd / For evr'y man's a Brother."[40]

In this vein, in *Absalom and Achitophel*, Dryden satirizes Shaftesbury's strategy for gaining political power in Achitophel's bald attempt to manipulate the mob:

> By buzzing Emissaries, fills the ears
> Of listening Crowds, with Jealosies and Fears
> Of Arbitrary Counsels brought to light,
> And proves the King himself a *Jebusite*:[41]
> Weak Arguments! which yet he knew ful well,
> Were strong with People easie to Rebell.
>
> (210–15)

Of those Whigs he deems too far beneath contempt to name in his poem, Dryden writes, "Nor shall the Rascall Rabble here have Place, / Whom Kings no Titles gave, and God no Grace" (579–80).[42] Here, Dryden appropriates to Tory politics the insolent pose affected by the court wits in their poetry. A typical instance of this attitude occurs in John Wilmot, earl of Rochester's poem, "An Allusion to Horace, the Tenth Satyr of the first Book":

> I loathe the rabble; 'tis enough for me
> If Sedley, Shadwell, Shepherd, Wycherley,
> Godolphin, Butler, Buckhurst, Buckingham,
> And some few more, whom I omit to name,
> Approve my sense: I count their censure fame.
>
> (120–24)[43]

In general, the Tories stood on their loyalty to the king and their (supposed) superiority of social status to license their cause despite their behavior.

It is important to note that Whig and Tory did not divide along class lines; however, the propaganda on both sides employs a false class-consciousness. As we have seen, the Whig propagandists took up where the antimonarchists and parliamentarians left off in portraying courtier-aristocrats as a class of licentious, Papist wastrels. This portrait left room for Whigs of all degrees to feel pleased with the difference of character and station that separated them from the dissipated Tories.

The Tory disparagement of their opponents as small-minded commoners would have been self-defeating if it had been intended to sway the middling sort to their cause. In fact, the strategy works in quite the opposite way. It flatters those who are loyal, distinguishing them as members of an elite class (whether they were in actuality or not). At the same time, it is also a bitter attack on those aristocrats who allied themselves with the Whigs. It is in this spirit that Charles II referred to George Villiers, the second duke of Buckingham, as "Alderman George" for his relationship with London's Whigs.[44]

Villiers is a good example of the fact that the parties did not split according to class divisions. Villiers had been a close companion of Charles from childhood and had played an important role in the royalist cause during the civil wars and the Interregnum. After the Restoration, he had held a number of important offices and was a Knight of the Bedchamber, a position that placed him among the king's closest companions. Villiers had, however, offended the king on a number of occasions and was given to just the kind of wild debauchery that gave the court such a bad image during Charles's reign. Eventually, Charles stripped Villiers of all his offices, after which Villiers took up with Shaftesbury and the opposition. With this alliance Villiers repudiated his former loyalty to the court, intentionally positioning himself against the king.[45]

Another reminder that the Tory party did not simply evolve out of the notorious circle of court wits exists in the irony that although Wilmot remained the admired model of the attractive, arrogant, acerbic rake celebrated by Tory writers, he and several of the rakish gentlemen mentioned in his "Allusion to Horace" aligned themselves with Villiers in the late 1670s and early 1680s. Wilmot's ambivalent position as court insider siding with the opposition emerges in several of his most jaded verses, as when he lampoons the king's vassalage to his mistresses:

> Nor are his high desires above his strength:
> His scepter and his prick are of a length;
> And she may sway the one who plays with th'other,
> And make him little wiser than his brother.[46]

Wilmot's contempt for the king's brother and heir plays a key role in this critique and later helped define his alienation from the political circle which would emerge as the Tory party, but there is also a jaded sense of disillusionment with the king himself in the poem: "Restless he rolls about from whore to whore, / A merry monarch, scandalous and poor" (20–21). More bitter and more telling is the closing couplet of this poem in which the speaker declares: "All monarchs I hate, and the thrones they sit on, / From the hector of France to the cully of Britain" (32–33).

Villiers and Wilmot were not lonely in their Whiggism. Among the aristocrats and wits associated with the Restoration court, a surprising number lent their support to the Whigs. Charles Sedley and Charles Sackville, Lord Buckhurst, earl of Dorset, both allied themselves with the Whigs. Along with Villiers and John Wilmot, earl of Rochester, Sedley and Sackville were some of the most notorious courtiers of their day.[47] Renowned for their drunkenness and dissipation, their exploits included an incident in which Sedley and Henry Savile clashed with officers of the London customs' office when the courtiers tried to import a shipment of dildos. By their own report, members of the group also on occasion danced naked outdoors at Woodstock park, a Crown property entrusted to Wilmot's wardenship. Most notorious of all was the occasion when Sedley, Sackville and Thomas Ogle appeared to the public on the balcony of the Cock Tavern, naked and in "open day . . . acting all the postures of lust and buggery that could be imagined, and abusing of scripture."[48]

Clearly, Whig condemnation of the licentiousness of the Tory court cannot be reconciled with the Whig party's actual membership. The notorious exploits of certain Whigs added credibility to the Tory contention that the Whig character was one of moral hypocrisy covering a secret life of sin, although this characterization was less likely to be applied to former courtiers than to "true blue Protestants" and "Commonwealthsmen" like Behn's Sir Timothy Treat-all.

The partisan politics of the late 1670s and early 1680s not only divided the wits and the court, but divided loyalties and severed friendships in theatrical circles as well. Sackville, Sedley, Wilmot and Villiers had all involved themselves in the theater as writers, patrons and influential critics. During these years, however, their partisan allegiances and personal feuds diverted them from supporting the theater in the manner to which it had become accustomed. Wilmot quarreled with Dryden. Dryden lampooned Villiers. Thomas Shadwell, who initially sided with the Tories, became a vociferous and sharp-penned lampoonist for the Whigs in 1681.[49] Shadwell's change of party caused him to fall out with Dryden, occasioning one of the bitterest rifts within the theatrical community.[50] Elkannah Settle was another outspoken proponent of the Whig cause, but Thomas Otway sided with Dryden and Behn and the Tories.

Behn's Ambivalence

In addition to the turncoating and side-changing among the partisan wits, neither party commanded uniformity of opinion or agenda amongst its members. J. R. Jones has described the Whigs as a loose coalition of five groups that diverged in social and economic profile, differed significantly on many political issues, but which could be depended upon to act cohesively as a party as long as exclusion remained their central issue. Melinda Zook illustrates that the Tory party was as diverse as their opponents the Whigs: "not all Tories thought alike, and this was as true for politicians as it was for poets and playwrights."[51] Behn, especially, was a passionately partisan writer, but *The City Heiress*, its anti-Whig enthusiasm notwithstanding, demonstrates a decided ambivalence about its witty young Tories and their sexual prowess. Tom Wilding, in typical rake fashion, dallies with several women at once, and although it presents him as charming, the play asks its audience to consider Wilding's behavior from the point of view of the women whom it affects. More disturbing than Wilding's sexual adventurism, though, is Behn's depiction of Sir Charles Meriwill's "honorable" courtship of Lady Galliard. In Behn's play, sexuality is a disruptive force that makes a mockery of the social mechanisms designed to contain it.

Michael Neill suggests that the dashing rake with his aristocratic pedigree, "his turbulent energies and unashamed delight in power" was an ambivalent representation of "those destructive drives which were undermining the fragile constitutional calm of the Restoration settlement." Neill writes that "the best 'Restoration Comedy' is properly so called not merely from historical convenience, but because, in its sly, allusive fashion, it is actively concerned with the nature of 'restoration' itself, with the business of re-forming a civil order in the face of those 'barbarous' but 'natural' impulses towards revolution, anarchy, or tyranny which constantly threaten to destroy it."[52] In comedy, of course, restoration is conventionally effected through satisfactory marriages which check, if they do not reform, the compelling impulses of sexuality.

In Behn's play, though, marriage seems entirely inadequate to this task. The reasons for this failure are complex. In part, Behn's vision is a uniquely feminine critique of her society's treatment of sexuality and women and the institution of marriage.[53] In many respects, however, the jaundiced view of marriage in this play corresponds to that of Behn's male peers and is inflected with the same kind of political topicality that colors their work.[54]

Behn's portrait of the rake differs little from the representation of this stock character in the works of her male peers. As Neill remarks, the rake's delight in his ability to live by his wits (to con or seduce others into supporting him) and his refusal to restrain his sexual desires places cynicism about traditional property-system marriages at the center of most Restoration comic plots. Her Willmore and Loveless and Gayman and Wilding and the rest are every bit as dashing and every bit as parasitic as the rakes of Dryden or Wycherley or Etherege. And yet, to take Wilding as an example, her rakes do not all fit the mold of the careless (though cash-poor) aristocrat. Indeed, Wilding is a product of the City; he is an alderman's nephew who has come to his political senses and has learned to appreciate the clothes, women and witty companionship of the Tory lifestyle. Presumably this character innovation makes Wilding a model for each audience member's own admiration for Tory politics and values. But Behn also innovates in representing Wilding's depth of feeling for Lady Galliard. Yes, he juggles three women at once; yes, he lies shamelessly to each of them; yes, he exercises relentless coercion in order to get the widow to bed. However, the play goes out of its way to make poignant the fact that Wilding loses Lady Galliard, in whom, despite his frequent disparagements of marriage, he seems to see a mate worth having. He and she both really care that Sir Charles Meriwill snatches the widow from Wilding's embrace. This is not to say Behn would have her audience believe that Wilding would be faithful or Lady Galliard happy in matrimony, but she does insist that both regret the other's loss.

Behn's affection for her rakes has led Melinda Zook to assert that the playwright advances the interests of elite males above the interests of the women in her plays:

> Behn's royalism, articulated time and again in her work, revolved around an idealized aristocratic ethos that liberated the individual from the tyrannies of dull customs and traditions, things acceptable for the common castes of society, but which shackled the noble mind and heart. In better times, Behn may well have concentrated solely on the need to break those traditional shackles which so confined a woman's life. But in the climactic atmosphere of pre-revolution London, Behn's focus revolved around glorifying and defending the Cavalier culture of court and castigating its enemies, the Whigs and Dissenters.[55]

While Behn indeed shares with her male peers a commitment both to Tory politics and an infectious fondness for her rakes, I think Zook misses the striking ways in which Behn both attends to the "traditional shackles which so confined a woman's life" and insists that her audience note what Tory libertinism costs the women it embraces.

Behn is truly an anomaly among the playwrights of her day with respect to the sympathetic portraits she draws of her female characters. Her women, like the women in Dryden's comedies and Wycherley's and Etherege's and Shadwell's, have desires and pursue love interests. The difference between Behn's women and their contemporaries is the dignity she accords them. Contrast, for instance, her Lady Galliard, the rich, young widow who falls for Tom Wilding's charms, with Etherege's Mrs. Loveit, the graceless gentlewoman seduced by Dorimant, *The Man of Mode*'s irresistable rake. Behn gives her women a thoughtful interior life which the male dramatists often omit. She uses brief exchanges between her ladies and their serving-women not to demonstrate their vanity and admiration for finery, nor to develop the unpleasantness of their jealous furies, but to demonstrate their understanding of their circumstances.

Charlot Gett-all has an important scene (2.1) with Mrs. Clacket, the "City Bawd and Puritan" with whom Wilding has lodged her for his convenience. Through their conversation Behn shows several aspects of Charlot's character: her love for Wilding, her apprehension of his unfaithfulness, her intelligent grasp of her precarious situation as a woman who has eloped, but not yet married, and the wit with which she will manage these challenges.[56] Even the kept woman, Diana, is given asides and exchanges with her woman Betty, which demonstrate both her genuine feelings for Wilding and her understanding that she must look out for herself and marry Sir Timothy Treat-all if she can (3.1, 5.3). Similarly, when Behn's women suffer the indignities of betrayal and abandonment, they are not made laughingstocks for the audience's pleasure. Although Behn's Lady Galliard gives in to

Wilding's seduction, she is not treated with the contempt that Etherege allots his equivalent character, Mrs. Loveit, who has lost Dorimant's affection in *The Man of Mode*.

Behn reveals a particular sensitivity to the dangers sexuality holds for women in her society. Wilding jeopardizes Charlot's reputation and her prospects for marriage when he does not make good his promise to marry her after she has eloped with him. When she realizes that far from being a promising young heir, Wilding is notorious as "one of the leudest Heathens about Town," she faces the prospect of either returning to her family in disgrace or marrying a fortune hunter like Mr. Foppington, who has no wealth of his own and wishes to support himself with her inheritance (2.1, p. 219).

Behn's young heiress learns to her cost that young men like Wilding may pay lip service to romantic love, but their courtship is only a cynical mask covering straightforward economic or sexual goals. Wilding, it turns out, may also be in search of a wife "to buy him breeches," but he is a more clever speculator in the marriage market than Foppington.[57] Wilding has converted his charms into capital with more than one wealthy prospective bride and hopes to find a better settlement than Charlot can offer (2.1, p. 219). She accurately assesses her situation and sees that Wilding is keeping her in reserve "for a dead Lift, if Fortune prove unkind, or wicked Uncles refractory" (p. 223). Should Wilding find a better way to secure his fortune than through marriage with her, Charlot will find herself with a ruined reputation instead of a husband. Behn does not allow this young woman to be a mere victim of masculine manipulation; her Charlot Gett-all is no whining ninny. When she learns that she has a rival, she cons the bawd Clacket into disguising her so that she may covertly mingle in the company at Sir Timothy Treat-all's house and view not only her feminine competition, but also assess the state of Wilding's relation with his uncle. Armed with this knowledge, Charlot is in a better position to understand her predicament; the knowledge she gains gives her some leverage with Wilding.

Although less vulnerable than the unmarried Charlot, Wilding's other wealthy love-interest, Lady Galliard, also suffers the consequences of her involvement with him. She, too, has a reputation to protect while she considers remarriage. She has reason to fear that Wilding cannot be trusted to protect her "fame" should she become his lover. She presciently tells him that she cannot risk consummating their love because "when you weary of me, first your Friend, / Then his, then all the World" will learn of it from him (4.1, p. 264). In fact, he does not wait to tire of her before telling the world; after they make love, he immediately reports the event to several of his friends (5.1, p. 277).

Wilding is not the real threat that Behn designs for Lady Galliard, however. Galliard, because she is a widow with some experience of men and control of her own estate, is able to cope with Wilding. Though it costs her considerable anxiety, she makes her own decision whether to accept or reject him as a lover. As a widow, she derives a certain freedom from the fact that a second husband will not expect to find her a virgin. She has a luxury Charlot lacks: she is able to separate sexual decisions from marriage plans. The man Lady Galliard finds unmanageable is not Wilding, but Sir Charles Meriwill, the man who wants to marry her. As Behn presents them, his attempts on the widow's independence are more damaging than Wilding's attempts on her virtue.

Behn explores the paradoxical nature of sex and marriage in two scenes at the center of her play. In the first, Wilding woos Lady Galliard to become his willing lover; in the second, Sir Charles Meriwill forces her to become his unwilling wife. In act 4, scene 1, Behn mobilizes and then manipulates to new ends several conventions about women's desire. First, Behn allows Lady Galliard to fulfill conventional expectations that, as a lusty young widow, she will yield to her desire for Wilding. Then, when she does give herself to him, Lady Galliard insists on constructing a verbal fiction that casts her as virtuous victim of Wilding's overpowering force. Her choice becomes his imposition. It is a tenuous fiction at best, and Lady Galliard deconstructs it herself even as she tries to establish it:

> Lady Galliard: [*In a soft Tone, coming near him*]
>   I find I must be miserable — I wou'd not be thought false.
> Wilding: Nor wou'd I think you so; give me not Cause.
> Lady Galliard: What Heart can bear distrust from what it loves?
>   Or who can always her own Wish deny?
>   [*Aside*] My Reason's weary of the unequal Strife;
>   And Love and Nature will at last o'ercome.
>   [*To him in a soft Tone*]
>   — Do you not then believe I love you?
> Wilding: How can I, while you still remain unkind?
> Lady Galliard: How shall I speak my guilty Thoughts?
>   I have no Power to part with you; conceal my Shame,
>   I doubt I cannot, I fear I wou'd not any more deny you.
>   . . . .
>   Turn your Face away, and give me leave
>   To hide my rising Blushes: I cannot look on you,
>   [*As this last Speech is speaking, she sinks into his Arms by degrees*]
>   But you must undo me if you will —
>   Since I no other way my Truth can prove.
>
>   (4.1, p. 267)

Lady Galliard tries to displace responsibility for an act she knows to be of her own choosing onto "Love" and "Nature" and onto Wilding and his unreasonable pressure. At the same time, though, her speech is full of acknowledgments of her own agency. She stresses the force of his impatience ("What heart can bear distrust from what it loves?"), but admits that her own desire is as demanding ("Or who can always her own Wish deny?"). She emphasizes her powerlessness to oppose his will ("I have not Power," "I cannot"), but must also acknowledge that it is her will as well ("I wou'd not any more deny you"). When she speaks of "the unequal Strife" and uses words like "Power" and "o'ercome," she frames the moment as a combat she cannot win. Finally, she describes it as a rape, an act for which Wilding only is responsible ("you must undo me if you will"), but she undermines even this characterization, turning the rape into a testament to her "Truth" — an act for which she takes credit.

Lady Galliard invokes the idea of rape in order to justify her decision to have sex with Wilding. For her, "rape" is a useful social convention that enables her to overcome the restrictive concern for reputation that would otherwise force her to refuse sex despite her strong desire for Wilding. Sir Anthony Meriwill understands this convention and instructs his nephew to use it to advantage. Describing the widow, the older Meriwill tells his nephew, "I am mistaken if she be not one of those Ladies that love to be ravisht of a Kindness. Why, your willing Rape is all the Fashion" (4.2, p. 268).

Such a "willing" rape could preserve the woman's claim to virtue, while nonetheless allowing her to have sex. In Restoration comedy, this device frequently brings lovers together. A woman's "no," therefore, is often merely a code for "yes" in these plays. Uncomfortable as this moment is for contemporary feminist readers of Behn's play, this female dramatist shares the same view of women's disingenuousness her male colleagues held.[58] That women love to be ravished of a "kindness" is a ubiquitous truism in Restoration literature, a pattern of behavior believed to be so basic to feminine behavior that it was available as a common analogy to describe other types of feigned reluctance. Variations on this formula appear in play after play, as when Mr. Medley, in Etherege's *The Man of Mode*, likens Sir Foppington's feigned modesty about dancing to women's feigned chastity: "Like a woman, I find you must be struggled with before one brings you to what you desire" (4.1).

Dryden meditates on this paradox in his early tragicomedy, *The Rival Ladies* (1664), when the character Don Gonsalvo considers forcing himself on a woman who does not return his passion:

> Against her will the fair Julia to possess,
> Is not t'enjoy but Ravish happiness:

> Yet women pardon force, because they find
> The Violence of Love is still most kind:
> Just like the Plots of well built Comedies,
> Which then please most, when most they do surprize.[59]

The implication of Dryden's lines is that women do not always know their own minds, but once ravished will realize that they enjoyed both the experience of sex and the masculine initiative that made it possible. Gonsalvo marks himself out as a forward-thinking man able to credit women with the right to make their own sexual decisions. However, he no sooner earns credit for recognizing that force is abusive, than he reverts to the more conventional masculine position, shifting blame for rape to the women who pardon it as a necessary convention. In this speech, Dryden further trivializes rape by linking it to stage fiction, suggesting that rape is analogous to a well-contrived plot, pleasing for its craft and its innovation. This metaphor shifts women out of the position of participant-victim to play the role of audience-appreciator of the rapist's advances and the dramatist's craft.

Behn seems to espouse this same apology for rape in her portrait of Lady Galliard, who looks to Wilding to take the initiative and the responsibility for consummating their relationship. Through the insights of Sir Anthony Meriwill, Behn provides the audience with a possible reading of Lady Galliard's disposition. He calls attention to her preference for importunate, forward courtship:

> Sir Charles: I've tried all ways to win upon her Heart,
>   Presented, writ, watcht, fought, pray'd, kneel'd, and
>   wept.
> Sir Anthony: Why, there's it now; I thought so: kneel'd and wept!
>   a Pox upon thee — I took thee for a prettier Fellow—
>   You should have huft and bluster'd at her door,
>   Been very impudent and saucy, Sir,
>   Leud, ruffling, mad; courted at all hours and seasons;
>   Let her not rest, nor eat, nor sleep, not visit.
>   Believe me, Charles, Women love Importunity.
>   (1.1, p. 218)

Meriwill's observation is partly borne out by the fact that Lady Galliard seems slightly less bored with Sir Charles when he becomes drunk and impudent in act 4. However, Meriwill's formulation does not account for affection. Even when he is as direct and demanding in his courtship as his friend Wilding, Sir Charles can never supplant Wilding in Lady Galliard's heart. Behn insists on this romantic aspect of the widow's desire; she insists that women make distinctions between one man and another. While Lady Galliard indeed appreciates Wilding's forwardness, she loves more than generic "importunity": not every insolent, importunate man will do. In fact, what seems most important to Lady Galliard is that she choose her own mate, that she exercise her own will. Ultimately, Behn insists that women do not wish to be raped. She defends their right to use the word in self-serving ways on occasion to excuse consensual sex, but she insists that women also reserve the right to refuse sex, to say no and mean it.

In contrast to Wilding's successful "ravishment" of Lady Galliard, Sir Charles Meriwill's honorable courtship of her culminates in an ugly scene in which Behn stages his marriage proposal as a real rape, that is, as an imposition of his will and his person on Lady Galliard, who resists him with all her might to no avail. The Meriwills, uncle and nephew, arrive at Lady Galliard's house late in the night to press Sir Charles's suit with her. Their untimely entrance forces Wilding to flee and leaves the widow in a panic that she will be discovered to have consummated her affair with him. Sir Charles, drunk and loudly belligerent, forces his way into Lady Galliard's private quarters, declaring, "I am obstinately bent to ravish thee, thou hypocritical Widow, make thee mine by force, that so I have no obligation to thee, and consequently use thee scurvily with a good Conscience" (4.2, p. 274).

Sir Charles makes good this threat after a fashion. He forces himself on Lady Galliard, menacing her physically, pulling her toward her bed, even "offer[ing] to pull off his Breeches, having pulled off almost all the rest of his Clothes" (4.2, p. 276). She only succeeds in preventing him from doing so when she agrees to marry him. He has, in fact, ravished her of something dearer to her than her sexual liberty; Sir Charles Meriwill takes from her her legal and economic independence. Behn illustrates the extent of Lady Galliard's loss of independence through the defection of her servants. Mrs. Closet conspires with Sir Anthony to allow Sir Charles access to the widow, and later, her manservant, William, obeys Sir Charles's instruction to "know your Lord and Master," rather than obey Lady Galliard's command to "run to my Lord Mayor's, and require some of his Officers" to arrest Sir Charles for his trespass (5.5, p. 291).

Lady Galliard finds herself overpowered and outmaneuvered by Sir Charles. Even the best strategy her wit can provide fails to save her from his assault. Behn, who throughout the scene has played rape against the grain, portrays Lady Galliard's best hope as resting on the aspect of rape that usually endangers women: its secrecy. When it is clear that no other means will save her, Lady Galliard agrees to Sir Charles's demand that she marry him. In doing so, her hope rests on the probability that Sir Charles is too drunk to remember her promise the next morning. If he should remember, she knows that his claim against her will be a very weak one. She will be able to deny having made any such promise and the case will amount only to his word against hers. Behn, however, supplies witnesses (Sir Anthony and the maid, Closet), whose presence makes the widow's promise binding.

Behn's scene is a brilliant travesty of rape. The twin ideas that rape might be used to "honorable" ends (to arrange a marriage) and that marriage might seem as much a violation as rape possessed great comic potential for the Restoration stage. Yet the tone of Behn's scene is radically unstable. On the one hand, the presence of witnesses dilutes the danger and makes Sir Charles's actions farcical. On the other hand, Sir Anthony's "peeping" on the scene is lurid and his running commentary on the event is salacious: his presence suggests the extent to which Lady Galliard is out*manned*, overpowered and victimized.

The scene is alternately grotesque and hilarious; it is super-charged throughout. Sir Anthony's ebullient congratulations to Sir Charles are undercut by Lady Galliard's fury:

> How, upon the Catch, Sir! am I betray'd?
> Base and unkind, is this your humble Love?
> Is all your whining come to this, false Man?
> By Heaven, I'll be revenged. [*She goes out in a Rage with Closet.*]

The sexual triumphing of the uncle and nephew that closes the scene jars against Lady Galliard's just sense of injury. Sir Charles's hopeful vision that sex will bind her to him ("I'll not leave her now, till she is mine; / Then keep her so by constant Consumma-tion. . . . / There's one sure way to fix a Widow's Heart," 4.2, p. 277) is especially hollow in the face of Lady Galliard's contempt for him and passion for Wilding, who has already looked forward to cuckolding his friend.

Behn's juxtaposition of Wilding's tender scene with Lady Galliard against Sir Charles's brutal scene with her reveals the playwright's ambivalence about sex and marriage, and by an extension that the text makes very clear, it also reveals her ambivalence about the Tory party. On the one hand, she offers Wilding to seduce the audience to Toryism. The play proffers Wilding as much as Lady Galliard as an object for the audience's desire in his amorous scene with the widow. Wilding's passion and Lady Galliard's passion for him work to make him desirable to viewers of both genders either as a potent fantasy-self or as an object of erotic fantasy. His *déshabillé* during and after the seduction uses his desirable body and steamy sexual potency to sell his Tory wares. Sir Charles, on the other hand, doubles and undoes Wilding's charming re-presentation of the romance of Tory self-indulgence. What is "ravishing" in the first man is abuse from the second, and Sir Anthony's role as voyeur and coach intensifies the outrage prompted by their Tory male presumption. In the Meriwills' Tory masculinity is indeed an exercise of arbitrary power. At the height of his swaggering and bullying, Sir Charles Meriwill dares Lady

Galliard to call out the watch to arrest him, "Ay, do, call up a Jury
of your Female Neighbours, they'll be for me, d'ye see, bring in the
Bill *Ignoramus*, though I am no very true blue Protestant neither"
(4.2, p. 275). With this boast, Sir Charles reminds Lady Galliard
and the audience of his political allegiance and so claims for himself
all of the most unsavory characteristics attributed to Tories. He
brags about his conquest of citizens' wives even as he boldly seizes
a City fortune from its rightful owner.

In his treatment of the widow, Sir Charles reveals himself to be
a perfect Tory: a tyrant who deprives citizens of their rights and
their property. The same behavior is not problematic when Wilding
practices it against his odious uncle, Sir Timothy Treat-all, but
Behn reverses the flow of sympathy in the case of Sir Charles.
Lady Galliard is a far more sympathetic (and much more fully
developed) character than Sir Charles Meriwill, and his behavior
toward her complicates the play's politics.

Though she treats him romantically, Wilding is not exempt from
Behn's ambivalence, which reveals itself again when she has him
proudly announce his Tory credo:

> Let Politicians plot, let Rogues go on
> In the old beaten Path of Forty one;
> Let City Knaves delight in Mutiny,
> The Rabble bow to old Presbytery;
> Let petty States be to confusion hurl'd,
> Give me but Woman, I'll despise the World.
>
> (3.1, p. 258)

This is precisely the attitude attributed to Charles II by his detractors, who suspected that he would sell out the nation if doing so
would secure his pleasure. Wilding makes this speech as he departs
for his tryst with Lady Galliard, a moment when he is supposed to
be organizing the robbery that will secure his inheritance. He leaves
his faithful friends to risk themselves on his behalf while he pursues
his pleasure. The political allegory is clear and unflattering from a
Tory point of view; it also takes aim at the chief problem for Tories

during the Exclusion Crisis: Charles's superfluity of bastards and lack of a legitimate heir. While Charles ignored the world to enjoy his mistresses, the state lapsed into confusion, and his friends were left to risk themselves for a less than credible cause.

Charles's marriage to Catharine of Braganza had produced no live births, and as early as 1667 there were rumors that Charles would divorce the queen and remarry.[60] After James made his conversion to Catholicism public and the Whig push for an exclusion bill gained momentum, rumors resurfaced that the king might either seek a divorce and marry a woman who could provide a legitimate heir or that he might acknowledge a youthful marriage to Lucy Walters, the mother of his very popular bastard, the duke of Monmouth. The king's numerous and notorious affairs made it easy to discount his commitment to his marriage, but Charles never gave any sign of considering a divorce. On the contrary, he repeatedly and publicly denied the rumors of his marriage to Walters, which if it had existed would have provided him with both an heir and the grounds for a divorce from Catharine.[61]

Nonetheless, Charles's sexual pluralism suggested a complete disregard for anything but the form of marriage. Dryden credits Charles with transcending the slavery of matrimony, in which "one to one [is], cursedly, confin'd" (*Absalom and Achitophel*, 4). Behn's protofeminist sensibilities will not allow her to embrace libertine sexuality with quite the bravado Dryden does. Wilding's sexual appeal and his multivalent desire are liabilities as much as they are assets. The institution of marriage which ostensibly contains and legitimizes the sexuality of the dashing, dangerous young Tories of Behn's play is as hollow on her stage as it was at Whitehall.

Understandably, there has been a good deal of puzzlement articulated in recent criticism about what Behn could have found so appealing in Toryism in general and in the rake figure in particular that she would identify with elitist males so against her own interests as a woman.[62] Melinda Zook sees in Behn's work just this sort of self-abnegating loyalty: "Her work defended the world of those whom she admired, those who could obtain personal and public freedom, elite males."[63] One might equally well accuse a male dramatist like Dryden of being politically naive for romanticizing this avaricious and parasitic elite against his own class interests.

To this way of thinking, Behn would seem to have double reason to distance herself and her drama from this apparently naive subservience to aristocratic interests. By way of explanation, Zook seems to propose that Behn's admiration of a romanticized cavalier past, which in her later years was blurred with nostalgia for the days of her youth, makes her overlook the inconsistency of her allegiance to a cause that treated women with contempt. For instance, Zook claims that

> Behn's royalism, articulated time and again in her work, revolved around an idealized aristocratic ethos that liberated the individual from the tyrannies of dull customs and traditions, things acceptable for the common castes of society, but which shackled the noble mind and heart. In better times, Behn may well have concentrated solely on the need to break those traditional shackles which so confined a woman's life. But in the climactic atmosphere of pre-revolution London, Behn's focus revolved around glorifying and defending the Cavalier culture of court and castigating its enemies, the Whigs and Dissenters. . . . [Her] political philosophy hence centered around a celebration of the young elite male, the cavalier, the epitome of individual freedom.

Zook is certainly right that Behn glamorizes and seems to idealize (and perhaps yearn for) individual freedom ("freedom from want, freedom from customary behavior, and freedom from religious fanaticism").[64] However, I think this argument misses the point on two levels, and the comparison with Behn's male peers helps to clarify the issue. Why does Dryden idealize the rakes and aristocratic heroes of his plays? Because he has a clear economic stake in doing so. As does Behn. Both writers empathize with and idealize figures who represent a privileged class to which they did not and could not hope to belong, but their service to the royalist cause was not a matter of irrational misperception of their social place or their personal interests.

Behn (like Dryden and her other colleagues in the theater business) exploits the culture of envy that enlivened the theater of her day in order to sell Toryism as enviable, desirable, a political philosophy and way of life to be affected by all who wished to be thought cultured and intelligent — by all who themselves wished to be envied. Behn represents, promotes, and herself subscribes to the idea that a transcendent aristocracy of taste binds the witty, discerning elite within the middling ranks (represented in *The City Heiress* by Wilding and Lady Galliard) to the aristocratic wits of the royal court.

The Restoration theater was an institution built on this ideal, persuading men like Pepys to spend his hard-earned salary in order to sit in the presence of the court, persuading him that he shared a cultivated sensibility with those he envied. Sharing the jokes, the pastimes, the courtesans of the aristocracy, Pepys (for example) seems to have been persuaded that his interests were bound to theirs. This doesn't mean that Pepys never had a critical thought about the king or his administration of the country (or his sexual indulgence): the diary attests that Pepys did. Nonetheless, it also attests to the fact that Pepys admired the court and lusted after the courtesans and loved to see and be seen at the theater because it made him feel a part of this extended social circle. To a degree this was certainly a self-deceptive fantasy, a misperception of his real economic position and interests, and it is just this sort of fantasy of belonging that Behn works to cultivate.

To an extent, Behn, too, suffers from this same misidentification of self-interest, idealizing the aristocratic male, his lifestyle and political causes, when she as a woman and a working person is not well served by these men. They *are* parasites living off her labor and her devoted promotion of them through her poetic propaganda pieces, her loyal prefaces and her fictional representations of them on the stage. It strikes me, though, that some of the criticism that has dwelt on this inconsistency in Behn's thinking blames her anachronistically for not seeing the politics of this exploitation in materialist and feminist terms. We can, instead, credit Behn with seeing that, in fact, women in her plays and in her society pay an especially high price for their support of and complicity with Tory men. The vicarious access to aristocratic luxury and liberty they purchase is precarious, without tenure or severance package. Behn uses the rhetoric and imagery of violation to articulate her ambivalence, and, through her female characters in plays like *The City Heiress*, Behn demands that her audience notice what loyal Toryism costs women.

We should also acknowledge that Behn's self-interest is, in fact, closely tied to the Tories and the aristocratic male insofar as his patronage and his presence at the theaters drew audiences and raised Behn's share of box office receipts. She has a real stake in the aristocratic ideology she sells to the Pepyses and the apprentices in her audience. For her it is not merely self-delusion to believe herself linked to the courtiers, wits and royals. She serves them, yes, but also benefits from the association; she depends upon it for her livelihood.

Does she envy their leisure, their security, their masculinity? Undoubtedly. Does she fancy herself a participant in their trend-setting, sophisticated culture of pleasure and intellect? Indeed. Does she credit women with the intellect to hold their own in such company and the wit to be wary of such companions? Certainly. Behn recognizes the compromised position she and her female characters occupy in such a society — as subjects, as members of the middling ranks, as women. It is with open eyes that Behn hawks the wares of majesty and Tory politics; indeed, it is with undisguised ambivalence that she markets her enviable, desirable, shameless rakes. Finally, it is with open eyes that she asks her audiences to buy the merchandise she proffers.

AFTERWORD

*[N]ow by Gods good providence the traverse Curtain is drawn, and
the King writing to Ormond, and the Queen, what they must not
disclose, is presented upon the stage.*

— From Thomas Fairfax, *The Kings Cabinet Opened*

In 1978, Kevin Sharpe wryly observed that "historians of the
seventeenth century are not famous for their concordance."[1] This
observation is no less true today, and no less apt as a description of
literary historians. As we attempt to draw the traverse curtain aside
to glimpse the action that was life in seventeenth century England,
we must concede that what is visible is a partial scene at best, a
scene that will look different in each critic's hands. Of course, we
each court difference to a certain degree, combining different
elements, looking from new theoretical or disciplinary vantage
points, defining the limits of period to concentrate attention on
one rather than another set of events. This study courts difference
in two ways: first by aiming to highlight the literature and events
of the Restoration not by seeing them at the threshold of a long
eighteenth century, but by situating them at the end of a period
that began with the Reformation, a long and politically crucial
seventeenth century. Second, by adding female writers to the male
authors who are traditionally the leading actors in studies of the
period, I have attempted to reintroduce women to a stage from
which they have been long excluded. While early modern women's

361

writing has become an important and active field within literary studies, it has continued to be ghettoized as a separate subfield, rarely integrated with studies of the major canonical male writers and movements of the period.

That sort of separation seemed particularly untenable in this study, where the focus is on a popular political trope that likened the experience of English subjects to the experience of the victims of sexual abuse, an experience, which in the imaginations of the writers in question, belonged to women as well as to men. Women as well as men used the rhetoric of abuse, sometimes to similar, sometimes to different ends.

As we have seen, the representations of violation in the drama of early modern England owed much to Protestant polemic's critique of abusive authority, and London's playwrights were not the only writers to recognize the power and potential of this imagery. Rape and emasculation were resilient and malleable materials in the hands of political activists in and out of Parliament, on and off the stage. And this imagery was durable: generation after generation made use of it without dulling its edge. This cultural currency retained its value despite heavy circulation. In fact, it may well have gained in value as it passed from cause to cause. Certainly, many of the members of Parliament who adopted this rhetoric of abuse to resist what they believed were the encroachments of royal prerogative, relied on their constituents and their fellow members to hear the echoes of polemical print in their words. They quite deliberately cast themselves and England's subjects as the next generation of Protestant faithful vulnerable to a powerful monarch, to a corrupt church hierarchy, to foreign spies and to Roman Catholic assassins.

This rhetoric created strange bedfellows among those who used it. Indeed, it was not only the inherited idiom of religious activists and political agitators like William Prynne; it proved useful to and was shared by writers from wildly incompatible political stances. Just as Shakespeare and Chapman were able to appropriate the conventions, rhetoric and imagery of polemical print for their own secular critiques of the ruling class, members of Parliament borrowed it to lend emotive force to their efforts to preserve and extend the rights of England's property owners.

It was a rhetoric that cast women as dangerous underminers of men's property, but was also available for use by women as different as Anne Askew, Arbella Stuart, Margaret Cavendish and Aphra Behn, who used it to cast themselves and their female characters in a sympathetic light. Thus, in 1680, when the duchess of Portsmouth stood accused of attempting to undermine the kingdom by corrupting the king's body and soul, she was held up as the current incarnation of the whore of Babylon, the biblical figure of sin and death, which had been appropriated by Protestant polemicists reaching back to John Bale as a figure for the church of Rome. The duchess's relations with the king fit easily into a narrative of corruption and abuse that had been a staple of political and religious discourse since the beginning of the Reformation. This particular iteration of the formula casts a woman as the abuser of the royal and, by extension, the national body. It is in juxtaposition with this political rhetoric and in the context of this extended history of its use, that I chose to set the work of Margaret Cavendish and Aphra Behn, whose female characters tend to be sexually tempting and tempted, women who struggle to take their places in the midst of the high stakes political and property negotiations of their male relations and acquaintances. These women's texts are no less politically topical than those of their male peers, and it is now time to consider them as fully integrated players in the theater of early modern England.

Notes

Notes to Introduction

1. Susan J. Owen, *Restoration Theatre and Crisis* (Oxford: Clarendon Press, 1996), 2.

2. Throughout this study I will occasionally use the term "class" in this anachronistic sense for want of a truly better way to describe the middling ranks of early modern English society. See Raymond Williams, *Keywords* (New York: Oxford University Press, 1983), 61: "class as a would-be specific description of a social formation."

3. Richard Helgerson, *Forms of Nationhood: The Elizabethan Writing of England* (Chicago: University of Chicago Press, 1994), 252.

4. "An Exhortation concerning good Order, and obedience to Rulers and Magistrates," in *Certaine Sermons or Homilies appointed to be read in Churches, In the time of the late Queene Elizabeth of famous memory. And now thought fit to bee reprinted by Authority from the Kings most Excellent Majestie* (London: Printed by John Bill, Printer to the Kings most Excellent Majestie, 1623), 70. Hereafter cited in the notes as *Certaine Sermons*. There were at least fourteen editions of this volume between 1547 and 1595, followed by editions in 1623, 1633, 1635 and 1640.

5. Ibid., 69–70.

6. Ibid., 71; emphasis added.

7. "The second part of the Sermon of Obedience," in *Certaine Sermons*, 74–75.

8. "The third part of the Sermon of Obedience," in *Certaine Sermons*, 76.

9. "An Homily of the State of Matrimony," in *Certaine Sermons*, notes that women "must specially feel the grief and pains of their matrimony in that they must relinquish the liberty of their own rule" and in that they may well be required to submit to harsh or abusive husbands (243). While this homily is at pains to counsel husbands against abusing their wives, it is direct in its requirement that women submit to whatever

husband God has provided her. "Even so think you, if thou canst suffer an extreme husband, thou shalt have a great reward therefore: but if thou lovest him only because he is gentle and courteous, what reward will God give thee therefore?" (244).

10. Poole's tract is reprinted in *Lay by Your Needles Ladies, Take the Pen: Writing Women in England, 1500–1700*, ed. Suzanne Trill, Kate Chedgzoy and Melanie Osborne (New York: Arnold, 1997), 167–68. The tract is also available through the Brown Women Writers Project textbase, Renaissance Women On-line, available at http://www.wwp.brown.edu/ texts/rwoentry.html (by subscription).

11. Ibid., 168. In her essay, which accompanies the Renaissance Women On-line text of Poole's tract, Katharine Gillespie argues that Poole "gives this analogy a radical twist when she adds that the Council should divorce the king" instead of executing him for having "violated the terms of his 'marriage' by behaving abusively and tyrannically." Gillespie argues at some length that Poole's sectarian (Particular Baptist) theology led her to maintain "that there are limits to a husband's power over his wife and that a wife is justified in breaking a blighted marital contract." Divorce, a term Gillespie uses more than once, is inaccurate in relation to Poole's analogical argument. In fact, Poole quite purposefully proposes not divorce, but separation between the king and his spouse, the country, to be imposed by the godly parliament or Cromwell's godly army (Renaissance Women On-line).

12. Ibid., 168.

13. Ibid., 167, 168.

14. Ibid., 168.

15. In fact, Poole was invited twice to address the General Council with her prophecies. After the second of these addresses, however, there was a move to discredit her: her insistence on leaving the king to heaven's judgment did not suit Cromwell. See Manfred Brod, "Politics and Prophecy in Seventeenth-Century England: The Case of Elizabeth Poole," *Albion* 31, no. 3 (1999): 395–412.

16. *A Vision*, in *Lay by Your Needles Ladies*, 167, 168.

17. See *Epistle exhortatorye of an Englyshe Christiane unto his derelye beloued contreye of Englande against the pompouse popyshe Byshoppes therof as yet the true membres of theyr fylthye father the great Antichrist of Rome* ([Antwerp], 1544), 22; *The Image of bothe Churches after the moste wonderfull and heavenly Revelacion of Sainct John the Evangelist, contayning a very frutefull exposicion or paraphrase upon the same. Wherin it is conferred with the other scriptures, and most auctorised historyes. Compyled by John Bale an exile also in this life for the faythfull testimonye of Jesu* (1545), B2.

18. *Epistle Exhortatorye*, 22, 23v; *The Actes of Englyshe Votaryes* (1560; reprint, Amsterdam: Theatrum Orbis Terrarum, 1979), U4.

19. Bale picked up on the suggestions of violation in Askew's text and greatly amplified them in his "elucidations" of her narrative in his edition of her work. By comparison with Bale's inflammatory characterizations of the salacious, bloodthirsty men who persecuted this vulnerable woman, Askew's narrative seems tame. Read without Bale's interventions, as the narrative is presented by John Foxe, *The Actes and Monuments of these latter and perillous dayes, touching matters of the Church, wherein ar comprehended and described the great persecutions & horrible troubles, that haue bene wrought and practiced by the Romishe Prelates, speciallye in this Realme of England and Scotlande from the yeare of our Lorde a thousande, unto the tyme nowe present* (London: John Daye, 1563), Askew's text clearly, if subtly, manipulates the motifs of violation. Because Foxe's work went through many editions and its title varied (in content and spelling) in its various editions, it is now conventional to abbreviate the title as *Acts and Monuments* and to cite the editions by year and page number, a practice I will follow hereafter in text and notes.

20. *The Examinations of Anne Askew*, ed. Elaine Beilin (Oxford: Oxford University Press, 1996), 170, 186, 187.

21. Askew's influence on later writers may be glimpsed when John Foxe opens the section of the *Acts and Monuments* on flogging victims by locating the first case in the "time of Anne Ascue," rather than in the days of King Henry VIII, though his usual practice is to date his narratives with reference to the reigning monarch (1563 ed., 1682).

22. Philippa Berry, *Of Chastity and Power* (London: Routledge, 1989); Helen Hackett, *Virgin Mother/Maiden Queen: Elizabeth I and the Cult of the Virgin Mary* (Basingstoke, England: Macmillan, 1995); and Carole Levin, *"The Heart and Stomach of a King": Elizabeth I and the Politics of Sex and Power* (Philadelphia: University of Pennsylvania Press, 1994).

23. The quoted phrase belongs to Marina Leslie and Kathleen Coyne Kelly, whose introduction to *Menacing Virgins: Representing Virginity in the Middle Ages and the Renaissance*, ed. Leslie and Kelly (Newark: University of Delaware Press, 1999), helpfully explores the complex meanings of virginity in early modern English culture (18).

24. Although the public stage inherited the politics of violation, drama was, in fact, a key early venue for its articulation: both John Bale and John Foxe wrote polemical plays for the university stage along with their better-remembered prose works.

25. Scot was the author of anti-Catholic and anti-Spanish tracts, including *The Belgicke Pismire*, *Vox Dei*, and *Vox Populi*, which particularly influenced Protestant politics — and Protestant playwrights — during the 1620s. Several studies of militantly Protestant Jacobean playwrights include: Margot Heinneman, *Puritanism and Theatre: Thomas Middleton and Opposition Drama under the Early Stuarts* (Cambridge: Cambridge University Press, 1980); Julia Gasper, *The Dragon*

and the Dove: The Plays of Thomas Dekker (New York: Oxford University Press, 1990); Jerzy Limon, *Dangerous Matter: English Drama and Politics in 1623/24* (Cambridge: Cambridge University Press, 1986).

26. An important earlier example occurs in Chaucer's *Wife of Bath's Tale*, which places lustful friars under the bushes and marauding knights on horseback to prey on unsuspecting maidens and abuse the common folk. This tale not only enunciates an imagined woman's resistance to the misogyny of her culture, it also articulates key Lollard critiques of the church and aristocracy.

27. Aphra Behn, *Oroonoko*, ed. Joanna Lipking (New York: W. W. Norton, 1997), 64.

28. Janet Todd and Sara Mendelson both suggest that Behn turned to Roman Catholicism in her later years. Mendelson credits Gerald Duchovnay with this information. See Todd, *The Secret Life of Aphra Behn* (New Brunswick, N.J.: Rutgers University Press, 1997); Mendelson, *The Mental World of Stuart Women* (Amherst: University of Massachusetts Press, 1987), 117; Duchovnay, "Aphra Behn's Religion," *Notes and Queries* 221 (May–June 1976), 235–37.

29. This is not to say that Behn was uninfluenced by Catholic martyrologies — she may well have been. My argument in this paragraph is for the pervasive influence of *Acts and Monuments*, itself derivative of earlier works in the genre, and its impact on a range of discourses, which in turn were likely among the sources of the images Behn uses to glorify Oroonoko and to belittle his opponents in her work.

30. Lipking, *Oroonoko*, 64, 57.

31. Ros Ballaster, *Seductive Forms: Women's Amatory Fiction from 1684–1740* (Oxford: Clarendon, 1992), 81, argues persuasively that what is crucial about Oroonoko is his royalty, his social station: the deceit and craven mistreatment he receives from the colonists is "an indignity to his class rather than his race." Ballaster's argument contextualizes Behn's surprising sympathy for the dark-skinned slave.

32. Behn does code Oronooko's difference in terms of color. In a characteristic passage, Oronooko concludes that "there was no Faith in the White Men, or the Gods they Ador'd; who instructed 'em in Principles so false, that honest Men cou'd not live amongst 'em . . . with them a Man ought to be eternally on his Guard, and never to Eat and Drink with *Christians* without his Weapon of Defence in his Hand; and, for his own Security, never to credit one Word they spoke" (Lipking, *Oroonoko*, 56).

33. Much historical ink has been devoted to James I's conflicts with the House of Commons in each of his parliaments. Older histories of the period tended to see these conflicts as an irremediable ideological conflict between monarch and subject and to interpret the series of individual skirmishes as an unbroken and escalating chain of conflict leading

inexorably to civil war (see, for instance, the work of S. R. Gardiner, Wallace Notestein, even Lawrence Stone). In the past 30 years, a group of "revisionist" historians has questioned this teleological vision of events and has reexamined the composition of the House of Commons during the period to discover that many of the M.P.s worked to promote cooperation and reconciliation with the Crown (see, for instance, the work of G. R. Elton, Conrad Russell, Mark Kishlansky, Margaret Judson, J. P. Kenyon, Kevin Sharpe). This revision has itself been challenged by J. H. Hexter and Derek Hirst, who point out the seriousness and effectiveness of parliamentary resistance to James's wishes. See, for instance, Hexter, "Parliament, Liberty, and Freedom of Elections," in *Parliament and Liberty from the Reign of Elizabeth to the English Civil War*, ed. J. H. Hexter (Stanford: Stanford University Press, 1992); Hirst, *Authority and Conflict: England, 1603–1658* (London: Edward Arnold, 1986); Hirst, *England in Conflict, 1603–1660: Kingdom, Community, Commonwealth* (New York: Oxford University Press, 1999).

34. Frances E. Dolan, *Whores of Babylon: Catholicism, Gender, and Seventeenth-Century Print Culture* (Ithaca, N.Y.: Cornell University Press, 1999), 2.

35. Kevin Sharpe, *Faction and Parliament: Essays on Early Stuart History* (Oxford: Clarendon Press, 1978), 7–8.

36. Dolan, *Whores of Babylon*, 4.

37. Frank Whigham, *Seizures of the Will in Early Modern English Drama* (Cambridge: Cambridge University Press, 1996), 18. Whigham borrows the phrase "daily social intercourse" from Keith Wrightson, *English Society, 1580–1680* (New Brunswick, N.J.: Rutgers University Press, 1982), 58.

38. T. H. Howard-Hill, *Middleton's "Vulgar Pasquin": Essays on "A Game at Chess"* (Newark: University of Delaware Press, 1995), 22.

39. Wendy Wall, *The Imprint of Gender: Authorship and Publication in the English Renaissance* (Ithaca, N.Y.: Cornell University Press, 1993), 7.

40. Betty S. Travitsky and Anne Lake Prescott, *Female and Male Voices in Early Modern England: An Anthology of Renaissance Writing* (New York: Columbia University Press, 2000), redress not only the long-standing omission of women's voices from studies of the period, but also correct for the unfortunate way in which anthologies of women's writing and courses on early modern women writers have tended to "ghettoize" women's literature. Their opinion, and mine, is that it enriches the study of literature and literary history when women's writing and men's writing are viewed together.

Notes to Chapter 1

1. The Protestant tradition of associating the Roman Catholic church with the whore of Babylon has been amply documented and discussed by a number of recent literary critics. See, for instance, John N. King, *Tudor Royal Iconography: Literature and Art in an Age of Religious Crisis* (Princeton, N.J.: Princeton University Press, 1989), and *Spenser's Poetry and the Reformation Tradition* (Princeton: Princeton University Press, 1990); Julia Gasper, *The Dragon and the Dove: The Plays of Thomas Dekker* (Oxford: Clarendon Press, 1990). Similar rhetoric had been used by both Roman Catholics and Protestants early in the century in England and on the Continent. In England, Protestant writers found an important model for their depictions of priestly depravity in Chaucer's satirical treatment of his tale-telling Canterbury pilgrims. See John N. King, *English Reformation Literature: The Tudor Origins of the Protestant Tradition* (Princeton, N.J.: Princeton University Press, 1982), 50–52, 228–29, 323, 400; David Bevington, *Tudor Drama and Politics: A Critical Approach to Topical Meaning* (Cambridge, Mass.: Harvard University Press, 1968), 70–72, 98–101, 160–63; Donna B. Hamilton, *Shakespeare and the Politics of Protestant England* (Lexington: University Press of Kentucky, 1992), 18–19; Paul Whitfield White, *Theatre and Reformation: Protestantism, Patronage, and Playing in Tudor England* (Cambridge: Cambridge University Press, 1992), 30.

2. John Foxe's first effort at martyrology was a Latin treatise on the fifteenth century persecutions of English Wicklifites (Lollards) and of the followers of Hus and Savonarola on the Continent: *Commentarii rerum in ecclesia gestarum maximarumque per totam Europam persecutionum a Wicleui termporibus ad hanc usque aetatem descriptio* (Argentorati [Strasbourg], 1554). He extended the scope of this Latin chronicle to include the first accounts of Marian executions in a volume entitled *Rerum in ecclesia gestarum commentarii* (Basel, 1559). Foxe began work on *Acts and Monuments* while still in exile and published his first English edition in 1563. Foxe oversaw three subsequent editions in 1570, 1576 and 1583. After the martyrologist's death, the work was again revised and extended in 1596, 1610, 1631, 1641 and 1684. One difficulty in discussing this work is the fact that it was not a stable text by any means. With each new edition, Foxe not only added masses of new material, he deleted and reshaped earlier material to such an extent that the editions might almost be seen as separate works. See J. H. Smith, ed. and trans., *Two Latin Comedies by John Foxe the Martyrologist: Titus et Gesippus. Christus Triumphans* (Ithaca, N.Y.: Cornell University Press, 1973), 25–30; King, *English Reformation Literature*, 423; James Frederic Mozley, *John Foxe and His Book* (New York: Octagon Books, 1970).

3. Foxe did not distinguish between Protestants and the heretics of

earlier years who had died for proto-Protestant heresies regarding the authority of the pope, the nature of the sacrament or the translating, printing or reading of the Bible in vernacular languages.

4. John Foxe, "To the Persecutors of Gods truth, commonlye called Papistes, an other preface of the Author," in *Acts and Monuments* (1563). All quotations from the *Acts and Monuments* refer to the sixteenth and seventeenth century editions unless otherwise noted and are hereafter cited in the text and notes.

5. John R. Knott, *Discourses of Martyrdom in English Literature, 1563–1694* (Cambridge: Cambridge University Press, 1993). In this assurance, Foxe follows his mentor, John Bale, for whom the inviolability of the martyr's soul was a key tenet. See, for instance, *The Image of Both Churches* (London: Richard Iugge, 1548), where Bale reiterates this claim several times: "Farther extended not [the persecutors'] violence, than upon the poor bodies. The souls were in God's hands, whose mercy is never far off," Q8.

6. King, *English Reformation Literature*, 56. King devotes a long section of his chapter on "The Emergence of the Protestant Tradition" to Bale.

7. *The Epistle exhortatorye of an Englyshe Christiane unto his derelye beloued contreye of Englande against the pompouse popyshe Byshoppes therof as yet the true membres of theyr fylthye father the great Antichrist of Rome*, 17v–18; hereafter cited in the text. Bale used the pseudonym Henry Stalbrydge on the title page of this tract, which also bore the false imprint: "Imprynted at Basyll the yeare of owre lorde M.D.xliii. the xiiii. of September." The date was correct, but the volume was printed in Antwerp. The false imprint was apparently meant to minimize the risk to Bale that he would be pursued and silenced.

8. *Geneva Bible* translation. Use of predator imagery derives from New Testament warnings against false prophets (Matt. 7:15) and predictions of the dangers Jesus' followers will face from nonbelievers, especially civil authorities, as they spread the gospel (Matt. 10:16; Luke 10:3; Acts 20:29). In all of these passages (and in John 10:12, where the emphasis is on the Good Shepherd), believers are figured as sheep threatened by wolves. Luke 13:32 likens Herod to a fox, establishing the pejorative tone of that image and connecting it to an archetypal tyrant. As a tool of Reformation polemicists, predator imagery goes back at least to the early Protestant attacks on Henrician bishops written by William Turner and John Bale in the manner of beast fables. See Bale ["James Harrison"], *Yet a Course at the Romyshe Foxe* (1543); Turner ["William Wraughton"], *The Huntyng and Fyndyng Out of the Romishe Fox* (1543), and *The Rescuynge of the Romishe Foxe Other Wyse Called the Examination of the Hunter Devised by Steven Gardiner* (1645).

9. Knott, *Discourses of Martyrdom*, contends that the conduct of Protestant martyrs and their management of suffering was designed to

reveal "the limitations of the power of the church or state to control the subversive spirit" (8).

10. Huston Diehl, *Staging Reform, Reforming the Stage: Protestantism and Popular Theater in Early Modern England* (Ithaca, N.Y.: Cornell University Press, 1997), 24. Ritchie Kendall also discusses Foxe's (and Bale's) dramatic impulses in *The Drama of Dissent: The Radical Poetics of Noncomformity, 1380–1590* (Chapel Hill: University of North Carolina Press, 1986), esp. 122–31.

11. Diehl, *Staging Reform*, 25. John N. King, "Staging Reform, Reforming the Stage: Protestantism and Popular Theater in Early Modern England by Huston Diehl" *Renaissance Quarterly* 52.1 (1999): 269–70, criticizes Diehl in an otherwise positive review for overestimating Foxe's authorial responsibility for the work and for failing to recognize the extent of John Daye's contribution to the work. Diehl misrepresents Foxe when she asserts that he "repeatedly puts his reformed beliefs into the mouths of craftsmen, artists, millers, and runaway wives. . . . At the same time, he puts traditional religious beliefs into the mouths of powerful men — archbishops, inquisitors, and officers of the crown" (41–42). In this insinuation that Foxe fictionalized his accounts, Diehl ignores evidence that Foxe was a surprisingly faithful transcriber of official records. This is not to say that Foxe never heightens his material, but it would be inaccurate to suggest that Foxe often put words into his "characters" mouths. Foxe's technique was to allow historical figures to speak for themselves out of surviving documents.

12. *Acts and Monuments*, 1563 ed., 1604. In this passage's alliterative denunciation of "bloody byshops," who "practise pestilent policy" to bring English Christians to "serue their slauishe slaughter," Foxe's stylistic debt to Bale is especially evident.

13. Both Foxe and Bale asserted that the pope's ascendancy over temporal princes was a gross perversion of God's creation. Many copies of *Acts and Monuments* contained a series of illustrations depicting this allegedly egregious assertion of papal primacy: in one the pope steps on the neck of the emperor to demonstrate the superiority of the ecclesiastical hierarchy over the secular. Protestants writers attempted to cultivate resentment in their rulers and the aristocracy in passages like this one from Bale's *The Actes of Englysh Votaryes* (1560; reprint, Amsterdam: Theatrum Orbis Terrarum, 1979): "By thys meane, at last they [ecclesiastics] had theyr full purpose, and therby made the Christen prynces to become their slaues, yea, to hold their stiroppes wyth cappe in hande, to kysse their fylthie fete, and to leade their mules and their horses. Yea, they played with those worldly rulers, for al their great power and wysdome, as the bearwardes do with their apes and beares" (2:U2).

14. This woodcut does not purport to be a portrait of Sawtrey or even to depict the circumstances of his particular execution. In fact, it is one of

many generic illustrations that Daye uses in the volume. In later editions, a different generic illustration fills this space in the text. The point of the illustration, then, is not its particular witness to Sawtrey's death, but to the suffering and fortitude of English martyrs. See Luborsky, "The Illustrations: Their Pattern and Plan," in David Loades, ed., *John Foxe: An Historical Perspective* (Brookfield, Vt.: Ashgate Press, 1999), 67–84, for a nuanced reading of different kinds of illustrations included in *Acts and Monuments*.

15. Three, sometimes four, illustrations precede the Sawtrey woodcut: (1) Henricus the Emperor with his wife and child waiting barefoot in the snow outside the pope's palace, (2) Pope Alexander treading on the neck of Frederick the Emperor, (3) (in some copies) the poisoning of King John, (4) the exhumation and burning of Wycliffe's bones. None of these depicts the execution of a heretic. Even the Wycliffe illustration does not emphasize the bodily trauma or the burning: Wycliffe's bones are depicted as mere bones.

16. I'm indebted here to Susannah Brietz Monta, who discussed the effects of gender in Foxe's accounts in a talk delivered at the Group for Early Modern Cultural Studies conference, Chapel Hill, N.C., November 1997. See also Monta, "A Book of Martyrs: Representing Testimony in Early Modern England" (Ph.D. diss., University of Wisconsin, Madison, 1998).

17. 1563 ed., 678; *The Examinations of Anne Askew*, ed. Elaine Beilin (Oxford: Oxford University Press, 1996), 192.

18. I am grateful to David Frantz for this suggestion and to Steven Mullaney for his reading of this illustration at the John Foxe and His World colloquium, Ohio State University, May 1999.

19. Peter Stallybrass, "Drunk with the Cup of Liberty: Robin Hood, the Carnivalesque, and the Rhetoric of Violence in Early Modern England," in *The Violence of Representation: Literature and the History of Violence*, ed. Nancy Armstrong and Leonard Tennenhouse (New York, N.Y.: Routledge, 1989), 50, 46.

20. Ibid., 46.

21. Sir John Harington, *A Supplie or Addicion to the Catalogue of Bishops* (1608), ed. R. H. Miller (Potomac, Md.: Studia Humanitas, 1979), 45.

22. Stallybrass, "Drunk with the Cup," 46; Mikhail Bakhtin, *Rabelais and His World*, trans. Hélène Iswolsky (Cambridge, Mass.: MIT Press, 1968), 26.

23. Stallybrass, "Drunk with the Cup," 46.

24. Ibid., 46.

25. Ibid., 51.

26. For a discussion of the Protestant conflation of celibacy, sodomy and nonprocreative sex, see Donald N. Mager, "John Bale and Early Tudor

Sodomy Discourse," in *Queering the Renaissance*, ed. Jonathan Goldberg (Durham, N.C.: Duke University Press, 1994), 141–61.

27. Stallybrass, "Drunk with the Cup," 54. Although some critics see the carnivalesque as an ultimately conservative phenomenon, Stallybrass argues that far from being limited to the service of political orthodoxy, the carnivalesque in English popular literature and culture was "central to the symbolic repertoire of political subversion" (51). In response to an early version of my chapter (written for a 1997 Shakespeare Association of America seminar), Stallybrass suggested the alternative reading of Bonner's overblown codpiece as a sign not of sexual power, but of impotence.

28. Samuel Y. Edgerton Jr., *Pictures and Punishment: Art and Criminal Prosecution during the Florentine Renaissance* (Ithaca, N.Y.: Cornell University Press, 1985), 134, describes an explicitly Roman Catholic artistic tradition, but Edgerton's research into the status and representation of executioners seems analogous to English representations and attitudes. Kendall, *The Drama of Dissent*, discusses representations of ecclesiastical judges in early Tudor Protestant drama and in the polemical (as well as dramatic) writings of John Bale, who in their tyrannical zeal to persecute, "deny their proper vocation as judges and instead debase themselves by assuming the dress and calling of the executioner" (124).

29. Edgerton, *Pictures and Punishment*, 135; see also 133–34. Pieter Spierenburg, *The Spectacle of Suffering: Executions and the Evolution of Repression: From a Preindustrial Metropolis to the European experience* (Cambridge: Cambridge University Press, 1984), 16, 21, discusses the treatment of executioners as a defiled, untouchable class, and notes (as does Edgerton) that in Europe, at least, the office was often relegated to "persons of unfree descent" or "swarthy" foreigners. Spierenburg further observes that hangmen were often assigned auxiliary duties of similarly debased status: "Sometimes he had to catch dogs, clean the streets and public latrines, or, in the early modern period, take care of syphilis patients. Worst of all, he could be a skinner" (21). Alternatively, like Pompey in Shakespeare's *Measure for Measure*, he might combine the office of executioner with that of brothel keeper (16, 21). To the extent that these associations were available to the English readers of Foxe, Bonner's representation as an executioner connected him to a decidedly unsavory cultural sphere.

30. See Margaret Aston and Elizabeth Ingram, "The Iconography of the *Acts and Monuments*," in *John Foxe and the English Reformation*, ed. David Loades (Brookfield, Vt.: Scolar Press, 1997), 66–142.

31. Harington, *Supplie or Addicion*, 46.

32. A further example of Foxe's use of debased language to degrade Bonner occurs in the 1563 edition of *Acts and Monuments*, where Foxe and Daye flanked the woodcut with a series of Latin epigrams that

exuberantly mock the bishop's unruly corporeality even as they decry his physical cruelty to his Protestant victims. See Deborah G. Burks, "Polemical Potency: The Witness of Word and Woodcut in John Foxe's *Acts and Monuments*," in *Foxe and His World*, ed. Christopher Highley and John N. King (Brookfield, Vt.: Ashgate, 2001), 263–76.

33. Thanks to John King for his suggestions regarding this interpretation.

34. William Tyndale, *Obedience of the Christen Man (Antwerp)*, 1528 (Amsterdam: Theatrum Orbis Terrarum, 1977), 24.

35. Ibid., 23v; for a discussion of this section of Tyndale's work, see Stephen Greenblatt, *Renaissance Self-Fashioning: From More to Shakespeare* (Chicago: University of Chicago Press, 1984), 88.

Notes to Chapter 2

1. Jonathan Goldberg, *James I and the Politics of Literature: Jonson, Shakespeare, Donne, and Their Contemporaries* (Baltimore: Johns Hopkins University Press, 1983), 230. His reference to Greenblatt is to *Renaissance Self-Fashioning: From More to Shakespeare* (Chicago: University of Chicago Press, 1980), esp. 227–28, 252–54.

2. As Julia Gasper and Jerzy Limon have demonstrated, Foxe's history of England's sixteenth century reformers was a fertile source for seventeenth century playwrights who sought to use the stage as a platform from which to encourage further reform. See Julia Gasper, *The Dragon and the Dove: The Plays of Thomas Dekker* (Oxford: Clarendon Press, 1990); Gasper, "The Reformation Plays on the Public Stage" in *Theatre and Government under the Early Stuarts* (Cambridge: Cambridge University Press, 1993); Jerzy Limon, *Dangerous Matter: English Drama and Politics in 1623/24* (Cambridge: Cambridge University Press, 1986).

3. See Craig Bernthal, "Staging Justice: James I and the Trial Scenes *of Measure for Measure*," *SEL: Studies in English Literature, 1500–1900* 32, no. 2 (1992): 247–69; Goldberg, *James I*, 210–39; Greenblatt, *Shakespearean Negotiations: The Circulation of Social Energy in Renaissance England* (Berkeley and Los Angeles: University of California Press, 1988), 129–42; Leah Marcus, *Puzzling Shakespeare: Local Reading and Its Discontents* (Berkeley and Los Angeles: University of California Press, 1988), 160–211.

4. See, for instance, Roy Battenhouse, "*Measure for Measure* and King James," *CLIO: An Interdisciplinary Journal of Literature, History, and the Philosophy of History* 7 (1978): 193–215; Robert B. Bennett, "The Law Enforces Itself: Richard Hooker and the Law Against Fornication in *Measure for Measure*," *Shakespeare and Renaissance Association of West Virginia — Selected Papers* 16 (1993): 43–51; Jonathan Dollimore, "Transgression and Surveillance in *Measure for Measure*," in *Political Shakespeare: New Essays in Cultural Materialism*, ed. Jonathan Dollimore

and Alan Sinfield (Manchester: Manchester University Press, 1985), 72–87; John W. Draper, "*Measure for Measure* and the London Stews," *West Virginia University Philological Papers* 23 (1977): 5–17; Harry V. Jaffa, "Chastity as a Political Principle: An Interpretation of Shakespeare's *Measure for Measure*," in *Shakespeare as Political Thinker*, ed. John Alvis and Thomas G. West (Durham, N.C.: Carolina Academic Press, 1981), 181–213; Richard Levin, *New Readings vs. Old Plays: Recent Trends in the Reinterpretation of English Renaissance Drama* (Chicago: University of Chicago Press, 1979); Catharine F. Siegel, "Hands Off the Hothouses: Shakespeare's Advice to the King," *Journal of Popular Culture* 20, no. 1 (1986): 81–88; Leonard Tennenhouse, "Representing Power: *Measure for Measure* in Its Time," *Genre: Forms of Discourse and Culture* 15, no. 2–3 (1982): 139–56.

5. Marcus, *Puzzling Shakespeare*, 199. Marcus has proposed that the play cultivated two simultaneous currents of interpretive possibility for early modern audiences: a "King James Version" and what she dubs a "paranoid" alternative version — an interpretation of the play conducted from a Protestant point of view. The two versions (the KJV and its Other) existed side by side in every performance — available according to the predisposition of individual audience members to attend to different textual cues — and available to each audience member at various moments within a given performance. Levin, *New Readings Vs. Old Plays*, gave the "King James Version" its name. Marcus qualifies her use of the term "paranoid" by pointing out that this reading of the play was based (1) on real concerns about the new king's commitment to reformed religion and to the English constitution, and (2) on reasonable fears about the intentions of the Catholic Hapsburgs with whom James had just negotiated a peace.

6. I am indebted to Stephen Orgel for raising the issue of Shakespeare's representation of friars in his response to a paper on Foxe's relationship to early modern theater which I contributed to a Shakespeare Association of America session in 1997. See also Thomas Healy, "Selves, States, and Sectarianism in Early Modern England," *English: The Journal of the English Association* 44, no. 180 (1995): 193–213, which makes a case for the extent to which Isabella's and the duke's monasticism would have prejudiced the early modern English audience's perception of their characters.

7. Marcus, *Puzzling Shakespeare*, 164, 198–9.

8. *Measure for Measure*, 1.3.1–6. All quotations from Shakespeare come from *The Norton Shakespeare*, ed. Stephen Greenblatt (New York: W. W. Norton, 1997), and are hereafter cited in the text.

9. Harry Berger Jr., "Getting Oneself Unmasked: The Duke, the 'Friar,' and Lucio," in *Critical Essays on Shakespeare's "Measure for Measure,"* ed. Richard P. Wheeler (New York: G. K. Hall, 1999), analyzes the dichotomous "divided structure" of the duke's role as friar, which conflates

"spiritual advisor" with "intriguer" and shifts the duke's actions from "moralizing to machination" (217).

10. Quotation from Bale, *The Image of both churches after the moste wonderful and heauenly Reuelacion of Sainct John the Euangelist* (London: John Daye, 1550), B2. Bale's influence was long-lived; his belligerent tone, shocking imagery and rhetorical excesses echo clearly in William Prynne's polemical tracts in the 1640s.

11. A further discussion of the woodcuts appears in my "Polemical Potency: The Witness of Word and Woodcut in John Foxe's *Acts and Monuments*," in *Foxe and His World*, ed. Christopher Highley and John N. King (Brookfield, Vt.: Ashgate, 2001), 263–76.

12. It must be said that the moment would have played very differently at the Globe depending upon the duke's appearance. If the actor playing the duke was, in fact, bald-pated, his friarliness would have lingered beyond his unmasking and would have been more strongly discolored by Lucio's words. If, on the other hand, the cowl covered a full head of hair and — more potent still — if it somehow covered a full beard, the duke's appearance would have been comfortingly Protestant in its coding. In this case, Lucio's words would wash over, but not adhere to the duke; their significance would be short-lived.

13. Bale, *The Actes of Englysh Votaryes* (1560; reprint, Amsterdam: Theatrum Orbis Terrarum, 1979), 1:63.

14. Ibid., 2:U1. See Mager, "John Bale and Early Tudor Sodomy Discourse," 141–61.

15. John Bale had enhanced Askew's reputation when he linked her with Princess Elizabeth in the preface to *A Godly Medytacyon of the Christen Sowle* (1548), his unauthorized edition of Elizabeth's "Miroir of the Christen Soule." See Patrick Collinson, *Elizabethan Essays* (London: Hambledon Press, 1994), 98.

16. G. R. Elton, *England Under the Tudors*, 3d ed. (London: Routledge, 1991), takes special note of the Askew execution in his account of the last years of Henry VIII's reign (199). See also James K. McConica, *English Humanists and Reformation Politics under Henry VIII and Edward VI* (Oxford: Clarendon Press, 1965), 222–27; King, *English Reformation Literature: The Tudor Origins of the Protestant Tradition* (Princeton, N.J.: Princeton University Press, 1982), 71–75.

17. Because she was associated with the prominent circle of the queen, Askew's case was something of a cause célèbre in London, where there reportedly was a fair amount of outrage over the fact that Askew was taken to the Tower and racked by the lord chancellor, Thomas Wriothesley, and Sir Richard Rich, another member of the king's Privy Council. According to Elaine V. Beilin, ed., *The Examinations of Anne Askew* (Oxford: Oxford University Press, 1996), "such desperate measures taken

against a gentlewoman were against the law and unusual in practice." Beilin quotes a contemporary letter to document the degree of interest the trial generated and to substantiate her claim that the public perceived Askew's treatment as both extreme and surprising (xxvii).

18. In significant measure, Askew's lasting impact owes to her spirited first-person account of her arrests, examinations and various incarcerations. However, they also derived allure from the surreptitious circumstances of their publication. Bale's first volume arrived in England during the last months of Henry VIII's reign; to own it was to commit a subversive act. The second volume arrived in the first month of Edward VI's reign, as Protestants celebrated the young king's reforming zeal. Askew's story then became a reminder of what the nation had recently escaped. As evidence of the sustained interest in Askew's narrative, Beilin points to the fact that there were a number of early printings of Bale's editions. She also notes the hostile response of Stephen Gardiner, conservative bishop of Winchester, who wrote with annoyance to Protector Somerset in June 1547 complaining that the government was not doing enough to suppress the Askew narrative, copies of which were "common" in his diocese. Beilin conjectures that in addition to opposing Bale's texts on doctrinal grounds, Gardiner was annoyed at the dissemination of a text in which Askew likened him to Judas and Bale dubbed him "the popes great dansynge beare" (ibid., xxix).

19. Julia Reinhard Lupton, "Afterlives of the Saints: Hagiography in *Measure for Measure,*" *Exemplaria: A Journal of Theory in Medieval and Renaissance Studies* 2 (fall 1990): 375–401, writes that "the debates between male tyrant and female martyr [were] conventional in hagiographies," 378. See also Rebecca W. Bushnell, *Tragedies of Tyrants: Political Thought in the English Renaissance,* esp. chaps. 3 and 5.

20. Foxe, *Acts and Monuments* (1563), 669–78; Beilin, *Examinations,* 170. Bale's version of this same scene is included in Beilin, 40–41.

21. The title page calls Bale's editorial insertions "Elucydacyon." The interplay between these "elucidations" and Askew's text bears more consideration. Beilin, *Examinations,* has pointed briefly to their interesting gender implications.

22. Beilin, *Examinations,* 41, 42.

23. *Acts and Monuments* (1563) in Beilin, ibid., 168. Bale's version of the scene is slightly different. There, Askew writes, "he asked me, if I were shryven, I tolde hym no. Then he sayd, he wolde brynge one to me, for to shryve me. And I tolde hym, so that I myght have one of these iii" (Beilin, 32–33).

24. *Acts and Monuments* (1563) in Beilin, *Examinations,* 168. Bale's version of this scene is included in Beilin, 34. I owe thanks to John King, John Norman, Luke Wilson, Christopher Highley and other members of

the Renaissance Reading Group at Ohio State University for sharing their thoughts on Askew's text, particularly this present passage. See also John N. King, Introduction to *The Early Modern Englishwoman — a Facsimile Library of Essential Works, volume 1, Anne Askew,* ed. Betty Travitsky and Patrick Cullen (Brookfield, Vt.: Ashgate, 1996); Paula McQuade, "'Except that they had offended the Lawe': Gender and Jurisprudence in *The Examinations of Anne Askew," Literature and History* 3, no. 2 (1994): 1–14.

25. For another reading of this scene, see Charles Hallett, "Is There 'Charity in Sin'?: Sexual Harassment in *Measure for Measure," Shakespeare Bulletin: A Journal of Performance Criticism and Scholarship* 11, no. 4 (1993): 23–26.

26. "The foxes runne over the hyll of Syon (sayth Hieremye) because she is fallen from God, Threnorum [Lamentations] 5. "O Israel (sayth the Lorde) thy prophetes are lyke the wylye foxes upon the drye feldes, Ezechielis 13" (Beilin, *Examinations,* 39). For Bale's more usual list of savage beasts, see the *Epistle Exhortatorye,* 2v.

27. Beilin, *Examinations,* 40.

28. See William Babula, "Justice in *Measure for Measure," The Carrell: Journal of the Friends of the University of Miami Library* 11, nos. 1–2 (1970): 27–33; Bernthal, "Staging Justice"; Carolyn E. Brown, "Duke Vincentio of *Measure for Measure* and King James I of England: 'The Poorest Princes in Christendom'" *CLIO: A Journal of Literature, History, and the Philosophy of History* 26, no. 1 (1996): 51–78; Lynda Boose, "The Priest, the Slanderer, the Historian and the Feminist," *English Literary Renaissance* 25, no. 3 (1995): 320–40; Goldberg, *James I*; Greenblatt, *Shakespearean Negotiations*; Marcus, *Puzzling Shakespeare.*

29. In "Staging Justice," Craig Bernthal reads the blatant staging of justice and the less than persuasive exhibition of demi-divine ducal mercy in the play's denouement as a deliberately ambivalent response to James I's unsuccessful (indeed catastrophic) attempt at staging a pardoning drama in the case of the Main and Bye plotters a few months before the play opened.

30. I have analyzed this illustration in considerably greater detail in chapter 1, addressing the pictorial ambiguities of the scene, particularly the bishop's role and the trajectory of the infant, which seems to conflate two narrative moments: the moment of its birth and the moment of the bishop's casting it back into the flames.

31. Boose, "The Priest, the Slanderer," argues that this scene stages a gratuitous and overdetermined display of masculine authority.

Notes to Chapter 3

1. Chapman and Ben Jonson spent time in jail for their parts in writing this comedy. John Marston, a third collaborator on the play, escaped prison by leaving town until the king's anger abated.

2. I have unmoored this phrase from its syntax, but, as I will argue below, it is a misreading I believe the play promotes.

3. George Chapman, *Bussy D'Ambois*, in *Drama of the English Renaissance II: The Stuart Period*, ed. Russell A. Fraser and Norman Rabkin (New York: Macmillan, 1976), 1.2.9–13; hereafter cited in the text.

4. Arbella Stuart noted with disapproval that the "great and gratious Ladies" of the new court — those who wished to establish their place in that court, in other words — "leave no gesture nor fault of the late Queene unremembered." From a letter to Mary Talbot, countess of Shrewsbury, 23 August 1603, in *The Letters of Lady Arbella Stuart*, ed. Sara Jayne Steen (Oxford: Oxford University Press, 1994), 181.

5. Ralph Winwood, quoted by Wallace Notestein, *The House of Commons, 1604–1610* (New Haven, Conn.: Yale University Press, 1971), 56.

6. Neil Cuddy, "Anglo-Scottish Union and the court of James I, 1603–1625," *Transactions of the Royal Historical Society* 39 (1989): 108.

7. Cuddy, ibid., 111, here quotes a contemporary's report to Dudley Carlton.

8. James brought with him his Scottish favorite, Sir George Home (later earl of Dunbar). After Home's death in 1611, he promoted Robert Carr, another Scot, and after Carr's fall, the Scottish marquis of Hamilton. There were also English favorites, however: first, Philip Herbert, whom he made earl of Montgomery; later, and most famously, George Villiers, whom he elevated from cupbearer to marquis within a year's time (and later to duke of Buckingham). Cuddy argues that James was much more deliberate in the selection of favorites than is commonly thought, balancing Scottish and English favorites in order to achieve national parity. James's other subjects seem to have been singularly unimpressed by this programmatic evenhandedness: from their perspective favorites received the lion's share of the king's bounty — and after the favorites, the other Scots of the Bedchamber, leaving the English to fight for what seemed to them a meager remainder (ibid. passim).

9. I accept a date of first production close to the 1607 publication of the first known quarto of this play. Some have argued for a date of composition or production in 1604, which would make the play's topical allusions to James's policies and constitutional theories early indeed. There have even been arguments for Elizabethan dates for this play, but those seem least convincing. My argument hinges on the play's belonging to the early Jacobean period; beyond that I am not particularly invested in the dating

controversy. For discussions of this play's date, see Russell A. Fraser's introduction to the play in *Drama of the English Renaissance II*, 269; John Hazel Smith, "Notes on Two Renaissance Authors: On the Date of George Chapman's *Bussy D'Ambois*," in *Brandeis Essays in Literature* (Waltham, Mass.: Department of English and American Literature, Brandeis University, 1983), 30–36; Albert Tricomi, "The Dates of the Plays of George Chapman," *English Literary Renaissance* 12, no. 2 (1982): 242–66.

10. See Keith Cameron, "Henri III — The Antichristian King," *Journal of European Studies* 4, no. 2 (1974): 152–63; Cameron, *Henri III: A Maligned or Malignant King? (Aspects of the Satirical Iconography of Henri De Valois)* (Exeter: University of Exeter, 1978). There were competing representations of Henri in French sources, but the principal alternative version of the king as a zealously devout, almost monkish Roman Catholic was equally unlikely to appeal to English Protestants. In fact, from that perspective, the reports of Henri's religious devotion would have seemed to complement rather than refute representations of the king as a sodomite.

11. With the rise in 1607 of Robert Carr as the new young favorite of James I, this portrait of D'Ambois in his new (French) clothes monopolizing the king's ear must have taken on fresh and bitter significance. Carr, a Scot who had spent time in France and returned to the English court with French clothes and manners, swept James off his feet. As early as December 1607, John Chamberlain, *The Letters of John Chamberlain*, ed. Norman Egbert McClure (Philadelphia: The American Philosophical Society, 1939), 1:249, remarked on Carr's rise and his nationality in a letter to Dudley Carlton: "Sir Robert Carre a younge Scot and new favorite is lately sworne gentleman of the bed-chamber." See also David M. Bergeron, *Royal Family, Royal Lovers: King James of England and Scotland* (Columbia, Mo.: University of Missouri Press, 1991), 87. James had been notorious since his adolescence for promoting attractive young men and showering them with money and titles.

12. The attacks on Henri III included Huguenot propaganda pieces which may well have been known in English Protestant circles, as for instance, Agrippa D'Aubigné's *Les tragiques* (c. 1576) (particularly the section, "Les princes"), which compares Henri to Sardanapalus and dubs him an "homme femme," who would shave and powder his face after the manner of courtesans and adopt "le geste effeminé" so that viewers could not tell if he was "un Roy femme ou bien an homme Reyne." A similar attack, attributed to the Huguenot Nicolas Barnaud, *The Cabinet of the King of France containing Three Precious Pearls* (1581), complained of Henri's *mignons* as "shameless Ganymedes," quoted by J. H. M. Salmon, *Society in Crisis: France in the Sixteenth Century* (New York: St. Martin's Press, 1975), 64–67. See also Keith Cameron, "Henri III — The

Antichristian King," and *Henri III: A Maligned or Malignant King?* Cameron discusses the success of Huguenot and antimonarchist propaganda during Henri's reign and the ubiquity of its representation of the king as a homosexual.

13. Marlowe's *Massacre at Paris* had given flesh to the depiction of the duke of Guise in contemporary pamphlets and histories as chief villain of the French wars of religion, especially the 1572 Saint Bartholomew's Day massacre. In a prefatory letter to the "Papists" in the 1563 edition of *Acts and Monuments*, John Foxe retails the bloody deeds of these enemies of Protestantism, among whom he especially mentions Francis, the recently assassinated duke of Guise: "If killing and slaieng coulde helpe your cause, you see what an infinite sorte you have put to death, [amounting to] an hundred thousand persons slaine in Christendome of you . . . besides them in Queene Maries time here in Englande, and besides them within these two yeares slaine in Fraunce by the Guyse, which as you know commeth to no small summe." After 1563, the dukedom passed to Francis's oldest son, Henry, who inherited both his father's title and his villainous reputation. It is the son who figures in Marlowe's and Chapman's plays.

14. Monsieur's physiognomy was among the secondary reasons to avoid a French marriage offered up by John Stubbs in his pamphlet, "The discouerie of a gaping gulf vvhereinto England is like to be swallovved by another French mariage, if the Lord forbid not the banes, by letting her Maiestie see the sin and punishment thereof" [London: Printed by H. Singleton for W. Page], 1579. Stubbs lost his pen hand for his presumption in printing his opinion of the match. See also Mack P. Holt, *The French Wars of Religion, 1562–1629* (Cambridge: Cambridge University Press, 1995), 118.

15. Lawrence Stone, *The Crisis of the Aristocracy, 1558–1641* (Oxford: Clarendon Press, 1965), 74. Stone's statistics on promotions to the peerage are unusually vague (he describes this group as a "large number" rather than offering a precise figure), and the appendices (3–6) dealing with this subject offer conflicting numbers. Stone's anecdotal evidence, however, provides a clear and convincing picture of the early corruption of the process of peer creation in James's reign. Although critics have raised legitimate concerns about Stone's handling of some of his data, *The Crisis of the Aristocracy* remains the most comprehensive social history of the changes in the composition and conduct of the aristocracy in this period, and of the impact of James I's monarchy on that class. In "Social Mobility in England, 1500–1700," *Past and Present* 33 (April 1966): 16–55, Stone looks beyond the aristocracy to present a more comprehensive picture of social change during the period. Subsequent scholarship has extended and revised our knowledge of the textures of early modern society. See, for instance, Susan Dwyer Amussen, *An Ordered Society: Gender and Class in Early Modern England* (New York: Basil Blackwell, 1988); David

Underdown's *Revel, Riot, and Rebellion: Popular Politics and Culture in England, 1603–1660* (Oxford: Clarendon Press, 1985); Underdown, "'The Taming of the Scold': The Enforcement of Patriarchal Authority in Early Modern England," in *Order and Disorder in Early Modern England*, ed. Anthony Fletcher and John Stevenson (Cambridge: Cambridge University Press, 1985); Alan Everitt, "Social Mobility in Early Modern England," *Past and Present* 33 (April 1966): 56–73; and Keith Wrightson, *English Society, 1580–1680* (London: Hutchinson, 1982).

16. See Robert Ornstein, *The Moral Vision of Jacobean Tragedy* (Madison: University of Wisconsin Press, 1960); Joel B. Altman, *The Tudor Play of Mind: Rhetorical Inquiry and the Development of Elizabethan Drama* (Berkeley and Los Angeles: University of California Press, 1978).

17. Deborah Montuori, "The Confusion of Self and Role in Chapman's *Bussy D'Ambois*," *SEL* 28, no. 2 (1988): 287–99, discusses D'Ambois's elision of "they" and "we" in this speech. See also Jonathan Goldberg's analysis of D'Ambois's uncommunicative language, which he takes to be a function of the character's "absolutist" view of himself. See *James I and the Politics of Literature: Jonson, Shakespeare, Donne, and Their Contemporaries* (Baltimore: Johns Hopkins University Press, 1983), 147–61, esp. 155–56. J. W. Lever, *The Tragedy of State* (London: Methuen, 1971), takes a different view of D'Ambois's independence.

18. The 1607 quarto simply directs "Bussy solus." Presumably the direction "poor" refers to the condition and arrangement of D'Ambois's clothing, coif and carriage. "Poor," then, points to the production's material markers of D'Ambois's condition: his dress and behavior.

19. Fraser and Rabkin, *Drama of the English Renaissance II*, 269.

20. Indeed, he ranks far below the great nobles, but his presence at court is in no way presumptuous. His presumption is to ignore the ideology of rank, which held that place was determined by birth. Insofar as he behaves as though social order is a matter of competition rather than inheritance, he challenges that ideology.

21. The topical reference to kings who violate their pardons after parliaments have ended is also worth noting. I discuss this reference in greater detail in chapter 4.

22. James Heath, *Torture and English Law: An Administrative and Legal History from the Plantagenets to the Stuarts* (Westport, Conn.: Greenwood Press, 1982), examines contemporary documents and illustrations to reach the conclusion that there were probably several different devices that were used to stretch the limbs and which were all called "racks" or "breaks" (181–83). Thus, the exact nature of the device used to stage Chapman's play is uncertain, but its effect (and its general design) is made clear by Montsurry when he contemplates his wife's wounded body: "methinks the *frame* / and *shaken joints* of the whole world should *crack* / To see her *parts so disproportionate*" (5.1.170–72;

emphasis added). The effect is the same as that threatened by Escalus when he orders the friar/duke's torture: "To the rack with him. We'll touse him / Joint by joint, but we will know his purpose" (*Measure for Measure*, 5.1.349–50).

23. Sir Thomas Smith, *De republica Anglorum: A discourse on the Commonwealth of England* (1583) quoted by ibid., 80.

24. Smith's text may serve as part of the Elizabethan establishment's denial that it practiced many of the same methods its predecessors had used; in any case, it stands together with Foxe in condemning torture as a continental (hence, Roman Catholic) barbarity and in promoting a mythology of Elizabethan civility and justice. See also Heath's speculations about Smith's aims in this passage (ibid., 269, n. 36).

25. Foxe includes a woodcut illustration of Cutbert Simson's racking: *Acts and Monuments* (1563), 1651; Verstegan, *Theatrum crudelitatum haereticorum nostri temporis* (1588), 73. Thanks to Christopher Highley for alerting me to the Verstegan illustration.

26. This official fiction was challenged by texts like Askew's, which charged that two Privy Councillors lost control of themselves and racked her with their own hands, acting out of anger and a desire to hurt her, rather than in the strict interest of obtaining information; see Beilin, *Examinations*, 127–29. See also Retha M. Warnicke, *Women of the English Renaissance and Reformation* (Westport, Conn.: Greenwood Press, 1983), 72.

27. 5.1.166. This is the reading of the 1607 quarto (59). The 1641 quarto emends this line to read "kind, worthy man," presumably because "innocent" seemed too implausible an attribute for the friar (62).

28. Critics disagree about the tone of the play's ending, particularly about whether to read D'Ambois's death as legitimately heroic. Deborah Montuori, "Confusion of Self," makes a persuasive case for D'Ambois's failure to live up to his grandiose self-conception. Montuori is less clear, however, about whether this constitutes a failure on Chapman's part, or whether the play is to be taken, as she suggests early in her article, as "social satire rather than tragedy." Her belief that it is the former rests on her assumption that Chapman wrote the play for the Children of the Revels and a further assumption that the children did not perform in a serious tragic mode, but would have rendered D'Ambois "a misconcieved and rather absurd hero" (298–99, n. 10; 288–89). The early performance history of this play is mere conjecture, although it has often been confidently asserted by critics that the play was produced well in advance of its 1607 publication and that it was performed by two different companies during this early period. The latter inference seems, unfortunately, to be based on Russell A. Fraser's confusion of the 1607 and 1641 quartos in his interpretation of the prologue in his much-used edition of the play (*Drama of the English Renaissance II*).

29. Eugene Waith, *The Herculean Hero in Marlowe, Chapman, Shakespeare and Dryden* (New York: Columbia University Press, 1962), 104–6.

30. Though the two stage directions agree about Montsurry's costume, the 1641 quarto adds one detail neglected by the 1607 quarto: Montsurry's pulling Tamyra onstage by her hair. (Q1607, 54; Q1641, 57.)

31. Elaine Scarry, *The Body in Pain: The Making and Unmaking of the World* (Oxford: Oxford University Press, 1985). Chapman's fictional representation of torture does not conform to Scarry's model in all ways. Her conception that torture unmakes the world in the experience of its victim has tantalizing echoes in Chapman's language, but in the final analysis Chapman's woman is a fantasy whose agony and endurance are constructed from the audience's point of view and for its pleasure; her experience is not compassed by the play.

32. Beilin, *Examinations*, 127. Foxe supplies the "with" missing in Bale's transcription of Askew's narrative (187).

33. Ibid., 128.

34. Ibid., 129, 128.

35. Eve Kosofsky Sedgwick, *Between Men: English Literature and Homosocial Desire* (New York: Columbia University Press, 1985), offers a more sophisticated and detailed version of this analysis of women's function as markers in the rigidly structured interactions of men. Gayle Rubin, "The Traffic in Women: Notes on the 'Political Economy' of Sex," in *Toward an Anthropology of Women*, ed. Rayna R. Reiter (New York: Monthly Review Press, 1975), 157–210, laid the groundwork for this approach to reading the function of women in the world and of female characters in literature.

36. Chapman was only able to take the liberty of allowing such a threatening character to triumph in his play because the historical Monsieur was known to have died without ever becoming king. Chapman plays to the audience's knowledge of Monsieur's fate when he allows D'Ambois to tell the prince that he will never be king. When Chapman wrote his play, English Protestants were taking comfort in the fact that the Valois dynasty had come to grief. The present king, Henri IV, was a Huguenot by birth and political affiliation, though he had been forced to convert to Roman Catholicism as a condition for becoming king of France.

37. Elsewhere I have discussed the relation between Chapman's representation of the countess's torture and representations of women's suffering in early modern erotic texts, particularly Pietro Aretino's *I Ragionamenti*. See my "Boiling Passions, Bloody Hearts, Horrid Spectacle: Sexuality and Violence in the Theater of Seventeenth-Century England" (Ph.D. diss., Rutgers University, 1994), 13–23.

38. Beilin, *Examinations*, 7, 107.

39. Ibid., 129, 131. There is a further reference to her as a "godlye *yonge*

woman" (133). John R. Knott, *Discourses of Martyrdom in English Literature, 1563–1694* (Cambridge: Cambridge University Press, 1993), 57, discusses Bale's exploitation of feminine stereotypes in his elucidations of Askew's narrative.

40. Beilin, *Examinations*, 132. In *Redeeming Eve*, Beilin disentangles Askew's voice from Bale's repackaging. See also John N. King, *English Reformation Literature* (Princeton, NJ: Princeton University Press, 1982), 71–75.

41. Beilin, *Examinations*, 129, 132–33, 135, 153.

42. Ibid., 151, 153.

43. Robert Crowley, *The Confutation of the Thirteen Articles, Whereunto Nicholas Shaxton Subscribed* (1548), cited by John N. King in the introduction to *The Early Modern Englishwoman: A Facsimile Library of Essential Works*, vol. 1, *Anne Askew*, ed. Betty Travitsky and Patrick Cullen (Brookfield Vt.: Ashgate, 1996).

44. Beilin, *Examinations*, 191–92.

45. A similarly teasing substitution of tongue for genitals famously occurs in Shakespeare's *The Taming of the Shrew*, 2.1, when Petruchio and Kate meet and spar for the first time.

Notes to Chapter 4

1. Dympna Callaghan, *Woman and Gender in Renaissance Tragedy* (Atlantic Highlands, N.J.: Humanities Press International, 1989), examines the Renaissance construction of gender and explores the construction of women and of female desire as socially disruptive and dangerous:

> Desire is inscribed at every level (social, economic, political, sexual) as the motivation for change, upheaval, disruption, and crucially, for female tragic transgression. It is a force of disorder in terms of both conceptual and social systems. Importantly, defining the category of woman in terms of desire is a Renaissance preoccupation, and yet, paradoxically, it is one which ultimately threatens to unfix the categories of gender difference because . . . this is precisely the point where differential markers themselves become problematic.
>
> Voracious female desire was posited as the most conspicuous sign of gender difference, and was treated both as a disease and as a monstrous abnormality. (140)

Susan Dwyer Amussen discusses the substantive as well as metaphorical connections between women's role in the family and social order or disorder in both her book-length study, *An Ordered Society* (New York: Basil Blackwell, 1988), and her "Gender, Family and the Social

Order, 1560–1725," in *Order and Disorder in Early Modern England*, ed. Anthony Fletcher and John Stevenson (Cambridge: Cambridge University Press, 1985).

2. Middleton's poem, "The Ghost of Lucrece," was published in 1600. There were actually two dramatizations of *Appius and Virginia*. The first was an early Elizabethan interlude, the second is tentatively credited to John Webster and Thomas Heywood. See Leonard Tennenhouse, *Power on Display: The Politics of Shakespeare's Genres* (New York: Methuen, 1986), 111; Lee Bliss, *The World's Perspective: John Webster and the Jacobean Drama* (New Brunswick, N.J.: Rutgers University Press, 1983), 6.

3. Unless otherwise indicated, all references to *The Changeling* will be to the Russell A. Fraser and Norman Rabkin edition, *Drama of the English Renaissance II: The Stuart Period* (New York: Macmillan, 1976), 399–429; hereafter cited in the text.

4. The Jacobean public was treated to the scandalous tales of a number of real women of this stripe. The divorce and remarriage of Frances Howard in 1613 was perhaps the most publicized of these; she claimed incredibly to be a virgin after seven years of marriage in order to obtain the divorce and marry her reputed lover, Robert Carr, earl of Somerset. In 1615 it came to light that Howard had conspired to murder Carr's friend Sir Thomas Overbury for his opposition to her remarriage. She and Carr and a number of accessories were convicted of murder. In "Diabolical Realism in *The Changeling*," *Renaissance Drama* n.s. 11 (1980): 135–170, J. L. Simmons makes a case for the importance of the Essex divorce as an inspiration for *The Changeling*. He particularly remarks upon the coincidence of the earl and countess of Somerset's release from the Tower in January 1621–22 with the period at which Middleton and Rowley must have worked on the play which was licensed on 7 May 1622. Cristina Malcolmson, "'As Tame as the Ladies': Politics and Gender in *The Changeling*," *English Literary Renaissance* 20, no. 2 (1990): 320–39, Margot Heinemann, *Puritanism and Theatre: Thomas Middleton and Opposition Drama Under the Early Stuarts* (Cambridge: Cambridge University Press, 1980), and A. A. Bromham and Zara Bruzzi, *"The Changeling" and the Years of Crisis, 1619–1624* (London: Pinter Publishers, 1990), also discuss the importance of the Howard scandal to Middleton and Rowley's portrait of Beatrice-Joanna.

5. See James Sharpe, "The People and the Law," in *Popular Culture in Seventeenth-Century England*, ed. Barry Reay (New York: St. Martin's Press, 1985). Sharpe discusses popular enthusiasm for litigation in the Jacobean period and the tendency of British subjects to define their legal rights in terms of property holding and in contrast to the prerogative rights asserted by the Stuart monarchs. The popular understanding of the law as the "cement" that held English society together is evident in this passage quoted by Sharpe from the 1620 York Assizes: "[Without justice] the land

would be full of theeves, the sea full of pirates, the commons would ryse against the nobylytye, and the nobylytye against the Crowne, wee should not know what were our owne, what were another mans, what we should have from our auncestors, what wee should learn [sic] to our children. In a worde, there should be nothing certayne, nothing sure . . . all kingdomes and estates would be brought to confucyon, and all humane society would be dissolved" (246–47).

6. Penelope Corfield discusses the economic pressures of the early seventeenth century in "Economic Issues and Ideologies," in *The Origins of the English Civil War*, ed. Conrad Russell (New York: Barnes and Noble, 1973). Perez Zagorin sketches out the influence of these pressures on the English social hierarchy in "Social Structure and the Court and the Country," *The Court and the Country: The Beginning of the English Revolution* (London: Routledge and Kegan Paul, 1969). Lawrence Stone, *Crisis of the Aristocracy, 1558–1641* (Oxford: Clarendon Press, 1965), addresses these same issues. A number of historians expressly tie these economic stresses to pressures on the patriarchal family and the position of women within it. See, for instance, Keith Wrightson, *English Society: 1580–1680* (London: Hutchinson, 1982); David Underdown, *Revel, Riot and Rebellion: Popular Politics and Culture in England, 1603–1660* (Oxford: Clarendon Press, 1985); Underdown, "The Taming of the Scold: The Enforcement of Patriarchal Authority in Early Modern England," in *Order and Disorder in Early Modern England*, ed. Anthony Fletcher and John Stevenson (Cambridge: Cambridge University Press, 1985); Gordon J. Schochet, *Patriarchalism in Political Thought: The Authoritarian Family and Political Speculation and Attitudes Especially in Seventeenth-Century England* (New York: Basic Books, 1975); Stephen Ozment, *When Fathers Ruled: Family Life in Reformation England* (Cambridge: Harvard University Press, 1983). Lisa Jardine, "Wealth, Inheritance and the Specter of Strong Women," in *Still Harping on Daughters* (New York: Barnes and Noble, 1983), addresses some of the demographic and economic factors that placed stress on English views of female heirs to substantial estates (68–98).

7. In a letter to Sir Dudley Carleton dated 6 July 1616, John Chamberlain wrote that "Lord Cooke (by the Kinges expresse order delivered by Secretarie Winwood) was sequestered from the counsaile table, from riding his circuit, . . . and willed to review and correct his reports as many wayes faulty and full of novelties in points of law. This was the summe of the censure for his corrupt dealing with Sir Robert Rich and Sir Christofer Hatton in the extent of theyre lands and instalment of the debt due to the King." Coke offended the king when he ruled against the king's interest in a case challenging the royal prerogative. When the king called Coke and the other justices of the King's Bench to his presence and demanded that they reconsider their decision, Coke offended James again with his

"insolent behavior" and his refusal to reverse his decision in the case. See *The Letters of John Chamberlain,* ed. Norman Egbert McClure (Philadelphia: The American Philosophical Society, 1939), 2:14, 32–57, 64.

8. Modern accounts of the Coke-Villiers match can be found in Laura Norsworthy, *The Lady of Bleeding Heart Yard: Lady Elizabeth Hatton, 1578–1646* (London: Harcourt, Brace, 1935); Stone, *Crisis of the Aristocracy,* and *The Family, Sex, and Marriage: 1500–1800* (New York: Harper and Row, 1977); Antonia Fraser, *The Weaker Vessel* (New York: Vintage Books, 1985); and Roger Lockyer, *The Political Career of George Villiers Duke of Buckingham* (London: Longman, 1981). With the exception of Lockyer, these writers make much of an apparently apocryphal story that Frances was "tied to the Bedposts [by her father] and whipped 'till she consented to the Match" (see, for instance, Norsworthy, 62). This report does not seem to exist in any contemporary accounts of the event. The first reference to Coke's whipping of Frances (that I can discover) appears in the margins of an eighteenth century manuscript in the British Library collection (Cole's MSS, vol. 33, p. 10).

9. McClure, *Letters of John Chamberlain,* 2:88–89.

10. Chamberlain reports the public's interest in Coke's fall from favor: "The common speach is that fowre Ps have overthrown and put him down, that is Pride, Prohibitions, Premunire, and Prerogative" (ibid., 2:34). Coke was unpopular for the vehemence and excessively personal tone of his questioning of Sir Walter Raleigh at the latter's trial for treason against James I.

11. McClure, *Letters of John Chamberlain,* 19 July 1617, 2:88–89. The report of the Privy Councillors to Secretary Lake (who was at that time with the king in Scotland) indicates that Lady Hatton appeared before them on 13 July 1617, "complayning in somewhat a passionate and tragicall manner that . . . she was by vyolence dispossessed of her childe" by her husband, who, with his "sonne and 10 or 11 servantes weaponed in violent manner . . . with a piece of timber or forme broken open the doore and dragged [Frances] along to his coach." The Privy Council then preferred "an informacion into the courte of Starr Chamber against Sir Edward Coke for the force and ryott used by him"; see *Acts of the Privy Council of England, 1616–17* (Nendeln /Lichtenstein: Kraus Reprint, 1974), 35:315–16.

12. September 1617, *Letters from George Lord Carew to Sir Thomas Roe, Ambassador to the Court of the Great Mogul, 1615–1617,* ed. John Maclean (London: The Camden Society, 1860). It should be noted that Carew was a member of the Privy Council to which Lady Hatton pleaded her cause. Carew was among the signers of the letter sent via Secretary Lake to inform the king of the Coke affair.

13. Coke told the Privy Council that he suspected his wife of planning "to carry his daughter into Fraunce" in order to break the match with

Villiers. The council charged him with the burden of proving his charge against his wife for illegal "transporting," one of the legal terms for ravishment.

14. McClure, *Letters of John Chamberlain*, 2:100.

15. Women who experienced some measure of success with the courts included the countess of Shrewsbury, who defended her estate against the claims of her husband and stepsons; Lady Anne Clifford, who managed, after long years of legal wrangling, to regain her estates from her uncle's heirs; and Elizabeth Cary, who appealed successfully for separate maintenance from her husband.

16. In *The Lady of Bleeding Heart Yard*, Norsworthy claims that as a condition of their marriage, Coke promised Elizabeth Hatton that she would control her jointure properties and that she would be able to honor her husband's debts. After the wedding, Coke reneged on both promises.

17. Lady Hatton pressed her custody dispute in the Privy Council rather than in a formal court of law, and she was heard and humored by the council so long as it served their interests to favor her against her husband. When the king made it clear that he wanted the marriage to go forward, Lady Hatton found herself under arrest and in the end she was forced not only to reconcile herself to the fact of her daughter's marriage, but also to contribute the money and land that her husband had promised on her behalf.

18. Even married women seem to have been vulnerable to this crime if they could be used to extort property from their husbands. They might be held for ransom, or in some cases, the ravishment might be part of a larger theft of a man's property.

19. "Anno 3, Henry VII, cap. 2," in *A Collection in English, of the Statutes Now in Force, Continued from the Beginning of Magna Charta* (London: Thomas Wright, 1603), 170. Unless otherwise noted, all citations of statutes have been taken from this edition.

20. *The Rape of Lucrece*, 1.838. Nancy Vickers, "'The Blazon of Sweet Beauty's Best': Shakespeare's *Lucrece*," in *Shakespeare and the Question of Theory*, ed. Patricia Parker and Geoffrey Hartman (New York: Methuen, 1985), 95–115, finds plentiful evidence in *The Rape of Lucrece* for the depiction of rape as covetousness in Renaissance England's conception of the crime. According to Vickers, "Shakespeare's narrator specifically casts Tarquin's desire for Lucrece as desire for lucre," and she cites the following passage from the poem:

> Those that much covet are with gain so fond
> That what they have not, that which they possess
> They scatter and unloose it from their bond;
> And so by hoping more they have but less,
> Of gaining more, the profit of excess

> Is but to surfeit, and such griefs sustain,
> That they prove bankrout in this poor rich gain.
> (*Lucrece*, ll. 134–40)

Vickers's quote in the text is from p. 102.

21. Issues of physical assault and character defamation, though covered by statutes against mayhem (maiming) and murder, seem to have been settled out of court more often than in. Physical retribution continued to be a more direct way of dealing with such matters. The courts, which were slow and costly, were used to obtain monetary settlements in property disputes, but swifter and more personal retaliation was often sought in cases of physical affronts and assaults. Stone, *The Crisis of the Aristocracy*, discusses the continuance of personal violence in the period.

22. It is worth noting, too, that ravishment was defined primarily as a crime committed against women of substance, though some of the laws do remember "others" (the most important of these others being servants who might be ravished away from their employers' service). There were other laws that concerned themselves with the sexual behavior of poor women: bastardy laws, including a very strict law passed early in James I's reign, which punished indigent women for bearing children who would become a drain on their parish's charity. Ravishment statutes might be seen as rich women's bastardy laws. Martin Ingram discusses popular attitudes about fornication and bastardy in "The Reform of Popular Culture? Sex and Marriage in Early Modern England," in *Popular Culture in Seventeenth-Century England*, ed. Barry Reay (New York: St. Martin's Press, 1985), esp. 151–56.

23. Sir Edward Coke, *The Institutes of the Laws of England* (London: M. Flesher, 1644), offers two examples from the Parliament rolls of widows who were "shamefully" ravished and forced by "dures and menace of imprisonment" to marry men they did not wish to marry (cap. xi).

24. There seems to be almost uniform agreement among critics that Middleton was responsible for the main plot and that Rowley wrote the subplot. See, for instance, Lois E. Bueler, "The Rhetoric of Change in *The Changeling*," *English Literary Renaissance* 14, no. 1 (1984): 95–113, and N. W. Bawcutt, introduction to *The Changeling*, The Revels Plays (London: Methuen, 1958). The play's action, however, is so carefully integrated that it seems that this collaboration was a close one. For my purposes, I will treat the play as a joint effort, rather than attributing specific aspects to one of its authors or the other.

25. Christina Malcolmson, "'As Tame as the Ladies': Politics and Gender in *The Changeling*," *English Literary Renaissance* 20 (spring 1990): 320–39, offers quite a different reading of the play, finding in it a "critique of hierarchical social relations," exposing Vermandero in the main plot and Alibius in the subplot as inadequate and tyrannical governors.

Nevertheless, she notes the play's fear of sexual and political rebellion and points out the frequency of the play's use of invasion imagery to signal threats to the civil body and its tendency to displace those fears and that imagery onto women's bodies. Hence Vermandero's response to the sight of Beatrice-Joanna's wounds at the play's end: "An host of enemies entered my citadel / Could not amaze like this" (5.3.147–48).

26. Heinemann, *Puritanism and Theatre*, discusses Beatrice-Joanna's class inflected blindness with respect to DeFlores (175).

27. Leonard Tennenhouse, *Power on Display: The Politics of Shakespeare's Genres* (New York: Methuen, 1986), an essay contrasting the violence against women on the Elizabethan and Jacobean stages, asserts that "women on the Jacobean stage are tortured, hung, smothered, strangled, stabbed, poisoned or dismembered for one of two reasons: either they are the subject of clandestine desire or else they have become an object of desire which threatens the aristocratic community's self-enclosure. . . . [It] seems that women must be excessively punished when they have blurred within their bodies the distinction between what is properly inside and what must be kept outside the aristocratic community" (116).

28. Ann Jennalie Cook, *Making a Match: Courtship in Shakespeare and His Society* (Princeton: Princeton University Press, 1991), discusses marriage negotiations and their financial importance to sixteenth and seventeenth century families. Cook quotes from the wedding sermon of Lord and Lady Hay (1607) to illustrate the economic and political importance of marriage between propertied families: "to marie ioynes sex and sex, to marie at home ioynes house and house, but your marriage ioyneth land and land, earth and earth" (239). Nazife Bashar, "Rape in England between 1550 and 1700," in *The Sexual Dynamics of History: Men's Power, Women's Resistance*, ed. The London Feminist History Group (London: Pluto Press, 1983), notes that cases that claimed a substantive economic damage to the family of a rape victim were more likely to be successfully prosecuted than claims made by working-class families who could not claim much damage. She cites a case in which "Thomas Rockingham, an alehousekeeper, petitioned the King in the mid 16th century about the rape of his daughter Elizabeth, [complaining that] she 'haith lost hir maryag that she might have had and hir good name in that Contie'" (42). Other noteworthy work on property and alliance concerns in matchmaking includes Stone, *Crisis of the Aristocracy*; Ralph Houlbrooke, "The Making of Marriage in Mid-Tudor England," *Journal of Family History* 10, no. 4 (1985): 339–52; David Cressy, "Kinship and Kin Interaction in Early Modern England," *Past and Present* 113 (1986): 38–69; Martin Ingram, "Spousals Litigation in the English Ecclesiastical Courts," in *Marriage and Society: Studies in the Social History of Marriage*, ed. R. B. Outhwaite (New York: St. Martin's, 1981), 35–57; and Vivien Brodsky Elliott, "Single Women in the London Marriage Market:

Age, Status and Mobility, 1598–1619," in Outhwaite, *Marriage and Society,* 81–100. Volume 40 (1987) of *Renaissance Quarterly,* which was devoted to "Recent Trends in Renaissance Studies: The Family, Marriage, and Sex," includes Barbara Diefendorf, "Family Culture, Renaissance Culture" (661–81), and Linda Boose, "The Family in Shakespeare Studies; or, Studies in the Family of Shakespeareans; or, The Politics of Politics" (707–41).

29. In 1614, yet another bill to deprive adulterous women of their jointures was read in Parliament.

30. *A Discourse Upon the Exposicion & Understandinge of Statutes with Sir Thomas Egerton's Additions,* ed. Samuel E. Thorne (San Marino, Calif.: Huntington Library, 1942), 143. The *Discourse,* preserved among the Ellesmere papers in the Huntington Library, probably dates from the 1560s or 1570s.

31. See William Blackstone, *Commentaries on the Lawes of England* (New York: W. E. Dean, 1841). Blackstone notes that a girl within age "by reason of her tender years . . . is incapable of judgment and discretion," and that "a male infant, under the age of fourteen years, is presumed by law incapable to commit a rape, and therefore it seems cannot be found guilty of it. . . . [A]s to this particular species of felony, the law supposes an imbecility of body as well as mind" (4:212). Cook, *Making a Match,* 20, quotes Henry Swinburne, *A Treatise of Spousals, or Matrimonial Contracts,* 24, who termed the ages of consent the "Ripe Age" at which "abilitie and fitnesse for procreation" begin. Swinburne's work, though published in 1686, must predate his death in 1624. See also Ian Maclean, *The Renaissance Notion of Women* (Cambridge: Cambridge University Press, 1980); Stone, *Family, Sex and Marriage,* and *The Crisis of the Aristocracy;* and Ozment, *When Fathers Ruled,* for other discussions of the legal age of consent and its relation to physical maturity and sexual practices in the period.

32. Coke, *The Institutes of the Laws of England,* affirms at numerous points that penetration was necessary for a rape to have occurred. Ejaculation near but not within a woman's body did not constitute a crime. Similarly, sodomy was held to have occurred only in cases where anal penetration could be proven.

33. 4 & 5 Philip and Mary, cap. 8, my emphasis. Under this act, girls between the ages of 12 and 16 were still to be held accountable for their consent.

34. See Blackstone's interpretation of this statute in his *Commentaries.* For conveying a girl away from home, this statute prescribes either a fine or two years imprisonment. Deflowering her or marrying her against her parents' wishes carries the penalty of five years in prison or a (presumably stiffer) fine.

35. In *The Second Part of the Institutes* (London: M. Flesher and R. Young, 1642), cap. 7, Coke chronicles another dispute that arose as a legacy of the Marian rape law, which punished kidnapping separately from

forced marriage or forced intercourse. Elizabethan courts were left to decide whether there was a felony offense of illegal transportation of women. They decided in 26 Elizabeth that without marriage or defilement, carrying away could not be judged a felony.

36. *The Third Part of the Institutes* (London: M. Flesher, 1644), cap. 11. When Elizabeth Tudor came to the throne, there was much need for plain declaration with respect to laws passed or amended during her sister's reign. Elizabeth's first two Parliaments passed legislation revoking some Marian statutes, especially those concerning church governance and practice, and those giving Philip II of Spain power in the English state. At the same time, they also confirmed certain pre-Marian statutes, with the effect of turning back the legal clock on law and precedent. The rape statutes were among those to receive particular reconsideration, and in 5 Elizabeth, cap. 17, the statute of 3 Henry VII was reconfirmed. This left the law once again without a lesser category for elopements. In 18 Elizabeth, a bill was introduced which seems to have included measures to reinstitute penalties for seduction and secret marriages; see *The Journals of all the Parliaments During the Reign of Queen Elizabeth, both of the House of Lords and House of Commons. Collected by Sir Simonds D'Ewes. . . . Revised and Published by Paul Bowes* (London, 1682), 244. The bill failed, but the idea was floated again in 1604 prior to the first Jacobean Parliament; see Wallace Notestein, *The House of Commons, 1604–1610* (New Haven: Yale University Press, 1971), 52.

37. 18 Elizabeth, cap. 7: "An act for the repressing of the most wicked and felonious Rapes or ravishments of women, maides, wives, and damsels," in *A Collection of Sundrie Statutes, Frequent in Use*, ed. Fardinando Pulton (London: M. Flesher, I. Hauiland, and R. Young, 1632).

38. *Aristotle's Master-Piece*, an anonymous treatise on reproductive physiology, seems to have been hugely popular, although early editions of it are now extremely scarce. A Latin edition of 1583 and an English translation of 1595 are the earliest known printings of the work, which ran through numerous editions and remained in print into the eighteenth century. I quote from the Garland press facsimile of the 1694 edition: *Aristotle's Master-Piece; or, The Secrets of Generation*, ed. Randolph Trumbach (New York: Garland Publishing, 1986), 63.

39. Kathryn Gravdal, *Ravishing Maidens: Writing Rape in Medieval French Literature and Law* (Philadelphia: University of Pennsylvania Press, 1991).

40. Ibid., 5.

41. *Lucrece*, ll. 1650–52. Coppélia Kahn discusses Lucrece's complicity in "The Rape in Shakespeare's *Lucrece*," *Shakespeare Studies*, ed. J. Leeds Barroll III, Barry Gaines and Ann Jennalie Cook (New York: Burt Franklin, 1976), and "Lucrece: The Sexual Politics of Subjectivity," in *Rape and*

Representation, ed. Lynn Higgins and Brenda Silver (New York: Columbia University Press, 1992). Joost Daalder, "Shakespeare's *The Rape of Lucrece*," *Explicator* 55 (summer 1997): 195–97, argues against the reading Kahn and I have offered. He understands this line to imply that Tarquin's lust swears false testimony and that it is his lust's opinion (and not Lucrece herself) which blames her beauty. I read the line to suggest that Lucrece accepts the presence of Tarquin's lust *as* the evidence of her beauty's crime.

42. This reading of the playwrights' use of the term "will" owes much to Frank Whigham, who first called my attention to the significance of this scene.

43. Christopher Ricks, "The Moral and Poetic Structure of *The Changeling*," *Essays in Criticism* 10 (1960): 290–306, discusses the sexual connotation of the word "will" in the play. He also calls attention to the double meanings of several other recurrent terms, particularly "service," "blood," "act" and "deed," and discusses their function within the play. Bueler, "Rhetoric of Change," also discusses the rhetorical importance of these terms. The *OED* listings for "will" consume several pages and include most of the senses I have discussed. For the use of "will" as a reference to the penis (a pun that continues in current British usage), see Eric Partridge, *Shakespeare's Bawdy* (New York: Routledge, 1990), 218–19.

44. Karen Newman, "Renaissance Family Politics and Shakespeare's *The Taming of the Shrew*," *English Literary Renaissance* 16 (1986): 86–100, observes that women's rebelliousness was often presented as a linguistic protest against patriarchal authority. Beatrice-Joanna's articulate, but secret, rebellion against her father's will might be seen as an alternative to Kate's shrewishness.

45. Jardine, *Still Harping*, also notes the similar assumptions elicited from men by the behavior of Desdemona and Beatrice-Joanna. Jardine points out the undeniable sensuality of Desdemona's character, often forgotten or glossed over by modern critics (75).

46. It is significant that ravishment law does not punish ravished women as felons even when it finds them to be material accessories to the crime. Such women are to be ostracized rather than executed. In other words, the law seems to treat women as incapable of the felonious malice attributed to their ravishers. See Heinemann, *Puritanism and Theatre*, for a discussion of Beatrice-Joanna's moral deficiency (175–78).

47. Matthew Hale, *Pleas of the Crown* (London, 1678), reflects on this unknowableness when he explains why juries should be reluctant to convict defendants in rape trials: "It is true rape is a most detestable crime, and therefore ought severely and impartially to be punished with death; but it must be remembered, that it is an accusation easy to be made and hard to be proved, and harder to be defended by the party accused tho' never so innocent" (1:634). If men's guilt was difficult to establish, women's

complicity with their rapists, however it might have been suspected, even more persistently eluded the kind of proof the law craved. It remained a mystery of the most unsettling kind.

48. Michael Dalton, *The Countrey Justice* (London, 1618), 247. G. R. Quaife, *Wanton Wenches and Wayward Wives: Peasants and Illicit Sex in Early Seventeenth Century England* (New Brunswick, NJ: Rutgers University Press, 1979), quotes this statement as part of a larger passage from Dalton in his discussion of sexual violence. J. A. Sharpe also cites Dalton in the course of his helpful survey of rape cases prosecuted during the seventeenth century. See especially Sharpe, *Crime in Seventeenth-Century England: A County Study* (Cambridge: Cambridge University Press, 1983), 63–5. Other legal texts promoted this "conception-equals-consent" rule, including Sir Henry Finch, *Law, or a Discourse Thereof* (London, 1627); T. E., *The Lawes Resolution of Women's Rights* (London, 1632); and William Lambarde, *Eirenarcha, or Of the Office of the Justices of the Peace* (London, 1582).

49. *Aristotle's Master-Piece*, 22–25. The anonymous author of the *Master-Piece* disputes much of this Galenic biology, particularly the notion that women have seed (the author believes the egg is materially different rather than strictly analogous to the male sperm). Although the author does not specify whether orgasm is necessary to conception in his competing physiology, it seems likely that it is not, as it is his opinion that the woman's ovum is the passive recipient fertilized by the active male seed. Audrey Eccles, *Obstetrics and Gynaecology in Tudor and Stuart England* (Kent, Oh.: Kent State University Press, 1982), discusses at some length the transition from the Galenic theory of male and female seed to a theory of ovum and seed. Eccles demonstrates that even at the end of the seventeenth century the two theories still competed for popular acceptance, although the Galenic theory had been abandoned by most medical writers.

50. *Aristotle's Master-Piece*, 89.

51. Alsemero's medical guide seems to be a compilation of experiments selected out of other texts. Beatrice-Joanna mentions the name of one of the authors it cites, Antonius Mizaldus, a French physician whose works included precisely such potions and tests. Dale B. Randall, "Some Observations on the Theme of Chastity in *The Changeling*," *English Literary Renaissance* 14, no. 3 (1984): 347–66, has researched Renaissance metaphysical works for evidence that such tests were not uncommon, and reports on a substantive tradition of virginity and pregnancy tests. Of particular note is the fact that Randall finds waning confidence in such tests by the seventeenth century. He mentions Fortunato Fedeli's *De relationibus medicorum* which concludes that there are no sure signs of virginity, and Robert Burton's *The Anatomy of Melancholy* which dismisses virginity tests as cruel side effects of jealous melancholy. In a paper delivered at the University of Pennsylvania conference, "Renaissance

Subject / Early Modern Object," Marjorie Garber, "Glass M and Glass C: The Art of Drug-Testing Women,"contextualized Alsemero's desire for proof of Beatrice-Joanna's sexual status as part of a larger desire on the part of sixteenth and seventeenth century English men to discover and demystify women's sexual pleasure.

52. I owe a debt of gratitude to Emily Bartels for her thoughts on this point.

53. See, for example, Jardine, *Still Harping on Daughters*; Kathleen McLuskie, "The Act, The Role, and the Actor," *New Theatre Quarterly* 3, no. 10 (1987): 120–30; Phyllis Rackin, "Androgyny, Mimesis, and the Marriage of the Boy Heroine on the English Renaissance Stage," *PMLA* 102, no. 1 (1987): 29–41; Jean E. Howard, "Crossdressing, the Theatre, and Gender Struggle in Early Modern Europe," *Shakespeare Studies* 39 (1988): 418–40; Laura Levine, "Men in Women's Clothing," *Criticism* 28, no. 2 (1986): 121–43; Stephen Orgel, "Nobody's Perfect; or, Why Did the English Stage Take Boys for Women?" *South Atlantic Quarterly* 88 (1989); and J. W. Binns, "Women or Transvestites on the Elizabethan Stage?" *Sixteenth-Century Journal* 5 (1974): 95–120.

54. In *"The Changeling" and the Years of Crisis*, Bromham and Bruzzi are much more eager to ascribe direct political comment and detailed political allegory to this play. While their book does a superb job of demonstrating the multiple valences of political suggestivity in *The Changeling*, the study's flaw is in the very abundance of the contemporary connections they search out: the authors seem indiscriminate in their pursuit of political allusion, with the result that their arguments frequently stretch to the point of improbability.

55. The early optimism of the English is conveyed in several early comments. Ralph Winwood, for instance, wrote that James appeared to be a "prince wise, sober, discreet, nowise debauched, or given over to pleasures, pious and religious, more learned in all kinds of good letters than any prince whatsoever of whom stories either ancient or modern have left us any memory." John Chamberlain offered a similarly glowing early assessment in a letter to Dudley Carlton: "The King uses all very graciously. . . . These bountiful beginnings raise all men's spirits and put them in great hopes, insomuch that not only protestants but papists and puritans and the very poets with their idle pamphlets promise themselves great part in his favor." Both quotes are included by Wallace Notestein, *The House of Commons, 1604–1610* (New Haven, Conn.: Yale University Press, 1971), 56. I have found Notestein's now controversial history of the first Jacobean Parliament invaluable for his inclusion of primary materials and highly suspect in his interpretation of them.

56. James's speech to the House of Commons, 31 March 1607; quoted by Robert E. Ruigh, *The Parliament of 1624: Politics and Foreign Policy* (Cambridge, Mass.: Harvard University Press, 1971), 6.

57. In June 1604, at the end of the first session of Parliament, James

revealed his impatience with this uncooperative, untrusting body: "Contrary here [in England], nothing but curiosity from morning to evening to find fault with my propositions. There [in Scotland] all things warranted that came from me. Here all things suspected. . . . He that doth not love a Scotchman as his brother, or the Scotchman that loves not an Englishman as his brother is a traitor to God and the King. . . . He merits to be buried in the bottom of the sea that shall but think a separation, where God hath made such a Union" (Notestein, *The House of Commons, 1604–1610*, 85). What this speech revealed about James's expectations for exerting power in his new kingdom confirmed the worst fears of his English audience.

58. The Venetian ambassador reported discontent among M.P.s in 1606 when their inability to use the power of the purse to coerce James into redressing their principle grievances: "The members complain that, after granting subsidies, they have obtained nothing but an announcement of further expenditure; and the populace makes this shrewd remark, 'Three subsidies, much evil, no redress,'" *Calendar of State Papers Venetian* 10:353; quoted by Kurt Fryklund, "Supply and Grievances: The House of Commons and the Power of the Purse, 1604–1629" (M.A. thesis, The Ohio State University, 1987), 9. In a parliamentary speech in 1610, Thomas Wentworth remarked wryly that "wee would be glad to heare of Spayne, that the Kinge spent all upon his favorites and wanton courtiers" (quoted by Fryklund, 15).

59. Notestein, *The House of Commons, 1604–1610*, 57, 508, n. 15.

60. Ibid., 79.

61. Notestein, ibid., whose thesis is that James was a bumbling failure as king, notes that criticism of James took a number of forms, some of them surprisingly open: in December 1604, the Venetian ambassador "reported the distribution of papers accusing the King of neglecting the state" (60). Lampoons (*pasquils*) deriding James and his chief minister, Robert Cecil, were posted in public places (38). Samuel Calvert wrote to Ralph Winwood on 25 March 1605 that "the plays do not forbear to present upon the stage the whole course of this present time, not sparing either King, State, or religion, in so great absurdity, and with such liberty that any would be afraid to hear them" (16). The French ambassador sent a similar report to his master: "What must be the state and condition of a Prince whom the preachers publicly assailed, whom the comedians . . . bring upon the stage, whose wife attends these representations to enjoy the laugh against her husband" (16). See also, Alastair Bellany, "'Raylinge Rymes and Vaunting Verse': Libellous Politics in Early Stuart England, 1603–1628" in *Culture and Politics in Early Stuart England*, ed. Kevin Sharpe and Peter Lake (Stanford: Stanford University Press, 1993), 285–310.

62. J. H. Hexter, "Parliament, Liberty, and Freedom of Elections," in

Parliament and Liberty from the Reign of Elizabeth to the English Civil War, ed. J. H. Hexter (Stanford: Stanford University Press, 1992), 40. Hexter cites the *Commons Journal* for this quotation of the Speaker of the House of Commons' paraphrase of James's statement.

63. "The Form of Apology and Satisfaction," quoted in ibid., 41; emphasis Hexter's.

64. Hexter, "Parliament, Liberty, and Freedom," 43.

65. A further allusion to prerogative abuse occurs in the play when D'Ambois cautions the duke of Guise not to think his greatness a warrant for insolence or "a prerogative to rack men's freedom with ruder wrongs" (3.2.121–22). Again a hint of Jacobean significance shimmers within this line: James I was a cousin of the duke of Guise through his mother's mother.

66. Notestein, *The House of Commons, 1604–1610,* 126.

67. William Hakewill, quoted by Conrad Russell, *The Crisis of Parliaments: English History, 1509–1660* (London: Oxford University Press, 1971), 275. According to Elizabeth Read Foster, *Proceedings in Parliament 1610,* ed. Elizabeth Read Foster (New Haven: Yale University Press, 1966), xiv, Hakewill's speech was so famous and influential that a century and a half later Ben Franklin kept a copy in his library in Philadelphia.

68. See Hexter, "Parliament, Liberty and Freedom," 41–43, for a discussion of this language of property in the *Apology.*

69. "Violation" is a term that crops up repeatedly in the parliamentary debates of the early seventeenth century. John Selden chooses it to describe the subterfuge of the royal printer who published Parliament's 1628 Petition of Right without including the royal response, which would have given the petition validity. Selden described the petition as having "been lately violated" and complained that "the liberties for life, person and freehold" had been "invaded." Discussed by J. P. Sommerville, "The Ancient Constitution Reassessed: The Common Law, the Court and the Languages of Politics in Early Modern England" in *The Stuart Court and Europe: Essays in Politics and Political Culture,* ed. R. Malcolm Smuts (Cambridge: Cambridge University Press, 1996), 69.

70. Hexter, "Parliament, Liberty, and Freedom," 42.

71. McClure, *Letters of John Chamberlain,* 1:301, italics added. Discussed by Notestein, *The House of Commons, 1604–1610,* 321–27; Fryklund, "Supply and Grievances," 16.

72. Hexter, "Parliament, Liberty, and Freedom," 270.

73. Stephen D. White, *Sir Edward Coke and "The Grievances of the Commonwealth," 1621–1628* (Chapel Hill: University of North Carolina Press, 1979), 271–72.

74. Carole Pateman, *The Sexual Contract* (Stanford University Press,

1988), analyzes Renaissance patriarchal theories of social order and the emergence by the end of the seventeenth century of social contract theories of government.

75. Notestein, *The House of Commons, 1604–1610*, 52.

76. Foster, *Proceedings in Parliament 1610*, 2:258.

77. Ibid., 2:265.

78. *Commons Journal*, 466:34; reproduced in *Proceedings in Parliament 1614 (House of Commons)*, ed. Maija Jansson (Philadelphia: American Philosophical Society, 1988), 88.

79. Add. MS. 48,101, British Library. Reproduced in ibid., 91.

80. Quoted by Jansson, *Proceedings in Parliament 1614*, xxvi.

81. The play has been attributed to Webster and some have suggested a collaboration between that playwright and Thomas Heywood. See, for instance, Bliss, *The World's Perspective*, 6, 204.

82. See Hexter, "Parliament, Liberty, and Freedom," 93–101, for a discussion of liberty in terms of free versus bond status.

83. Thomas Scott, *Vox Populi; or, Newes from Spayne* (1620), 31; quoted and discussed by Zara Bruzzi, "Political Iconography and the Spanish Marriage," in Bromham and Bruzzi, 64. Her discussion of the literature of the Spanish match and its relation to *The Changeling* is invaluable. While I do not agree with her reading in all parts, I have found it tremendously helpful.

84. *An Experimentall Discoverie*, 33–35; quoted in ibid., 56.

85. I have borrowed the term, but not its context, from their argument. It is King James that they call a "central absence" and a "repressed protagonist." As I will explain, I do not believe that James stands behind the text in the way these critics claim (57).

86. All we know about Vermandero is that he is the keeper of a castle (he calls it "*my* citadel"), but there is no indication that we are to take him as more than a regional feudal lord. He is never identified as a territorial ruler (king or duke, for example). He may, in fact, keep the citadel in the service of some greater lord.

87. Sir Edward Coke, *Reports of Sir Edward Coke* (London, 1658), 3.

Notes to Chapter 5

1. George Chapman quoted by Barbara Kiefer Lewalski, *Writing Women in Jacobean England* (Cambidge, Mass.: Harvard University Press, 1993), 81. Epigraph from *The Letters of Lady Arbella Stuart* ed. Sara Jayne Steen (Oxford: Oxford University Press, 1994), 254; hereafter cited in the text as *Letters*, followed by page number.

2. Dudley Carleton, 13 July 1610, in Sir Ralph Winwood, *Memorials*

of the Affairs of State in the Reigns of Queen Elizabeth and James I, 3 vols., ed. E. Sawyer (London, 1725), 3:124. See also Lewalski, *Writing Women*, 84.

3. Elizabeth Talbot is usually referred to as "Bess of Hardwick" by historians needing an easy way to distinguish her from the other Elizabeths of her period. I prefer to avoid this moniker, which seems to me to diminish the woman.

4. Steen, *Letters*, 15. See also Phyllis Margaret Handover, *Arbella Stuart: Royal Lady of Hardwick and Cousin to King James* (London: Eyre and Spottiswoode, 1957); David N. Durant, *Arbella Stuart: A Rival to the Queen* (London: Weidenfeld and Nicholson, 1978).

5. The English Lennox estates had been the dowry bestowed by Henry VIII on his niece, Margaret Douglas, when he arranged her marriage with the exiled earl of Lennox, Matthew Stuart. Margaret was the daughter of Henry's sister, Margaret, and her second husband, Archibald Douglas.

6. The grounds on which Elizabeth made this demand rested on a statute created to address the dynastic complications of Henry VIII's reign. 28 Henry VIII, cap. 24 prohibited anyone to "espouse marry or take to wife any of the King's children [being lawfully born or otherwise commonly reputed or taken to be his children,] or any of the King's Sisters or Aunts of the part of the Father, [or the lawful children] of the King's Brothern or Sisters [not being married,] or contract marriage with any of them, without the special license assent consent and agreement first thereunto had and obtained of the King's Highness in writing under his great seal, [or defile or deflower any of them not being married]" (brackets in original). The language of this law was constructed to cover the nearest claimants to the throne during Henry VIII's lifetime. Under the childless Elizabeth, the nearest claimants stood at a greater remove of relation than the law specifies, but this is clearly the legal ground on which Elizabeth, and later James, demanded control of Arbella Stuart's marriageability. From *Statutes of the Realm, from Magna Carta to the End of the Reign of Queen Anne . . . from the original records and authentic manuscripts* (London, 1810–28); quoted in Whigham, *Seizures of the Will in Early Modern English Drama* (Cambridge: Cambridge University Press, 1996), 25.

7. Elizabeth responded to that elopement by arresting and imprisoning the couple, then declaring the marriage invalid. The couple made a strategic error when they overlooked the need for witnesses to corroborate their claim that a wedding ceremony had taken place in proper order. The children of the union were declared illegitimate, but this did not stop contemporaries from considering them possible claimants to the throne, since the circumstances of their illegitimacy were so patently a matter of state politics and royal convenience. Hertford was released from the Tower following his wife's death (Lewalski, *Writing Women*, 71, 352 n. 17).

8. There is circumstantial evidence that Stuart did not act solely on

her own in this matter, but acted on the advice and with material support from her uncles, William and Henry Cavendish. The tone of Stuart's correspondence with her extended family and with her retainers, John Dodderidge and (especially) George Chaworth, suggests that she and they understood her actions to have familial support. Henry Cavendish's attempt to free Stuart from Hardwick Hall with the help of an armed escort suggests that he did not view her actions as either ill-founded or irrational and attests to the danger he was willing to incur by implicating himself in her affairs. Her grandmother, on the other hand, immediately distanced herself from Stuart's actions, demonstrating loyalty to the Crown by disciplining and disinheriting the granddaughter she once called her "jewel."

9. Both Steen, *Letters*, 34, and Lewalski, *Writing Women*, 71, put forward versions of this interpretation of events.

10. Stuart suggests this interpretation in a letter to Sir Henry Brounker (Steen, *Letters*, 173–74). Stuart's correspondence with many individuals during this period of house arrest was collected in an intelligence file by Robert Cecil, Elizabeth's chief counselor; the Cecil Papers are now archived at Hatfield House library.

11. Whigham, *Seizures of the Will*, 1.

12. In fact, though Stuart does convey fleeting moments of triumph or thrill at dominating others (her grandmother, her interrogators), she principally signals that she feels violated in the aftermath of her failure to elope with Seymour. This seems to be an important variation on the phenomenon Whigham studies in his book.

13. This document was Brounker's report of his interrogation of Stuart. Steen supplies the word "lands" to fill a blank in the original document.

14. The appeal was directed to Sir Thomas Fleming, lord chief justice of England and Sir Edward Coke, lord chief justice of common pleas; see BL Harley MS 7003, f. 152; Steen, *Letters*, 255–56.

15. Stuart was, in fact, 32 rather than 28 at the time of this report. See *Calendar of State Papers, Venetian*, vol. 10 (1603–07), 514; quoted in Lewalski, *Writing Women*, 82. Steen discusses contemporary reactions to Stuart's behavior in "The Crime of Marriage: Arbella Stuart and *The Duchess of Malfi*," *Sixteenth Century Journal* 22 (1991): 61–76.

16. Quoted in Lewalski, 352 n. 22. Elizabeth Talbot used the phrase "so wilfully bent" to describe Stuart in another letter directed to Sir John Stanhope and Sir Robert Cecil (quoted in Lewalski, 353 n. 32).

17. Whigham, *Seizures of the Will*, 28, 29.

18. Ibid., 30.

19. In 1610, when James separated her from her husband, Stuart Seymour again represents herself as a victim of conflicting ideological demands (to marry and to refrain from marriage at the command of the monarch). Again she constructs herself as a dutiful early modern woman

obedient to her culture's imperative that she marry an appropriate husband, and in this instance she reconstructs the royal demand on her not as a reasonable request that she defer to the dynastic needs of the ruling monarch, but as a tyrannous expectation that she must renounce what her Protestant culture defines as womanhood's only valid end.

20. This annotation appears on one of three copies of the letter in Cecil's files (Steen, *Letters*, 149).

21. Lewalski, *Writing Women*, 71–77.

22. Steen, *Letters*, 144. Lewalski, *Writing Women*, 74, speculates that "James was perhaps the one man in the kingdom who could not be harmed by her naming, since no one would credit this long-married known homosexual as Arbella's secret lover."

23. Brounker told George Chaworth that he found Stuart to be of "a hundred minds," and reported to the Privy Council on the "distempering of her brains apparent enough by the multitude of her idle discourses" (quoted in Steen, *Letters*, 38, 36).

24. Lewalski, *Writing Women*, 75.

25. Steen's translation (*Letters*, 155).

26. Foxe, *Acts and Monuments* (1563), 1712.

27. Steen, *Letters*, 170; Foxe, *Acts and Monuments* (1563), 1715. Foxe uses a version of this formula earlier in the Elizabeth account: "thought, woorde, and deede" (1712).

28. Askew, "The Latter Examination of the worthy servant of God, mastres Anne Askew, the yonger doughter of sir William Askew knight of Lincon shire, lately martired in Smithfield, by the wicked sinagoge of Antichrist," in *The Examinations of Anne Askew*, ed. Elaine Beilin (Oxford: Oxford University Press, 1996); Foxe, *Acts and Monuments* (1563), 669–80.

29. Steen, *Letters*, 170–71. Her last phrase, which reveals that the torture she bears is "exile with expectation," rather deflates the effect of her rhetoric.

30. A further hint that Stuart has been reading Foxe is her allusion to Queen Mary's reputed assertion that when she died her embalmers would find "Calais" written upon her heart. "I know it would be so much to your satisfaction and credit to find and understand this concealed truth which seek and examine and torture whom you list you shall never find but in my heart," she writes to Brounker, "and oh that you would seek it there where it is as deeply printed and in the same Characters of undeserved redressless unkindness as Calais in Queen Mary's." This allusion to a famous anecdote from the end of Foxe's section on Princess Elizabeth's ordeal is linked in Stuart's mind (and sentence) with her echo of the "examinations" and "rackings" at the opening of Foxe's account.

31. Foxe, *Acts and Monuments* (1563), 1712. Bale was especially fond of constructions that portrayed his enemies as simultaneously licentious

and bloodthirsty (as in "that bawdy bloody Synagogue of Satan") and was a master of conveying the pleasure he supposed those enemies took in their tortures and executions ("horrible fury of Antichrist," "mortal malice," "this hungry wolf practiceth by all crafty ways possible to suck the blood of this innocent lamb," "this Babylon Bishop, or bloodthirsty wolf," "their bloody behove").

32. Among the passages referenced here are Isaiah 2:22, Psalm 37, Matthew 7:1; Luke 6:37.

33. Quoted on the title page of *The first two partes of the Actes or unchaste examples of the Englyshe Votaryes, gathered out of theyr owne legendes and Chronycles by Jhon Bale, and dedicated to oure moste redoubted soueraigne kyng Edwarde the syxte* (1560).

34. Letter to Arbella Stuart from Lady Jane Drummond, BL Harley MS 7003, ff. 64–65; Steen, *Letters*, 292. Steen discusses James's remark in her introduction (71).

35. BL Harley MS 7003, f. 82; Steen, *Letters*, 254.

36. BL Harley MS 7003, f. 57; Steen, *Letters*, 254.

37. The analogy is also interesting insofar as it plays against James's fondness for thinking of himself as a modern-day Solomon. Solomon was the son of David's union with Bathsheba. Stuart's allusion, then, reminds James of the seamier side of the figure he has reverenced and suggests that she thinks David is the more apt precursor for this king — and not David in his more admirable moments, but David at his behavioral nadir.

38. Quoted by Conrad Russell, *The Crisis of Parliaments: English History, 1509–1660* (London: Oxford University Press, 1971), 275; *The Letters of John Chamberlain*, ed. Norman Egbert McClure (Philadelphia: The American Philosophical Society, 1939), 1:301. For more on these issues, see my chapter 4. James's unrelenting harshness may be explained in part by remembering that 1610 was also the year in which Henry IV of France was murdered by a Roman Catholic fanatic, an event that made James fear that Arbella's marriage was part of a grand scheme by Catholic plotters planning to usurp the throne in her name. (Steen discusses this context of James's reaction to Arbella's marriage in her introduction (*Letters*, 65–66.)

39. King James to William James, bishop of Durham, 13 March 1611, BL Harley MS 7003, f. 94; quoted in Steen, *Letters*, 71.

40. Francis Bacon's characterization of Stuart's behavior during his prosecution of Mary Talbot, countess of Shrewsbury. See *The Letters and the Life of Francis Bacon*, vol. 4, ed. James Spedding (London: Longman, 1861–74), 297–98; also discussed by Steen, *Letters*, 71.

Notes to Chapter 6

1. William Prynne, *Newes from Ipswich* (London: T. Bates, 1641).

2. Among the changes in the liturgy was the omission of prayers for the king, whose position as head of the Anglican church denied the authority of the pope. Also absent from Laud's worship book were prayers for Charles's sister, the Protestant queen of Bohemia. Laud's opponents made much of such omissions. See Eliabeth Skerpan, *The Rhetoric of Politics in the English Revolution, 1642–1660* (Columbia: University of Missouri Press, 1992), 44–45. These material innovations in the churches and the worship service were the outward signs of Laud's "arminian" attack on the established Calvinism of the English church. For a discussion of the tenets of arminianism and Laud's campaign to uproot Calvinism, see Nicholas Tyacke, "Puritanism, Arminianism and Counter-Revolution," in *The Origins of the English Civil War*, ed. Conrad Russell (New York: Barnes and Noble, 1973), 119–43. See also Christopher Hill, "The Protestant Nation" and "From Grindal to Laud," in *The Collected Essays of Christopher Hill*, vol. 2 (Amherst: University of Massachusetts Press), 24, 63–82.

3. In her *Memoirs of the Life of Colonel Hutchinson*, ed. James Sutherland (London: Oxford University Press, 1973), Lucy Hutchinson uses "godly" as a more appropriate term for Calvinist Protestants than "puritan" (38). In his edition (1806) of Hutchinson's work, Julius Hutchinson noted that "godly" was "the name always given by the Puritans to those of their own party" (quoted in Sutherland's edition, 299). Now as then, "Puritan" evokes a stereotype of separatist, religious zealotry, which was never an accurate description of many of the people to whom it was applied. John Pym, a central figure in the godly party, argued in Parliament in 1621 against the use of "that odious and factious name of Puritans" to label religious reformists like himself. See Tyacke, "Puritanism," 129. In the interest of avoiding this stereotype, I will refer to the somewhat loose party of Protestant reformers as the "godly party" rather than as "Puritans." This group was predominantly Calvinist in theology and included Presbyterians as well as a variety of separatist sects who came together in the cause of resisting the Anglican movement toward Catholicism (although their ultimate goals varied). For my purposes, the term emphasizes the explicitly political methods used by this group to achieve their reformist objectives. For further examples of seventeenth century objections to the categorizing of people as "Puritans," see Anonymous, *A Discourse Concerning Puritans: A Vindication of Those, Who Unjustly Suffer by the Mistake, Abuse, and Misapplication of That Name* (London: Robert Bostock, 1641), and Hutchinson, *Memoirs*, esp. 43–44.

4. Lawrence Stone makes this point in *The Crisis of the Aristocracy, 1558–1641* (Oxford: Clarendon Press, 1965). He believes that the excess of horror with which the public seems to have viewed the Prynne, Burton and Bastwick disfigurements is the result of their having been condemned to suffer physical punishments inappropriate to their social station (29–30). J. P. Kenyon agrees that public hostility to the Court of Star Chamber was probably fueled by the harshness of its sentences for upper-class offenders. He focuses on aristocratic prisoners punished by that court rather than on middle-class figures like these three pamphleteers. See J. P. Kenyon, *The Stuart Constitution, 1603–1688* (Cambridge: Cambridge University Press, 1986), 105.

5. In *Discipline and Punish: The Birth of the Prison*, trans. Alan Sheridan (New York: Vintage Books, 1979), Michel Foucault discusses the danger that a public execution might be read by the public as a spectacle of the state's oppression rather than as an enactment of justice. Foucault describes the delicate balance that must be maintained so that the tide of shame meant to be cast on the condemned individual does not turn backwards onto the executioner and the state authority represented by his office.

6. John Bastwick, *The Letany of John Bastwick* ([London], 1637), A4. That Burton, Prynne and Bastwick borrow their language of abuse from John Bale and John Foxe is particularly clear in this passage's pointed recollection of the heretic burnings at Smithfield.

7. *A Speech Made by Captain Audley Mervin to the Upper House in Ireland. With Certaine Articles of Treason Against Sir Richard Bolton and Others* (London: Hugh Perry, 1641), 5, 9.

8. *An Honourable and Worthy Speech: Spoken in the High Covrt of Parliament, by Mr. Smith of the Middle-Temple, October 28. 1641. Concerning the Regulating of the Kings Majesties Prerogative, and the Liberties of the Subjects* (London: Barnard Alsop, 1641). Brian Manning, *The English People and the English Revolution, 1640–1649* (London: Heinemann, 1976), identifies this Mr. Smith, noting that he was allied to the court party through his association with the duke of Richmond — obviously a troubled alliance given his critical remarks in the speech quoted here (82, 94, 135).

9. See, for instance, Manning, *The English People*. Christopher Hill, in *Reformation to Industrial Revolution* (London: Weidenfeld and Nicolson, 1967) and elsewhere, and Lawrence Stone, *The Crisis of the Aristocracy*, offer alternative — and conflicting — views of the relationship between economic crisis and the outbreak of war.

10. Skerpan, *The Rhetoric of Politics*, looks at particular moments and strategies of the partisan literature generated by parliamentary supporters, royalists and religious radicals; Lois Potter, *Secret Rites, Secret Writings: Royalist Literature, 1641–1660* (Cambridge: Cambridge University Press, 1989), offers a comprehensive study of the methods, modes and means of

production of royalist propaganda. Both discuss the importance of the London audience of this literature to the development and outcome of the conflicts of the 1640s and 1650s.

11. Anonymous, *Archy's Dream, Sometimes Iester to His Maiestie; but Exiled the Court by Canterburies Malice* ([London], 1641), A2; Anonymous, *A New Play Called Canterburie His Change of Diot* ([London], 1641), A2, A2v.

12. E. M. Yearling, ed., introduction to *The Cardinal* (Manchester: University of Manchester, 1986), 3. Excerpts from the play are from this edition and hereafter cited in the text.

13. In April and again in December 1641, Charles was discovered to have conspired with some members of the army to suppress parliamentary opposition by force. The plots, however, were revealed to Parliament and exposed in the public press before they could reach fruition. See Conrad Russell, *The Fall of the British Monarchies, 1637–1642* (Oxford: Clarendon Press, 1991), 291–95; Hutchinson, *Memoirs*, 50–51; Manning, *The English People*, 74–76; 102–3.

14. See Russell, *The Fall of the British Monarchies*, 454–524.

15. Shirley's association with the Catholics among the court literary coteries is documented and discussed by Sandra Burner, *James Shirley: A Study of Literary Coteries and Patronage in Seventeenth-Century England* (New York: University Press of America, 1988), 101–3. Her evidence for believing Shirley to have been Catholic in the 1640s seems fairly weak. It is true that he was libeled by Captain Thomas Audley in the 4–11 January 1644 issue of *Mercurius Britannicus* as "Frier Sherley," but any Anglican with court connections would have smelled of Catholicism to Audley. Suffice it to say that Shirley, with his court friends and work for the theater, would have been suspected of crypto-Catholic leanings by those of the godly party — and in the 1640s suspicion was enough.

16. Russell, *Fall of the British Monarchies*, details the ebb and flow of support for Charles during the first years of the 1640s, noting that the king's popularity was generally at its highest in the months when he was most idle. In fact, the peak of his popularity seems to have been during the months of August to November 1641 when Charles was in Scotland (303–4).

17. There seems to be a critical consensus that Carolinian theater audiences were a wealthier and somewhat more homogenous group than the audiences drawn to plays in earlier periods. R. Malcolm Smuts, *Court Culture and the Origins of a Royalist Tradition in Early Stuart England* (Philadelphia: University of Pennsylvania Press, 1987), notes that "under Charles, the Crown had to take steps to alleviate the jams of aristocratic coaches clogging the entire Blackfriars district whenever a new play opened" (63). See also Alfred Harbage, *Shakespeare and the Rival Tradition* (London: Macmillan, 1952); W. A. Armstrong, "The Audience of the

Elizabethan Private Theaters," *Review of English Studies* n.s. 10, no. 39 (1959): 234–49; Andrew Gurr, *The Shakespearean Stage, 1574–1642* (Cambridge: Cambridge University Press, 1970); Michael Neill, "'Wits Most Accomplished Senate': The Audience of the Caroline Private Theaters," *SEL* 18 (1978): 341–60; Ann Jennalie Cook, *The Privileged Playgoers of Shakespeare's London* (Princeton: Princeton University Press, 1981); Martin Butler, *Theatre and Crisis, 1632–1642* (Cambridge: Cambridge University Press, 1984); Stephen Orgel and Roy Strong, *Inigo Jones: The Theater of the Stuart Court* (Berkeley and Los Angeles: University of California Press, 1973).

18. See Smuts, *Court Culture*, 110 n. 30.

19. Jonson had been in trouble in 1603 for the presumed topicality of *Sejanus* and its depiction of tyranny, and in 1605 Jonson and George Chapman spent time in prison for their anti-Scottish satire in *Eastward Hoe*, a play on which John Marston had also collaborated.

20. Dugard, quoted in Potter, *Secret Rites*, 74.

21. William D'Avenant, *Sir William D'Avenant, the Seige of Rhodes: A Critical Edition*, ed. Ann-Mari Hedbäck (Stockholm: Uppsala University Press, 1973).

22. In his introduction to the play, Yearling points out that *The Cardinal* would have been too late to warn Charles against Laud, who had already been impeached and was in the Tower awaiting trial. For Yearling, the fact that the play follows Laud's arrest proves that the play has no political intentions despite its topical allusions. It seems to me, however, that the play joined a number of Charles's critics in Parliament, urging the king to learn from his experience with Strafford and Laud that he must change his approach to Parliament and his mode of government if he hoped to avoid war. Whether these hopes were merely political posturing, or the product of a real belief that Charles could still avert a conflict with Parliament, is not clear. Nonetheless, *The Cardinal* was an active voice within the political arena of that last year before the fighting began.

23. Lucius Carey, second Viscount Faulkland, *A Speech Made to the Hovse of Commons Concerning Episcopacy by the Lord Viscount Faulkeland* (London: Thomas Walkely, 1641), 3–4.

24. William Prynne, *A Brief Survay and Censure of Mr. Cozens His Couzening Devotions* (London, 1628), 7–8; quoted in John Dykstra Eusden, *Puritans, Lawyers, and Politics in Early Seventeenth-Century England* (New York: Archon Books, 1968), 75; emphasis Prynne's.

25. Richard Ward, *The Principal Duty of Parliament Men* (London: J. R., 1641), 24.

26. The authors of these tracts are uniformly male, and the audience they assume is male as well, despite the cross-gender identification that this imagery then requires of its readers.

27. Anonymous, *The Times Dissected; or, A Learned Discourse of*

Severall Occurences Very Worthy of Speciall Observation, to Deter Evill Men, and Incourage Good ([London], 1641), 6; Anonymous, *Canterbvries Pilgrimage; or, The Testimony of an Accused Conscience for the Bloud of Mr. Burton, Mr. Prynne, and Doctor Bastwicke and the Just Deserved Sufferings He Lyes Under: Shewing the Glory of Reformation, Above Prelaticall Tyranny* (London: H. Walker, 1641), A3v.

28. *A Speech Made by Captain Audley Mervin*, 5.

29. Prynne, *Newes from Ipswich*.

30. Anonymous, *A Rent in the Lawne Sleeves; or, Episcopacy Eclypsed, by the Most Happy Interposition of a Parliament Discoursed Dialogue-wise Betweene a Bishop and a Iesuite* (London: Iohn Thomas, 1641), 3; Smith, *An Honourable and Worthy Speech*, 2; emphasis mine.

31. *Articles Ministred by His Majesties Commissioners for Causes Ecclesiasticall. Presented to the High Court of Parliament Against John Gwin, Vicar of Cople in the County of Bedford* (London: V. V., 1641).

32. London, 1641.

33. At least three tracts were published in 1641 on the subject of John Atherton's trial, confession and execution for sodomy: *The Life and Death of John Atherton Lord Bishop of Waterford and Lysmore* (London); *A Sermon Preached at the Bvriall of the Said Iohn Atherton* (Dublin); *and The Penitent Death of a Woefvll Sinner; or, The Penitent Death of John Atherton* (Dublin: Society of Stationers).

34. *A Rent in the Lawne Sleeves*, 4.

35. *Petition of the Weamen of Middlesex . . . with the Apprentices of Londons Petition* (London: William Bowen, 1641), A2v. There was a legend, particularly popular during the Reformation, that one of the popes had been a woman who had successfully masqueraded as a man until her licentiousness led to pregnancy and she was discovered in childbirth. This story combined several favorite slanders on Catholic priests: that they were effeminate, that they were sexually voracious, that they were easily duped, and that the succession of the popes from Saint Peter was a sham, or at least hopelessly corrupted.

36. Anonymous, *Anatomy of Et cætera* (London, 1641), 3; *Canterbvries Pilgrimage*, A3v.

37. It was largely fear of the unknown that made Catholicism so frightening. Given their expansive definition of popery and their restrictive understanding of properly reformed Protestantism, the godly party, though living in a Protestant nation, saw themselves as an isolated and persecuted minority. Robin Clifton offers a valuable discussion of the distrust and alarm with which Catholicism met in the early 1640s. Clifton, "Fear of Popery," in *The Origins of the English Civil War*, ed. Conrad Russell (New York: Barnes and Noble, 1973), examines the depth and sources of that fear in the political crisis of 1641–42.

38. Anonymous, *A Discovery of the Notorious Proceedings of William*

Laud. Archbishop of Canterbury, in Bringing Innovations Into the Church, and Raising Up Troubles in the State, His Pride Riding in His Coach When the King Himselfe Went Along on Foot, and Being Reproved, Would not Alight. With His Tyrannicall Government Both in Himselfe and His Agents. Confessed by John Browne a Prisoner in the Gatehouse, Twice Examined by a Committee of Six from the Honourable House of Commons (London: Henry Walker, 1641), A2v; Anonymous, *Wrens Anatomy. Discovering His Notorious Pranks, and Shamefull Wickednesse* ([London], 1641), 2; Anonymous, *Old Newes Newly Revived; or, The Discovery of all Occurrences Happened Since the Beginning of the Parliament* ([London], 1641), A3.

39. See, for instance, the lampoon on bishops and courtiers in the anonymous *Fortunes Tennis-ball* (London, 1640).

40. Prynne's use of the phrase "tyrannizing Lordly prelates" in *Newes from Ipswich* is characteristic of his writing and may have identified him as the tract's author. In 1641, when the debate over the bishop's role in Parliament was heating up, *Newes* was reprinted, and a new tract, *The Antipathy of the English Lordly Prelacy* (London, 1641), indicated Prynne's continuing involvement in the debate.

41. In part, this fear was fueled by the fact that Charles allowed a number of known recusants and several Jesuits places at his court. Another continuing provocation was the royal marriage settlement that entitled Henrietta Maria to maintain a private chapel and to keep priests (she had four Capuchins in addition to a confessor) in her household. It also became public knowledge that the pope had sent an envoy to the English court who had been in the country secretly for some time before his presence was known. It did not help matters that during the years of his personal rule, Charles had not enforced the laws against recusants. In some quarters there was worry that the king might himself be a crypto-Catholic; certainly he seemed inclined to grant papists special protection. Thomas Hobbes, *Behemoth: The History of the Causes of the Civil Wars of England*, ed. William Molesworth (New York: Burt Franklin, 1963), discusses contemporary reaction to the Catholic influences at Charles's court. See also, Russell, *Fall of the British Monarchies*, 23, 229–30, 259, 352–54; Clifton, *Fear of Popery*, 152; Quentin Bone, *Henrietta Maria: Queen of the Cavaliers* (Urbana: University of Illinois Press, 1972), 99–119.

42. Anonymous, *The Black Box of Roome Opened* ([London], 1641), 18. Clifton, *Fear of Popery*, points out that there was some truth in this characterization. Priests tended to come from landed, monied families who could afford to send their sons abroad to attend seminary. When these men returned home, they sought out their own class and ministered and made converts in that company (152–53).

43. See Russell, *Fall of the British Monarchies*, 291–92; Manning, *The English People*, 22–23, 71–78; Donald Pennington, "The Making of War,"

in *Puritans and Revolutionaries: Essays in Seventeenth-Century History Presented to Christopher Hill*, ed. Donald Pennington and Keith Thomas (Oxford: Clarendon Press, 1978), 161–63, 172–75, 178.

44. Anonymous, *The Svcklington Faction; or, Sucklings Roaring Boyes* ([London], 1641).

45. The long, curled hair that was fashionable among aristocratic men was a particular target of the godly, who wore their hair short and unadorned, earning them the name "roundheads." Prynne wrote *The Unlovelinesse of Love-Lockes* (London, 1628) maintaining that it was sinful for men to wear their hair long. See Edmund Miller, introduction to *Mount-Orgueil (1641) by William Prynne*, ed. Edmund Miller (Delmar, N.Y.: Scholar's Facsimiles and Reprints, 1984), iii.

46. The only scene in *The Cardinal* that occurs outside the court is set in the army camp, an extension of the king of Navarre's sphere, populated by commissioned officers who, in peacetime, are inhabitants of the court. The play does not acknowledge a larger nation with rural and urban interests in addition to the tight little world in which the king and his courtiers live. I will argue later, however, that class remains an implicit issue in this play. Although the setting ignores the existence of a layered society, the ambivalence of the play toward its wealthy, courtier characters is a product of the class hostilities in London in 1641.

47. For discussions of the early modern English usage of the term "effeminacy," see Alan Bray, *Homosexuality in Renaissance England* (London: Gay Men's Press, 1982); Bruce Smith, *Homosexual Desire in Shakespeare's England: A Cultural Poetics* (Chicago: University of Chicago Press, 1991); Gregory Bredbeck, *Sodomy and Interpretation: From Marlowe to Milton* (Ithaca, N.Y.: Cornell University Press, 1991); Valerie Traub, *Desire and Anxiety: Circulations of Sexuality in Shakespearean Drama* (London: Routledge, 1992); and Jonathan Goldberg, *Sodometries: Renaissance Texts/Modern Sexualities* (Stanford, Calif.: Stanford University Press, 1992).

48. John Milton, *Eikonoklastes*, in *Complete Prose Works of John Milton*, vol. 3, ed. Merritt Y. Hughes (New Haven, Conn.: Yale University Press, 1962), 570–71. Milton's association of court life with "effeminacy" belongs to a well-established Protestant tradition going back at least to Stephen Gosson and the antitheatrical writers of the 1570s and 1580s. Gosson, *The Schoole of Abuse* (London: Thomas Woodcocke, 1579), uses effeminacy as a charge to attack courtiers who spent their days in flattery and artistic pursuits, preferring to exchange witticisms with ladies rather than to engage in martial exercise:

> [Once,] english men could suffer watching and labor, hunger and thirst, and beare of al stormes with hed and shoulders, they vsed slender weapons, went naked, and were good soldiours. . . . But the

> exercise that is nowe among vs, is banqueting, playing, pipyng, and
> dauncing, and all suche delightes as may win us to pleasure, or rocke
> vs a sleepe.
>
> Oh what a wonderfull chaunge is this? Our wreastling at armes,
> is turned to wallowyng in Ladies laps, our courage to cowardice,
> our running to ryot, our Bowes into Bolles, and our Dartes to Dishes.
> (B8–C1)

Gosson makes even more explicit the objection that at court men consort
with women and delight in womanish entertainments and diversions.
Gosson, writing 60 years earlier than Milton, holds military pursuits
forward as an ideal of masculine conduct. Milton has no such fondness
for combat.

49. Anonymous, *Mercurius Britanicus*, 10–17 June 1644, 307; Potter,
Secret Rites, 46.

50. "Malignant" was a favorite tag that godly pamphleteers hung on
the king's supporters.

51. Christopher Hill, *A Nation of Change and Novelty: Radical Politics,
Religion and Literature in Seventeenth-Century England* (London:
Routledge, 1990), 24–34, discusses the artificiality and disingenuity of
opposition writers's strategic avoidance of criticizing Charles. In *Eikonoklastes*, Milton announces that this strategy of displacing criticism
of Charles onto his accessories is no longer necessary nor effective: "As
[Charles I] to acquitt himself, hath not spar'd his Adversaries, to load
them with all sorts of blame and accusation, so to him, as in his Book
alike, there will be us'd no more Courtship then he uses; but what is
properly his own guilt, not imputed any more to his evil Counsellors, (a
Ceremony us'd longer by the Parlament then he himself desir'd) shall be
laid heer without circumlocutions at his own dore" (341).

52. Hutchinson, *Memoirs*, 42.

53. Hutchinson, *Memoirs*, 46. Villiers was not the only favorite with
whom James was reputed to have had a homosexual relationship, but he
was the last and most powerful of the king's favorites, and the most hated.
His power continued when Charles succeeded his father on the throne.
Villiers was assassinated in 1628.

54. See Henry Wotton, *A Parallell Betweene Robert Late Earle of Essex,
and George Late Diuke of Buckingham* (London, 1641), 7, 8; *James I: By
His Contemporaries*, ed. Robert Ashton (London: Hutchinson, 1969), 124;
David M. Bergeron, *Royal Family, Royal Lovers: King James of England
and Scotland* (Columbia: University of Missouri Press, 1991). Goodman's
account, which seems not to have been published until 1839, was written
in the early 1650s as a response to Anthony Weldon's violently anti-Stuart
Court and Character of King James (London: R. I. to be sold by J. Collins,
1651). See also Royce Macgilivray, *Restoration Historians and the English
Civil War* (The Hague, Netherlands: Martinus Nijhoff, 1974), 28.

55. Margaret Cavendish offers a version of this same unease with the behavioral and occupational roles open to gentlemen in her play, *The Sociable Companions* (published 1668, possibly written some years earlier), where a soldier is made to observe of men with a courtly, poetic bent, that "Wit makes the minds of men soft, sweet, gentle, and effeminate; insomuch as those that have Wit, are not fit for Soldiers; for Soldiers should have resolute minds, cloudy thoughts, hard hearts, rough speeches, and boisterous actions" (2.5). As these lines suggest, Cavendish not only critiques the courtly man but the martial man in her play, here ironically scripting the soldier's lines to identify his own unpleasant characteristics. See Cavendish, *The Sociable Companions; or, The Female Wits: A Comedy*, ed. Amanda Holton (Oxford: Seventeenth Century Press, 1996), 37.

56. As Hill, *Collected Essays*, points out, "railing off the altar . . . emphasized not only the real presence [of Christ's body in the Host] but also the mediating role of the priest. Puritans wanted the communion table to be in the center of the church, with the *minister* attending on seated communicants, not the *priest* mediating the miracle of the mass." See particularly "The Protestant Nation," 24, and "From Grindal to Laud," 63–82.

57. Manning, *The English People*, 46–70.

58. Edmund Waller, *A Speech Made by Mr. Waller Esquire, in the Honourable House of Commons, Concerning Episcopacy, Whether It Should be Committed or Rejected* ([London], 1641), 4–5.

59. Manning, *The English People*, describes this emerging middle class and their interests in some detail (112–62; see esp. 152–62).

60. Catherine Belsey, *The Subject of Tragedy: Identity and Difference in Renaissance Drama* (New York: Methuen, 1985), 101.

61. Ibid., 101.

Notes to Chapter 7

1. The bibliographic history of the *Eikon Basilike* is understandably complex and fraught with difficulty given its circumstances of publication and its status as a dangerous text in the aftermath of the king's execution. The best account of its publication history is Francis F. Madan, *A New Bibliography of the Eikon Basilike of King Charles the First* (Oxford: Oxford University Press, 1950). I have also consulted Philip Knachel's introduction to *Eikon Basilike: The Portraiture of His Sacred Majesty in His Solitudes and Sufferings*, ed. Knachel (Ithaca, N.Y.: Cornell University Press, 1966), and Merritt Y. Hughes's discussion of the *Eikon* and *Eikonoklastes* in *The Complete Prose Works of John Milton*, vol. 3, ed. Don M. Wolfe (New Haven: Yale, 1962). The epigraph to this chapter is from "Last Instructions to a Painter. London, 4 September 1667"

(885–906). Attributed to Marvell. See *Andrew Marvell*, ed. Frank Kermode and Keith Walker (Oxford: Oxford University Press, 1990).

2. The ghostwriter was John Gauden, who reputedly drafted *Eikon Basilike*, then submitted it to Charles for his approval. Two editions of the text were released; the second apparently bore Charles's revisions of Gauden's text. See Christopher Hill, *A Nation of Change and Novelty* (London: Routledge, 1990), 108–12; "John Gauden," in *The Longman Anthology of British Literature*, vol. 1, ed. David Damrosch et al. (New York: Longman, 1999), 1701. In discussing *Eikon Basilike*, I will observe the fiction that Charles I himself writes and speaks the text's words as the work's contemporary audience appears to have believed this to be the case. In the sections of his rebuttal quoted here, Milton, too, finds it convenient to accept the attribution of the work to Charles because it allows him to blame Charles for the work's hubris. Milton did, however, question Charles's authorship on stylistic grounds and hinted that the text might be fraudulent. This was a both/and accusation: Milton holds Charles accountable for all of the offensive material in the text, then holds unnamed royalist partisans responsible for perpetrating a fraud against the reading public.

3. Lois Potter, "Royal Actor as Royal Martyr: the *Eikon Basilike* and the Literary Scene in 1649" in *Restoration, Ideology, and Revolution*, ed. Gordon J. Schochet, Patricia E. Tatspaugh and Carol Brobeck (Washington, D.C.: The Folger Shakespeare Library, 1990), 217–40, examines the authorship, intentions and reception of the *Eikon*. Thomas N. Corns, *Uncloistered Virtue: English Political Literature, 1640–1660* (Oxford: Clarendon, 1992), also examines the careful design and political effectiveness of the *Eikon* in a chapter of his work.

4. Knachel, introduction to *Eikon Basilike*, 12, 14.

5. Milton, *Eikonoklastes*, in Hughes, *Complete Prose Works*, 3:356; hereafter cited in the text by page number. Corns, *Uncloistered Virtue*, examines Milton's strategic reading of the *Eikon Basilike*, presenting Milton's work as a well-executed deconstruction of the King's Book (see esp. 212–20).

6. The whole of the passage from the *Eikon Basilike* which Milton paraphrases runs as follows. It is the opening paragraph of that work.

> This last Parliament I called, not more by others' advice and necessity of my affairs then by my own choice and inclination, who have always thought the right way of Parliaments most safe for my crown and best pleasing to my people. And although I was not forgetful of those sparks which some men's distempers formerly studied to kindle in Parliaments (which, by forbearing to convene for some years, I hoped to have extinguished), yet resolving with myself to give all just satisfaction to modest and sober desires, and to redress

all public grievances in church and state, I hoped, by my freedom and their moderation, to prevent all misunderstandings and miscarriages in this; in which, as I feared affairs would meet with some passion and prejudice in other men, so I resolved they should find least of them in myself, not doubting but by the weight of reason I should counterpoise the overbalancings of any factions. (3)

7. Knachel, *Eikon Basilike*, 3–5.

8. In his discussion of the occasion of Milton's writing *Eikonoklastes*, Hughes accepts Milton's account of the council's motivations for urging the author to take up the project. Hughes discusses the parliamentarian fear of *Eikon Basilike*'s power to sway the populace toward a revived royalist cause and places Milton's work within the context of the tract war that raged over the authenticity and authority of the "King's Book" (150–61).

9. Milton claims in the preface to *Eikonoklastes* that he expects his volume will not draw many readers in comparison with the *Eikon Basilike* because it will not have the king's name to sell it. This remark, however true it may have been, is part of Milton's strategy to woo his readers to his point of view. He casts the readers of the King's Book as "the blockish vulgar" and "the Common sort," but compliments his own readers as "those few, such of value and substantial worth, as truth and wisdom, not respecting numbers and bigg names, have bin ever wont in all ages to be contented with" (339–40). Milton intends to draw some of "the blockish vulgar" who had read the *Eikon* to prove themselves valuable and substantial by reading his work and abandoning their uncritical sympathy for the king.

10. A number of recent studies have examined what Steven N. Zwicker, "Lines of Authority: Politics and Literary Culture in the Restoration," in *Politics of Discourse: The Literature and History of Seventeenth-Century England*, ed. Zwicker and Kevin Sharpe (Berkeley and Los Angeles: University of California Press, 1987), calls the "literary assertions of cultural authority," which is to say the complex interactions of politics and literature, after the Restoration.

11. Cavendish's most famous early critic was Dorothy Osborne, who wrote her lover, William Temple, first to express her eagerness to read the duchess's first book of poems ("For God's sake if you meet with it send it me, they say it is ten times more Extravagant than her dress"), then wrote again with her review of the volume ("There are many soberer people in Bedlam, I'll swear her friends are much to blame to let her go abroad"). See Kathleen Jones, *A Glorious Fame: The Life of Margaret Cavendish, Duchess of Newcastle, 1623–1673* (London: Bloomsbury, 1988), 95, 99. Andrew Marvell offers a sour comparison of Henrietta Maria to Margaret Cavendish in lines 49–50 of his "Last Instructions to a Painter; London, 4

September 1667": "Paint then again Her Highness to the life, / Philosopher beyond Newcastle's wife," an uncomplimentary look at both women, which nonetheless speaks to the notoriety not only of Cavendish's person, but her works. See Kermode and Walker, *Andrew Marvell*, 126.

12. In fact, Cavendish would have been appalled to think her work might bear any similarity to the works of parliamentary partisans. Of these writers, she says, "Good Fortune is such an Idol of the World, and is so like the golden Calf worshipped by the Israelites, that those Arch-Rebels never wanted Astrologers to foretell them good success in all their Enterprises, nor Poets to sing their Praises, nor Orators for Panegyrics; nay, which is worse, nor Historians neither, to record their Valour in fighting, and Wisdom in Governing." See *The Life of the Thrice Noble, High and Puissant Prince William Cavendish* (London: A. Maxwell, 1667), D1r.

13. These propaganda tracts did not attack Charles directly, but attacked his courtiers and councillors and the hierarchy of the English church instead. See my chapter 5.

14. Anonymous, *The Life and Reigne of King Charls; or, The Pseudo-Martyr discovered* (London: W. Reynold, 1651), A3r, A3v; hereafter abreviated as *The Pseudo-Martyr discovered* and cited in the text by page number. The comparison of Charles to Tarquin was a popular allusion. Henry Burton likened Charles under the influence of Archbishop Laud and other Arminian bishops to the Tarquins. See Burton, *For God and for the King* (1636), 96.

15. *The Pseudo-Martyr discovered*, 114; John Cook, *Monarchy No Creature of Gods Making* (Waterford, Ireland: Peter de Pienne, 1652).

16. M. Cary, *The Little Horns Doom and Downfall; or, A Scripture-Propheseie of King James, and King Charles, and of this Present Parliament, Unfolded* (London, 1651), 11. For a discussion of the work and life of the Fifth Monarchist minister, Mary Cary, see Rachel Warburton, "Contextual Materials for 'The Little Horn's Doom and Downfall,' and 'A New and More Exact Map' by Mary Cary" Renaissance Women On-line, Brown Women Writer's Project, September 1999; available at <http://www.wwp.brown.edu/texts/rwoentry.html>, access by subscription.

17. *The Pseudo-Martyr discovered*, 23; Thomas May, *History of the Parliament of England* (London, 1647), 11.

18. Cook, *Monarchy*, 2. Milton asserted that under Charles's rule, "all Britain was to be ty'd and chain'd to the conscience, judgement, and reason of one Man . . . meanwhile, for any Parliament or the whole Nation to have either reason, judgement, or conscience, by this rule was altogether vaine, if it thwarted the Kings will" (*Eikonoklastes*, 359).

19. "Voluptuous" is, of course, related to "will" through a common linguistic root.

20. Peyton, *The Divine Catastrophe of the Kingly Family of the House of Stuarts* (London: Giles Calvert, 1652), 4.

21. Thomas May, *A Breviary of the History of the Parliament of England* (London: J. Cottrel, 1655), 46–47.

22. Anthony Weldon, *A Brief History of the Kings of England, Particularly Those of the Royal House of Stuart, of Blessed Memory* (London: T. Williams), 11.

23. Anonymous, *Britania Triumphalis: A Brief History of the Warres and Other State-Affairs of Great Britain, from the Death of the Late King to the Dissolution of the Last Parliament* (London: Samuel Howes, 1654), 2–3.

24. Lucy Hutchinson, *Memoirs of the Life of Colonel Hutchinson*, ed. James Sutherland (Oxford: Oxford University Press, 1973), 42. Hutchinson wrote her memoir sometime after the Restoration, apparently from notes or journals she had kept of the wars and of her husband's participation in events of those years. The *Memoirs* were not published until 1806.

25. Ibid., 42. She does mention the "Catamites" of James's court, and when she speaks of George Villiers, the duke of Buckingham, she notes that he was "raised from a knight's fourth son to that pitch of glory, and enjoy[ed] great possessions acquired by the favour of the King upon no merit but that of his beauty and prostitution" (46). Royce Macgillivray, *Restoration Historians and the English Civil War* (The Hague, Netherlands: Martinus Nijhoff, 1974), discusses Hutchinson's political and religious allegiances, their influence on her *Memoirs*, and the position of that work within the genre of antimonarchist histories.

26. Francis Osborne, *Traditionall Memoyres on the Raigne of King James* (London: Thomas Robinson, 1658), 72, 127–29.

27. Weldon, *The Court and Character of King James. Whereunto is Now Added the Court of King Charles: Continued Unto the Beginning of These Unhappy Times, With Some Observations Upon Him in Stead of a Character* (London: R. I., 1651), 94. Alan Bray *Homosexuality in Renaissance England* (London: Gay Men's Press, 1982), points out the need for caution in discussing homosexuality in the early modern period. Bray demonstrates that homosexuality did not exist as a separate, alternative sexual identity. Although he argues persuasively that effeminacy was a complex term, which was often allusive of heterosexual practices rather than homosexual behaviors, these accounts of James's homosexual relationships repeatedly define his homosexual behaviors as a type of effeminacy. Some of the texts describe James as womanish; in others, his male lovers appear (or seek to appear) womanish. These descriptions hold James's behavior up to a standard of normative heterosexuality and find his conduct monstrous.

28. Anthony Weldon, *The Character of King James*, quoted by Jonathan

Goldberg, *James I and the Politics of Literature* (Baltimore: Johns Hopkins University Press, 1983), 55.

29. Anonymous, *The None-such Charles His Character: Extracted Out of Divers Originall Transactions, Dispatches and the Notes of Severall Publick Ministers, and Councellours of State as Wel at Home as Abroad* (London: R. I., 1651), 20–21.

30. Goldberg, *James I*, 150.

31. Peyton uses the term in his title: *The Divine Catastrophe of the Kingly Family of the House of Stuarts: or, A Short History of the Rise, Reign, and Ruine Thereof. Wherein the most secret Chamber-abominations of the last two Kings are discovered, Divine Justice in King Charles his overthrow vindicated, and the Parliaments proceedings against him clearly justified.*

32. [Charles I], *The Kings Cabinet Opened; or, Certain Packets of Letters and Papers, Written with the Kings Own Hand, and Taken in His Cabinet at Nesby-Field, June 14, 1645 by Victorious Sr. Thomas Fairfax* (London: Robert Bostock, 1645), A4v.

33. The popularity of these metaphors also owes to the fact that the theaters were rumored to be sites of homosexual activity. Several of the Elizabethan antitheatricalist writers were very direct in charging such a connection. Philip Stubbes, *Anatomie of Abuses* (London: Richard Jones, 1583), warned that theatergoers took home with them the inclination to "play the Sodomites or worse" (166). John Rainolds, *Th'Overthrow of Stage-Playes* (London, 1599), cautioned against the sight of boys playing women's roles, by which "the senses are moved, affections are delighted, hearts though strong and constant are vanquished" and by which "men are made adulterers" (18). Alan Bray examines the evidence linking the theaters with homosexual prostitution in *Homosexuality in Renaissance England*. Bray calls attention to Ben Jonson's discussion of the subject in *Poetaster* where Ovid learns of his son's intention to become a player and remarks, "Shall I have my son a stager now, an ingle for players?" Bray defines an "ingle" as a male prostitute in early modern English terminology (53, 55). Jonathan Goldberg quotes Sir Simonds D'Ewes's discussion of sodomy in "this wicked city" and of "boys . . . grown to the height of wickedness to paint" (*The Diary of Sir Simonds D'Ewes, 1622–1624*, 92–93, cited in Goldberg, *James I*, 143). One Restoration event stands out as evidence of the continued association of homosexuality with the stage (and the court). In December 1670, Sir John Coventry was the victim of an assault in retribution for libeling the king in Parliament, where he wondered aloud "whether the king's pleasure lie among the men or the women that acted." For this sexual slander, Coventry had his nose very nearly sliced off in the attack. Charles Sackville refers to this incident in a letter to John Wilmot; Jeremy Treglown provides details of the incident in the notes to his edition of Wilmot's correspondence, *The Letters of*

John Wilmot, Earl of Rochester (Chicago: University of Chicago Press, 1980), 61.

34. Osborne, *Traditionall Memoyres*, 128.

35. Janet Todd, *The Sign of Angellica: Women, Writing and Fiction, 1660–1800* (New York: Columbia University Press, 1989), 68.

36. James Fitzmaurice, introduction to *Margaret Cavendish: Sociable Letters*, ed. James Fitzmaurice (New York: Garland, 1997), xix. Cavendish discusses the pressures of the couple's life in exile in *The Life of the Thrice Noble, High and Puissant Prince William Cavendish* (London: A. Maxwell, 1667). See also Jones, *A Glorious Fame*.

37. Margaret Cavendish, "To the Reader," *Poems and Fancies* (London: T. R. for J. Martin and J. Allestrye, 1653), 3r; citations from *Poems and Fancies* hereafter cited in text.

38. In a characteristic passage from her memoir of her husband, Cavendish articulates her opinion that William was ill repaid for his sacrifices: "I have heard [William] say several times, That his love to his gracious Master King Charles the Second, was above the love he bore to his Wife, Children, and all his Posterity, nay to his own life: And when, since His Return into England, I answer'd him, That I observed His Gracious Majesty did not love him so well as he lov'd Him; he replied, That he cared not whether His Majesty lov'd him again or not; for he was resolved to love him" (*The Life of William Cavendish*, 179). Here Cavendish protects her husband from any part in her critical attitude toward the king and the royalist party; however, she does intimate that William may have shared her sense of his unjust suffering even if he would not place blame where blame was due: "Also I have heard him say, That he was never beholding to Lady Fortune; for he had suffered on both sides, although he never was but on one side" (177).

39. Ibid., 3v.

40. William Cavendish, "To the Lady Marchioness of Newcastle, on her Book of Tales," in Margaret Cavendish, *Nature's Pictures Drawn by Fancies Pencil to the Life* (London: J. Martin and J. Allestrye, 1656), B1v.

41. Hilda L. Smith, "'A General War amongst the Men . . . but None amongst the Women': Political Differences between Margaret and William Cavendish," in *Politics and the Political Imagination in Later Stuart Britain*, ed. Howard Nenner (Rochester, N.Y.: University of Rochester Press, 1997), 143–60, discusses Margaret Cavendish's differences of political thought from her husband, William, and offers the first critical look at Margaret's sometimes surprising departures from standard royalist thinking.

42. There is little doubt that Margaret Cavendish was deeply steeped in the aristocratic ideology with which she had been raised. Nonetheless, it is necessary to note her extraordinary sympathy for common folk, especially women of the lower orders, which manifests itself in many of

her works. She reserves her contempt for those like parliamentary politicians who, in her opinion, overreach their station to usurp rule and social preeminence from the aristocracy.

43. "An epistle to Mistress Toppe," *Poems and Fancies*, 1r; "To the Reader," *Poems and Fancies*, 3v.

44. Taylor, who counted Ben Jonson among his mentors, borrows the phrase from Jonson's *A Tale of a Tub* (1639). The phrase, which first signified "an apocryphal tale, a 'cock and bull' story" (OED), easily lent itself to the disparagement of Noncomformist preaching, stereotyped as the purview of ill-qualified, lower-class types who fancied themselves preachers and who, lacking a pulpit from which to speak, would settle for even so base a platform as an overturned tub. That tubs were also infamously associated with the sweating cures for syphilis in this period lent further color to the term.

45. Elaine Hobby, "'Discourse so unsavoury': Women's Published Writings of the 1650s," in *Women, Writing, History: 1640–1740*, ed. Isobel Grundy and Susan Wiseman (University of Georgia Press, 1992), 16–32, discusses Cavendish's ambivalence toward the public political and religious activities of contemporary women.

46. "An Epistle to my Readers," in Cavendish, *Nature's Pictures*, C1r.

47. See, for instance, Lois Potter, *Secret Rites and Secret Writing: Royalist Literature, 1641–1660* (Cambridge: Cambridge University Press, 1989).

48. Much has been written about her open bid for fame; more has been said about the utopian fictions in which Cavendish reserves center stage for the female hero she imagines herself to be. See Ellayne Fowler, "Margaret Cavendish and the Ideal Commonwealth," *Utopian Studies* 7 (winter 1996): 38–48; Judith Kegan Gardner, "'Singularity of Self': Cavendish's True Relation, Narcissism, and the Gendering of Individualism," *Restoration: Studies in English Literary Culture, 1660–1700* 21 (fall 1997): 52–65; Rosemary Kegl, "'The World I have made': Margaret Cavendish, Feminism and *The Blazing World*," in *Feminist Readings of Early Modern Culture: Emerging Subjects*, ed. Valerie Traub, M. Lindsay Kaplan and Dympna Callaghan (Cambridge: Cambridge University Press, 1996), 119–41; Marina Leslie, *Renaissance Utopias and the Problem of History* (Ithaca, N.Y.: Cornell University Press, 1998).

49. *The Life of William Cavendish*, D1r.

50. Cavendish, *Nature's Pictures*, C2r, C2v.

51. Ibid., C2v.

52. Henry Burton, *For God and for the King* (1636), 47–48.

53. William Prynne, *A Looking-Glass for all Lordly Prelates* (1636), especially 54–55. Both Prynne and Burton, ibid., owed much of their rhetoric to John Bale.

54. *The Convent of Pleasure and Other Plays*, ed. Anne Shaver

(Baltimore: Johns Hopkins University Press, 1999), p. 220, act 1, scene 2. Hereafter cited in the text by act, scene and, where applicable, page number.

55. James Fitzmaurice, introduction to *Margaret Cavendish: Sociable Letters*, xiii–xiv; Anne Shaver, introduction to *The Convent of Pleasure and Other Plays*, 10–14; Ann McGuire, "Margaret Cavendish, Duchess of Newcastle, on the Nature and Status of Women," *International Journal of Women's Studies* 1, no. 2 (1978): 193–206; Sara Heller Mendelson, *The Mental World of Stuart Women: Three Studies* (Amherst: University of Massachusetts Press, 1987), 12–61.

56. *The Sociable Companions; or, The Female Wits*, ed. Amanda Holton (Oxford: Seventeenth Century Press, 1996), 59; "Assaulted and Pursued Chastity," in *The Blazing World and Other Writings*, ed. Kate Lilley (New York: Penguin, 1994), 59. Both plays hereafter cited in the text by page number.

57. The young lady uses similar language a second time in her letter of farewell to the prince's aunt: "Madam, it is too dangerous for lamb to live near a lion; for your nephew is of so hungry an appetite, that I dare not stay" (76). Again, when the prince joins a crew of pirates, Cavendish makes it clear that his disposition perfectly suits him to such companions, who let "nothing escape which they can get to make advantage on, so ravenous is their covetous appetite," an appetite the prince soon proposes to feed by recommending that they "go a-piracing for women, . . . which prizes, if we get, will bring us more comfort, pleasure and profit than any other good" (87).

58. *Andrew Marvell*, ed. Frank Kermode and Keith Walker (Oxford: Oxford University Press, 1990), 146.

59. "The Contract," in Lilley, *The Blazing World*, 29. Hereafter cited in the text by page number.

60. Catherine Gallagher discusses the uncomfortable paradoxes of Tory women's royalism with their feminism in "Embracing the Absolute: The Politics of the Female Subject in Seventeenth-Century England," *Genders* 1, no. 1 (1988): 24–39, which begins its analysis with an examination of Margaret Cavendish.

61. Lady Happy asks this question in act 1, scene 2 of *The Convent of Pleasure* (218).

62. In Cavendish's *The Sociable Companions*, a young woman, aptly named Prudence, voices a similar assessment of young cavaliers as poor marital prospects:

> I'le rather choose an old Man that buys me with his Wealth, than a young one, whom I must purchase with my Wealth; who, after he has wasted my Estate, may sell me to Misery and Poverty. Wherefore, our Sex may well pray, From Young Men's ignorance and follies, from their pride, vanity and prodigality, their gaming, quarelling,

drinking and whoring, their pocky and diseased bodies, their
Mortgages, Debts and Serjeants, their Whores and Bastards, and from
all such sorts of Vices and Miseries that are frequent amongst Young
Men, Good Lord deliver Us. (65).

63. "A note Containing the opinion of on[e] Christopher Marly
Concerning his Damnable Judgment of Religion, and scorn of gods word,"
facsimile in A. D. Wraight, *In Search of Christopher Marlowe: A Pictorial
Biography* (London: Macdonald, 1965), 309. A similar gesture denotes Piers
Gaveston's sodomitical relationship with Edward II in Marlowe's play,
where Gaveston is described by the earl of Warwick as "leaning on the
shoulder of the King" (1.2.23); at the beginning of the play, Gaveston
anticipates a similar gestural intimacy with the king, "upon whose bosom
let me die" (1.1.14).

64. Weldon, *The Character of King James*, quoted by Goldberg, *James
I,* 55.

65. In her introduction to this edition, Holton discusses the Hobbesian
qualities of the men in Cavendish's plays. For a more sustained discussion
of Cavendish's relationship to Hobbes and Hobbesian thought, see Anna
Battigelli, "Political Thought/Political Action: Margaret Cavendish's
Hobbesian Dilemma," in *Women Writers and the Early Modern British
Political Tradition,* ed. Hilda L. Smith (Cambridge: Cambridge University
Press, 1998), 40–55, and *Margaret Cavendish and the Exiles of the Mind*
(Lexington: University of Kentucky Press, 1998).

66. Marina Leslie offers a reading of this text's construction of the
heroine's gender which complements my reading of its construction of
aristocratic masculinity: "Evading Rape and Embracing Empire in Margaret
Cavendish's *Assaulted and Pursued Chastity,*" in *Menacing Virgins:
Representing Virginity in the Middle Ages and Renaissance,* ed. Kathleen
Coyne Kelly and Marina Leslie (Newark: University of Delaware Press,
1999).

67. "Assaulted and Pursued Chastity" ends with this gynocratic
arrangement; in *The Blazing World,* Cavendish explores in much greater
depth the beneficial rule of a monarch's wife.

68. The play twice makes the point that the prince has failed in his
duty to his kingdom. In act 4, scene 1, the prince has a soliloquy in
which he confesses this neglect: "my Kingdom wants me, not only to
rule, and govern it, but to defend it: But what is a Kingdom in comparison
to a Beautiful Mistress? Base thoughts flie off, for I will not go; did not
only a Kingdom, but the World want me" (239). Then, in act 5, scene 1,
the Embassador confronts the prince with his dereliction of duty: "the
Lords of your Council sent me to inform your Highness, that your Subjects
are so discontented at your Absence, that if your Highness do not return
into your Kingdom soon, they'l enter this Kingdom by reason they hear

you are here; and some report as if your Highness were restrained as Prisoner" (243).

69. Shaver, introduction to *The Convent of Pleasure,* 14.

70. Some have argued that Cavendish coveted aristocracy, that her biographical writings reveal her to have come from an acquisitive, aspiring family, and that her own work reveals a deep-seated envy and relish for the status and perquisites of rank. See Janet Todd, *The Sign of Angellica: Women, Writing and Fiction, 1660–1800* (New York: Columbia University Press, 1989), 58–59.

Notes to Chapter 8

1. "Order for Stage-plays to cease," *Acts and Ordinances of the Interregnum,* ed. C. H. Firth and R. S. Rait (London: H. M. Stationery Office, 1911), 26–27.

2. *The Divine Catastrophe of the Kingly House of Stuarts; or, A Short History of the Rise, Reign and Ruin Thereof. Wherein the most secret and Chamber-abominations of the last two Kings are discovered, Divine Justice in King Charles his overthrow vindicated, and the Parliaments proceedings against him clearly justified* (1652), 33.

3. Lucy Hutchinson, *Memoirs of the Life of Colonel Hutchinson,* ed. James Sutherland (Oxford: Oxford University Press, 1973), 42.

4. Charles II's personal connection with the theater was extensive. He is known to have been an active critic of plays, who sometimes offered advice for particular revisions to plays in progress and who, on occasion, suggested ideas for plays to certain playwrights, including Dryden. More appreciated, no doubt, was the willingness of the king and his courtiers to lend their state robes to the theaters in order to allow the players to represent nobles and monarchs more convincingly. In October 1661, Charles lent his coronation robes to Betterton to wear in the Duke's Company production of D'Avenant's *Love and Honour.* See *The London Stage 1660–1800, Part 1: 1600–1700,* ed. William Van Lennep (Carbondale, Ill.: Southern Illinois University Press, 1965), 41, 92; Nancy Klein Maguire, *Regicide and Restoration: English Tragicomedy, 1660–1671* (Cambridge: Cambridge University Press, 1992), 17, 93, 118, 180, 199.

5. Samuel Pepys, *The Diary of Samuel Pepys,* ed. Robert Latham, and William Matthews, 11 vols. (Berkeley and Los Angeles: University of California Press, 1970–1983), reveals his fondness for mingling with the upper classes at the playhouses. In fact, his diary tells us much about the composition of the audience and the snobbish appeal it had for the middling sort, who attended in order to place themselves in proximity to their betters. Evaluations of Restoration audiences include Emmet L. Avery and Arthur H. Scouten's introduction to *The London Stage;* Avery, "The

Restoration Audience," *Philological Quarterly* 45 (1966): 54–61; Harold Love, "The Myth of the Restoration Audience," *Komos* 1, no. 2 (1967): 49–56. More recent studies of this audience include Peter Holland, "The Text and the Audience," in *The Ornament of Action: Text and Performance in Restoration Comedy* (Cambridge: Cambridge University Press, 1979); Harry William Pedicord, "The Changing Audience," in *London Theatre World: 1660–1800*, ed. Robert D. Hume (Carbondale, Ill.: Southern Illinois University Press, 1980), 236–52, reviews the primary sources, and David Roberts, *The Ladies: Female Patronage of Restoration Drama 1660–1700* (Oxford: Clarendon Press, 1989), discusses the presence of women in the Restoration audience.

6. Susan Staves sees the genre in this light in *Players' Scepters: Fictions of Authority in the Restoration* (Lincoln: University of Nebraska Press, 1979). See also Maguire, *Regicide and Restoration*, for an insightful analysis of Dryden's role as "mythographer" for the restored monarchy (190–214).

7. Staves, *Players' Scepters*, 52.

8. This dual plot, characteristic of heroic drama, has produced two schools of criticism so opposed in their readings of the genre as to seem irreconcilable. For a long time, critics of heroic drama argued that it was the least political of all genres. Because they paid attention primarily to the exotic settings and the pretentious rhetoric of the plays, these critics saw them as escapist fantasies or as contributions to a larger genre of moral literature. This criticism includes Bonamy Dobree, *Restoration Tragedy: 1660–1720* (Oxford: Clarendon Press, 1929); Montague Summer, introduction to *Dryden: The Dramatic Works*, ed. Summers (London: Nonesuch Press, 1931); D. W. Jefferson, "The Significance of Dryden's Heroic Plays," in *Restoration Dramatists, a Collection of Critical Essays*, ed. Earl Miner (Englewood Cliffs, N.J.: Prentice Hall, 1966); Sarup Singh, *The Theory of Drama in the Restoration Period* (Bombay: Orient Longmans, 1963). All of these studies insist on the romantic and, hence, "unreal" qualities of heroic plays. See, too, Eric Rothstein, *Restoration Tragedy: Form and the Process of Change* (Madison: University of Wisconsin Press, 1967), and Anne Righter, "Heroic Tragedy," in *Restoration Theatre*, ed. John Russell Brown and Bernard Harris (New York: Capricorn Books, 1967), 135–57. These studies have espoused similar opinions about the apoliticism of Restoration serious drama.

As literary critics have become more attuned to the political function of literature, critics of heroic drama have "discovered" that in working and reworking themes of political factionalism, civil war, loyalty and betrayal, and restoration of monarchy, these plays dealt with the important political concerns of their moment. John Loftis, *The Politics of Drama in Augustan England* (Oxford: Oxford University Press, 1963), and his

"Political and Social Thought in the Drama," in *The London Theatre World*, ed. Hume, 236–52; Anne T. Barbeau, *The Intellectual Design of John Dryden's Heroic Plays* (New Haven: Yale University Press, 1970); Geoffrey Marshall, *Restoration Serious Drama* (Norman: University of Oklahoma Press, 1974); Staves, *Players' Scepters*; J. Douglas Canfield, "The Significance of the Restoration Rhymed Heroic Play," *Eighteenth Century Studies* 13 (1979): 49–62, and his "Ideology of Restoration Tragicomedy," *ELH* 51 (fall 1984): 447–64; Nicholas Jose, *Ideas of the Restoration in English Literature: 1660–71* (Cambridge, Mass.: Harvard University Press, 1984); and Richard W. Bevis, *English Drama: Restoration and Eighteenth Century, 1660–1789* (New York: Longman, 1988) have argued the political relevance and purpose of this drama. Staves comes close to reconciling the two strains of criticism by arguing that the lavish stagings and exotic stories of heroic drama were, indeed, the stuff of fantasy, but rather than escapism, these fantasies encouraged audiences to process the traumas of their own recent social strife. Unfortunately, Staves, who marvels at the blindness of earlier critics who saw *only* the romance in heroic plays, is unable to account for those love plots in her reading and chooses to ignore their presence. More recently, in *Regicide and Restoration*, Maguire discusses Dryden's split plot as being analogous to the masque and antimasque elements of court entertainments. In her reading, the "masque" plot of plays like *Tyrannic Love* and *The Conquest of Granada* treats the martyrdom of Charles I and the threats of civil war, but she sees this plot as being overtaken by "the sexual low plot, the Charles II plot" — the "anti-masque" (203).

9. John Dryden, *The Conquest of Granada, Part II*, in *The Works of John Dryden*, vol. 11, ed. John Loftis and David Stuart Rodes (Berkeley and Los Angeles: University of California Press, 1978), 171, 4.3.192–94.

10. We do not know precise dates for the first performances of either part of *The Conquest*. A number of people who saw it commented on it, including both Mr. and Mrs. Evelyn and Lady Mary Bertie. From these records, it seems that the first part opened in December 1670 and was revived in January 1671 when part 2 was produced so that audiences could see the whole *Conquest* over two nights of theater. For more on the performance history of the play, see H. T. Swedenberg Jr. and Alan Roper, commentary in the Loftis and Rodes edition (411–12) and Montague Summers's headnote to the play in his Dryden (13–14).

11. When the second part of the play was published in 1672, its title page bore the amended title, giving precedence to the love plot.

12. The convention was already old when Petrarch appropriated it for his sonnets, which later proved formative in the development of English love literature.

13. It is in this same vein that Middleton and Rowley convey

Vermandero's shock at his daughter's promiscuity through his exclamation, "A host of enemies entered my citadel could not amaze like this" (*The Changeling*, 5.1).

14. Dryden, *The Conquest of Granada, Part 1*, in *The Works of John Dryden*, vol. 11, ed. John Loftis and David Stuart Rodes (Berkeley and Los Angeles: University of California Press, 1978), 4.2.390–400, 406–7. Hereafter cited in the text.

15. Donne's poem, "The Apparition," which contains a particularly memorable version of this image of ghostly ravishment, seems to have had an active afterlife in Interregnum and Restoration literature. Margaret Cavendish uses the image in "The Contract," in *The Blazing World and Other Writings*, ed. Kate Lilley (New York: Penguin, 1994), where her central male character threatens his beloved with just such a violent haunting should she marry after his death (29).

16. In this essay, I attempt to distinguish between a generic use of the word "love" and Dryden's almost allegorical sense of "Love" by retaining his capitalization of the L and by placing the word in quotation marks.

17. The significance of Almanzor's name was noted by contemporaries. Wycherley pays sly homage to the name and character of Almanzor in the person of Manly, the huffing, straight-talking hero of *The Plain Dealer*. George Villiers also alludes to Almanzor with *The Rehearsal*'s Drawcansir. The conspicuous etymological game played by Villiers in "Draw-can-sir," suggests that "All-man-sir" was a joke in at least some circles.

18. There is a pun on "will" in this passage, as well, playing on "will" as a slang term for the penis. For a discussion of this slang usage, see chapter 4 above.

19. Lucy Hutchinson, a severe a critic of the Stuarts, pays Charles a grudging compliment in her *Memoirs of the Life of Colonel Hutchinson*, admitting that he "was temperate and chast and serious; so that the fooles and bawds, mimicks and Catamites of the former Court grew out of fashion, and the nobility and courtiers, who did not quite abandon their debosheries, had yet that reverence to the King to retire into corners to practise them" (*Memoirs*, 46).

20. *The Coppy of a Letter of Father Philips, the Queenes Confessor, Which Was Thought to Be Sent Into France, to Mr. Montague; Discovered and Produced to Be Read in the House of Commons, by Mr. Prynne, the 25. Of June, 1641. To This Effect. Lamentably Complaining of the Times and Present State of Things, and This Was Written Presently After Piercy and Jermyn Fled* ([London], 1641), 3–4. Whether the letter can be taken at face value is difficult to discern. Its strategy of apparent revelation of dissension within the king's party is so convenient as to suggest a cleverly crafted counterfeit; however, in the present context, this issue is irrelevant.

21. Potter, *Secret Rites*, discusses the seizure in 1644, by parliamentary forces, of a painting that was interpreted to depict "the king of England

offering a scepter to the queen," who, in turn, offers it to the pope. This painting was brought to London and put on public display in the Star Chamber, where it symbolically proclaimed the triumph of the Parliament over effeminate Charles and his overruling wife. Potter quotes a pamphleteer who interpreted the painting as a depiction of "the weaker sexe triumphing over the stronger, and by the help of a Miter, thou hast seen a scepter doing homage to the Distaffe" (46, 47).

22. *The Kings Cabinet Opened; or, Certain Packets of Secret Letters and Papers, Written with the Kings Own Hand, and Taken in His Cabinet at Nesby-Field, June 14, 1645. By Victorioius Sr. Thomas Fairfax* (London: Robert Bostock, 1645).

23. *Three Speeches Spoken at a Common-Hall, Thursday the 3. of July, 1645. By Mr. Lisle, Mr. Tate, Mr. Brown, Members of the House of Commons: Containing many Observations upon the Kings Letters, Found in His Own Cabinet at Nasiby Fight, and Sent to Parliament by Sir Thomas Fairfax, and Read at a Common-Hall* (London: Peter Cole, 1645), 27. It is worth noting that among royalist women, Henrietta Maria's leadership was given a positive value. Margaret Cavendish works with this image in her play *Bell in Campo*, where Lady Victoria convinces her husband, "Lord General, to take her to the battlefront, where she outperforms him in his own arena as the 'Generaless' of a tightly trained army of 'Heroickesses,' winning back strongholds her husband and his troops have lost" (11). Cavendish's stepdaughters, Elizabeth Brackley and Jane Cavendish, include a similarly admiring comment on the queen in their poem "On hir most sacred Majestie," which applauds Henrietta Maria's ability to conquer "Armyes of Rebells." "Your Eye if look, it doth an Army pay / And soe, as Generall, you doe lead the way." Quoted in Susan Wiseman, *Drama and Politics in the English Civil War* (Cambridge: Cambridge University Press, 1998), 95.

24. *The Kings Cabinet opened*, 43.

25. See Frances E. Dolan, *Whores of Babylon* (Ithaca, N.Y.: Cornell University Press, 1999), 122–27.

26. *Britania Triumphalis; a Brief History of the Warres and Other State-Affairs of Great Britain from the Death of the Late King, to the Dissolution of the Last Parliament* (London: Samuel Howes, 1645), 3.

27. Anonymous, *The Life and Reigne of King Charls; or, The Pseudo-Martyr discovered* (London: W. Reynold, 1651), 129.

28. Throughout his heroic plays, Dryden imagines the will as the site of an almost Manichaean battle between Love and Honor. See also, in *The Works of John Dryden*, vol. 12, ed. Vinton A. Dearing (Berkeley and Los Angeles: University of California Press, 1994), where the villainess, Nourmahal, describes her struggle against Love in these terms: "I fought it to the last: and Love has wonn: / A bloudy Conquest; which destruction brought, / And ruin'd all the Countrey where he fought" (3.1.373–75).

29. *The History of Great Britain, Being the Life and Reign of King James the First* (London: Richard Lownds, 1653), A3; italics in original.

30. Loftis and Rodes, *The Works of John Dryden*, 11:14, 16.

31. Ibid., 7.

32. Ibid., 427.

33. Maguire, *Regicide and Restoration*, 206.

34. Tim Harris, *London Crowds in the Reign of Charles II: Propaganda and Politics from the Restoration until the Exclusion Crisis* (Cambridge: Cambridge University Press, 1987), has suggested that Charles "could not live up to his image of 1660 — a majestic and semi-divine monarch; in reality, he proved to be a rather debauched, worldly man, preoccupied with venereal delights" (94). John Miller, *Popery and Politics in England: 1660–1688* (Cambridge: Cambridge University Press, 1973), depicts Charles as having potentially much more power than he ever effectively used, noting that "the traditional picture of Charles putting pleasure before business is far from inaccurate" (92). Roger Thompson, *Unfit for Modest Ears: A Study of Pornographic, Obscene and Bawdy Works Written or Published in England in the Second Half of the Seventeenth Century* (Totowa, NJ: Rowman and Littlefield, 1979), espouses this traditional view, maintaining that Charles II exhibited a case of arrested development caused by the extended idleness and uncertainty of his twenties and thirties when he sojourned in the courts of other kings and had little better to do than cultivate his wit and indulge his amorous whims. Thompson blames the Restoration settlement for not better employing the king when he returned to England. Charles II never laid aside his sensual diversions, but collected about him a group of men and women only too happy to spend his leisure with him. Thompson likens the literature produced by this group to "the wit of the school magazine, the satire of the student newspaper, the smutty parody or obscenity of the lavatory wall, parochial, personal, adolescent" (119). Miller, "The Later Stuart Monarchy," in *The Restored Monarchy: 1660–1688*, ed. J. R. Jones (London: Macmillan, 1979), reiterates this view, asserting that Charles's "conduct of government was characterized by indolence and cynicism" (37). In the same volume, Jennifer Carter, "Law, Courts and Constitution," 71–93, and J. R. Jones in his introduction, also take up the issue of Charles's power and his effectiveness as an administrator of government. Paul Seaward writes about the economics and power struggle of the settlement in his work on *The Restoration, 1660–1688* (New York: St. Martin's Press, 1991), 11–39, and in his introduction to *The Cavalier Parliament and the Reconstruction of the Old Regime, 1661–1667* (Cambridge: Cambridge University Press, 1988). A contemporary commentary on Charles, the court and the king's pleasure occurs in Pepys's *Diary* entry for 26 April 1667, when he reports a conversation he had with John Evelyn (the other well-known Restoration diarist). The two men talked for two hours "of the badness of the

Government, where nothing but wickedness, and wicked men and women command the King: that it is not in his nature to gainsay any thing that relates to his pleasures; that much of it arises from the sickliness of our Ministers of State, who cannot be about him as the idle companions are, and therefore he gives way to the young rogues" (8:181).

35. Dedications to heroic dramas (and other ceremonial addresses to the royal family) are full of this language. In his dedication of *The Conquest* to James duke of York, Dryden writes that "Poets, while they imitate, instruct. The feign'd Hero inflames the true: and the dead virtue animates the living" (Loftis and Rodes, *The Works of John Dryden*, 3). The reiteration of James's acts of "worth and valour" and Dryden's suggestion that his fictions might inspire James to even greater deeds in the future seem to be part of his larger project of Stuart mythmaking. Rather than seeking to improve the prince's moral character "by precept and Example," Dryden is advertising James's merits to a dubious public.

36. Jocelyn Powell, *Restoration Theatre Production* (London: Routledge and Kegan Paul, 1984), discusses the effect of Dryden's casting of Gwyn as Almahide and of Hart as Almanzor. She also points out the comic prologue spoken by Gwyn in a broad-brimmed hat, although she does not develop the contrast this sets up between Prologue and Almahide.

37. Gwyn was at least the third actress the king had lured from the stage. Elizabeth Farley (a.k.a. Mrs. Weaver) and Mary Davis preceded her. Charles Hart, one of the leading men of the King's Company and a former lover and costar of Nell Gwyn, was widely reputed to have had an affair with Lady Castlemaine, herself a cast-mistress of the king (Pepys, *Diary*, vol. 9, 7 April 1668). Other romantic links between the court and the stage included Sir Philip Howard's relationship with Elizabeth Hall of the King's Company and Sir Charles Sedley's affair with Margaret Hughes, also a player with the King's Company (mentioned by Pepys 7 May 1668). Hughes later left the stage to have a daughter by Prince Rupert; see John Harold Wilson, *All the King's Ladies: Actresses of the Restoration* (Chicago: University of Chicago Press, 1958), 150. Elizabeth Barry came to the stage as the mistress of John Wilmot, earl of Rochester, and in the course of her long career was reported to have had many lovers (115). Samuel Pepys, a hanger-on at court to whose diary we owe much of our information about the Restoration theater, spent much recreational time with actresses, but the only one he seems to have had sex with (though his attempt may not have been successful) was Mary Knepp (May 1668). Much more scandalous than the extramarital liaisons between players and aristocrats was the marriage of the earl of Oxford to Hester Davenport, famous for creating the role of Roxolana in the second part of Davenant's *The Siege of Rhodes* (Wilson, 138).

38. Gwyn's most successful roles had been in romantic comedies (particularly Dryden's *Secret Love* and *An Evening's Love*) in which she

and Charles Hart had developed the enormously popular formula of the "witty couple," the gold mine of Restoration comedy. Their appearance together in *The Conquest of Granada* was a reprise of their well-loved pairing and Almanzor and Almahide's sparring and bantering echoes their earlier comic material.

Prior to her relationship with the king, Gwyn had left the stage for an interval while she was mistress to Charles Sackville, Lord Buckhurst, an event that Pepys notes as news "that troubles me" (*Diary*, vol. 8, 13 July 1667). In his next entry he writes, "Poor girl! I pity her; but more the loss of her at the King's house" (14 July 1667).

39. *The Rehearsal* testifies to the popularity of heroic drama (the Duke's Company thought it popular enough to spoof) and, I believe, depends on the campiness of the genre to make its satire work. If we accept that audiences recognized and enjoyed the gap between heroic drama's love and honor rhetoric and its undisguised eroticism, we may guess that Buckingham's play was designed to appeal to the same audience, which came to laugh at itself as much as at the genre or at its practitioners.

40. See Katherine M. Quinsey, "Almahide Still Lives: Feminine Will and Identity in Dryden's *Conquest of Granada*," in *Broken Boundaries: Women and Feminism in Restoration Drama*, ed. Quinsey (Louisville: University Press of Kentucky , 1996), 141–42.

Notes to Chapter 9

The first epigraph is from Aphra Behn, *The City Heiress; or, Sir Timothy Treat-all* (1682), 4.2, in *The Works of Aphra Behn*, vol. 2, ed. Montague Summers (London: William Heinemann, 1915), 268. References to *The City Heiress* appear hereafter in the text, followed by act, scene, and page number. Summers's edition does not assign line numbers to the text. The second epigraph is from *The Rival Ladies*, 2.2.148–51, in *The Works of John Dryden*, vol. 8, ed. John Harrington Smith and Dougald MacMillan (Berkeley and Los Angeles: University of California Press, 1962). The third epigraph is from *Absalom and Achitophel*, lines 467–74, in *The Works of John Dryden*, vol. 2, ed. H. T. Swedenberg Jr., Earl Miner, Vinton A. Dearing and George R. Guffey (Berkeley and Los Angeles: University of California Press, 1972); hereafter cited in the text by line numbers.

1. For accounts of Shaftesbury's presentment of James and Kéroualle, see J. R. Jones, *Charles II: Royal Politician* (London: Allen and Unwin, 1987), 157–58, as well as Jones, *The First Whigs: The Politics of the Exclusion Crisis, 1678–1683* (London: Oxford University Press, 1961), 126–33, and John Pollock's *The Popish Plot: A Study in the History of the Reign of Charles II* (London: Duckworth, 1903), 247–50. See also Shaftesbury Papers VI B (Public Record Office), 420–24; Narcissus Luttrell,

A Brief Historical Relation of State Affairs (Oxford: Oxford University Press, 1857), i.49; BM, Sloane MSS. 2496, f. 55. For discussions and clarification of the partisan terms "Whig" and "Tory," see Robert Willman, "The Origins of 'Whig' and 'Tory' in English Political Language," *Historical Journal* 17, no. 2 (1974): 247–64; and Susan J. Owen, *Restoration Theatre and Crisis* (Oxford: Clarendon, 1996), xi.

2. "Recusancy" was the crime of not attending Church of England services. While it applied to Protestant dissenters as well as to Catholics who refused Communion in the state church, in practice, the law's enforcement was almost always aimed at suppressing Catholicism and the term "recusant" was used colloquially to refer to Catholics.

3. *A Collection of Scarce and Valuable Tracts, on the most Interesting and Entertaining Subjects: But chiefly such as relate to the History and Constitution of these Kingdoms. Selected from an infinite number in Print and Manuscript, in the Royal, Cotton, Sion, and other Publick, as well as Private Libraries; Particularly that of the late Lord Somers* (London: J. Cogan, 1748), 1:4.436.

4. Jones, *The First Whigs*, claims that the duchess was presented as "a common nuisance" (127); in this characterization of the charges, he echoes Pollock's assertion in *The Popish Plot* that she was charged with being "a national nuisance" (247). In *Charles II: Royal Politician*, Jones does point more clearly toward the sexual nature of the accusations, but his statement that she was to be tried as "a prostitute" is hardly an adequate representation of the substance of the charges (157).

5. Francis E. Dolan, *Whores of Babylon: Catholicism, Gender and Seventeenth-Century Print Culture* (Ithaca, N.Y.: Cornell University Press, 1999), mentions de Kéroualle only in passing, but sees the charges leveled against her as one instance of the demonization of Roman Catholic women (218).

6. Historians including Pollock and Jones have noted that both of these cases really targeted James. While some in the Whig party would no doubt have rejoiced to see de Kéroualle's judicial murder, Shaftesbury saw her as a useful pawn in the service of his party's real design: the exclusion of James from the royal succession. Shaftesbury used the (very credible) threat of prosecution in addition to a very large bribe to ensure that de Kéroualle would use her influence with the king to encourage Charles to acquiesce to the Parliament's efforts to pass an Exclusion Act. Their money and her influence proved ineffectual in this case.

7. In addition to Jones and Pollock, see J. P. Kenyon, *The Popish Plot* (New York: St. Martin's, 1972); John Miller, *Popery and Politics in England 1660–1688* (Cambridge: Cambridge University Press, 1973); Jonathan Scott, "England's Troubles: Exhuming the Popish Plot," in *The Politics of Religion in Restoration England*, ed. Tim Harris, Mark Goldie and Paul Seaward (Oxford: Basil Blackwell, 1990); O. W. Furley, "The Whig

Exclusionists: Pamphlet Literature in the Exclusion Campaign," *Cambridge Historical Journal* 13 (1957): 19–36; Paul Seaward, *The Restoration, 1660–1688* (New York: St. Martin's Press, 1988).

8. Quoted by Maureen Duffy in *The Passionate Shepherdess: Aphra Behn, 1640–89* (London: Jonathan Cape, 1977), 169; a similar report of the incident appears in Christopher Hill, *The Century of Revolution, 1603–1714* (New York: W. W. Norton, 1980), 198.

9. The strategy of criticizing the king indirectly was an old one. For instance, this book has discussed it at length with regard to attacks on Charles I's Privy Council and on Henrietta Maria (see chapters 7 and 8). Tim Harris, *London Crowds in the Reign of Charles II: Propaganda and Politics from the Restoration until the Exclusion Crisis* (Cambridge: Cambridge University Press, 1987), writes of this indirect mode of Whig propaganda that, "although the logic of the whig exploitation of the Popish Plot led them to claim they were protecting Charles II, their propaganda could carry an implicit criticism of the king" (117).

10. "Dialogue" [c. January 1675/6], in *The Complete Poems of John Wilmot, Earl of Rochester*, ed. David M. Vieth (New Haven: Yale University Press, 1968), 129–30. Portsmouth, of course, is de Kéroualle; (Mary) Knight is another of Charles's mistresses renowned for her singing; George Porter, a knight of Charles II's bedchamber, is evoked here in relation to his mistress, (Jane) Long, who was one of the founding actresses of the Duke's Company; Mazarin is the king's other French Catholic mistress, Hortense Mancini, who was brought to court and mentored by Philibert, comte de Grammont, a Frenchman long in residence and favor at the English court (see Vieth's notes on the poem).

11. Both of these contemporary opinions are quoted by Richard L. Greaves, *Secrets of the Kingdom: British Radicals from the Popish Plot to the Revolution of 1688–1689* (Stanford: Stanford University Press, 1992), 49.

12. This is one of the chief issues for Andrew Marvell in *An Account of the Growth of Popery and Arbitrary Government in England* (Amsterdam, 1677). In the introduction to *The First Whigs*, Jones describes the Whigs as a single-issue coalition of five groups who diverged significantly on other points, but who were able to act cohesively as a party as long as exclusion remained their chief objective.

13. Seaward, *The Restoration*, 109. Though Charles II did not attempt to impose Catholicism on his Protestant subjects, nor publicly align himself with Rome, he did act precisely as the Whigs feared he would when he ended the Exclusion Crisis by negotiating a pension from the French king that allowed him to rule England without summoning another Parliament from 1682 until his death in 1685. It is important to remember that we know this with the benefit of hindsight unavailable to the Whigs during the early 1680s; however, historians frequently invoke this

hindsight view to note that the Whigs were not wrong in their suspicions.

14. Harris, *London Crowds*, 110.

15. J. S., *Popery Display'd in its Proper Colours* (London, 1681), 4. Quoted at greater length and discussed by Tim Harris, "The Parties and the People: The Press, the Crowd and Politics 'Out-of-Doors' in Restoration England," in *The Reigns of Charles II and James VII and II*, ed. Lionel K. J. Glassey (New York: St. Martin's Press, 1997), 129.

16. Harris, "The Parties and the People," 130.

17. Ibid., 130.

18. Jones, "Parties and Parliament," *The Restored Monarchy*, 66, discusses the sometimes uncomfortable relationship between Charles and the Tories for which Charles's cynicism and perceived unreliability were largely responsible.

19. Todd, *The Secret Life of Aphra Behn* (New Brunswick, N.J.: Rutgers University Press, 1997), 277.

20. Michael Neill, "Heroic Heads and Humble Tails: Sex, Politics, and the Restoration Comic Rake," *The Eighteenth Century (Theory and Interpretation)* 24, no. 2 (1983): 118, 120. Neill suggests that "theater audiences in the post-interregnum period were more extensively politicized than at any other time in English history, and the crises of the period directly affected lives of many of the dramatists who catered to them. . . . If these conditions encouraged close censorship of the drama by the authorities and a natural circumspection on the part of the dramatists, they also created an audience exceptionally alert to political nuances."

When Neill wrote his article, it was necessary to argue the political relevance of what critics had long taken as an escapist literature. Neill makes the case persuasively, and criticism has moved on to accept that the Restoration stage participated actively in its political moment. Susan Staves, *Player's Scepters: Fictions of Authority in the Restoration* (Lincoln: University of Nebraska Press, 1979), remains the foundational study of theater's political relevance in Restoration society. Susan J. Owen's extensive work on the sexual politics of Behn's drama and the gendered politics of Behn's Tory activism has refined and developed Neill's point. See especially her *Restoration Theatre and Crisis* (Oxford: Clarendon, 1996); "Interpreting the Politics of Restoration Drama," *Seventeenth Century* 8, no. 1 (1993): 67–97; "'Suspect My Loyalty When I Lose My Virtue': Sexual Politics and Party in Aphra Behn's Plays of the Exclusion Crisis, 1678–83," *Restoration: Studies in English Literary Culture, 1660–1700* 18 (spring 1994): 37–47; "'He that should guard my virtue has betrayed it': The Dramatization of Rape in the Exclusion Crisis," *Restoration and Eighteenth Century Theatre Research* 9, no. 1 (1994): 59–68; "Sexual Politics and Party Politics in Behn's Drama, 1678–83," in *Aphra Behn Studies*, ed. Janet Todd (Cambridge: Cambridge University Press, 1996), 15–29.

21. Neill's article opens an important discussion of the political

implications of the rake-hero of Restoration comedy, but he does not satisfactorily account for the partisan politics of either the rakes themselves or of the dramatists who created them.

22. For a detailed, astute and class-sensitive discussion of the propaganda of both parties in the Exclusion Crisis, see Harris, *London Crowds*.

23. Owen discusses Lee's tragedy in "'He that should guard my virtue.'" The play was banned shortly after it opened in 1681, presumably because its representation of monarchy in terms of Tarquinian lust was unacceptable to the king.

24. See Harris's discussions of this play in *London Crowds*, 109, and "The Parties and the People," 129.

25. Quoted by Owen in "'He that should guard my virtue'" 65. I accept her argument that *Venice Preserv'd*, a famously ambivalent play, uses the near rape in its plot to demonstrate that rebellion is unruly, unpredictable and likely to be as arbitrary in its use of power as the tyranny it offers to overturn.

26. Ibid., 65.

27. Arlen Feldwick, "Wits, Whigs, and Women: Domestic Politics as Anti-Whig Rhetoric in Aphra Behn's Town Comedies," in *Political Rhetoric, Power, and Renaissance Women*, ed. Carole Levin and Patricia A. Sullivan (Albany: SUNY Press, 1995), 229.

28. Chris Cook and John Wroughton, *English Historical Facts, 1603–1688* (Totowa, N.J.: Rowman and Littlefield, 1980), 62–63, 88; Jones, *The First Whigs*, 8; Seaward, *The Restoration*, 118–19.

29. Regarding Shaftesbury's much-lampooned designs on the elective Crown of Poland, see Duffy, *The Passionate Shepherdess*, 212, and Montague Summers, ed., *The Works of Thomas Shadwell* (London: Fortune Press, 1927), clvi, clxvii. The "whole Bag of Knavery, damn'd Sedition, Libels, Treason, Successions, Rights and Privileges, with a new fashion'd Oath of Abjuration, call'd the Association" (5.1, p. 282), which Foppington and Wilding find during the robbery and with which they threaten Treatall, seem forgotten by the end of the play when Wilding simply produces the binding documents in which his uncle transferred his estate to Wilding.

30. Stephen N. Zwicker, "Lines of Authority: Politics and Literary Culture in the Restoration," in *Politics of Discourse: The Literature and History of Seventeenth-Century England*, ed. Kevin Sharpe and Stephen N. Zwicker (Berkeley and Los Angeles: University of California Press, 1987), 230–70, discusses Dryden's representation of the Tory victory over Whiggism in *Absalom and Achitophel* in similar terms.

31. Janet Todd, *The Secret Life of Aphra Behn* (New Brunswick, N.J.: Rutgers University Press, 1996), 280.

32. J. Douglas Canfield, "Tupping Your Rival's Women: Cit-Cuckolding as Class Warfare in Restoration Comedy," in *Broken Boundaries: Women and Feminism in Restoration Drama*, ed. Katharine M. Quinsey (Lexington: University of Kentucky Press, 1996), 113–28, takes this plot element

quite seriously, noting the centrality of citizen cuckolding in royalist and Tory drama.

33. Marvell, *An Account of the Growth of Popery*, 6.

34. "Porridge" was a familiar derogatory term for the sacrament in nonconformist polemic of the Restoration, a protest against the ceremonies of the state church which were too "popish" in the opinion of the opposition. Harris, *London Crowds*, quotes a tract from the period which frames the critique in these terms: "It is Mass, 'tis Porridge, 'tis Bibble babble; 'tis Will-worship; 'tis Superstition" (73).

35. This profile of Whig behavior is offered by Sir Charles Meriwill in an attempt to persuade Sir Timothy that his nephew, Wilding, is following the uncle's example. Again, Marvell's *Account of the Growth of Popery* is a representative example of the partisan position Behn lampoons in Treat-all.

36. Treat-all's recollection of an act against boasting refers to an actual Commonwealth law that made "the detestable sins of incest, adultery and fornication" felonies to be punished by death. See *Acts and Ordinances of the Interregnum*, 10 May 1650, quoted by Keith Thomas, "The Puritans and Adultery: The Act of 1650 Reconsidered," in *Puritans and Revolutionaries: Essays in Seventeenth-Century History Presented to Christopher Hill*, ed. Donald Pennington and Keith Thomas (Oxford: Clarendon Press, 1978), 257.

37. Zwicker, "Lines of Authority," discusses Dryden's use of Scripture.

38. Owen, *Restoration Theatre and Crisis*, 179.

39. Harris, *London Crowds*, 161.

40. Quoted by ibid., 137, and by Seaward, *The Restoration*, 115.

41. In Dryden's adaptation of the Absalom story, Jebusites stand in place of Roman Catholics.

42. For further analysis of Dryden's political propagandizing, see J. R. Moore, "Political Allusions in Dryden's Later Plays," *PMLA* 73 (1958): 36–42; Philip Harth, *Pen for a Party: Dryden's Tory Propaganda and Its Contexts* (Princeton: Princeton University Press, 1993).

43. Ironically, Wilmot and several of the rakish gentlemen celebrated in this passage, a group whose behavior had contributed much to the court's reputation for debauchery, aligned themselves as Whigs in the late 1670s and early 1680s. It is also worth noting that Dryden is one of the victims of this particular satire. Wilmot had long been one of his patrons, but their relationship deteriorated into acrimony. Wilmot's poem opens with the lines: "Well, sir, 'tis granted I said Dryden's rhymes / Were stol'n, unequal, nay dull many times." See *The Complete Poems of John Wilmot, Earl of Rochester*, ed. David M. Vieth (New Haven, Conn.: Yale University Press, 1968), 120.

44. Quoted by H. T. Swedenberg Jr. in his "Commentary" on *Absalom and Achitophel*, in *The Works of John Dryden*, 2:258.

45. Swedenberg offers a good biographical sketch of Villiers in his

commentary, ibid. See also John Harold Wilson, *A Rake and His Times: George Villiers, Second Duke of Buckingham* (New York: Farrar, Straus and Young, 1954), and *The Court Wits of the Restoration: An Introduction* (Princeton, N.J.: Princeton University Press, 1948).

46. Wilmot, "A Satyr on Charles II," in *The Complete Poems*, 60–61; hereafter cited in the text by line numbers. This poem undoubtedly circulated in manuscript among Wilmot's friends. In fact, it circulated into the hands of Charles II — Wilmot accidentally delivered a copy to the king when he meant to share another, less damaging verse. Tradition has it that Wilmot was forced to flee the court for a period of time until the king's anger subsided. Vieth has pointed out, however, that "Charles's displeasure cannot have been serious, for on 27 February 1673/4 and 2 May 1674 Rochester secured the coveted offices of Ranger and Keeper of Woodstock Park" (xxvii). This incident and its sequel illustrate Wilmot's vacillating fortunes at court, which were undoubtedly linked to the ebb and flow of his disenchantment with the king.

47. Contemporary comment on Villiers's decadence included Samuel Butler's (the author of *Hudibras*) portrait of him in "A Duke of Bucks":

> [He] is one that has studied the whole Body of Vice. . . . His Appetite to his Pleasures is diseased and crazy, like the Pica in a Woman, that longs to eat that, which was never made for Food, or a Girl in the Green-sickness, that eats Chalk and Mortar. Perpetual Surfeits of Pleasure have filled his Mind with bad and vicious Humours (as well as his Body with a Nursery of Diseases) which makes him affect new and extravagant Ways, as being sick and tired of the Old. (Swedenberg, in *The Works of John Dryden*, 2:258, 259)

Dryden satirized Villiers in the character of Zimri in *Absalom and Achitophel*, depicting him as

> A man so various, that he seem'd to be
> Not one, but all Mankinds Epitome.
> Stiff in Opinions, always in the wrong;
> Was everything by starts, and nothing long:
> But, in the course of one revolving Moon,
> Was Chymist, Fidler, States-Man, and Buffoon:
> Then all for Women, Painting, Rhiming, Drinking;
> Besides ten thousand freaks that dy'd in thinking.
>
> (545–52)

Wilmot's political allegiance in the late 1670s is less clear than Sedley's and Sackville's. He is assumed by Duffy, *The Passionate Shepherdess*, 180, to have had Whig leanings, though she reports that he addressed the

House of Lords with a speech against exclusion in 1678. In this respect, Duffy seems to repeat an error of attribution common to other accounts of Wilmot's life, including *John Wilmot, Earl of Rochester: His Life and Writings*, ed. Johannes Prinz (Leipzig: Mayer & Müller g.m.b.h, 1927), 296, and John Adlard, *The Debt to Pleasure: John Wilmot, Earl of Rochester, in the Eyes of His Contemporaries and in His Own Poetry and Prose* (Cheadle, Cheshire: Carcanet Press, 1974), 122. According to Jeremy Treglown, *The Letters of John Wilmot Earl of Rochester* (Oxford: Basil Blackwell, 1980), 31, and John Harold Wilson, ed., *The Rochester-Savile Letters, 1671–1680* (Columbus: University of Ohio Press, 1941), 22, the speech was made by Lawrence Hyde, who was given the title "Earl of Rochester" in 1682 after the Wilmot line died out and who was consistently a leading opponent of exclusion. Montague Summers, *The Works of Thomas Shadwell* (London: Fortune Press, 1927), clxvi, includes Wilmot in his list of Tories associated with the theater for certain passages in his revision of Beaumont and Fletcher's play, *Valentinian*. However, Wilmot's participation in politics and his association with the theater were both severely curtailed by illness at the end of the 1670s. Wilmot died at his country home in July 1680. Wilmot's quarrel with Dryden makes his party allegiance even harder to place. See also John Hayward, *The Collected Works of John Wilmot Earl of Rochester* (London: Nonesuch Press, 1926), xlv.

Sedley, Sackville, Wilmot and Henry Savile were among the members of a group that called themselves "the Ballers." Pepys remarks on his acquaintance with this group (*Diary*, 30 May 1668) and Savile refers to their exploits in a letter to Rochester 26 January 1671. See Treglown, *Letters*, 63.

48. Regarding the customs' office, see letter from Savile to Rochester, 26 January 1671, in Treglown, *Letters*, 62–64. For incidents at Woodstock park, see an exchange of letters between Wilmot and Henry Savile written in October 1677, in Treglown, *Letters*, 156–60. On the Cock Tavern episode, see Pepys, *Diary*, 1 July 1663. Pepys relates the incident in some detail, reporting that Sedley, who was tried for public lewdness, "preach[ed] a Mountebanke sermon from that pulpitt, saying that there he hath to sell such a pouder as should make all the cunts in town run after him — a thousand people standing underneath to see and hear him. And that being done, he took a glass of wine and washed his prick in it and then drank it off; and then took another and drank the King's health." Another account of the incident can be found in Anthony á Wood, *Life and Times, Collected from His Diaries by A. Clarke* (Oxford: Oxford Historical Society's Series, 1891). Vivian de Sola Pinto relates the episode in the biography of Sedley, *Sir Charles Sedley: 1639–1701: A Study in the Life and Literature of the Restoration* (New York: Boni and Liveright, 1927), 61–63.

49. On the changeable party loyalties of the wits and playwrights, see de Sola Pinto, *Sir Charles Sedley*; Brice Harris, ed., introduction to *The Poems of Charles Sackville Sixth Earl of Dorset* (New York: Garland, 1979); Montague Summers, introductions to *The Works of Thomas Shadwell, The Works of Aphra Behn*, and *John Dryden: The Dramatic Works*, ed. Summers (London: Nonesuch Press, 1932); Angeline Goreau, *Reconstructing Aphra: A Social Biography of Aphra Behn* (New York: Dial Press, 1980); and Duffy, *The Passionate Shepherdess*.

50. Dryden pilloried Shadwell with his 1682 poem, *Mac Flecknoe; or, A Satyr upon the True-Blew-Protestant Poet, T. S.*

51. Jones, *The First Whigs*; Melinda Zook, "Contextualizing Aphra Behn: Plays, Politics, and Party, 1679–1689," in *Women Writers and the Early Modern British Political Tradition*, ed. Hilda L. Smith (Cambridge: Cambridge University Press, 1998), 77.

52. Neill, "Heroic Heads," 120, focuses primarily on Shadwell's *The Libertine* (1675) and on Etherege's *The Man of Mode* (1676).

53. Elaine Hobby discusses Behn's critique of marriage in *Virtue of Necessity: English Women's Writing, 1649–88* (Ann Arbor: University of Michigan Press, 1989). Yvonne Shafer provides a social history of women in the period in "Restoration Heroines: Reflections of Social Change," *Restoration and Eighteenth-Century Theatre Research* 2, no. 1 (1987): 38–53.

54. Several recent articles trace Behn's dual identity as "Tory" and "feminist," particularly Donald R. Wehrs, "*Eros*, Ethics, Identity: Royalist Feminism and the Politics of Desire in Aphra Behn's *Love Letters*," *SEL: Studies in English Literature, 1500–1900* 32 (summer 1992): 461–78, and Nancy Copeland, "'Who Can . . . Her Own Wish Deny?': Female Conduct and Politics in Aphra Behn's *The City Heiress*," both in *Restoration and Eighteenth-Century Theatre Research* 8 (summer 1993): 27–49; Elizabeth Bennett Kubek, "'Night Mares of the Commonwealth': Royalist Passion and Female Ambition in Aphra Behn's *The Roundheads*," *Restoration: Studies in English Literary Culture, 1660–1700* 17 (fall 1993): 88–103.

55. Zook, "Contextualizing Aphra Behn," 77–78.

56. Despite the conventionality of her name, Charlot Gett-all is not the acquisitive, social-climbing belle that moniker would imply, and the play treats her sympathetically. By contrast, Mrs. Clacket, the Puritan bawd, is exactly as her name defines her: talkative and sexually available. She is a conventional stage Puritan (like Treat-all and his housekeeper, Mrs. Sensure), who speaks piety and acts lechery. She is, according to Lady Galliard's assessment, "a most devout Bawd, a precise Procurer; / Saint in the Spirit, and Whore in the Flesh; / A Doer of the Devils work in Gods Name" (4.1.35–37).

57. The difference between rakes and fops is worth noting: for all their similarity of economic circumstance, Wilding possesses sexual allure

Foppington can only envy. The fop must attempt to substitute modish clothes and phrases for his lack of roguish sex appeal. The fop attaches himself to the rake's entourage, hoping to support himself by his companion's wit and good looks. This is especially true in Behn's representation of this stock figure: her Foppington hopes to beat Wilding at his own game by exposing his womanizing to Charlot, then marrying her on the rebound. Foppington's aim is to steal the crumbs from Wilding's table before he has even swept them aside, but of course he can neither outwit nor outwoo the rake.

58. Even more uncomfortable are the passages where Behn puts this logic in women's mouths, as when she innovates in her translation of Oenone's lament from Ovid's *Heroides*. In Behn's hands Oenone castigates Helen as an adulteress vainly trying to salvage her reputation by calling her elopement with Paris a rape: "Rape hides the Adult'rous Deed. / And is it thus Great Ladies keep intire / That Vertue they so boast, and you admire? / Is this a Trick of Courts, can Ravishment / Serve for poor Evasion of Consent?" Quoted and discussed by Todd, *The Secret Life of Aphra Behn*, 257.

59. *The Rival Ladies*, 2.2.146–51, in *The Works of John Dryden*, vol. 8, ed. John Harrington Smith and Dougald MacMillan (Berkeley and Los Angeles: University of California Press, 1962). To be fair (both to Gonsalvo and to Dryden), it must be said that the character rules out rape on the grounds that "constraint Love's noblest end destroys, / Whose highest Joy is in anothers Joys" (2.2.152–53).

60. Miller, *Popery and Politics*, 128.

61. Jones, *The First Whigs*, 80–81.

62. For instance, Goreau, *Reconstructing Aphra*, 272–73; George Woodcock, *Aphra Behn: The English Sapho* (Montreal: Black Rose Books, 1989), 151–52; Arlen Feldwick, "Wits, Wigs, and Women," 225–26; Judith K. Gardiner, "Aphra Behn: Sexuality and Self-Respect," *Women's Studies* 7 (1980): 67–78.

63. Zook, "Contextualizing Aphra Behn," 79.

64. Ibid., 77–78.

Note to Afterword

1. Sharpe, *Faction and Parliament: Essays on Early Stuart History* (Oxford: Clarendon Press, 1978), 1.

Index